The U.S.
Crusade in China, 1938-1945

The U.S.
Crusade in China, 1938-1945
Michael Schaller

Columbia University Press · New York · 1979

Library of Congress Cataloging in Publication Data
Schaller, Michael, 1947–
    The U.S. crusade in China, 1938–1945.

    Bibliography: p.
    Includes index.
    1. United States—Foreign relations—China.
2. China—Foreign relations—United States.
3. China—Politics and government—1937–1945.
4. World War, 1939–1945—China. I. Title.
E183.8.C5S325   940.53′22′73   78-15032
ISBN 0-231-04454-2

Columbia University Press
New York   Guildford, Surrey

Dedicated to my parents, Edith and Lawrence Schaller

Contents

Preface

FOR ALMOST TWO uninterrupted decades, China suffered the concurrent agony of invasion and civil war. Japan's seizure of Manchuria in September 1931 and the proclamation of the People's Republic in October 1949 were primarily important to China. Nevertheless, these episodes also demarcated a period in which the United States became massively involved in China's destiny. By the late 1930s American leaders believed successful Japanese aggression in China was a prelude to a direct assault on other American interests and allies in the Pacific. The Communist victory of 1949, on the other hand, appeared as the loss of China behind the iron curtain of Soviet conquest.

Since the late nineteenth century, American concern with China had been a curious, usually glib amalgam of missionary zeal, reformist interest, and dreams of a boundless market. The vaguely defined Open Door was less an operative plan than a wish that neither Russia nor Japan would establish hegemony over China. Meanwhile, American diplomacy rested on the hope that developments within China and private American influence would contribute to the evolution of a politically and economically integrated nation along the democratic capitalist model exemplified by the United States.

During the 1930s the revival of a powerful Chinese revolutionary movement and Japan's aggression challenged an essentially passive American policy. In their separate ways, each of these forces first came to frustrate American hopes for China and then appeared to make China itself a threat to the United States. Late in 1938 President Franklin D. Roosevelt and his top advisors concluded that Japanese control of China endangered the security of both the United States and its de facto European allies

ix

with Asian colonial interests. American policymakers increasingly linked Japanese aggression with its German and Italian counterparts in Europe. Accordingly, they set their policy on a new course, one designed to actively aid and support the Kuomintang (KMT) regime of Generalissimo Chiang Kai-shek. American aid, they hoped, would enable Chiang to withstand Japan's assult and improve his position against his major domestic rivals, the Chinese Communists. If the KMT were assured of this support, American liberals hoped that it would undertake political reforms to make itself a more popular and effective government. Hopefully, it could then serve as a long-term American ally, able to assist in the gradual, orderly transition of political power in Asia from closed empires toward a system of self-governing, stable nations.

While most Americans concerned with policy formulation shared a belief in the broad outlines of this idea, its very breadth inevitably led to a variety of interpretations. Competing bureaucracies, each with a different perspective and approach, clashed over the application of tactics and the interpretation of events in China. Also, as the military and political landscape within China underwent change after 1938, it severely strained the previous consensus to bolster Chiang's position against his domestic enemies.

New developments became even more important once the United States entered the war. The emergence of the Soviet Union and the Chinese Communists as major contenders for power in northeast Asia, the crumbling of the European empires, and the likely elimination of Japanese power all presented a radically new set of factors imposing themselves on an American policy which already showed signs of ossification. Moreover, Chiang's regime, which the United States wished to continue in power, was drastically affected by the impact of war and American aid. Enervated by corruption, it was quickly losing its frail base of power and legitimacy to the Communists.

Even before the Japanese surrender of August 1945, the central question affecting China was over the likely course of revolutionary social change. The United States needed to assess the impact which revolution would have on the goals it had pursued since the late 1930s. Should these goals be altered? Whether altered or not, could they best be realized by supporting the Communists or the Nationalists, or perhaps by remaining neutral? How should the United States respond to growing Soviet power? Unfortunately, the American response to these issues was disjointed, contradictory, and almost totally incapable of achieving positive results.

The time during which the United States both formulated and locked itself into a tragic policy spans the years from 1938 to 1945. Although full-scale civil war did not erupt until 1946 or terminate until 1949, the template cut during World War II set the pattern for American policy toward the Chinese Communist victory and the subsequent revolutionary and nationalist upheavals in Asia. This study, I believe, offers a new approach to the history of U.S.-Chinese relations. Both my own analysis of political events during World War II and access to new source material have led me to revise many standard interpretations of this period.

The literature on American policy toward China is of an unusually high quality. Since the early 1950s there have appeared major studies by Herbert Feis (*The China Tangle*), Charles Romanus and Riley Sunderland (*The History of the China-Burma-India Theater*), Tang Tsou (*America's Failure in China*), and Barbara Tuchman (*Stilwell and the American Experience in China*). While all these studies make valuable contributions (and on many points I take no issue with them) my own interpretations and conclusions are frequently at variance with theirs.

With the exception of Tuchman's work, which reflects a liberal's disillusion with the Vietnam war, all were written during the 1950s or early 1960s. They express the predominant influence of cold war liberalism, a belief in the monolith of Sino-Soviet Communism, and an assumption that all revolution is a conspiracy. Overemphasizing the naivete of American diplomacy, they attribute policy failures almost solely to Soviet, Communist, and KMT scheming which bedeviled a benevolent, idealist, but bumbling American policy.

Building on a core of information presented in some of the previous studies, this work probes several basic but unanswered questions. Why did the KMT's conservative nationalism appeal to American planners concerned with the future of Asia? What factors prejudiced Americans against the Chinese Communists? Why and how deeply did various American factions become involved in the power struggle between the Nationalists and Communists? Would the policies of either President Roosevelt or General Stilwell, if realized, have contributed to China's progress or would they have instead led to a more "efficient" dictatorship of modern militarists and technocrats? Answers to these questions may help us to understand the legacy of conflict in Asia willed to the people of China and the United States since 1945.

Many individuals and institutions contributed to this project. Among those who helped most with my gaining access to materials were the staffs of the Modern Military Branch of the National Archives, the Federal Records Center at Suitland, Maryland, the Franklin D. Roosevelt Presidential Library, the Hoover Institution, the Center for Naval History, the Center for Military History, and the Western History Collections of the University of Oklahoma. Research funds were made available at various times by the Center for Chinese Studies of the University of Michigan and the National Endowment for the Humanities. The manuscript was typed by Mrs. Wiladene Stickel and Mrs. Marilyn Bradian.

I owe the greatest obligation to those friends and colleagues who read and criticized the work in its formative stage. My thanks to Professors Bradford Perkins (who supervised the dissertation), Dorothy Borg, Albert Feurwerker, Ernest Young, Marilyn Blatt Young, Robert Schulzinger, William E. Leuchtenburg, and Leonard Dinnerstein. I alone remain responsible for any errors which remain.

Material in chapter 4 originally appeared in *American Quarterly*, vol. 28 (Spring 1976), No. 1. Parts of chapter 11 first appeared in *Pacific Historical Review*, vol. 44 (November 1975), No. 4. The author acknowledges permission to use these. Quotations from the Henry L. Stimson Papers appear with permission of the Sterling Memorial Library, Yale University.

The U.S.
Crusade in China, 1938-1945

Chapter 1
Images of China

FOR A CENTURY before World War II, the American imagination fed upon the mystique of China. Its wonderfully strange language and culture, the lure of its potential market, pulled like a magnet across the horizon of the Pacific Ocean. England's victory in the Opium War (1839–42) cleared the path into the isolated Middle Kingdom. Successive assaults by Western powers and Japan through the rest of the century brought along in their wake an invasion of merchants, missionaries, soldiers of fortune, and travelers. The foreigners enjoyed immunity from Chinese law through the imposition of an arrangement ponderously known as "extraterritoriality." Special protection and privileges stimulated the growth of Western-style cities, or treaty ports (eventually totaling several dozen), along China's coasts and rivers. Gradually, China's cultural, political, and economic independence slipped away until it occupied a hazy ground just short of formal colonialism.

Because their soldiers and sailors took no part in the several pre-1900 wars with China, most Americans assumed that they enjoyed a special relationship with China. The fact that the United States demanded and acquired all the imperialist privileges which others wrung from the Chinese government seemed a mere technicality. Conventional wisdom affirmed that America helped China by sending missionaries, educators, merchants, and friendly diplomats who protected her territory against imperialist encroachment. When Chinese revolutionaries overthrew the decrepit Ch'ing Dynasty in 1912, Washington supposedly supported the new republican government. The culmination of this trend came with U.S. recognition of

Chiang Kai-shek's new regime in 1928, the Republic of China.

The standard version of Sino-American relations explained very little of what happened between the 1840s and 1940s. The "special relationship" could not readily be seen in the Chinese Exclusion Act of 1882, which barred all Chinese from immigrating to America. Nor was it evident in the endemic anti-foreign and anti-missionary riots which swept China right through the 1930s. Practically no Americans understood the immense cultural distance actually separating Chinese society from themselves. In 1949, when China's "century of dishonor" came to an end with the creation of the People's Republic, the predominant reaction in the United States was a feeling of dismay that the Chinese had betrayed their benefactors. Few in America understood Mao Tse-tung's meaning when he declared that the Chinese people had "stood up" and that China would never again be an "insulted nation."

During the first half of the twentieth century, an almost unimaginable chaos engulfed China. As the traditional political system and culture died, pent-up social forces, conflicting nationalisms, and rival imperialisms transformed China into the world's greatest battlefield. Yet, aside from a handful of missionaries proselytizing in the interior, the epic was fought far beyond the gaze of Americans. Even those U.S. citizens actually in China remained largely confined to the treaty ports, dealing with atypical Chinese. The policy of the American government left most activity in China to private efforts by missionaries, educators, and merchants. The much discussed China Market remained a chimera, for exports to China hardly ever surpassed 3 percent of total U.S. trade. In the 1930s the average American's concept of China could not have been much more than the corner laundry, an exotic restaurant, or perhaps the simple, stoic peasant of Pearl Buck's bestseller, *The Good Earth* (1931). As Harold Isaacs concluded in a study of public opinion, most Asians were scarcely more than "scratches on our mind."[1]

Yet, in the decades following the British assault on China, a cataclysm fell upon the Middle Kingdom. Imperial decay, a population explosion, civil war (the T'aip'ing Rebellion of the 1850s, for example, killed an estimated twenty million people!), growing regionalism and foreign pressures so completely undermined the existing system that by 1912 it essentially fell apart. In the four decades which spanned the years between the fall of the Ch'ing Dynasty and the creation of the People's Republic, the five hundred million peasants of China suffered a seemingly endless series of civil conflicts and foreign invasion. The banditry, warlordism, disease, hunger, and taxation which were the peasant's lot comprised the real China which few Americans knew.

More than any other factor, the social crisis of the masses determined China's political evolution and its eventual relations with the United States. Yet almost all contemporary American observers ignored this point. In the 1930s China's population approached one-half billion, 90 percent of whom were peasant farmers. Among these, two-thirds could be classified as "poor peasants," those who owned or rented a tiny plot that yielded a harvest near the subsistence level. The poor and even the slightly better off peasant lived with three onerous facts of life: rents, taxes, and usury. Tenants often paid rents averaging 45 percent of the harvest; taxes were levied on everything from land to cooking pots, windows, and doors. In Szechuan province, a favorite prize of competing warlords, the taxes due in 1971 were collected in 1933! In order to pay both rents and taxes, the peasant had to raise cash from usurers— who frequently doubled as the rent or tax collector. Annual interest rates of 30–100 percent were common. Within the village, the landowners, or gentry, often served as the civil authority, under both the old imperial order and its successors. After 1928 the Kuomintang (KMT) regime exercised authority on the local level simply by incorporating existing elites into the party and government apparatus. The resulting class and political oppression led the French social historian and Sinologist, Lucien Bianco, to conclude that "poverty, abuse and early death were the only prospects for nearly half a billion people" in China.[2]

Only a handful of journalists and missionaries saw and understood these conditions. Before the late 1930s, American diplomats seemed largely indifferent to or ignorant of social forces. Living in Peking, Nanking, or a few other Westernized cities, they knew little of China's vast interior. Their concerns centered on protecting the lives and commercial interests of American citizens. Officials in Washington saw China as a pawn among the major nations with interests in the Pacific. They focused attention on Japanese and Soviet behavior in China, or possible threats which might emanate from radical political movements. The State Department engaged in scarcely any planning for contingencies and had few expectations that positive developments might occur.

The overthrow of the Ch'ing Dynasty in 1912 and the forces unleashed by the nationalist movement, the Bolshevik Revolution, and World War I required the Great Powers to reach new agreements to protect the Far Eastern balance of power. The United States played a major role in forging a new framework of order by promoting the treaties of the Washington Conference (1921–22) and the Pact of Paris, or Kellogg-Briand Pact (1928). By the terms of the several Washington treaties, the major powers of the West (minus the Soviet Union) and Japan agreed to a program of naval limitations, acceptance of the colonial status quo, and peaceful competition for economic and political influence in China. The divided Chinese nation had to endure the continuation of extraterritoriality and the unequal treaties of the nineteenth century. Although the nationalist political and military upheavals which swept China in the mid-1920s tempted foreign, especially Japanese, intervention, the uneasy international arrangements held. When in 1927 KMT General Chiang Kai-shek purged his erstwhile Communist allies and Soviet advisors, the foreign powers felt reassured that intervention had proved unnecessary. Chiang's restrained nationalism and effort to win Western support erased the label of "Red general" which some unfriendly observers had placed upon him.

The leader of the newly proclaimed Republic of China won further credit upon his conversion to Methodism and marriage to the Wellesley-educated Soong Mei-ling, sister of Dr. Sun Yat-sen's widow. He reversed the trend toward anti-missionary agitation and recruited American missionaries to assist the spiritual-political reform program known as the New Life Movement. The Treaty Powers acknowledged Chiang's moderation by agreeing to Chinese demands for tariff autonomy and by promising to abrogate other parts of the unequal treaties sometime in the future. But the stability which the new regime had initiated in China was soon undercut by the world depression and domestic crisis. Moved by its dire need for new markets and raw materials, and fearful of Chiang's early successes in reasserting national authority, Japan began an armed assault on Chinese territory which would culminate in the Pacific war.

The Japanese army attacked Manchuria while the United States experienced the most severe economic crisis in its history. As the foundations of the strongest industrial power shook, events in the Far East seemed distant and marginally important. Few Americans sympathized with Tokyo; fewer still assumed the United States should become directly involved. What frightened Secretary of State Henry Stimson and President Herbert Hoover in September 1931 was not so much China's fate as the specter of the great powers seizing new empires to rescue themselves from economic depression. If Japan, or other nations, saw fit to ignore the constraints of the Washington Treaties and Pact of Paris, the carefully balanced stability of the world was doomed.

At the same time, neither the Administration, Congress, nor (said the polls) public opinion seemed at all interested in challenging Japan. Many Americans hoped that "moderates" in Tokyo would regain the upper hand in due course. Others understood that the United States simply lacked the will or military means to confront Japan in the Pacific. Reflecting these attitudes, Stimson and Hoover chose to seize the high moral ground of diplomacy. In January 1932 Stimson declared that the United States would not "recognize any situation, treaty or agreement which may be brought about by means contrary to the Pact of Paris." In short, Washington refused to accept the legitimacy of Japanese control of Manchuria or any future conquests.[3]

But the Nonrecognition or Stimson Doctrine of 1932 marked the essential limit of the response to Japanese aggression. America declared it found Tokyo's policy politically and morally abhorrent but not worth fighting over. Later comments by Stanley Hornbeck, the rather pompous and opinionated State Department Asia expert, substantiated this point of view. While the United States deeply sympathized with China's suffering and opposed Japanese military expansion, Americans had nothing to gain by aiding China and playing Santa Claus in Asia.[4] Thus American policymakers felt relieved when the Chinese and Japanese finally reached a truce agreement by themselves in May 1933 which at least temporarily halted Tokyo's advance south into China.

Any hope within China that the newly inaugurated President, Franklin D. Roosevelt, planned to revise American policy was at best misguided. Though FDR enjoyed charming his listeners with colorful stories about his grandfather's adventures as a China merchant, Roosevelt had no intention of involving the United States more deeply in East Asia. Certainly, before 1937 one of Roosevelt's diplomatic priorities was avoiding conflict with Japan by limiting any danger of a confrontation. This meant actively discouraging the Chinese government from anticipating any material assistance against Japan. Initially, FDR, like most of his advisors, felt China's fate was of no great importance to nor a responsibility of the United States.

The public and private adulation which Roosevelt and other Americans would heap on Nationalist China during World War II could not have been foreseen by earlier observers. Before 1937 a large number of official reports on Chiang's regime were highly critical. The Nanking embassy's diplomatic staff and attachés both frequently complained of the KMT's misguided priorities. While Japan continued to press southward from Manchuria, Chiang insisted on using his limited armed strength against rival warlords and Communists in south-central China. When in 1933 Ambassador Nelson Johnson appealed to H. H. Kung (Chiang's brother-in-law, banker, and sometime finance minister) to counter the appeal of Chinese Communists by actively supporting land and tax reforms, his pleas were deprecated. The solution to peasant discontent, Kung indicated, was greater military power and a stepped-up campaign against the Reds.[5]

Kung's dictum might well serve as the paradigm for the entire Nationalist regime. During the so-called Nanking Decade, 1927–37, China made little progress in any field. The Kuomintang, or National People's Party (KMT), which was essentially the government, exercised firm control only in two provinces and partial control in eight others. This left eighteen provinces under the rule of semi- or fully independent provincial officials and warlords. The formal government administration and bureaucratic organs remained weak and lacked clearly defined authority. At the local level the KMT depended on the support of established elites, usually landlords, thus alienating the peasantry. Power within the party devolved into a smaller and smaller group clustered around Chiang Kai-shek. The Military Council, headed by Chiang, held almost exclusive power.

The Generalissimo ruled through the adroit manipulation of party factions, encouraging them against one another. This prevented any combination of cliques from becoming strong enough to challenge the center. It also left the KMT too divided to deal effectively with any major problem. Government policy could only be exercised in a few regions, especially in the cities and modern economic sector. Rural China, with 90 percent of the population, lay largely outside the realm of Nanking. Model reform laws affecting rents, taxes, and usury were passed and routinely ignored by provincial officials and landlords. Chiang's ruling circle neither could nor wished to challenge vested interests. After all, they themselves might be the first victims of profound social and economic change.

In place of real reform, Generalissimo and Madame Chiang sponsored a pet project called the New Life Movement. Wrapped in the verbiage of conservative Confucian philosophy and some Christian doctrines, the New Life Movement implored the Chinese masses to respect authority, refrain from spitting in public, and correct their posture. Chiang Kai-shek seemed to possess a single motivating vision, that of ultraconservative nationalism. Under his own leadership he would forge a united China whose source of strength lay in military power. Neither economic modernization nor social change had a place in this transformation.

The conservative and militaristic tone of political power found echoes among all KMT factions. The C.C. Clique (so named for its leaders, the Ch'en brothers), the Blue Shirts, the Political Study Group, the Whampoa Clique, and others each adhered to Chiang's ideas. Their differences reflected their control of certain aspects of government—the army, secret police, education, propaganda, bureaucracy, etc.—rather than clashing ideologies. They competed to gain influence with the Generalissimo, not to alter the direction in which he led China.[6]

Nothing better epitomized the internal chaos of China in the middle 1930s than did the protracted battle between the Nationalists and the Chinese Communists. Despite Japan's imperialist threat, a revolutionary civil war smoldered on. American diplomatic observers realized that any Chinese ability to resist Tokyo would require some form of unity. Yet there was scant hope that this was in the offing. In 1927 Chiang Kai-shek had established his supremacy within the KMT largely on the basis of purging the Communists from the first united front alliance. By 1931, when a remnant of the CCP under Mao Tse-tung's leadership had created a new Soviet base area in mountainous Kiangsi province, Chiang declared its destruction his priority. During the next four years the Generalissimo threw the bulk of his armed forces against the Reds in a series of massive but unsuccessful "bandit suppression" campaigns.

China's internal warfare took place in the interior, making it extremely difficult for Americans to get first-hand information. Most reporting on the Communists tended to be hearsay, gleaned from the Nationalist side. Despite these limitations, at least two consular officials managed to send reports to the State Department which identified several of the fundamental issues in the revolutionary struggle. In 1932, for example, O. Edmund Clubb prepared a lengthy report suggesting that poverty, not international Communist intrigue, was the "breeding ground" of revolution in China. The KMT, unwilling or unable to help the mass of poor peasants, might be swept out of power by the Communists as well as by the Japanese, Clubb observed.[7]

Walter Adams, consul-general at Hankow, supplemented Clubb's report in 1934. Having stumbled upon Mao's influential "Report to the Provincial Soviet in Kiangsi," Adams believed he had evidence to advance a novel theory about "Chinese Communist ideology and aims." Communism in China, he reasoned, was not merely a Soviet puppet nor a cover for banditry as many Americans supposed. Rather, it was an increasingly popular revolutionary movement with its "Chinese character indelibly marked upon it by its environment and the obstacles it faces." Adams predicted that "in the absence of reform of the economic and political conditions that gave birth to the subversive movement," KMT efforts to exterminate the Communists would be "an exceptionally difficult matter." He further reasoned that even if the Kiangsi Soviet, Mao's headquarters, were destroyed, the Communists would adopt guerrilla warfare in new areas.[8]

The commentaries of Clubb and Adams made little impression within the State Department. Mired in the conviction that all Communist movements were creatures of Moscow, field reports on Chinese Communism were forwarded to the Russian, not Chinese, experts within the Department. There, we may assume, they were filed and forgotten. In Clubb's case, however, this cannot have been completely so. Years later, in 1950, he would be declared a security risk and discharged from service in part because his 1932 report on the CCP was adjudged too radical.[9]

During 1934 American concern with the Communists grew as the pace of civil war increased. Chiang launched another massive assault on Kiangsi which compelled the Communists to begin the yearlong, 6,000-mile retreat known afterwards as the Long March. Of the 100,000 original marchers, nearly 75 percent perished along the route before reaching remote Shensi province. An American journalist, Edgar Snow, emerged as chronicler of this epic (and Mao's first biographer) when his *Red Star over China* appeared in 1938. But even before this, diplomatic officials endeavored to follow the political and military consequences of the Communist retreat. If the Communists should survive as a military force, Chiang would probably continue to use his armies against them. If they were eliminated, he might finally turn his attention toward the Japanese in the north.[10]

During 1936 problems within China and between China and Japan mounted. The Communists held onto their new base in northwestern Shensi, while Chiang marshaled his strength for a renewed attack upon them. Meanwhile, Japanese policy became more bellicose. Tokyo had already made plain its intention of increasing naval power in the Pacific when, on November 25, 1936, it joined the European fascist states in the Anti-Comintern Pact. The Japanese apparently intended to use the suppression of Communism as yet another defense for their drive to dominate China.

Despite this menacing development, Chiang pressed on with his own effort to eradicate the Communists. In December 1936 he took the fateful step of flying to the city of Sian in the northwest. There he would prod the hesitant Manchurian warlord and erstwhile KMT ally, Chang Hsueh-liang, to step up the flagging campaign against the Communists, now headquartered in the city of Yenan. On December 12, 1936, news from Nanking revealed that Chiang Kai-shek was under detention in Sian, pressed by Chang to abandon the civil war and accept the Communists into an anti-Japanese united front.[11] The Communists had earlier called for such an alliance and now found support in parts of the Nationalist camp.

A subtle but remarkably important change in Chinese politics and American sensibilities occurred over the next two weeks. Within China and in the capitals of the Western nations came the realization that for all his many faults, Chiang Kai-shek was the single figure who might lead a united national defense against Japan. The Chinese Communists lacked a sufficient base and most of Chiang's rivals within the KMT were even less disposed than he to confront the Japanese. By a process of elimination, all the parties to the Sian incident, direct and indirect, sought to convert Chiang into sharing their belief in the importance of a United Front.

The drama in Sian created a strange alliance which would last, in distorted form, until the end of World War II. The Chinese Communists sent representatives to meet with the Generalissimo and his captors. The latter, apparently, were urged to spare his life, while Chiang himself was pressed to join an anti-Japanese front. From the Soviet Union came public and private warnings that Chiang's elimination would "weaken China's defences" (and consequently Moscow's) against Japan. Ironically, Chiang's two greatest enemies, the Chinese and Soviet Communists, helped save his life from jealous rivals and transform him into the symbol of Chinese unity and political legitimacy. As his life was put in jeopardy, the Generalissimo eclipsed all other claimants for power in China.[12]

Americans in China and Washington agonized over the possible consequences of Chiang's death. President Roosevelt personally reviewed the State Department's communications to the Nanking embassy. The situation, read Ambassador Johnson's instructions, was of concern not only to China "but to the whole world." Chiang's survival was a "key element" in preserving the precarious peace of Asia.[13] Ambassador Johnson and senior military officials feared Tokyo would seize upon the crisis to increase its pressure on Chinese territory. Johnson now described Chiang as a figure "psychologically necessary" for China; he was a "man of destiny" who "personified leadership."[14]

These characterizations, which continued to escalate over the next several years, would have been unimaginable only a few months earlier. Similarly, diplomatic officials reacted with glee to Chiang's release at Christmas, realizing that he must have made at least an implicit promise to form a United Front. In fact, over the next several months, Nationalist officials kept the Nanking embassy apprised of developments in the KMT-CCP discussions aimed at reaching a formal agreement.[15] (This came only in September 1937, following Japan's attack on China.) At Sian, both the Nationalists and Communists gained increased respect in American eyes.

Finally, after years of civil war and drift, China appeared to be achieving a semblance of political unity. American officials believed this to be the sine qua non of stopping Japanese expansion. Furthermore, a united China might restrain the Japanese imperialists from further aggression in Asia and the Pacific. Now, with little danger to itself and no outlay of resources, the United States might have an ally of sorts in the Far East. The commander of the Asiatic Fleet, Admiral Harry Yarnell, typified the optimistic mood among American officials in the aftermath of Sian. In a letter written to thank a friend for the gift of Carl Crow's *400 Million Customers* (a classic China Market tract), the admiral proclaimed that the present time was unique in China's history. The unity and power personified by Chiang Kai-shek would inevitably form the bulwark of peace and American influence in Asia.[16] However, Yarnell neglected to consider Tokyo's perception of the situation. The realization of an anti-Japanese United Front would frustrate the developing idea of integrating China into a Japanese empire. Five weeks after the admiral predicted prolonged peace and prosperity, the Japanese army in Manchuria launched its invasion of China proper.

The fighting which began on July 7, 1937, at the Marco Polo Bridge north of Peking soon engulfed China and, in time, forced the United States to take heed of its own danger. As in 1931, a minor armed clash between Japanese and Chinese forces served as a pretext for military escalation. Japanese truce terms demanded the virtual separation of the northern provinces from Nanking's control, a condition Chiang could not accept. Despite some spirited resistance by Chinese units, the Japanese overran Peking on July 25, a sign of China's grave military weakness and Tokyo's expanded horizon. During the next year Japan's army overran most of northern China, the coastal areas, and major riverine ports. Constantly retreating inland, the KMT army and government traded space for time.

American officials had almost as little to say about the new war in China as they had had about the 1931 Manchurian Incident. Secretary of State Cordell Hull issued an official statement on July 16, an extremely bland pronouncement admonishing all nations to adhere to international treaties and commit themselves to the principles of peace and nonaggression.[17] Hull's inertia reflected the communications between the State Department and the ambassadors in Tokyo and Nanking. All agreed the United States could do little to affect the situation, that the drama must be played out in China, and that Chinese officials should be told to expect no significant American economic, political, or military assistance.[18]

During the first four months of the Sino-Japanese War, American officials were so quiescent that President Roosevelt's address in Chicago on October 5 (subsequently called the Quarantine Speech) caused a public sensation. No one had been prepared to hear FDR suggest that the peaceloving nations of the world might be forced to quarantine aggressors, just as health authorities isolated disease carriers. The President's strong words inspired a short-lived public debate, the idea receiving both praise and criticism. But when asked directly to expand on his speech and its policy implications, Roosevelt refused to offer an explanation. After numerous "clarifications," FDR had so muddled the question that it ceased to be discussed seriously.

However, the President was not reluctant to take decisive steps ensuring that the United States would not move against Japan in any way. Within weeks of his Chicago speech, FDR had to dispatch delegates to attend the Brussels Conference on the Far Eastern crisis. It was a consultatory gathering of the signatories to the Nine Power (Washington) Treaty of 1922. Roosevelt determined that the American delegates' instructions would prohibit them from assuming any position of leadership against Japan. The Japanese government was similarly informed through Ambassador Joseph Grew in Tokyo.[19] As was generally the case with China, leading Americans had no intention of substituting action for talk.

To criticize Roosevelt's retreat from the trial balloon of the Quarantine Speech is not to suggest that the President was suppressing a ground swell of activism in America. His own cautious and somewhat contradictory views of the events in Asia were typical of those within the Administration and Congress, and among the public. A headline appearing in the Hearst press during the earlier Manchurian crisis was just as applicable in 1937: "We sympathize. But it is not our concern." Had the President been willing and able to focus national attention on China and to win support for some form of American intervention on its behalf in 1937, it would have been a truly remarkable thing.

The political climate within the United States precluded immediate change. China remained an abstract concept in the minds of most Americans, a largely disorganized and unimportant foreign state. Japan, though a potential menace, on its own might still return to a policy of national self-restraint. Moreover, many diplomatic officials remained convinced that in the long run, Japan, despite its faults, was a necessary "stablilizing influence" in Asia. The prospect of leading a Western bloc against Japan had little appeal to American leaders sceptical of the value of collective security. Secretary Hull voiced a common opinion when he suggested that the British and French hoped to cajole the United States into a confrontation with Japan in order to safeguard their own vulnerable Asian colonies.[20]

Even beyond these policy considerations lay the more diffuse but equally real influence of isolationism and its hold on both Congress and the public. Congressional investigations into the origins of the Great War, a series of binding neutrality acts, vocal antiwar citizens' movements, all revealed the depth of American disillusionment with active world involvement. At the same time, the United States retained major overseas interests and several thousand citizens and soldiers in China. The ambiguities of this position appeared on December 12, 1937, when Japanese planes attacked and sank the U.S. Navy gunboat *Panay* on the Yangtze river. Briefly, it forced public and official minds to concentrate on the question of American interests in China.

The *Panay*, one of many Western gunboats sailing China's rivers, had been escorting barges of the Standard Oil Company. Though plainly marked as American, the ship was repeatedly strafed and then sunk with the loss of several lives. Not surprisingly, this lethal Japanese attack on a U.S. ship shocked and offended most Americans. High officials in Washington briefly considered some form of retaliation; Congress and the press demanded vengeance or justice. But when Tokyo rushed to aplogize and offer compensation for the lost lives and property, there was virtual unanimity in agreeing to accept it. Shortly thereafter, public opinion polls indicated a preference for withdrawing all American forces from China to prevent future incidents.[21]

An informed observer, witnessing both this latest event as well as the record of American inaction since 1931, would probably conclude that the United States had all but abandoned its interests in China. Washington had chosen to take no action whatever which might involve itself in the Sino-Japanese War. General and strategic trade with Japan continued without interruption. China's coastline was rapidly being sealed off by Japan's armies, isolating the Nationalist regime from normal trade. The Roosevelt administration had come under growing pressure to withdraw the small naval and military forces stationed in China by treaty. Suffering mounting losses on the battlefield and with little likelihood of foreign assistance, China seemed on the threshold of defeat. Within a year, perhaps, the Nationalist government would be replaced by a Japanese puppet regime, transforming all China into a vast Manchukuo.

Chapter 2
The Economics of
Containment, 1938-1940

THE SOMBER PREDICTIONS which doomed all China to Japanese domination never came to pass. Nor did the United States continue its attitude of benign neglect toward the Sino-Japanese War. During 1938 the tide of opinion reversed and China emerged as something of a symbol of American-sponsored resistance to Japanese aggression. This basic shift in perspective and policy demonstrated the new way in which American officials looked at both the importance of the Chinese Nationalist regime and the likely consequences of a Japanese victory. Gradually, as 1938 wore on, the outline of a new policy appeared, one predicated on the maintenance of a pro-American China which might be a bulwark against Japan. The United States hoped to use China as the weapon with which to contain Tokyo's larger imperialism. Economic assistance, Washington hoped, could achieve this result.

A variety of complementary factors transformed American attitudes and policy between late 1937 and December 1938. Singly, none sufficed to reverse the appeal of doing nothing; taken together, they had a great impact. Among the more important reasons, the most emotional must have been public shock at reports of the brutality of the Japanese army in China. The terror attacks on Shanghai and Nanking, civilian targets, outraged a generation of Americans not yet immune to total warfare. Another factor was the belief, gaining ground in Washington, that Japanese policy in China actually reflected a determination to control all Asia and the Pacific. If so, the stakes were much greater than merely the preservation of an independent Chinese regime. Also during 1938, the global military balance shifted momentously. Nazi Germany's re-emergence as a great armed power raised fears of a new European war and seriously reduced the deterrent value of British, French, and Dutch colonial forces in the Pacific. This left China and the United States as the two major sources of power which might resist Japan. When, late in 1938, fear grew in Washington that Chinese resistance might collapse, the need to sustain the Nationalist regime through American loans became obvious. The resulting policy decision became one of the several milestones on the road to Pearl Harbor.

Following the Japanese destruction of the *Panay* in December 1937, Ambassador Johnson sent several messages to Secretary Hull and Stanley Hornbeck (the Department's highest authority on Asian affairs) which revealed his personal fear. The attack on American property and personnel, he felt, had an aim quite apart from insuring victory over the Chinese. Instead, the Japanese were driven by a vision of eliminating "all western influence among the Chinese." In the face of what appeared to be American indifference, Johnson suggested, Nationalist leaders might move toward an accommodation with Tokyo or, alternatively, with Moscow since the Soviet Union had begun to extend credits and equipment to the KMT.[1]

Johnson's view, that the future of American influence in China hung in the balance, appeared a minor concern beside the warning sounded by Admiral Yarnell. The commander of the Asiatic Fleet alerted the Navy Department to his belief that Tokyo intended to eliminate American interests everywhere in the Pacific. To Yarnell, the fate of China, the Philippines, and future economic opportunities throughout Asia were all a single issue. His reports to Admiral William Leahy admonished the chief of naval operations that to permit a Japanese conquest of China was tantamount to abandoning the mainland of Asia and control of the Pacific Ocean. The only way to frustrate Japan's scheme, Yarnell believed, was to aid Chiang and maintain him in power, while initiating trade sanctions against Japan. America's most important ally—and its defense bulwark in Asia—must be Nationalist China.[2]

While Yarnell's apocalyptic vision might be dismissed as an overly pessimistic reaction to the Navy's loss of the *Panay*, senior staff took it quite seriously. Admiral Leahy, a powerful figure in both the Roosevelt and later the Truman administrations, saw to it that Yarnell's reports circulated among high officials in the State and War departments and among the President's staff. He even hand carried many directly to the President. One in particular warned that only Chinese resistance, led by "Generalissimo and Madame Chiang," stood between Tokyo's legions and California. The United States must begin to support China, Yarnell wrote, "not only for those sound moral and political reasons but for the really tremendous trade possibilities which such supported stability would bring." China Market rhetoric, it seemed could always substitute for sound strategy. In any case, wrote Admiral Yarnell, if Japan were not soon stopped, "the white race would have no future in Asia."[3]

If Roosevelt shared Yarnell's nightmare, he did not say. The President's view of the war in China, and most other foreign policy questions at this time, remained a cipher. Neither his own papers nor the memoirs of aides provide much insight into whether he believed new policies must be devised. One useful index of FDR's thought, however, can be derived by examining the people to whom he turned for information. The President often preferred to rely on private sources, rather than regular government or State Department officials, for reports on problem areas. This no doubt reflected his deep suspicion of bureaucrats and desire to remain uncommitted to any particular faction. From 1938 until his death in 1945, FDR dispatched nearly a dozen "special" emissaries to serve as his eyes and ears in China. These presidential agents represented a diverse group, in terms of their skills and political philosophies. But all were linked directly to the President, not to an intermediary bureaucracy. The impact of these individuals upon Roosevelt and American policy would range from the trivial to the catastrophic.

The first such mission to China fell upon the able shoulders of Marine Captain Evans F. Carlson. A former intelligence officer in China, Carlson had met Roosevelt while a member of the presidential honor guard at Warm Springs, Georgia. They became good enough acquaintances for Roosevelt to later urge his son to serve under Carlson's command during World War II. But in 1937 the President had a different design. Knowing that the captain was slated to return to China, FDR asked him to gather intelligence especially for the White House. Communications between the two men were routed through the President's secretary, Marguerite Le Hand.

On his own initiative, Carlson determined to investigate the aspect of the war in China most shrouded in mystery: the Communist guerrilla campaign. He was eager to learn how, with even fewer material resources than the KMT, the Communists were managing to sustain a vast if ill-defined battle front in north China. Sucn an investigation meant Carlson would have to cross into Communist territory, *terra incognita* to most Americans. Fortuitously, he could rely on past friendships with Edgar Snow (for contacts with the CCP) and Chiang's Australian political advisor, W. D. Donald, for KMT permission. During most of 1938 this rugged Marine officer tagged along with the Communist Eighth Route Army, making friends with its commanders and preparing reports for Roosevelt.[4]

Carlson's letters to the White House provided vivid accounts of the "miracle" he discovered among the Communists. With no outside assistance, they had organized a guerrilla army based on massive peasant support. In Communist territory he saw little of the defeatism and corruption which had paralyzed the KMT's war effort. While the Communists were undoubtedly social revolutionaries, Carlson wrote, they were also bona fide nationalists who were eager to cooperate with the United States to defeat Japan and reconstruct China. Aid to the Communists, Carlson told the President, would help defeat Japan and secure the friendship of the most dynamic and progressive political group in China.[5]

Did these reports have any serious impact on Roosevelt? FDR admitted to Secretary of the Interior Harold Ickes that Carlson's letters excited his imagination and provided a stirring picture of the value of guerrilla warfare. Ickes, too, had just become familiar with the existence of the Chinese Communists through reading Snow's recently published *Red Star over China*. Roosevelt took up the suggestion that he read the book and quickly became a fan of Snow. Several times, over the subsequent years, the journalist received invitations to discuss Chinese politics with the President.[6] But, as was so often the case, FDR's discussions with Ickes and Snow demonstrated his thirst for information. He said almost nothing to reveal his own thoughts or uncertainties.

The issues posed by the arguments of Carlson and Snow made the dilemma of China policy all the greater, if that were possible. Explicit in their discussions with the President was the assertion that the United States must become selectively involved in China. Merely to assist the Nationalist regime might be insufficient or counterproductive. The Communists, too, had a claim on American support, for they had mobilized millions of Chinese to fight the enemy. Just how Washington could politically justify (or physically deliver) aid to the Communists was unclear. Certainly, as all subsequent events showed, Chiang would never permit it. But the question of which Chinese should receive aid for use against Japan became an obvious problem months before a decision to begin assistance was made.

Unfortunately for Carlson, his own commitment to the Communists became a political liability. As he explained to his friend, Ambassador Johnson, conservative elements in the Navy Department and in the KMT regime bitterly resented his suggestions that the Communists deserved military support. Increasingly isolated, Carlson believed his usefulness as an intelligence officer had been undercut. Late in 1938 he resigned his commission and returned to the United States to begin working as a journalist lobbying for aid to China.[7] The Nationalists so feared his partisanship that they objected to his return to China for the rest of the war years, and, according to rumors, suspected the entire Marine Corps of harboring Communist sympathizers.

As of early 1938, the Chinese Nationalist regime could still count on very little from America. Dramatic warnings continued to reach the State and Navy departments from Ambassador Johnson and Admiral Yarnell. The Japanese, it seemed, would conquer Asia or "die trying." Similarly, Admiral Leahy confided to his diary the conviction that, to turn an interesting phrase, China's battle was a desperate defense of "western civilization." Captain Carlson, too, peppered the White House with news from the war front and pleas that the United States assist China. But the only demonstrable affect the Sino-Japanese War had so far upon influential Americans was seen in Henry Luce's (son of a missionary family) decision to place Generalissimo and Madame Chiang on the cover of *Time* magazine as 1937 "Man and Wife of the Year."[8]

America's priorities were outlined in April 1938 in a memorandum sent by Stanley Hornbeck to the British Foreign Office. Though an unofficial communication, the Far Eastern advisor to the Secretary of State explained it represented a consensus within the department. The United States, he wrote, deplored Japanese aggression in China; Washington would continue to honor the principles of nonaggression and territorial integrity embodied in the Nine Power Treaty. Hopefully, Japan would come to see the error of its ways. In the meantime, Washington saw no advantage in any attempt at Anglo-American mediation or intervention, and neither the risk nor cost of war with Japan was acceptable. While some junior officers in the department questioned whether China could carry on the fight alone very much longer, no senior official seriously discussed the logical alternatives of aiding China and imposing economic sanctions on Japan.[9]

Of course, the Chinese desperately sought foreign economic assistance from all sources. Since the KMT derived the bulk of central government revenues from the modern economic sector and treaty ports, the early loss of these areas and the move inland deprived the regime of its economic base. Diplomatic representatives in London and Washington pled with their host governments for support, though their methods of operation did little to enhance the cause. A fierce factional and household battle had been waged within the KMT administration for years centering upon Chiang's rival brothers-in-law, H. H. Kung and T. V. Soong. Soong, with his superior command of English and American Ph. D. degree, had stronger support among the diplomatic and commercial communities in England and the United States. Foreign friends often "complimented" him as a white man in a yellow skin! Right through the Communist victory, the two brothers-in-law would battle for influence over Chiang by demonstrating their superior ability to woo foreign aid. During early 1938, as the naval attaché in China, James McHugh, reported, each spread rumors that they had succeeded in securing large foreign loans. The object apparently was to embarrass one's rival, whatever the effect on China.[10] When American aid, weapons and personnel finally did arrive, this contest escalated to a dizzying intensity and seriously undermined the war effort. In 1938 it only succeeded in delaying the initial decision by the United States to assist China.

By the summer of 1938, while the Western European democracies compromised Czechoslovakia's independence to preserve peace, the pace of the war in China also quickened. The Japanese army resumed its offensive, closing in on the Nationalists who had retreated toward the interior. Nanking was quickly lost and the major cities of Canton and Hankow were threatened. In essence, the KMT's base area—the coastal provinces and the lower Yangtze region—would be controlled by Japanese forces. Many Chinese and foreigners doubted that the regime could take root in the backward and mountainous western provinces controlled by semiautonomous warlords. A peace faction emerged around the person of Wang Ching-wei, Chiang's old rival within the KMT, and strains appeared in the infant United Front with the Communists. Chiang's survival appeared to hinge on both a successful retreat to the interior and visible signs of new outside support.

These circumstances prompted American officials to act before Chinese resistance collapsed. In July Secretary of State Hull, who seldom initiated important policies on his own, told Ambassador Joseph Kennedy in London to inform the British of American interest in possible joint economic aid to China. Hull's Far Eastern advisor, Hornbeck, soon met with Warren Pierson, president of the Export-Import Bank, to discuss aid strategies. Hornbeck told the bank president that American security required continued Chinese resistance to Japan. Therefore the bank, ought to consider extending credits to the Nationalist government for the purchase of vital material. Pierson endorsed the principle of a "political loan" to China and promised to go along if the President and State Department requested it.[11]

The official who finally drove through a new policy, however, was neither State nor Navy, but the energetic Secretary of the Treasury—and Roosevelt intimate—Henry Morgenthau, Jr. A man who went out of his way to influence every decision remotely relating to economics, Morgenthau particularly believed in the need for the United States to play a more active role in resisting Nazi and Japanese aggression. He had already gotten a foot in the door of China policy through the reports he received from a few special Treasury agents in China. While traveling in Europe during August, he contacted Chinese representatives and encouraged them to have the influential Chinese banker K. P. Chen sent to Washington to discuss trade credits.[12] By the time the Chinese agreed to send Chen, later in August, the military situation had grown even more desperate. H. H. Kung, Nationalist finance minister, provided Chen instructions which reflected a mood of desperation. He was to seek an immediate cash loan to prevent the collapse of the Chinese currency and the consequent political repercussions.

Chen also was to seek aid from "big U.S. companies with China interests."[13]

Morgenthau played a pivotal role in forging a new China policy, one which the State Department, under Hull, could not. The Secretary of the Treasury enjoyed a special relationship with the President and used the access it provided to the limit. Morgenthau had a thinly veiled contempt for Hull (which Roosevelt probably shared) and believed most diplomats too cowardly and slow witted to stand up to fascist aggression. Moreover, the Treasury Secretary believed that the President needed a gadfly to prod him to take risks in foreign affairs, a role Morgenthau cast for himself. Between 1938 and early 1941 Morgenthau secured a leading role for the Treasury Department in supervising economic aid to China. Only with the passage of Lend-Lease in 1941 did FDR take back the reins.

During the fall of 1938 Morgenthau supervised the Treasury Department's negotiations with K. P. Chen. Roosevelt received progress reports on the talks which doubled as Morgenthau's lobbying effort. Economic aid to China, he claimed, would do much to deter not only Japanese but German aggression as well. "What greater force for peace could there be," he asked FDR rhetorically, "than the emergence of a unified China?"[14] To secure this end, the Treasury wished to grant China a $25 million commodity credit. If Roosevelt approved, Morgenthau explained, the Export-Import Bank would extend a loan secured by China's promise to eventually deliver a suitable quantity of tung oil (used in varnish and paint) for sale in the United States. The actual cash would be given to the Universal Trading Corporation (UTC) a Chinese government front, to purchase American trucks and vital supplies.[15]

Before reaching a decision, Roosevelt first asked the Chinese for a promise to continue resisting Japan (which they eagerly gave) and then went through the formality of polling the State Department. Both Secretary Hull and Maxwell Hamilton, head of the Division of Far Eastern Affairs, spoke against the proposal. These two men feared a hostile reaction by isolationists in Congress and a technical violation of the neutrality laws. The loan, they claimed, would antagonize Japan without doing very much for China. Hamilton spoke for both when he declared [the loan] "would not vitally affect the outcome of hostilities. If the United States wishes to do that it must throw its whole weight behind China." [16]

The inconvenience of this opposition by the Secretary of State and the head of the Far Eastern division was overcome when Hull agreed to permit Stanley Hornbeck to communicate a dissenting opinion to the President. Hornbeck, as one of the most senior Asian experts in the department (and Hull's personal advisor), possessed sufficient seniority to mitigate the other statements of opposition to the loan. He argued forcefully that the proposal to grant immediate credits to China was a tremendous blow against Japan's "predatory imperialism." If Japan was not stopped in China, the United States would soon be facing Tokyo's forces closer to home. This aid, Hornbeck explained, ought only to be the first step in a "diplomatic war plan" that should include denouncing the 1911 commercial treaty with Japan, repealing the Neutrality Act, restricting trade with Tokyo and bolstering American naval strength in the Pacific to "show we mean business." Hornbeck concluded his memorandum to the President by stating that the decision at hand should not be judged solely by its immediate significance, nor its current impact on China. The credits should be granted "on the basis of and in the light of a decision by the American Government to exert itself actively and intensively toward throwing the weight of this country's capacity into a general effort to halt Japan's predatory advance." [17]

Morgenthau's lobbying efforts, Hornbeck's support for the project, and the American shock at the recent German dismemberment of Czechoslovakia consequent to the Munich agreement all magnified the importance surrounding the argument over whether to grant China economic credits. In addition, by late November, the Treasury Secretary added a new arrow to his quiver. The Chinese had begun receiving significant military aid from the Soviet Union and passed the word to Americans that dependence on the Soviets would influence the Nationalists' political stance. Morgenthau, when informed of this, advised colleagues in several executive agencies that the delayed loan decision had come close to driving Chiang into the "hand of Russia" and communism.[18] American officials, it seemed, did not want to save China from Japan by permitting it to be "lost" to Russia.

Not surprisingly, the Japanese themselves provided the final impetus which prodded the American government toward decisive action. In November 1938 Tokyo declared that it no longer considered the Open Door an operative principle for economic conduct in Asia.[19] Apparently this meant that Japan formally claimed the right to challenge and exclude the Western powers from their entrenched positions throughout Asia. This ominous statement coincided with Japanese military victories at the supposed Nationalist strongholds of Hankow and Canton. Desperate for the signs and substance of American support, KMT officials informed their confidant, Naval attaché James McHugh, that Chiang might have to consider making peace with Japan.[20] Whether a bluff or not (realistically, Chiang had no future if Japan succeeded), American officials scurried to meet this crisis.

As usual, Morgenthau led the campaign for action within the administration. As soon as Secretary of State Hull left Washington for a conference in Lima late in November, Morgenthau conferred with Under-Secretary of State Sumner Welles. As both a friend of the President and a diplomat disposed to act more boldly than Hull, Welles agreed to cooperate with Morgenthau in pressing FDR for a quick decision on the aid question. On November 30, 1938, they jointly presented their arguments to Roosevelt and received his approval for the credits. No one bothered to inform Hull until December 2.[21] During the next three years Morgenthau would relish the story of how he outfoxed Hull by taking action when the Secretary of State was "at sea."

On December 15, after the details of the aid program had been clarified, the State Department released notice of an agreement between the Export-Import Bank and the UTC for extension of a $25 million credit. By granting some Treasury Department funds to the Bank of China for "currency stabilization," Morgenthau was able to supplement the sum slightly.[22] However, the total funds were not the major issue in what was essentially a political decision to adopt a new policy toward China. Led by Morgenthau, activists in Washington had finally pried open (if only a trifle) the coffers of American aid. The President apparently agreed that maintaining Chinese resistance to Japan served as a first line of American defense. Looked at from a slightly different perspective, Morgenthau and Hornbeck had formulated a primitive domino theory which postulated Nationalist China as the pivot in the defense of the Pacific. A Japanese victory would undermine the entire Western position right across Southeast Asia and the Pacific.

Tokyo reacted vociferously to the credits, denouncing foreign interference in China and warning that the action endangered Japanese-American relations.[23] Tokyo particularly objected to the timing of the loan, not merely its substance. In December, Wang Ching-wei resolved to join the Japanese and create a rival "Kuomintang" government. This act, many thought, might split Chiang's supporters and solidify peace sentiment in China. The almost simultaneous American decision to grant credits to Chiang's regime cushioned the impact of Wang's defection. Some time later China's ambassador in Washington, Dr. Hu Shih, told Hornbeck that the December loan played a major role in sustaining Chiang's grip on the KMT.[24]

The official as well as the private Nationalist reaction to American policy reflected Hu's assertions. This at last evidenced real material commitment to China. The major KMT press organ, *Chung-yang Jih-pao* (Central Daily), labeled the

American aid (and the small English sterling credit which followed) a "decision to preserve the Open Door" and China's independence. Over the days which followed, editorials and feature articles heralded the small loan as an end to America's appeasement of Japan. U.S. power, the implication stressed, backed China.[25]

Yet the most revealing Chinese reaction may have appeared in a confidential message sent by one of the Chinese negotiators to Finance Minister Kung. He stated that

the $25 million is only the beginning. . . . Further large sums can be expected . . . this is a political loan . . . America has definitely thrown in her lot and cannot withdraw. We will have two years [of a] sympathetic Washington administration, possible six. Our political outlook is now brighter.[26]

The Chinese representative's joy apparently extended to include both the immediate circumstances and the possibility of a third Roosevelt administration.

While the message to Kung overstated the case, the decision to extend a loan certainly represented a major change in American attitudes and policy. Roosevelt endorsed the view of his advisors who favored utilizing China as a vehicle to contain Japan. Maintaining an independent Chinese regime now had real meaning, rather than the traditional lack of meaning associated with the Open Door. But, all in all, the tung oil credits represented only a tiny contribution to China's economic and material needs. To have any effect, American aid would have to be much more substantial and combined with parallel economic pressures against Japan. Such a policy, in turn, required that the Roosevelt administration reorganize the foreign-policymaking bureaucracy. The rather sluggish State Department represented a drag on policy innovations. Within the executive branch only Morgenthau's Treasury Department seemed able and willing to advance bold initiatives. But all that it did was ad hoc, dependent on Morgenthau's stamina and FDR's willingness to let the Secretary push ahead.

The problem of overlapping authority and bureaucratic rivalry remained unresolved right down through the beginning of the war with Japan. State and Treasury department planners frequently worked at cross purposes, only to discover the War and Navy departments moving in a third direction. By 1941, as Roosevelt and the White House staff became more concerned with personally formulating policy, a fourth dimension was added to the puzzle. The split between civilian and military planners widened when they had to consider America's relative military weakness in the Pacific. Though they might agree on essential goals, military commanders realized the severe limitations under which the United States labored. Even after naval expansion began in 1936, sea and land forces in the Pacific remained small, poorly equipped, and unprepared for conflict with Japan.

Strategic planners looked upon Europe and Nazi Germany as the major potential threat to the United States. Until the conclusion of the Nazi-Soviet Pact in August 1939 and the German blitz of the following spring, most presumed that the European colonial powers in Asia would augment American forces and that Tokyo might press north, toward Siberia, rather than southward. While maintaining a delicate balance, the Roosevelt administration had to be mindful of not provoking a war with Japan over its China aid policy. A fundamental reason for assisting China, after all, was to put physical constraints on Japanese military expansion. Any action which might lead to war must be avoided. Six months after the initial loan of December 1938, the United States gave Tokyo the required six-month notice of terminating the 1911 commercial treaty. Yet no actual economic and trade sanctions began until another half-year had passed. This caution also restrained a second infusion of aid to China before March 1940. The long gaps in imposing trade sanctions and assisting China resulted from a temporary easing of the military crisis in China as well as from an American concern with the escalating crisis in Europe. After the European war began in September 1939, American officials proved even more reluctant to provoke a confrontation with Tokyo, for war in the Pacific now meant essentially a struggle between the United States and Japan.

During 1939, while the war of attrition in China continued, American officials pondered the question of why China was so important to the United States. Hornbeck of the State Department took the lead. He circulated an article in the department which propounded a domino-like theory that both China and Southeast Asia were areas absolutely essential for American economic security. China, Hornbeck believed, was really the key to Southeast Asia because it was the base of strategic control for the whole region. With its abundant concentrations of vital raw materials such as oil, rubber, and tin (all of which Japan desperately required), the United States would have to fight "any power that might threaten to sever our trade lines with this part of the world." The twin goals of preserving Western domination of Asian resources and preventing Japan's access underlay Hornbeck's rationale. Not surprisingly, he took the personal initiative of urging American corporations and banks to cease business with Japan.[27]

Others in the State Department, such as the rising star among the China hands, John Carter Vincent, also spoke of the need to impose economic sanctions on Japan combined with increased aid to China. In Vincent's opinion, American security in the Pacific required "keeping in existence an independent Chinese government . . . independent of Soviet Russia as well as Japan." At a February meeting with the President, Ambassador Johnson expressed his view that the United States must assume the mantle of world leadership as the heir to the British Empire in Asia. Only the United States could "lead the world out of the chaos in which it is now struggling."[28]

During 1939 the Treasury Department, too, developed a rationale to convince itself of China's strategic importance to the United States. As early as May 1939 Morgenthau's aide, Harry Dexter White, recommended granting China a "well publicized loan" which might deter Japanese aggression elsewhere and insure that the United States would win the bulk of "reconstruction work" and trade with postwar China.[29] This evolved into a plan to lend China money in return for future tin shipments. Yet, for the remainder of that year, Morgenthau found it impossible to shake Secretary Hull out of his fear of further antagonizing Japan. The Treasury Secretary even quipped that the best strategy would be to send Hull abroad for another conference and get to Welles and Roosevelt while he was "at sea." But even when Morgenthau did broach the idea of a new loan directly with the President, he found little support. Roosevelt complained that "isolationists" in Congress would seize upon his granting additional aid to China as warmongering.[30] Thus, through the beginning of 1940, arguments favoring increased assistance to Chiang's regime still could not overcome the deeply rooted fear of provoking Japan. Similarly, the administration refused to restrict strategic sales to Japan until after Tokyo occupied northern French Indochina.

As had been true in December 1938, Japan's actions tipped the scales in favor of bolder American policy. Early in the spring of 1940, Wang Ching-wei established the pro-Japanese Nanking puppet regime, a move destined to undercut the loyalty of Chiang's shaky coalition. Tokyo's intentions frightened American leaders for now there seemed little hope of Japan ever agreeing to reach a settlement with the Chungking regime. Instead, the Japanese appeared more determined than ever to gain control over all China. Both Roosevelt and Hull quickly overcame their earlier reservations that additional aid to Chiang would antagonize Tokyo. Instead, they felt it more important to signify their support for Chiang and opposition to Wang's puppet regime. His hand freed, Morgenthau sprang ahead and by March 7, 1940, concluded arrangements to grant China—actually UTC—$20 million in return for future tin shipments.[31]

Largely staffed by American lawyers formerly employed in the White House, the Treasury Department, and federal regulatory agencies, UTC acted as the business agent of the Chinese government. It serviced orders placed in the United States by Chinese agencies, paying with funds made available from American credits. Although the credits of December 1938 and March 1940 were legally restricted to nonmilitary purchases, by the end of 1941 an estimated $25 million had actually been used to buy military supplies. The responsible American officials collaborated in this subterfuge by having UTC obscure its military purchases by subcontracting through another "front," the Criterion Trading Corporation.[32]

Not surprisingly, having succeeded in obtaining the additional credits of March 1940, the Chinese pressed Washington for still more aid. They transmitted warnings of imminent currency collapse and used unofficial channels to bring pressure on the Treasury Department. Some of the Chinese tactics, such as having Arthur Young, the American financial advisor to Chiang, request Hornbeck to ask Morgenthau for additional aid, angered Morgenthau. The Treasury Secretary felt loans had to go through proper channels, and he much preferred to deal only through K. P. Chen: "Everything that a story book Chinese businessman should be and most of them aren't." At least among his close associates in the Treasury Department, Morgenthau admitted that he liked Chen "because he will keep his word, but the rest of them are just a bunch of crooks." Nevertheless, the Secretary continued to remain an ardent supporter of aid to China, believing that the maintenance of some form of pro-American, anti-Japanese regime was crucial.[33]

In any case, the Chinese demands for aid were not diminished by Morgenthau's personal scruples or his belief that aid funds should primarily be granted in the form of credits rather than of subsidies to Chinese currency. T. V. Soong, Chiang's personal envoy to Washington (Ambassador Hu Shih was merely a figurehead), continued a dialogue on aid projects and developed a novel scheme. He proposed a three-way trade in raw materials and cash among China, the United States, and the Soviet Union. Profits from American purchases and resale of Russian and Chinese raw materials would be funneled back through Russia to China, to the tune of $140 million. Although somewhat confusing, the plan marked a significant political development. It appears to be the first time that the Chinese Nationalists attempted to involve both Washington and Moscow in a scheme to aid the Nationalists. Such a plan would not only benefit the KMT economically but would certainly transmit a major political message to Chiang's adversaries, both in Tokyo and in Yenan.

Morgenthau showed interest in exploring this idea, which might lead to stockpiling strategic materials, helping China, and improving relations with the Soviet Union. Encouraged by Roosevelt's having "specifically said to go ahead," the Treasury Secretary circulated the proposal around Washington and sought the reaction of the Russian ambassador. The Soviet representative evidenced some interest and agreed to conduct further discussions. However, Sumner Welles of the State Department raised such violent objections to the suggestions of trafficking with Russia (then nominally allied to Germany) that Morgenthau finally abandoned the effort.[34]

This interdepartmental quibbling over the form of aid and the "morality" of American dealing with the Soviets became a nonaffordable luxury by the fall of 1940. The collapse of France, Japan's move into northern Indochina, and her adherence to the Axis alliance all had a cumulative shock effect on Washington. Not only was Japan's grasp stretching beyond China—as Hornbeck and Morgenthau had long predicted—but it now directly endangered the colonial lifelines of England to Singapore, Malaya, India, and the Dutch East Indies. China's supply lifeline, the Burma Road, lay exposed to easy conflict. Japan's control of Southeast Asian resources would eventually virtually free Tokyo from foreign economic dependence and eliminate the effectiveness of the strategy of economic warfare which the United States was about to commence. In Hornbeck's phrase, the United States now faced a "two-front war."

Policymakers in both Tokyo and Washington realized that rhetoric on the legitimacy of the Open Door was about to be replaced by a slugfest. The first round began in July 1940 with the imposition of American export restrictions on high grades of steel and gasoline.[35]

The Western European collapse and Japanese advance of mid-1940 further altered the pace of Sino-American cooperation. Both Chungking and Washington feared the implications of the British decision of September 1940 temporarily to close the Burma Road. To induce a sign of American support, Chiang responded to this act by proposing to Roosevelt and Morgenthau that the United States accept an economic protectorate over certain areas of China which it would be expected to defend against Japan.[36] Chiang followed this idea with a suggestion that the Chinese sign a formal and comprehensive alliance with the United States and Great Britain. In return for several hundred million dollars, one thousand airplanes, and the dispatch of American military advisors, the generalissimo would grant the United States generous postwar rights to Chinese naval facilities. These staggering proposals, politely disregarded by Washington, were nonetheless important in indicating the direction in which Chinese thought had moved. The desire to acquire sophisticated airplanes and the technicians to operate them, and offers for postwar port facilities, were all efforts to gain immediate and tangible benefits as well as to create a network of American support for long-term involvement on behalf of Chiang.

However, American plans still focused on economic aid for China, not open-ended and dangerous military support. During September 1940 Morgenthau approached Hull with suggestions that more aid be given China. Hull responded favorably, indicating he, too, had it in mind to "get tough with the Japs" by imposing sanctions against Japanese exports to the United States. When Hull also suggested extending additional credits to China, Morgenthau and his staff jested that they might not be "sober."[37] Hull and Morgenthau arranged for Federal Loan

Administrator Jesse Jones to grant China $25 million with the "implication given to the Chinese" that more aid would follow. T. V. Soong managed to interfere with the planning by first insisting that the loan be at least $50 million. After some talking-to by Arthur Young, Hornbeck, James McHugh, and Jesse Jones, Soong graciously accepted a loan of $25 million on behalf of the Central Bank of China on September 26. Careful observers of the announcement probably noted that the text omitted any restriction on possible military uses of the American funds.[38]

This loan was quickly augmented by still greater American aid. Late in November the Chungking crisis mill geared up in response to Tokyo's formal recognition of the previously established Wang Ching-wei puppet regime in Nanking. Since recognition of Wang by Tokyo indicated a hardening of the Japanese position, Ambassador Johnson warned of imminent collapse in Chungking unless Washington moved to bolster Chiang by extending renewed financial and political support.[39]

Roosevelt himself now took the initiative in pressing his subordinates for quick action. On the morning of November 29, 1940, the President phoned Morgenthau with the message that "he is worried about China and he is evidently worried about something going on between Wang and Chiang, and he wants me to make a stabilization loan of fifty million dollars to the Chinese in the next 24 hours." In addition, Roosevelt wanted the Export-Import Bank to make an equally large commodity credit available to China. Morgenthau did not disagree with Roosevelt's goal but was placed in a personally awkward position by the fact that he had promised to consult Congress before any large currency stabilization funds were granted to a foreign nation.[40] Roosevelt's twenty-four-hour time limit made such a procedure impossible. Morgenthau naturally disliked being cast as the spoilsport, attempting to delay announcement of the loan before consulting with key senators and members of the House. Meanwhile, Chinese supporters in Washington and pro-Chiang Americans in Chungking began to circulate rumors of impending collapse in China.

Morgenthau called in T. V. Soong on November 30 to determine just why an immediate loan was so urgent. Soong, never renowned for his modesty, told Morgenthau that Chiang actually wanted "between two and three hundred million dollars" but would settle for one hundred million for the time being. The importance of an immediate loan, Soong explained, was to demonstrate American defiance of Tokyo's recognition of Wang's regime. Anything short of one hundred million dollars would cause Chiang to lose both face and power, Soong implied.[41] By this time, threats of surrender had become standard KMT negotiating practice.

Momentarily frustrated by Morgenthau's efforts to delay announcement of the loans until he had consulted Congress, Soong flitted over to the State Department. There he managed to enlist the support of Welles and Hull for an immediate announcement. Welles met with the Treasury Secretary and after some discussion persuaded the reluctant Morgenthau to agree to release a statement that same day (November 30) that the Treasury Department had the "intention to ask Congress" for approval of the $100 million for China. Soong had successfully undercut Morgenthau's pledge of honor to go before Congress before making any such deals.[42]

The Treasury Secretary of course bitterly resented the comparative ease with which Soong had manipulated the White House and State Department. He worried—with good cause—that the Chinese had learned a technique to manipulate the American bureaucracy. The only favorable result of the deal, Morgenthau believed, was that Treasury Department representatives would be authorized to go to China in an attempt to supervise use of the stabilization funds. Still more importantly, they could then prepare economic and political reports exclusively for the Treasury Department, freeing Morgenthau from complete dependence on the State Department's Foreign Service, which he distrusted.[43]

Morgenthau's frustration with the November 1940 loan episode revealed both present and emergent problems of the China aid program. Within the Roosevelt administration, lines of authority remained blurred as various agencies claimed jurisdiction over setting and implementing policy. The resulting confusion both interfered with coherent, long-range planning and allowed Chinese lobbyists, such as T. V. Soong, to manipulate decisions more easily. As the confrontation between the United States and Japan tensed at the end of 1940, President Roosevelt resolved to take a more direct role in redressing these problems. Through his White House staff, Roosevelt for the first time asserted central control over China policy. The President set out to forge a tightly administered program designed not only to expedite economic aid but also to transform China into a useful military and political ally of the United States. At the time, virtually no one in Washington glimpsed the quagmire into which America had stepped.

Chapter 3
American Aid and Chinese Politics, 1939-1941

MILITARY AND DIPLOMATIC crises crowded in upon the United States during 1941. Both German advances in Europe and Japanese moves in Asia threatened to destroy America's new allies just as Washington resolved to underwrite their war effort. The desperate economic and military positions of Great Britain, China, and (after June) the Soviet Union impelled Roosevelt to again mobilize the nation as he had in the early days of the New Deal. Having declared that America must be the "arsenal of democracy," FDR sought to give the words meaning in the Lend-Lease bill he sent to Congress in January 1941. By its terms, Washington would finance the purchase and supply of military equipment to any government "whose defense the President deems vital to the United States." Under Lend-Lease Roosevelt could dispense more aid, quickly, without the need to press several sluggish agencies into action. For the rest of the war, Lend-Lease proved the vital political and military link between the United States and its allies.

The challenges of supporting Great Britain and the Soviet Union were fully matched by the problems of the weakest ally, China. Even as the U.S. commitment to China grew, China's own United Front and war effort began to disintegrate. Civil war, smoldering since 1927 and only briefly suspended in 1937, appeared about to explode. Chiang and his allies remained determined to exterminate the Communists at almost any cost. The generalissimo allegedly described the Japanese as a mere "disease of the skin" but the Communists as a "disease of the heart." The fundamental hostility between the two dominant Chinese factions posed a dilemma which the United States faced with neither the British nor the Soviets. The same Amer-

39

ican aid which might spur resistance to Japan could—and probably would—spark internal warfare. Right through Japan's surrender in 1945, American planners struggled to devise a formula to solve China's growing domestic turmoil. Nor surprisingly, the twin crises, civil war and the war against Japan, fused together for the Americans as it already had for the Chinese combatants.

Despite the hopes of many Americans and Chinese, the heralded United Front reached its zenith shortly before the first tung oil loan reached China. During 1938 the Nationalists had relaxed slightly their anti-Communist campaign. This involved abandoning the assault on Yenan and establishing political liaisons. A heavily censored Communist paper, *Hsin-hua Jih-pao* (New China Daily), was permitted limited circulation in KMT areas and a handful of CCP representatives were permitted to reside in the Nationalist capital, then being moved from city to city before the Japanese advance. Chiang also granted "legal" status to some of the Red military forces operating in north China and behind Japanese lines. But the cooperative effort faded quickly as the two factions split on the questions of basic military and political strategy. In the summer and fall of 1938, the KMT rejected the Communists' idea of organizing the workers and peasants around the provisional capital and major city of Hankow to resist Japan. Chiang preferred to abandon the city, which he believed doomed, and to withdraw the bulk of his forces to distant Chungking in Szechuan province. There the army would be needed to establish supremacy over the western warlords. The Communists not surprisingly felt that Chiang wished to avoid any real cooperative effort against Japan.[1] In fact, within a few months the Nationalists reassigned several hundred thousand of their best troops to blockade the Communist base areas in the north, a blockade maintained through 1945.

Initially, American officials in both China and Washington knew very little about this growing split, and not much more about Communist policies than they had in earlier years. The view of Sumner Welles was more or less typical. In 1938 he instructed the consul at Hankow to collect Communist publications, warning the diplomat that the CCP remained a Russian puppet plotting to colonize China on Moscow's behalf.[2] However, the staff of the American embassy in China felt less certain than did Welles of the Communists' ultimate designs. In fact, they were somewhat in awe of the early success of the Communists in organizing guerrilla armies from ignorant and untrained peasants. The tactic of combining resistance to a foreign invader with basic social reform obviously had much more appeal than did the KMT press gangs which roamed the countryside.[3]

The rapid growth of Communist strength both within and behind Japanese lines proved the source of renewed internal warfare. The Nationalists feared the Communists' success in assuming the mantle of political legitimacy and nationalism in the wake of the KMT retreat from its former base areas. By the summer of 1939 the Nationalists, now entrenched in Chungking, decided to restrict the areas in which the Communists would be permitted to operate. They hoped to keep the Reds as isolated as possible in areas to the north of the Yangtze River. An early result of this decision was a series of battles fought in Shantung province during the summer of 1939. KMT spokesman explained the situation to America diplomats by declaring the Communists Russian puppets who would be fully exterminated "as soon as hostilities with Japan were ended."[4]

This reference to Soviet meddling in China should have struck the Americans as ironic, for the facts of the case were quite reversed. In the two years prior to the end of 1939, the Soviet Union had extended over $500 million in military credits to the KMT, and even provided a fighter squadron flown by Russian pilots. Yenan, however, received little or no Soviet assistance before August 1945. Nevertheless, the KMT seemed to feel that raising the specter of Soviet interference might win American support for operations against the Chinese Communists. By the end of 1940, Chiang explicitly linked his determination to destroy his Communist rivals with the KMT's position vis-à-vis Moscow and Washington.

As CCP-KMT relations deteriorated during 1940, the deployment of the Communist New Fourth Army south of the Yangtze River emerged as the most volatile flash point for the two factions. While the Nationalists put pressure on the Communists to move north (which meant into Japanese-held territory!), Chiang invited Ambassador Johnson to hear the Chungking regime's side of the story. The generalissimo made no attempt to hide the fact that he hoped to strike against his partners in the United Front. Rather, he spoke of the factors which had heretofore limited his flexibility. Since the Soviet Union remained a major arms supplier of the Nationalists (though the level of aid had declined and soon would end due to Russia's own growing needs and desire to placate the Japanese), Chiang believed that attacking the Communists before securing new patronage would be dangerous.[5]

However, the Chinese leader went on, if the United States offered China a comprehensive military and economic aid package, he would act swiftly. Chiang envisioned a large loan, one thousand military aircraft, and American volunteer pilots. All this would allow him to deal with China's "real" enemy, the one within.

It is not the Japanese army which we fear, because our army is able to deal with it, but the defiant Communists. American economic assistance plus the aid of the American Air Force can stabilize our unsteady economic and social conditions, thus making it impossible for the Communists to carry out their schemes.[6]

Chiang's description of these plans, along with his sudden fascination with air power (discussed in the following chapter), were confirmed by remarks of the generalissimo's influential minister of war and chief of staff, General Ho Ying-chin. The National government, he declared, would use force to move the Communists north of the Yangtze.

Johnson's report to the State Department concluded that

the "two contending groups must eventually come to grips in a military struggle" and that the "scattered and ill equipped Communists" stood little chance against the KMT. And even as the confrontation along the Yangtze loomed, a loan decision made in Washington, on November 30, 1940, gave Chiang the financial reassurance he desired from the United States. Though Roosevelt and Morgenthau intended the $100 million loan to bolster the Nationalists against the repercussions of Japan recognizing Wang's puppet regime, its effect within China was more general. A KMT spokesman soon told an embassy official that Chungking no longer had to "appeas[e] the Communists."[7]

Fearful that increasing American aid would embolden the KMT, Communist representatives in Chungking appealed to the embassy for assistance. The CCP's chief spokesman in Chungking, Chou En-lai, told one member of the embassy staff that "even if the New Fourth Army complied with the instructions" to move to north China it "would probably be attacked by Government forces." On December 23 a Communist delegation visited Ambassador Johnson to plead that he intercede with Chiang on behalf of their trapped comrades. The Ambassador, with Hull's approval, refused to interfere with what he called "problems of an internal character."[8] A few days later the Nationalists attacked and destroyed most of the New Fourth Army, marking the end of any real cooperation between the KMT and CCP. From that point on, until the renewal of full-scale civil war after the Japanese surrender, the United Front remained a convenient fiction. Only the common threat of Japan, and constant prodding by the United States, contained the scale of fighting.

American officials and private observers familiar with these events quickly split into two antagonistic camps. Those like Edgar Snow and Evans Carlson, sympathetic to the Communists, urged that the United States revise its policy of dealing exclusively with the Nationalists. They advocated instead that aid by granted directly to armies in the field which were fighting Japan, regardless of their political affiliations.[9] Ambassador Johnson, shortly to leave China, denounced any suggestion of circumventing the KMT. The Nationalists, he believed, represented China's future, while the Communists only subverted unified resistance to Japan. He insisted Chiang was a true democrat worthy of a full commitment.[10] Americans who thought otherwise, like Edgar Snow, were actually pro-Communist agents subverting U.S. policy, according to the ambassador.[11]

Johnson's strident views dovetailed with reports from the influential naval attaché in Chungking, James McHugh. Because he enjoyed a personal friendshp with the Soong family, the State Department and White House frequently consulted McHugh's messages. The attaché, an extreme anti-Communist, blamed virtually all of China's problems on the CCP, those sowers of "disorder and lies." McHugh was alarmed by suggestions that aid be given directly to all anti-Japanese groups, regardless of their politics. The suggestion of circumventing Chungking in doling out future aid, McHugh wrote,

boils down to a thesis that we should set up a puppet show of our own here in competition with the Japs, insisting however that ours is a righteous one. Anybody who professes to know China knows that it cannot be done and anyone who knows the U.S.A. knows that we are the last people to attempt such a thing.[12]

McHugh warned the State Department that pro-Communist Americans wanted nothing more than to use American aid to China as a way of destroying the Kuomintang.[13]

Although Chiang's supporters clearly dominated the diplomatic and journalistic channels, not all Asia experts agreed to consign the Communists to the inferno. At least one junior officer in the State Department's Division of Far Eastern Affairs, John Patton Davies, showed an early penchant for analysis which first advanced and then destroyed his career in the Foreign Service. After reading whatever materials he could gather on the CCP and interviewing those few Americans who had first-hand contact with the Party, Davies suggested to his superiors that the outbreak of internal conflict signified the immense and unresolved dimensions of the social crisis in China.

It seemed clear to Davies in early 1941 (as it would to several historians and political scientists from the perspective of the 1960s) that the Communists had succeeded brilliantly in alloying their doctrine of social revolution to an upsurge of peasant nationalism in the wake of Japan's invasion. As the KMT armies and government administration withdrew from the countryside to the relative safety of the interior, the Communists rushed in political and military cadres to fill the leadership void. A report from American military intelligence described the process in some detail:

Wherever the Eighth Route Army (Communist) penetrated, its retinue of propagandists, social and economic workers, school teachers, etc., immediately started organizing and training the peasant masses for resistance through guerrilla warfare. Their central idea in all these efforts was that the social and economic level of the peasants had to be improved in order to maintain morale and to instill among the people a will to resist Japan and support their own armies. [14]

Since the KMT relied primarily on the support of landlords, the possibility of its organizing peasants was anathema. Davies reasoned that the war of resistance against Japan had already taken on the unmistakable trappings of a revolutionary civil war. Logically, then, internal fighting could only be expected to increase. [15]

While Davies' particular analysis had no great audience or impact upon officials in Washington, it spoke to a dilemma that others did begin to take note of. In reality, two competing regimes existed within China, each with its own army, political administration, and territory. Only one, however, the Republic of China led by Chiang Kai-shek, enjoyed the support of the United States. The de facto Communist regime and its "liberated areas" of several million inhabitants existed in a limbo as far as America was concerned. Both the Nationalists and Communists played a vital role in containing several million Japanese troops in mainland Asia. Yet, at any given moment, after the January 1941 New Fourth Army incident, large-scale internal warfare between the two factions might resume. This would only ease the Japanese task of solidifying control over China and freeing its forces for action in other areas.

Washington faced a dilemma posed by the fact that everything it did to bolster Chiang's position vis-à-vis the Japanese could easily prompt the KMT to move against the Communists. Soviet assistance, which many had thought restrained KMT moves to attack Yenan, had dwindled by the beginning of 1941. With the signing of the Soviet-Japanese nonaggression pact in April, it virtually ceased. During March, American embassy staff in Chungking heard reports that Chiang had told his followers to expect a sudden war between Japan and the United States which would free his hand to dispose of the Communists. These rumors so disturbed officials in London and Washington that the Department of State and British Foreign Office both addressed a message to Chiang urging him against a total break with the Communists.[16]

Amidst the pitfalls of conflict within China, a Japanese military buildup in Southeast Asia, and Britain's grave danger from Nazi air and sea assaults, Roosevelt introduced Lend-Lease legislation to Congress. This proposal to allow the President wide discretionary authority in supplying vast amounts of military aid to de facto allies revolutionized American foreign and defense policy. As Roosevelt described the concept to Ambassador Grew in Tokyo, it would be part of a global policy of self-defense against aggression.[17] In addition, Lend-Lease (if Congress agreed) was designed to make the White House the center of military and economic aid to Great Britain and China. No longer would aid proposals have to be channeled through the often competitive bureaucracies of the State and Treasury departments, the Export-Import Bank, or Congress. Henceforth, the President himself could direct the transfer of strategic aid directly to allies.

Although the new program specifically aimed at alleviating Britain's financial crisis, it held equal promise for the Chinese. T. V. Soong, Chiang's brother-in-law and the leading KMT representative in Washington, sensed this immediately. No sooner had Lend-Lease legislation been introduced in January than Soong urged Roosevelt to dispatch a special personal envoy to Chungking. Though the Chinese failed in their effort to have Harry Hopkins sent to China, the outcome of the mission must have pleased the KMT.

Roosevelt appeared to relish the opportunity to send a personal envoy to confer with Chiang Kai-shek. Forging a special link between the White House and important foreign allies emerged as a Roosevelt trademark during the war. The President seemed to feel that having this own man confer with foreign leaders permitted him to avoid the delays, leaks, and pressures that inevitably followed working through the State Department. Furthermore, a personal envoy might discuss a wide range of political topics which would be considered taboo under more formal circumstances. In the case of China, Roosevelt almost certainly desired to discuss the Communist problem and the internal political difficulties of the KMT regime. Thus a special envoy in the spring of 1941 appealed both to the President's style and the Nationalists' desire to forge links to the White House.

Roosevelt chose an intriguing and skilful aide for the complicated mission, economic advisor Dr. Lauchlin Currie. After serving as an aide to Marriner Eccles of the Federal Reserve System (where he became a leading apostle of Keynesian economics), Currie caught the President's eye and received appointment to an advisory post in the White House. Although formally trained as an economist, Currie quickly involved himself in many aspects of domestic policy and, eventually, foreign affairs. As an extremely capable and ambitious assistant, Currie identified China policy as a tremendously important question and one Roosevelt desired to devote greater attention to. Moving rapidly to carve out China as his area of special expertise under the President, he became in essence the first of several "fixers" whom Roosevelt would send to patch up the fissures in China and steer that troubled nation toward the liberal political transformation which was FDR's dream for postwar Asia.[18] The tragedy of Roosevelt's China policy grew from the fact that the quick fix became the permanent solution.

During an extended visit to the Chinese capital in February and March 1941, the dual purposes of the Currie mission clearly emerged. Chiang demanded another infusion of American money, $50 million this time, and a promise to deliver to China a modern air force. Were such aid denied, dire results might ensue. Even as Currie and the generalissimo spoke, Madame Kung, wife of the finance minister, told naval attaché Jame McHugh (who was in close contact with Currie) that her husband had just received new Japanese peace feelers. She tactfully explained that the Nationalists must know the enemy's terms if further resistance became impossible. On a personal level, the Kungs may have feared for their own financial future, since in Washington T. V. Soong was slated to become China's Lend-Lease agent. This would surely cut the Kungs out of whatever money would be made in the arrangement.[19]

Upon his return to Washington, Currie met with the President and, fortunately, prepared a written report of his mission. The record revealed Currie's—and probably Roosevelt's—growing concern over the political situation within China, especially the KMT-CCP rift. The American envoy explained that he stove to impress upon Chiang Washington's concern over a renewal of civil war. Internal fighting would only benefit Japan, he warned. Rather than meet the Communist "problem" with force, Currie suggested that Chiang follow "Roosevelt's example" of promoting liberal economic reforms to undercut the appeal of the left and right. Unfortunately, Currie added in his report to the President, Chiang seemed uninterested in following such a course. Instead, he almost reflexively preferred to increase repression to destroy his enemies. The result was nearly complete disgust toward the KMT from all Chinese left of center, Currie noted. As events were going, both China and the United States would be lucky if full-scale civil war could be postponed until after the Japanese threat abated.

If the United States wished to preserve and increase China's value as a barrier against Japanese expansion, Washington had no choice but to play a more direct role in Chinese politics. Currie believed that America's willingness to grant aid served in part to justify this intervention. He then outlined a program that the President might consider. Hopefully it would succeed in prodding the KMT regime along the path of liberal reform he believed vital for both the current effort and longer-term international relations.

Currie envisioned the appointment of a team of American experts, from the fields of economics, politics, and transportation, to supervise what would surely be an increasing flow of aid. These advisors would serve as a professional back-up team to the notoriously corrupt and inefficient Chinese bureaucracy. At the very pinnacle, Roosevelt might appoint a "liberal advisor" to assist Chiang's political judgment. Basic economic and political reforms, Currie argued, would also make China a far more attractive postwar economic partner for the United States.

Changes within China comprised only part of this scheme. Currie feared that Chiang enjoyed far too little support among the American liberal community and public. Roosevelt might alter this by personally championing the generalissimo, by "saying nice things about him," and by referring to China as a democracy and a great power. The White House could use the press in this sales campaign by leaking "inspired stories from Washington" extolling Chiang's virtue. Currie concluded with an appeal to his boss's vanity: since Chiang looked upon the President as "the greatest man in the world," Roosevelt had a unique power to influence the man who commanded the most populous nation in the world.[20]

Even accounting for the hyperbole of Currie's recommendations, he had done for the administration what no one attempted before: to draw the broad outlines of a China policy. China, he argued, should be treated as a major ally and future great power; Chiang should simultaneously be supported in power and encouraged to reform. America's overall goal should be to encourage a political evolution which both prevented civil war and discouraged a Chinese Communist victory. Though FDR never formally adopted Currie's report, it clearly served as an informal agenda during the next several years, locking official policy into an increasingly rigid mold.

In retrospect, the glibness of Currie's arguments are striking. (They would be questioned increasingly as the war proceeded.) He twisted the Chinese experience to fit his own vision of reform. As the New Deal had attacked the bastions of the old economic order, Americans would train Chinese Keynesians to smash the legacy of rural poverty and political oppression. Currie seemed completely unaware of the fundamental class and land struggle which underlay China's crisis. He possessed no sense of what forces the KMT represented, or why the Communists could successfully appeal to the peasantry. Moreover, to expect any political group in China to accept the indignity of subordinating themselves to foreign advisors was to totally misunderstand the direction of Chinese nationalism since the 1911 revolution. Finally, Currie ignored the possible domestic consequences of wildly inflating the importance of a foreign ally who had a tenuous grip on power. It gave the "puppet" a powerful hold over the strings of American public opinion, encouraging Chiang to believe that the United States felt his personal survival more important than the nation he represented.

Currie's advocacy of American support for Chiang also seemed at variance with his own observation that the generalissimo, in his heart, rejected democracy. To make matters even more peculiar, the presidential envoy had not formed his judgment of the Communists at second or third hand. While in Chungking, Currie arranged a secret meeting in the British embassy between himself and Communist representative Chou En-lai. Unfortunately, neither party left a record of this discussion. Afterwards, Currie remarked in an offhand manner to a member of the American Embassy staff that Chou personally impressed him, as did the pragmatic policies advocated by the Communists. In his formal report to the President, however, no mention of the meeting appeared. What Currie did stress, in terms of "secret meetings," was of an opposite political nature. He arranged for naval attaché James McHugh, known for his intimacy with the Chiang and Soong clans, to serve as a special conduit between China's leading families and the White House. Currie encouraged McHugh to send his own reports directly to the President and to pass on messages from Chiang which were best kept from regular channels.[21]

The policy advocated by Currie and gradually adopted by Roosevelt created a symbiotic tie between the United States and the Nationalist regime. Soon the relatively straightforward challenge of supporting Chinese resistance to Japan became overwhelmed by a host of new considerations. A long-range goal of reforming China's political system and linking to it to an American alliance in postwar Asia seemed feasible, though no one could yet suggest how this might be accomplished. Currie and Roosevelt believed, or more likely hoped, that the creation of a "special relationship," increased aid, and the dispatch of advisors might achieve fundamental change within China. Such a policy would perhaps prevent civil war and reduce the likelihood of a successful Communist revolution.

The events of 1941 quickly put the new program to a test. In March Congress passed Lend-Lease, setting the stage for vastly increased foreign military assistance. Also, the Roosevelt administration accepted the need to send advisors to China to oversee the aid and attendant reform programs. In a sense, these two approaches of aid and reform represented two poles—Chiang's need and Washington's desire. Few Americans yet understood their inherent contradiction.

In mid-April, a few weeks after Currie's return to Washington, an impatient Chiang Kai-shek directed Soong to press Roosevelt for a firm promise of new aid. The desired items included military supplies, military aircraft (which Chiang had requested since late 1940), and a $50 million "loan."[22] These requests were vigorously endorsed by McHugh, in Chungking, who lost little time utilizing his new White House entré. The naval attaché urged Currie to seek the President's approval, even though the money would go "down the drain and the planes [would soon be] cracked up." The aid must be given in order to "boost Chinese morale." The Chungking regime, he explained, had been shaken by the recent conclusion of the Soviet-Japanese nonaggression pact and the growing reluctance of the Treasury Department to pump unregulated currency stabilization funds into China.[23]

McHugh's complaints about Treasury policy stemmed from a growing dispute between Morgenthau and Soong over the means and timing of economic assistance. The Chinese wanted lump-sum, unregulated infusions of dollars. The Treasury Secretary had insisted that aid be given in small, periodic, and regulated amounts to discourage speculation. If Chungking objected to this procedure, Morgenthau angrily told his staff, they could "go jump in the Yangtze." Now Soong, McHugh, and Currie made an end run around the Treasury and succeeded in having the White House endorse the Nationalist's demands.[24]

However, in a compromise move Currie and Morgenthau both agreed on the need to send American advisors to China in order to oversee the funds and alleviate other problems in the aid program. The transportation bottleneck along the Burma Road particularly vexed American planners, since it was the sole means of moving supplies into China. Thus by the summer of 1941 a group of financial and transportation advisors had been sent out by the Treasury. Their achievement, however, was negligible. The Chinese bitterly resented this foreign interference and succeeded in nullifying it. The advisors were isolated and ignored by KMT officials, kept ignorant of vital facts, and forced to sit by helplessly while their hosts routinely pilfered supplies along the Burma Road.[25]

Currie thought it might be possible to amend these practices from the top down by placing an American political advisor in Chiang's headquarters. A man of the right political instincts, he told Roosevelt, might steer Chiang in the direction of the New Deal. Exactly what a political advisor ought to do and the degree to which he could count on White House support remained unspecified. Currie seemed to feel that merely placing an American at Chiang's side would begin to transform the KMT—a judgment which was highly unrealistic to say the least. Nevertheless, the name of Owen Lattimore, a liberal and noted Asian scholar, passed from Currie to Roosevelt, who endorsed the appointment.[26]

Given Chiang's staunch pride and noted dislike of foreign meddlers, the question arises why he agreed to such an indignity. The generalissimo initially may have felt it to his advantage to grant consent. First of all, the President obviously supported the plan, which made it awkward to reject it out of hand. Second, since Lend-Lease would be run through the Executive branch, it made practical sense for Chiang to deal directly with the source of power. If this was insufficient reason, the appointment of a new ambassador to Chungking gave Chiang added cause. Early in 1941 the rather pliable and affable Nelson Johnson was succeeded by Clarence Gauss, who had logged many years in Chinese consular posts. Gauss, a dour and taciturn figure, bore little affection for the KMT, and the Nationalists reciprocated the feeling. The appointment of a presidential advisor to Chiang provided an alternative channel to the American embassy, now considered (as it would be through 1945) to be in "unfriendly hands."[27]

The actual outcome of Lattimore's mission disappointed both parties to the arrangement. His stay in China proved both brief and unproductive. Put most simply, Lattimore was not the man Chiang expected. As McHugh reported from Chungking, the generalissimo anticipated a politically adroit Roosevelt crony who would ask no embarrassing questions and plead the case for more aid. Instead, Chiang found himself saddled with a scholar versed in Chinese history who carried virtually no weight with the President. The Chinese leader wanted "the Henry Luce type who will sing praises and give lots of money with no questions asked." Chiang, while personally cordial to Lattimore upon his arrival, had nothing further to do with him. In fact, articles immediately appeared in the KMT press hinting that Lattimore held pro-Communist views and had come to force a compromise with Yenan. Shortly thereafter, Chiang hustled Lattimore back to Washington with the suggestion that he use his scholarly expertise to lobby for a large American loan.[28]

The reason why Lattimore and the technical advisors sent to China failed to make an impact is not difficult to understand. They had little to offer but meddlesome advice and represented the tradition of imperialist dictation. Their effort to clean up graft on the Burma Road, to suggest tax and economic reform, ignored the fact that the KMT survived through corruption and the bargains it struck with existing elites. Changing any single part of the system risked a collapse of the entire structure. Chiang did not need outside advice on reform but guns, planes, and money. Sadly, this simple lesson made little impression on the President or his top aides for quite some time.

Despite the initial failure of part of Currie's program, the Americans and the Chinese Nationalists discovered common ground in the Lend-Lease program. Soon after its passage in March 1941, Roosevelt and Hopkins designated Lauchlin Currie to expedite new aid to China.[29] The White House advisor worked closely with T. V. Soong, whom Chiang had designated as his personal representative in Washington. Soong in turn ran the Chinese aid mission through an organization called China Defense Supplies (CDS) which resembled a mercantile corporation as much as a government agency. As with most KMT operations, the lines between private business and politics frequently crossed. During World War II rumors continually surfaced of kickbacks passing between contractors and CDS officials.

The rather complicated arrangements for the transfer of Lend-Lease aid to CDS were further confused by the staff Soong assembled. A glance at CDS's roster would lead one to assume FDR or Hopkins had created yet another New Deal alphabet agency. Former members of the White House staff, the Federal Power Commission, the Army Air Force, China missionaries, and businessmen with links to major industrial corporations could all be found listed as employees of the Chinese government. The most prominent names included Thomas Corcoran, William Youngman, Claire Chennault, and Roosevelt's distant cousin, Joseph Alsop, who served as a public relations aide. Soong had carefully selected a staff with close links to various executive agencies to insure a sympathetic reception for Chinese aid requests. He also succeeded in forging a lasting relationship between the Washington establishment and the Chinese Nationalists, a marriage later known as the China Lobby.[30]

Soong's methods reflected both the prevailing Chinese belief that influence held the key to receiving aid, as well as his own family's preference for conspiratorial politics. Madame Chiang, for example, insisted that important messages from the White House to the Chinese government be sent through personally selected Americans (such as McHugh) rather than through the American or Chinese embassies. Similarly, her cables would go to Currie for delivery to the Treasury Department or President. When Currie notified Morgenthau of her preferences, the Treasury Secretary remarked bitterly to his staff that "the trouble with Mr. Currie is, I don't know half the time whether he is working for the President or T. V. Soong, because half the time he is on one payroll and the rest of the time he is on the other." Trying to keep track of the Chiang and Soong families' demands became such a bother that Morgenthau's staff composed a sarcastic rhyme entitled "Sing a Song of Six Soongs."[31]

The object of these Chinese intrigues, of course, was military aid. During the six months before the Japanese attack at Pearl Harbor, the American military posture in China and the western Pacific grew increasingly bold as Roosevelt bolstered the naval, air, and ground forces in Hawaii and the Philippines. Simultaneously, the quantity and quality of military assistance to China improved. As the pace of rearmament quickened, American planners even approved the secret creation of Chiang's long-sought air force. (This act, a milestone in clandestine warfare, will be discussed in the following chapter.)

China's formal tie into the Lend-Lease pipeline began on March 31, when Soong applied for three categories of aid. He requested sufficient arms and equipment for thirty divisions, construction equipment to build a railroad and highway network between India-Burma and China, and one thousand airplanes and pilots under the command of Claire Chennault. Unlike the former requests, an air force could be used for offensive strikes against the Japanese home islands, thus adding a new dimension to the American aid program. Eventually, Roosevelt decided to proceed with this plan in great secrecy.

The Chinese requests put an additional strain on American military production as well as upon the rather awkward transportation route that lay between the United States, Rangoon, and western China. The transportation problem defied full solution until the end of the war. Allocating supplies proved almost as great a challenge. Currie pressed the War Department to quickly meet Soong's order. Yet military experts discovered that the Chinese often failed to specify exactly what weapons and supplies they needed. Much of what they did specify proved currently unavailable or totally inappropriate for Chinese capabilities. Soong, for example, wanted heavy tanks and trucks which would have collapsed China's primitive roads and bridges. Other equipment required specially trained personnel for operation and maintenance, which China lacked. After agile pruning, the War Department certified a weapons shipment valued at $45 million which Roosevelt approved on April 23. A second shipment valued at $100 million followed shortly.[32]

Appropriating aid solved one problem, but the problems of delivery and utilization remained. Supplies would take several months to reach China and then would have to be distributed to largely untrained military units. Anticipating major bottlenecks down the road, the army chief of staff, General George C. Marshall, convinced Roosevelt to approve creation of an American Military Mission to China (AMMISCA) early in July. General John Magruder, its commander, received instructions to keep his unit "camouflaged until we get into this war actively."[33] Magruder, previously an attaché in China, expected to devote his time to improving the Burma Road transportation network and overseeing the distribution and use of Lend-Lease aid.

Marshall, however, had more in mind than efficiency when he proposed the creation of an army mission in Chungking. Like Morgenthau before him, the general had grown worried over the Chinese penetration of the policymaking bureaucracy. The links between Soong, Currie, CDS, and numerous current and former officials seemed to endanger the sanctity of American control over military aid. The War Department's role in questions of aid to China had been reduced to filling orders drafted by Soong and Currie. By establishing his own group in China, Marshall believed, he could ensure army influence over aid requests and utilization. Furthermore, regular army officers might better restrain some of the more adventurous proposals for strikes against Japan originating with the Chinese.

Not surprisingly, Currie and CDS employees suspected that AMMISCA's creators in the War Department hoped to circumvent their influence over the President. Claire Chennault went so far as to warn Madame Chiang that Magruder had been sent to break the influence of Currie and Soong over Lend-Lease. Regular army planners, he asserted, cared only about Europe and would give China as little aid as possible.[34] Chennault only exaggerated a bit, for in July the desperate plight of both England and the Soviet Union convinced Marshall and his aides that a war in the Pacific could not be risked. When Magruder's mission began operations in October, it pressed the Chinese to improve the quality of their military training and logistic system. Magruder discouraged requests for high-technology offensive weapons that might inadvertently provoke a Japanese attack on American possessions in the Pacific.

The simultaneous strains of assisting two European and one Asian ally, of rearming at home, and of slowly bolstering the small military forces in the Pacific required caution in dealing with Japan. At least through November, American leaders believed it might be possible and certainly desirable to postpone a war with Japan. For this reason, the Roosevelt administration approved negotiations with the Japanese. As with so many of the administration's decisions, however, the talks proceeded without much coordination among the civilian and military departments. For some time, Roosevelt even permitted Postmaster General Frank C. Walker and two Catholic priests who had served in Japan to conduct semiofficial discussions with private Japanese emissaries. Neither group of participants really represented their government's policies, and the episode only further confused relations.[35]

Official negotiations began in earnest in July 1941, continuing right up to the outbreak of war. Roosevelt recalled the long-slighted Cordell Hull from diplomatic limbo to lead the discussions with special Japanese envoy Admiral Nomura. Hull, it seemed, was the only senior cabinet official not publicly linked to a hostile or hard-line position toward the Japanese, though by July he basically concurred with Stimson and Morgenthau. A cynic might suggest that Roosevelt selected Hull because the task facing him seemed insoluble. Knowing the slight chance for success, the President may have preferred to reserve the time of more respected associates for other duties.

In the end, personality counted for very little. During July the Japanese swept down upon southern French Indochina, a strategic position endangering the remainder of colonial Southeast Asia. The most important American response came on July 26, when Roosevelt ordered the licensing of all trade between the United States and Japan. As administered by Morgenthau, the directive served to embargo all oil sales to the Japanese.[36] When the British and the Dutch East Indies governments followed suit, oil deliveries to Japan virtually ceased. Since Tokyo possessed very limited reserves, the American embargo effectively imposed a deadline on war or peace. The Japanese could meet American demands or risk striking out to seize oil supplies in Southeast Asia.

This new crisis provided the backdrop for the Japanese-American negotiations in Washington. Tokyo labored under an unalterable deadline imposed by the cutoff of oil. The United States had to first resume sales and then extricate itself from supporting Chiang. This would permit Japan to impose a peace settlement on China. The American position as voiced by Hull revealed a reversed perspective. The United States, he explained, could only agree to resume strategic trade following a resolution of outstanding disputes. Put most simply, Hull demanded a Japanese evacuation of all territory occupied by force since 1931, a pledge against future armed expansion, and the abrogation of the Tripartite Alliance with Berlin and Rome.

From July until late November, the two negotiating positions hardly varied. The Americans refused to entertain any suggestions short of complete fulfillment of their demands. When Japanese Prime Minister Konoye, considered a relative moderate, proposed a meeting between himself and Roosevelt, the pedantic Stanley Hornbeck convinced both Hull and the President to spurn the offer. Tokyo, Hornbeck claimed, actually feared a war. The real purpose of a "summit" meeting was to lull the United States with false promises and to tarnish American prestige.[37]

In November, as Japanese oil reserves continued to fall, Nomura offered two additional proposals, Plan A and Plan B. The first entailed the resumption of oil sales followed by a comprehensive settlement in Asia. It further presumed American approval of de facto Japanese domination of China and Southeast Asia. This suggestion, of course, got nowhere. Nor did the more "modest" Plan B. By its terms, Japan promised to begin a phased withdrawal from Indochina if the United States resumed oil sales and guaranteed access to a continued flow of vital raw materials. Furthermore, the United States would have to end military assistance to Chiang and assist Japan in imposing a favorable peace settlement on China.

American leaders, with increasingly little faith in the value of any Japanese promises, found these suggestions totally inadequate. Tokyo, it appeared, remained determined to bring all China under its political and economic if not military domination. Nomura's plans called upon the United States to abandon the regime it had assumed sponsorship of in China. Washington assumed, perhaps incorrectly, that Japan would only wait for the proper moment to resume expansion across the Pacific. From this perspective it appeared that Tokyo had offered Washington nothing, just as the Japanese must have felt nothing had been offered them.

Despite their bitter reactions, Roosevelt, Hull, and the War and Navy departments understood the vulnerability of the United States. American armed forces in the Pacific could not yet effectively resist or deter a full-scale Japanese advance. War in the Pacific would seriously impair the American effort to assist Great Britain and the Soviet Union in their desperate holding actions against Germany. As Roosevelt remarked, he simply lacked "enough navy to go around." Prudence dictated that the United States at least explore the possibility of achieving a temporary modus vivendi with Japan, some arrangement that would postpone what now seemed an inevitable war. Perhaps the resumption of oil sales on a limited basis would freeze the crisis until the European war front stabilized and American forces in the Pacific increased. Despite Hornbeck's typical rejection of this idea, Hull and Roosevelt considered it during November.[38]

In the final analysis, China again emerged as a crucial

sticking point in Japanese-American relations. The belief had become deeply entrenched in Washington that any sort of compromise with Japan could lead to the political or military collapse of Chinese resistance. Since the maintenance of a pro-American, independent regime was now considered a fixture of policy, taking an action to appease Japan or cut off aid to Chungking seemed contrary to the basic goals of American policy in East Asia. The Japanese, who had spent a fortune in money and an awful price in lives, similarly could not tolerate a settlement which left China still fighting and the recipient of growing American aid. All parties to the issue had invested so heavily in the outcome of events that they could not imagine abandoning China.

Aware of this sentiment in both Tokyo and Washington, and somewhat fearful that in the unlikely event of a compromise China might be the sacrifice, the Nationalist regime did all it could to publicize its case to American leaders. Communicating to Washington through every available channel— the regular embassies, General Magruder, James McHugh, T. V. Soong, Hornbeck, Hull, Morgenthau, Stimson, and Roosevelt—the Chinese warned of an impending Japanese plan to invade western Yunnan province and knock China out of the war by closing its supply lines to the west. Tokyo had prepared such an attack, Chiang insisted, because of a belief that Washington might abandon its support for China. To dispel these rumors and confound the Japanese, the generalissimo urged the United States to launch a preemptive attack on Japan!

A typical message of this period, in both content and means of delivery, passed from Chiang to Soong to Stimson and then to the State Department on November 25. Chiang desired to explain to the American government the "gravity of the situation." Were there any relaxation of the embargo or freezing regulations, or if

a belief of that gains ground, then the Chinese people would consider that China has been completely sacrificed by the United States. The morale of the entire people will collapse and every Asiatic nation will lose faith . . . in democracy. . . . The Chinese army will collapse and the Japanese will be enabled to carry through their plans. . . . Such a loss would not be to China alone. . . . The certain collapse of our resistance will be an unparalleled catastrophe to the world, and I do not indeed know how history in future will record this episode.[39]

Administration officials were both confused and angered by the blitz of warnings and threats coming from China. Chinese suspicions were ill founded and only added to the extreme pressures under which the State Department was operating. Hull complained to the British ambassador that Chiang Kai-shek had "sent numerous hysterical cable messages to different Cabinet officers and high officials in the Government other than the State Department, and sometimes even ignoring the President, intruding into a delicate and serious situation with no real idea of what the facts are."[40]

During November Morgenthau, too, worried lest China actually be deserted by Washington in some compromise deal. He forwarded to Hull and Roosevelt a fanciful proposal developed by his assistant, Harry Dexter White, which would guarantee China's independence as part of any deal with Tokyo. In return for a nonaggression pact and favorable trade, credit, and loan arrangements with the United States, Japan would agree to completely withdraw from China and Indochina. In addition, Tokyo would virtually break off relations with Berlin and "sell the United States up to three quarters of her current output of war materials on a cost-plus basis." The remarkable idea which Morgenthau advanced appeared to request the Japanese to join in the struggle against Germany as an American and Chinese ally.

Late in November Morgenthau reacted to Soong's allegations that an anti-Chinese plot was afoot in Washington by drafting a letter to Roosevelt imploring that there be no compromise with Japan at China's expense. As Morgenthau quickly discovered, it was unnecessary to deliver this plea.[41] The final terms which Hull delivered to the Japanese on November 26 again called for the complete abandonment of the Japanese bargaining position. The Japanese were told to withdraw from China and Indochina, renounce the use of force, and give pledges to respect the status quo throughout colonial and non-colonial Asia and the Pacific. Only then would the United States consider the resumption of normal trade. Neither China nor anything else would be abandoned by the United States.

The tenacity with which the United States countered all Japanese bargaining proposals during the last half of 1941 culminated the series of policy decisions undertaken since December 1938. The United States had moved forward, first to underwrite the Chinese Nationalist regime morally and then to sustain it materially against Japan. China had been linked to the preservation of the American and European foothold throughout Asia and the Pacific. The Japanese advance into southern Indochina in July 1941, combined with American knowledge (obtained through the breaking of Japanese codes: MAGIC) of Japanese preparations for further expansion, served to confirm the domino-like predictions which Hornbeck had been making for years. By 1941 Morgenthau, Hull, Stimson, Currie, and their numerous subordinates generally shared this vision. American leaders believed that Japan intended to bring China under its control as the first stage in the conquest of all Southeast Asia and the entire Pacific region. Since Tokyo's goal appeared infinite to them, compromise over China or other territory was both immoral and unrealistic. By the end of 1941 the linchpin of American policy in East Asia had become the preservation and support of Nationalist China. In a direct way, this attitude led to a decision by Roosevelt to support the creation of a secret American air force in China to compel Japan's acceptance of America's will. In the last months before the attack at Pearl Harbor, the Sino-Japanese War and the initiation of a secret American air war against Japan began to merge.

Chapter 4
American Air Strategy and the Origins of Clandestine Warfare

POPULAR WISDOM PLACES the beginning of active American practice of the techniques of clandestine warfare at some point soon after 1945. Military intervention and the proliferation of U.S.-sponsored counterinsurgency programs are heralded as a pragmatic response to Communist subversion in the underdeveloped countries. There has long been a reluctance to trace these policies and tactics back to the origins of World War II. This reluctance probably stems from a desire not to cast aspersions on the inherent virtue of the struggle against fascism. But self-imposed political censorship (benign as its intentions may be) is fundamentally anti-historical. For the origins of the contemporary American intelligence establishment, along with the tactics of covert warfare, were spawned during the struggle against Germany and Japan.

This assertion applies particularly to a series of military measures adopted by the United States against Japan. After the end of World War II, a bitter historical and political debate erupted over charges that the Roosevelt administration had precipitated the Japanese attack on Pearl Harbor through political conspiracy or clandestine military provocation. The argument, however, said more about the participants' view of the New Deal than about the origins of the war. Critics on the right decried a "needless" war whose legacy was Soviet expansion. Liberal internationalists in sympathy with the New Deal countered with a vigorous and widely accepted defense of Roosevelt's policies.[1]

Yet on both sides there appeared a willingness to concentrate on issues of personal guilt, all the while searching for

65

some crucial document that would confirm or refute the charges that the President and his staff formally sat down to hatch a plot to provoke war with Japan. The historical and political debate over this issue quickly became barren as it continually wrenched evidence out of meaningful context. The pro- and anti-conspiracy hounds of the 1940s and 1950s ignored the reality of how complex bureaucracies like the U.S. government operate. Policy is debated and devised at many levels and frequently at cross purposes. Because of the way they are applied (or the influence of objective conditions), many policies achieve vastly different purposes than those for which they were conceived. Similarly, American policymaking does not conform to the ideal that the War Department would make military policy and the State Department political policy. Policies of importance in all fields are frequently conceived and carried out by individuals and groups outside the regular bureaucratic structure, or by regular bureaucrats acting outside their official capacities. Franklin D. Roosevelt's personal style made such irregular decisionmaking even more prevalent.

The very essence of covert military activity required the development of special government organs. During the war this was formally acknowledged by the creation of the Organization of Strategic Services (OSS), while the Cold War later spawned the Central Intelligence Agency. However, even before Pearl Harbor the Roosevelt administration saw a need to utilize informal or semiofficial agents and agencies to spearhead an attack on an enemy it could not yet formally challenge. This development of covert tactics served two functions. Not only did it camouflage clandestine military operations—an obvious prerequisite for many activities—but it also insulated top officials and bypassed frequent opposition from the more tradition-bound factions within the foreign-policymaking bureaucracy.

With these considerations in mind, during 1940–41 influential American officials worked closely with quasi-private individuals and special-interest groups associated with the Chinese

Nationalists to develop at least two plans for clandestine attacks upon Japan. Approaching the problem from an intellectual framework which in the later Vietnam war would be called "protective reaction," these plans involved the use of ostensibly private American planes and pilots to assist the Chinese in a joint effort against Japan. As conceived in Washington, the project had implications for the broader Japanese-American confrontation in the Pacific. Developed largely outside the State and War departments, these activities were looked upon as a possible military deterrent to a general war with Japan. Americans considered this a method of bolstering Chinese morale and warning Japan directly of the risk it ran in provoking the United States. Yet these activities themselves escalated the military confrontation in the Pacific and set precedents for the use of clandestine military means as an active element of American foreign policy.

Initial American military aid to China, though it embittered Japan, posed no immediate threat to Tokyo's larger expansionist strategy. By gradually taking economic and military control of Southeast Asia, the Japanese believed they could isolate and eventually crush Chinese resistance. The only threat to Japan proper or to its overseas forces which could come from China would arise if China became the recipient of an advanced American air force capable of attacking Japanese forces in China, Japanese shipping, or the Japanese home islands. However, the military disorganization and technological backwardness of the Nationalist armies virtually insured that no Chinese force, as then constituted, could mount an offensive even if they possessed American planes.

Theoretically, an American-piloted air force in China might be able to hamper Japanese ground movements, harass shipping, and take the initiative of bringing the war back to Japan. In 1938 a train of events was set in motion which had precisely these objectives. Gradually expanding economic and military aid to Chiang and the number of American advisors associated with him, the United States moved to subsidize a "proprietary" air force in China. After December 1940, President Roosevelt, Secretary of the Treasury Henry Morgenthau, Jr., White House aide Lauchlin Currie, and Colonel Claire Chennault arranged with the Chinese Nationalists to pursue plans for the firebombing of Tokyo and other Japanese cities by American planes and pilots operating from secret air bases in China.

Two bombing proposals, of December 1940 and July 1941, were conceived by individuals outside the normal military and diplomatic channels of the U.S. government. In this instance, the Executive branch provided funding for a private corporation linked to the Chinese government to acquire an air force to be used against Japan. This technique both minimized overt involvement by Washington and mollified opposition expressed by regular military planners. Accordingly, it foreshadowed the style, if not substance, of future policies in Asia and is an important link with policies the United States pursued during the later Indochina war.

Equally striking is the continuity of personnel engaged in America's clandestine air wars. One individual and his entourage figure in these activities over a period of almost fifteen years. Colonel (later General) Claire Chennault has enjoyed wide publicity for his World War II gallantry but there has been little scrutiny of his pre- and postwar political-military activities. His wartime service in China was troubled by a fundamental dispute with General Joseph Stilwell, the China Theater commander. Where Stilwell stressed military and political reforms of the Chinese armies as the key to defeating Japan, Chennault championed the almost exclusive use of American air power. Chennault lost the strategic argument and he has suffered at the hands of liberal historians as well.[2]

Before 1936 Claire Chennault had enjoyed a successful and controversial career in the U.S. Army Air Force. He was a prominent advocate of the importance of the fighter plane operating both independently and as a bomber escort. But when the Army Air Force adopted the contrary strategy based on the use of unescorted bombers, Chennault quickly lost influence. When questions were raised about Chennault's physical fitness (he suffered a hearing disability), the colonel retired from active duty.

Unhappy with this premature retirement, Chennault's interest was engaged by reports he received from friends who were serving as flying instructors in China. News of Chennault's aviation skills was brought to Madame Chiang Kai-shek's attention through this channel. Shortly before the outbreak of the Sino-Japanese War in 1937, Madame Chiang, who served on the board overseeing the Chinese air force, persuaded Chennault to accept a position as an air defense advisor. Nominally, however, Chennault's employer was the Bank of China. This technically avoided an overt violation of American neutrality statutes. In addition, the arrangement linked Chennault to the wider circle of Chinese Nationalist family politics since T. V. Soong, Madame Chiang's brother, ran the bank and later served as a key Chinese official in Washington.

Chennault was greeted upon his arrival in Nanking by Madame Chiang and the generalissimo's Australian political advisor, W. D. Donald. The aviator became enamored of both his sponsors. He described Madame Chiang as a "princess" and idolized the arrogant Donald (who boasted of having lived for years in China without tasting Chinese food or learning a word of the language) as a modern Marco Polo, battling Oriental corruption. Acting together, all three might join in a crusade to lead China toward Western reform and progress. Chennault took personal pride in the fact that he would displace the influence of an Italian air mission then serving Chiang.

When war broke out between Japan and China in July 1937, Chennault offered his skilled services to the generalissimo. During the next year the American advisor trained the Chinese pilots who flew the ramshackle assortment of outdated planes which comprised Chiang's air force. But, as Chennault noted with uneasy admiration, far more effective was the large

Soviet air contingent which Stalin lent to Chiang in 1937–38. Even in his memoirs, written several years later, Chennault abandoned his characteristic anti-Communist rhetoric to praise the Russian fliers who fought heroic air battles that Chennault undoubtedly believed should have been fought by heroic Americans. In response to China's need and his own sense of duty, by late 1938 Chennault himself had set out to organize a small "international squadron" composed of European, U.S., and Latin American pilots.[3]

Even all of this activity could hardly stem the Japanese tide. As Russian aid diminished, the Chinese became more aware of the absence of substantial American assistance. The loan which had been extended to China in December 1938 had not been followed by meaningful economic or military aid. This hiatus resulted from disagreement between the State and Treasury departments. While Secretary of the Treasury Henry Morganthau, Jr., favored increased support, Secretary of State Cordell Hull warned that American involvement would push Japan to take "rash action" and thus should be kept to a minimum. Late in November 1940, however, in a long-delayed move, the Japanese formally recognized the regime of their Chinese puppet, Wang Ching-wei. This not only boosted Wang's standing but indicated a Japanese determination to destroy the Nathonalist regime as well as Chiang personally. Ambassador Nelson Johnson had already concluded that this would make war between the United States and Japan all but inevitable.[4] Acting with unusual speed, Roosevelt responded to Johnson's warnings and Chiang's pleas for help by telling Morgenthau to give China $100 million within the next twenty-four hours. Although it actually took forty-eight hours to accomplish the task, the Chinese received what they wanted and needed.[5]

Within the week the State Department had also altered its position and had come around to support more direct American aid. The Chinese embassy in Washington received a note which explained that the State Department was developing a program supporting extensive military aid to China. The program would probably include the supply of planes and pilots. In any case, the note stated, the U.S. government would no longer discourage American volunteer pilots from going to China as mercenaries.[6]

These substantially new American initiatives were closely associated with the activities of Chennault and his powerful sponsor, T. V. Soong, both of whom had lobbied for a reversal of standing policies. Soong had come to Washington to act as China's chief pleader. Though not technically ambassador, he had full power to speak for China. (After Pearl Harbor, Soong was named foreign minister and spent much of his time in Washington.) Chennault and Chinese General P. T. Mow had been sent by Chiang to Washington in October 1940 to pursue American aid. There they worked under Soong and were introduced to another Soong retainer, Joseph Alsop. Alsop, a journalist, was a distant cousin of Franklin D. Roosevelt and would often serve as intermediary between Chennault and the White House.

Between August and December 1940, Soong, Chennault, and Alsop lobbied actively among Washington's policymakers. Soong had warned Secretary of War Henry Stimson that America's limited aid to China might turn the KMT in the direction of the Soviet Union. He also shuttled between Stimson and Morgenthau, persuading both to accept the principle of sending some American planes to China.[7] As mentioned earlier, Chiang Kai-shek had only recently stated that American planes could be used to suppress the Chinese Communists.

On November 30, as the $100 million loan was being approved, Soong submitted to Morgenthau a proposal which Chennault had developed. The plan was a primitive blueprint for strategic bombing and made the claim that if Chennault and China were given a force of five hundred planes piloted, supplied, and maintained by the United States, the Chinese could virtually annihilate the Japanese forces within China and neutralize Japan's naval striking ability. This "special Air Unit," operating from bases in China only six hundred and fifty miles from Tokyo, "could operate independently in attacking Japan proper." An offensive strategy, Soong assured Morgenthau, would undermine Japanese civilian morale. The most severe Japanese response would only be increased bombing of China, according to Soong.

Morgenthau had long been the leading administration advocate of aid to Chungking, both as a means of restricting Japanese expansion elsewhere and in order to sustain a pro-American, non-Communist regime in China. The Treasury Department was already serving as the main conduit of American economic aid, and Morgenthau leaped at the opportunity to assist the development of a military aid policy aimed against Japan.[8] However, since the diversion of any planes to China would mean the reallocation of planes committed to Great Britain, Morgenthau took the initiative of approaching the British ambassador, Lord Lothian, on December 3. The Secretary suggested that China be given bombers and trained crews "with the understanding that these bombers are to be used to bomb Tokyo and other big cities." At first enthusiastic, Lothian encouraged Morgenthau to continue his discussions with Soong.[9] Although the British, undoubtedly troubled by the diversion of planes, soon expressed misgivings, Morgenthau resolved to pursue the question further.

After lunching with Roosevelt on December 8, Morgenthau met again with Soong. He first swore the Chinese representative to secrecy, receiving a pledge that only Chiang Kai-shek would learn the contents of their discussion. Morgenthau had not yet learned that, in addition to being a master of subterfuge, Soong was a master of indiscretion. In any event, he told Soong that the grant of anything approaching five hundred planes was impossible, though a substantial number might become available sometime in 1942. Meanwhile, "what did he [Soong] think of the idea of some long range bombers with the understanding that they were to be used to bomb Tokyo and other Japanese cities?" Soong, of course, was delighted with the offer, especially when Morgenthau stretched the truth a bit to intimate that the idea came directly from Roosevelt. In fact, Morgenthau noted in his diary, Roosevelt had only suggested to him that "it would be nice if the Chinese would bomb Japan." Between themselves, Soong and Morgenthau agreed that such a bombardment would "change the whole picture in the Far East," and they agreed to consult further.

At this stage Morgenthau finally felt the need to sound out the opinion of the War and State departments. Meeting with Hull, he was startled by the Secretary of State's enthusiasm for the bombardment of Japan. The normally dour and cautious Hull, previously so reluctant to back up words with action, now declared that he would love to see five hundred American planes "start from the Aleutians and fly over Japan just once." So much the better "if we could only find some way to have them drop some bombs on Tokyo." Upon hearing this, Morgenthau related the contents of his own discussions with Soong.

The similarity between Hull's ideas and Morgenthau's previous discussions makes it quite likely that Hull either had access to the original Chinese proposal or had learned of the communications which Soong had sent to Chiang. In any case, Morgenthau left the meeting elated and confided to his diary that he would suppress some of his well-cultivated dislike for Hull. In fact, he intended to "see a lot more of Hull because we evidently are thinking absolutely along the same lines as to what are necessary steps to take to get this country ready to defend itself." [10] In the minds of two cabinet members, then, the bombing of Tokyo was considered a defensive act.

Pressure from the Chinese to gain approval for this plan immediately increased. Chiang Kai-shek cabled both Roosevelt and Morgenthau stressing the urgency with which he awaited an affirmative decision sending bombers to China. Chiang's messages prompted Roosevelt to encourage Morgenthau to wind up the proposals. Morgenthau discussed the proposal before the President and the Cabinet at a meeting on the morning of December 19. Roosevelt, according to Morgenthau's notes, responded enthusiastically and believed that such an operation might have a positive effect not only upon the Asian situation but in Europe as well.[11]

Following the cabinet meeting, Roosevelt summoned Morgenthau, Hull, Secretary of War Henry Stimson, and Secretary of the Navy Frank Knox to a further discussion of the plan to have American bombers, operating from China, attack Japan. Morgenthau's notes reveal that they all favored the plan, and he proceeded to inform Soong that he was now looking "for a man who knew how to fly these four engine bombers. . . ." In further discussions with Frank Knox, Morgenthau pursued the problem of how to get War Department approval for the sending of scarce bombers and Curtiss-Wright P-40 fighter planes to China. Stressing the need to keep the whole operation "hush-hush," they resolved to meet with State, War, and Chinese officials over the next several days.[12]

Morgenthau, along with an aide, Philip Young, resumed his talks with Soong, General Mow, and Colonel Chennault. He announced that Roosevelt wanted to send Flying Fortresses to China and had asked the Chinese to provide some specific ideas for their use. Chennault explained his belief that long-range bombers, assisted by fighters, could successfully attack Japan. He preferred Flying Fortresses over Lockheed Hudson bombers since their greater range would allow them to reach Tokyo as well as Nagasaki, Kobe, and Osaka. Though no definite number of bombers was mentioned, Chennault thought that about two hundred fighters would be needed to protect Chinese airfields used by the bombers. Soong, less concerned with such details or logistics, made clear his willingness to accept all planes in any combination.

As envisioned by Chennault, the crews would be composed of an American bombardier, pilot, and five mechanics for each plane. Morgenthau believed the bombers could be flown in from the Philippines and that the "Army would release enough men from active duty at $1,000 per month to help the Chinese with the ships." The Secretary wanted to know the specifics of the bombing plan. For example, could incendiary bombs be used, "inasmuch as the Japanese cities were all made of just wood and paper. Chennault said that a lot of damage could be done using this method, and that, even if the Chinese lost some of the bombers, it would be well justified."[13]

While Morgenthau and Chennault discussed the terror bombing of Japanese cities and civilians, they seem to have given little thought to a Japanese counterattack against the United States. Nor did they seem troubled by any moral objections. Beyond this, both appear to have been deceived by their own smoke screen. They ceased to look upon this as an "American" operation, for it was to be carried out by a private group in the service of the Chinese government. The origins of the fliers, their equipment, funding, and support were simply ignored.

As was often the case, however, bureaucratic competition aborted Morgenthau's and Chennault's grand strategy. Stimson was growing ever more troubled by Soong's freewheeling style and strategy. He believed Morgenthau, Hull, and Roosevelt were being swept up in Chinese dreaming and would commit the United States to a recklessly provocative policy. Stimson took the initiative of calling together all the principals to meet with General George Marshall in order to "get some brains into it [the Chinese air plan] before we get committed to it." The involvement of the army chief of staff was crucial, for he was known to oppose the diversion of scarce bombers to China and believed air support should be limited to a grant of fighter planes.[14]

Marshall's vigorous objections carried weight with all the Americans in decisionmaking positions. This was made plain the next day when Morgenthau, Hull, Knox, Stimson, Marshall, and Admiral Harold Stark met to formulate a definitive policy. In an effort to forestall more loose talk of sending scarce bombers to China, Marshall strongly advocated that the United

States transfer from the British to the Chinese one hundred P-40 fighter planes which had not yet been delivered. Those present all seem to have agreed, as did the President, who now charged Morgenthau with the responsibility of informing Soong and Chennault that the air strategy had been altered.[15] The Secretary explained to them that, despite his own support, the army would not sanction the release of long-range bombers. Perhaps some of the Chinese representatives' disappointment was tempered by the news that they would soon receive one hundred fighter planes.[16]

The delivery of these planes, and the additional military aid which was expected to follow the passage of the Lend-Lease Act, required that the Chinese expand and reorganize their aid mission in Washington. Previously Soong had operated as an official Chinese purchasing agent dealing through the Chinese-owned Universal Trading Corporation (UTC), the company which used the American credits which had been extended to China from December 1938 through December 1940 to buy supplies in the United States. In response to expanded aid, Soong created a new corporation in early 1941. China Defense Supplies (CDS) supplanted UTC and became China's designated Lend-Lease agent in April 1941. As noted earlier, the many tentacles which Soong used to reach into government agencies prompted Morgenthau to remark that when dealing with CDS and its supporters he could not tell who was working for the United States and who for China.[17]

Among the most important members of CDS were Claire Chennault, Joseph Alsop, Thomas Corcoran, William Youngman, Harry Price, and William Pawley, all devotees of the Chinese Nationalists and of air power. Between January and April 1941, the CDS staff was absorbed in arranging for the transfer of military equipment to China and in negotiating an extensive Lend-Lease request. By late spring about $150 million worth of military equipment had been allocated to China. Yet delivery was a problem, for many of the supplies would not be available before 1942 and shipping space was scarce for what was available.[18] To break this bottleneck the Chinese pushed to secure the immediate delivery of the promised planes and pilots.

Chennault, who was working in Washington for CDS, played a major role in seeking a solution. After consulting with Knox, Morgenthau, and White House aides, Chennault decided to create an American Volunteer Group (AVG) to fly for China. Chennault and Pawley developed a scheme to recruit American military personnel who would resign their commissions and sign contracts with a private corporation, the Central Aircraft Manufacturing Corporation (CAMCO), which was, of course, a front. Jointly owned by Chinese Finance Minister H. H. Kung (Madame Chiang's brother-in-law) and Pawley, CAMCO's operating funds came from CDS and originated as U.S. Lend-Lease aid.[19]

CAMCO recruited pilots and crews at military bases throughout the United States. Chennault and Pawley eagerly accepted fliers who would agree to resign their commissions and sign on with CAMCO, and Roosevelt signed an Executive Order permitting the "resignations." By late September 1941, over one hundred pilots plus mechanics had signed contracts. The first contingent began their journey to China via Rangoon on June 9 aboard a Dutch freighter escorted by American naval vessels. This was done under orders of Admiral Harold Stark, who delared their safe arrival was "essential to the United States support of China."[20] Within a few months these men and their P-40 fighter planes would become famous as the Flying Tigers.

This secret creation of an American tactical fighter force in China was only one aspect of developing a program for clandestine air war. Creation of the AVG had only opened the path to more comprehensive planning. Lend-Lease had centralized military aid granting authority with the President and his agents. This transferred the initiative from Morgenthau's Treasury Department to the White House. Accordingly, the President named his special assistant, Lauchlin Currie, to take charge of expediting aid to China. Currie was no stranger to this task, having already visited Chungking and consulted with Chiang Kai-shek regarding military assistance. Currie's vociferous support for increased aid to China increasingly centered on military support, expecially in the form of air power. As coordinator of China aid, Currie worked closely with Chennault, Soong, and naval attaché James McHugh. Because of his personal ties to the Soong family, McHugh served as Currie's "ambassador" in Chungking.[21] Currie received numerous suggestions from all these sources on plans to resurrect the bombing proposal which Morgenthau had supported the previous December.

Early in May 1941, Currie forwarded a new proposal (afterwards identified as JB 355) to the Joint Aircraft Committee, which sent it on to General Marshall and the Joint Board for consideration. As first presented, Currie's proposal stressed the role that an air force in China could play in defending Singapore, the Burma Road lifeline to China, and the Philippines against Japanese attack. This defense could be accomplished without directly involving the United States or endangering its Pacific Fleet. The mere existence of such an air force, Currie suggested, would be a constant threat to a Japanese advance anywhere in Southeast Asia. Not only might this force inhibit new Japanese moves but it also could take the offensive since "Kobe, Kyoto, Osaka as well as Yokohama and Tokyo could be attacked by bombers operating from existing airfields in China."

Similar to recommendations made by Chennault in December 1940 and again in October 1942, this proposal called for an air force of five hundred war planes and additional transports. Through a gradual buildup, the force would reach full strength during 1941. In addition to the previously allocated P-40s, two hundred and fifty fighters and one hundred and fifty bombers would be sent to China to commence operations during November 1941. Currie noted that Chennault and CAMCO were already recruiting American crews for these planes and that future pilots might be drawn from Chinese trained in the United States.

Among the "tactical objectives" Currie listed were occasional raids on Japanese industrial complexes and support of offensive operations by the Chinese army. Among the "strategic objectives" were the "destruction of Japanese factories in order to cripple production of munitions and essential articles for maintenance of economic structure in Japan."[22] A trained economist, Currie frequently emphasized the economic consequences of strategic bombing in the proposals he submitted to the Joint Board. He believed bombing would erode Japan's will and ability to undertake military expansion.

Currie slightly amended the scope of these proposals almost as soon as he drafted them. On May 12 he informed Marshall that he was developing a revised short-term program and asked that the Joint Board defer consideration of the matter until they had received the amendments.[23] Currie forwarded the amended proposal to Frank Knox on May 28, suggesting that the desired planes might be drawn from existing stocks or planned production and scaling down the number of aircraft to a little more than half the original five hundred. Currie again explained that the pilots would be American reserve officers working under Chennault and Chiang. He also raised an important new point: It would be of immense value for "our men to acquire actual combat experience." The overall value of this plan, however, was not only the gains to be made in striking Japan. It was partly a psychological strategy to bolster the Chinese Nationalists and partly a deterrent strategy aimed at frightening the Tokyo militarists against further expansion by communicating American opposition through the "occasional incendiary bombing of Japan."[24]

While this proposal remained under consideration by the Joint Board during June and July, major problems had yet to be resolved. The acute shortage of all planes, especially bombers, and the paucity of trained crews made the army hesitant to offer very much to China or for use in China. America's meager airplane production was largely committed to filling British needs as well as to reinforcing General Douglas MacArthur's position in the Philippines. The branches of the armed services and policymakers had to discuss any suggestions to divert planes to China, coordinating the decisions with the British.

The China air force proposal received encouragement as the fragile military stalemate existing in Southeast Asia began to crumble in June and July. Japanese advances into southern French Indochina followed the German attack upon the Soviet Union in June 1941. The Japanese were not only moving toward control of vital resources which would free them from dependence on American supplies, they were also threatening Singapore and the Burma Road supply line over which American aid reached China. Anticipating these frightening developments, Currie and Chennault increased their efforts to win Joint Board approval for the Chinese air program. On June 11 they again urged the Joint Board to act on the May 28 proposal that China be given two hundred and sixty-nine fighters, sixty-six bombers, and thirty-five transports. In addition, Currie recommended that the United States begin to train Chinese pilots.[25] These requests, combined with evidence of an impending Japanese move against southern Indochina, led the Joint Planning Committee to recommend, on July 9, that the full Joint Board approve the Chinese air program.

The report issued by the Planning Committee supported the idea that American volunteers, flying for China, attack Japan on several fronts. The committee accepted the premises of the Currie-Chennault proposal and urged that the requested planes, advisors, and other assistance (such as the training of Chinese pilots) be given to China as soon as possible. This program, it stated, could play a decisive role in the defense of Singapore, the Burma Road, and China. Yet the recommended timetable for the delivery of the planes indicated that few if any bombers would be sent to China before November 1941 at the earliest.[26]

On July 12 the Joint Board approved Currie's "Short Term Aircraft Program for China," which called for the "incendiary bombing of Japan" by Americans flying under contract for a Chinese-American front corporation.[27] Secretary Knox and Acting Secretary of War Patterson formally notified the President of their endorsement of the plan on July 18. Undoubtedly influenced by Currie, Roosevelt affixed his initials to the Secretaries' letter on July 23. The President included the notation, "but restudy military mission versus the attaché method."[28] He perhaps referred to a related aid mission concurrently being dispatched to China by the War Department. Still extremely wary of air strategies, General Marshall had moved to send an army group to China under General John Magruder; its job would be to study the organization and supply requirements of the Chinese army.[29]

Here again was an example of both clandestine military operation and the opposition of the regular army to the air strategy being pushed by "outsiders" like Currie and Chennault. Chennault himself saw Magruder's mission as a tool of Marshall and the "regular" War Department planners who hoped to push a ground strategy in China, undercutting plans for offensive strategic bombing of Japan. Magruder allegedly warned Marshall that Chenault's proposed attack might lead to a rapid Japanese response directly against the United States.[30]

Chennault had returned to the Far East shortly before the approval of JB 355. In Burma, where the recently arrived AVG were undergoing training and assembling their first P-40s, Chennault received the news from Currie. The White House aide explained that sixty-six bombers were to be made available to China before the end of the year, with twenty-four to be sent immediately. In addition, the United States would begin training Chinese pilots to assume a combat role as more planes arrived.[31]

Between August and November, Chennault in Burma and Soong and Currie in Washington wrote frequently and continually explored ways to expedite the delivery of the bombers. Chennault told Generalissimo and Madame Chiang that he was beginning the recruitment of a second volunteer group in the United States specifically trained to fly the thirty-three Lockheed Hudson and thirty-three DB-7 (Douglas) bombers which were now promised.[32] T. V. Soong and Chennault also discussed the best way to recruit trained Americans and fly the airplanes from the United States to China.[33] Although the recruitment drive proceeded, the delivery of the planes continued to be delayed. This resulted from both production and shipping bottlenecks. On November 22 Currie wrote from the White House explaining that he and certain of Chennault's supporters in the War Department were now hopeful of sending the planes by year's end.[34] Chennault himself attributed the delay largely to intense hostility among other factions in the War Department and the competing demands of the British and MacArthur in the Philippines. Still, the AVG commander believed that with White House backing the bomber squadron could be operative by late December.[35]

These hopes, as well as expectations of receiving a special shipment of supplies which MacArthur had promised from the Philippines, were shattered by the Japanese attack upon Pearl Harbor on December 7, 1941. Chennault was left stranded with only his fighter group in Burma and western China. On into January 1942, Chennault still pleaded with Currie to send the bombers so that he could immediately "begin attacks on Japan's industry."[36] Japan's rapid conquest of Southeast Asia and the Pacific precluded this possibility. Still, for the next three years Chennault would fight a rearguard action pleading for the creation of a special air force in China under his command and sniping at the American army's ground strategists, Stilwell and Marshall. Chinese airfields did finally play an indirect role in bombing Japan in the spring of 1942, when the aircraft carrier launched planes of the Doolittle raiders attempted to land in China after bombing Tokyo.

The Japanese attack upon the U.S. Pacific Fleet changed the entire basis of American military planning and obviously eliminated the imagined deterrent aspect of the plan to bomb Japan's cities. But the very existence of the plan raises questions as to the extent, if any, of Japanese foreknowledge. Granted that the larger causes of the war lay in the overall incompatibility of Japanese and American interests in the Pacific and that the de facto American oil embargo of July 26, 1941, provided an immediate cause, the secret American air strategy may still have influenced the course of events. Certainly the information which the Japanese government did possess about Chennault's activities was a source of great concern in Tokyo.[37]

In one sense the story of abortive decisions to bomb Japan ends with the double question of what might have been if the bombers had become available before December 7, and what influence the mere existence of the plan had on Japanese policy. However, this narrative should also compel historians to look forward in time and refrain from the tendency to dismiss JB 355 and Chennault's activities as merely discarded contingency plans.

Between December 1940 and July 1941, agents and agencies of the United States did conspire with private military entrepreneurs and the Chinese Nationalists to develop a program for secret air warfare. This appears to have set a major precedent for U.S. military and political planning, not merely in style but in terms of creating a core of personnel and an organizational structure which could function on a continuing basis. Moreover, the individuals most active in the AVG—Chennault, William Pawley, Tom Corcoran, Whiting Willauer, and Joseph Alsop—continued their partnership during World War II, either working for Chennault's 14th Air Force in China or Soong's CDS in Washington. At the end of the war, Chennault, Corcoran, and Willauer (who later served as ambassador to Honduras and helped direct the CIA-sponsored air attack and coup against the leftist Arbenz regime in Guatemala)[38] joined forces to resurrect the AVG as Civil Air Transport (CAT). CAT used many former AVG fliers and, following pressure from Washington, received an UNRRA contract for relief work in China. With planes purchased from American military surplus at bargain prices, CAT soon began flying military airlifts to beseiged Nationalist garrisons in north China. When the Communist victory of 1949 compelled a Nationalist withdrawal to Taiwan, CAT went along.[39]

Although nominally a private firm incorporated in the state of Delaware, CAT functioned as a paramilitary arm of the Central Intelligence Agency. In 1959 CAT was transformed into Air America and expanded its operations throughout Southeast Asia. Documents appearing in the *Pentagon Papers* make it clear that CAT–Air America played an active combat military role during the French and American wars in Vietnam, from the early 1950s until 1975.[40]

A force originating in December 1940 as an effort to punish Japan and perhaps deter its further aggression had transformed itself along with the political environment of East Asia and the growth of American globalism. By 1946 the United States already possessed a cadre of Asia experts and revolution fighters able to carry out national policy through the agencies of private armies, air forces, and multinational corporations. This major development in the tactics of clandestine intervention was inaugurated in the decisive months preceding Pearl Harbor and should not be rationalized or dismissed as merely another development of the Cold War. The long-term implications of Chennault's AVG were of course imagined only dimly, if at all, in December 1941. But in the context of America's China policy at that time, these plans evidenced a much deeper involvement with the Nationalist regime than is usually imagined. Given the willingness to sponsor a covert attack upon Japanese forces and Japan itself, it is increasingly difficult to believe that anything short of general war could have emerged from the Japanese-American confrontation of 1941. The necessary political, military, and economic sinews of an alliance had been stretched between Washington and Chungking. It only awaited a catalyst to emerge. Tokyo itself dramatically provided this on December 7, 1941.

Chapter 5
Allies in a New War

JAPAN'S LIGHTNING AIR RAID upon the Pacific Fleet at Pearl Harbor destroyed the possibility that the United States could continue to utilize China as a military proxy against Tokyo. Within days of the initial attack, Germany joined the war upon America and Japanese forces began a rout of British, Dutch, and American troops scattered throughout the islands and archipelagos of the Pacific. The shock of this attack, though eventually it proved a rallying point, struck fear and self-doubt in the minds of countless Americans. Two days after war began, an editorial appearing in the *New York Times* voiced hope that despite its early losses, the United States "did not stand alone."

We have as our loyal ally China, with its inexhaustible manpower—China which we did not desert in her own hour of need—China from whose patient and infinitely resourceful people there will now return to us tenfold payment upon such aid as we have given. In the presence of these allies we shall find the key to the strategy of the Pacific. . . .[1]

Understandably, perhaps, the editorial board of the *Times*, which wished to draw upon the good will and manpower of China, viewed things differently than did a weary Chinese leadership in Chungking. After suffering five years of war, most Chinese were merely relieved that some other people would absorb Japan's attention. The long-range implications of the Japanese-American conflict led KMT officials in Chungking to celebrate news of the war almost as loudly as must have been the case in Tokyo. The Chinese writer Han Suyin recalled the event in this way:

It was Pao [a KMT officer and the author's husband] who returned, almost as soon as he had left for his office that morning, and told me; bringing the newspaper with him. Almost immediately there were noises in the street; newsboys shouting extras, people surging out of their houses to buy the newspapers, crowding together, the sounds of their voices above the hum of the traffic. Pao was radiant; the Military Council was jubilant; Chiang was so happy he sang an old opera aria and played Ave Maria all day. The Kuomintang government officials went around congratulating each other, as if a great victory had been won. From their standpoint, it was a great victory, what they had waited for, America was at war with Japan. At last, at last, America was at war with Japan! Now China's strategic importance would grow even more. American money and equipment would flow in; half a billion dollars, one billion dollars . . . Now Lend-Lease would increase. . . . Now America would *have* to support Chiang, and that meant U.S. dollars into the pockets of the officials, into the pockets of the army commanders, and guns to Hu Tsung-nan for the coming war against Yenan.[2]

The stark contrast between the projections of the *Times*'s editorialists and the Nationalists' actual reactions to Pearl Harbor could serve as a reference point to the tragedy of Chinese-American relations during World War II. The allies had joined together, but had begun two different wars. While American planners expected to use Chinese manpower as a vast force against Japan, the Nationalist regime hoped to utilize its alliance to accumulate reserves of money, weapons, and influence which would help achieve domestic supremacy. Americans who supposed that aid could be used as a lever to encourage reform confronted a Chinese leadership convinced that foreign assistance obviated the need for reform. These contradictions cast the first of many long shadows over the imaginary "key to the strategy of the Pacific."

Even as Japan overran the scattered American outposts of the Pacific, military and diplomatic officials in China sought to warn Washington against the danger of attributing too much importance to the Chinese alliance. General John Magruder, head of AMMISCA, predicted that the Nationalists would conclude a de facto truce with Japan, leaving Americans to carry on the war. The KMT intended to horde American aid "largely with the idea of post-war military action." To expect the Chinese to launch an offensive was an "alluring fiction," an extension of the Chinese tendency to "believe in the world of make-believe." Chiang, Magruder, explained, regarded his soldiers and equipment as "static assets, to be conserved for assistance in fighting against . . . fellow countrymen for economic and political supremacy."[3]

Naval attaché James McHugh, writing to the Navy Department and the White House, offered no more hopeful prognosis about China's current military value. Nevertheless, consistent with his political support of the KMT, McHugh warned Washington not to begrudge the Chinese substantial military and economic assistance. To do so would run the risk of turning Chiang "anti-foreign." American strategy, the attaché argued, must accommodate Chiang's demands for aid while supplying the Generalissimo's protégé, Claire Chennault, with an air force to fight Japan.[4]

Another somber judgment came from the diplomatic corps, headed by Ambassador Clarence Gauss. By nature a brooding man, and especially skeptical about the KMT, Gauss cautioned his superiors in the State Department against believing that China was or would soon become an effective military ally. Chiang, he declared, suffered from "a touch of unreality derived from a somewhat grandiose or 'ivory tower' conception of his and China's role." Following Japan's attack on the United States, Gauss noted, Chiang actually moved to enhance the power of reactionary elements of the KMT. The ambassador recommended that the United States do nothing to buttress the ruling hierarchy of Chungking, such as granting it a blank-check endorsement. Instead, American policy should be directed toward identifying and supporting liberal elements in the KMT coalition.[5]

These reports from Chungking, though quite dissimilar in political content, attested to the dubious military value of

China in the current war effort. The judgment they rendered upon Chinese politics showed scant trace of the romantic or heroic propaganda which had dominated popular discussions about China. To understand why these and most later recommendations from "experts" in China were ignored, we must look again at Franklin D. Roosevelt, the individual most responsible for charting the course of American diplomacy. Early in the war, Roosevelt adopted an Asian strategy centered upon elevating Nationalist China to "great power" status, something Lauchlin Currie had previously urged him to do. This decision had major implications for both the conduct of the war and postwar diplomacy.

Not surprisingly, Roosevelt assumed that following Japan's eventual defeat Asia would enter a new stage of political evolution. Japan would be gone as a dominant military power, but so would the mighty British, Dutch, and French empires—soon if not immediately. Two major forces would probably rush in to fill this power vacuum: Soviet power extending from northeast Asia and nationalist political movements emerging within the former colonial and neocolonial societies. Wartime decisions made by the United States could influence the pace of decolonization, the dimensions of the Soviet sphere, and, perhaps most importantly, the nature of Asian nationalism. Neither Roosevelt nor his advisors were deadset against any of these developments, since they hoped that a carefully reordered Asia would contribute to world stability and prosperity. But they were determined that the United States should play a major role in outlining the contours of postwar Asia.

Constraining this concern, however, was the demand imposed upon American resources by the global war. The massive battlefronts of Europe and the Pacific, deemed strategically more vital than mainland Asia, meant that the American war effort in China stood in third place. Neither the best minds in Washington, sufficient materiel, nor many troops would be spared for the China front. Yet for a variety of reasons, both pragmatic and romantic, Roosevelt sought to include China among the ranks of the Grand Alliance. Encouraged by the advice of such men as Lauchlin Currie, Harry Hopkins, James McHugh, Claire Chennault, Joseph Alsop, and Chiang Kai-shek, the President believed he could join American power to the KMT and thereby create an effective wartime and postwar ally. This policy, he believed, might encourage the development of a liberal, pro-American China to replace the influence of the imperialist powers in Asia and counter the appeal of revolutionary doctrines among the masses of the East. A thought expressed by Roosevelt and Hopkins at several points during the war clinched the argument: "in any serious conflict of policy with Russia," Nationalist China "would line up on our side."

Roosevelt's concern, however, was not fixated upon a Soviet or revolutionary threat. During the war American planners were equally concerned with easing the European imperialists out of Asia. The British in particular feared that American policy had determined to pull down the foundations of the empire even before a final verdict was rendered. Throughout the war the British growled about extending aid to Chiang Kai-shek, largely because they saw Chinese nationalism as a direct threat to colonialism. Churchill believed Roosevelt's game was to make China strong enough to "police" Asia while remaining essentially dependent upon the United States. The prime minister complained to subordinates that the Americans expected to use China as a "faggot vote on the side of the United States in an attempt to liquidate the British overseas Empire."[6]

Before fulfilling either Roosevelt's hope or Churchill's fear, the United States had first to succeed in prodding the Nationalist regime to begin the military and political reforms which might transform China into a powerful and unified state. Without change, little could be expected of China. Yet Roosevelt never really understood that in his effort to forge a new order in Asia he had linked the United States to a crumbling regime, a situation reminiscent of the Austrian "corpse" to which Germany found itself allied in World War I. From 1941 on, despite a brave façade, the KMT's claim to popular support and power grew only weaker. The party and government apparatus devolved from an instrument of class and military rule to a jumble of family-oriented cliques and semi-independent military commanders. As this occurred, the forces of social revolution grew consistently stronger, accelerating the internal crisis and unraveling the web of American policy. The demise of the United Front and Nationalist power removed the buffer between the Chinese Communists and the United States, placing these two powerful forces on a collision course.

In the immediate aftermath of the Pearl Harbor attack, Chiang Kai-shek sought to secure the support of the Western allies for his regime and for the war against Japan. On December 8, 1941, the generalissimo held an audience with the American and Soviet ambassadors, suggesting that both nations commit their armed forces—naval, air, and ground—to pushing the Japanese out of China. Chiang seemed especially eager to secure a Soviet commitment to assist China against Japan. Implicitly, this involved getting Moscow to declare itself resoundingly on the side of the KMT. In addition, a thoroughgoing Soviet-American involvement in China would prevent the British from drawing off resources to Europe or for the battle to retake lost colonies. This was a particularly stinging issue for the Chinese, since British authorities in Rangoon had already begun to confiscate China-bound Lend-Lease supplies and had requisitioned the AVG for the defense of Burma.[7]

Chiang's strategy held out little appeal to any of the allies. The Soviet Union faced far too desperate a struggle in Europe to open an Asian front against Japan. The British had no desire to sacrifice anything on China's behalf. In fact, only the United States possessed the will and ability to do anything for China. Yet even Roosevelt remained most uncertain about what form American assistance should take. Stalling for time, the President suggested to Chiang that the allies not commit themselves to a strategy until a military conference could be held in Chungking later in December.[8]

The delay in setting a course for aid to China stemmed, in part, from the determination of Roosevelt and Army Chief of Staff General George C. Marshall to concentrate on the defeat of Nazi Germany. This priority determined close cooperation between the United States and Great Britain and, to a lesser degree, the Soviet Union. In planning strategy and distributing aid, China was expendable. Roosevelt and Churchill met in Washington late in December at the ARCADIA Conference, which established the framework for coalition warfare. The two leaders created a Combined Chiefs of Staff (CCS) and a Munitions Assignment Board to allocate Lend-Lease supplies. The Chinese were neither invited to participate in these organs nor consulted when the CCS decided to establish a China-Burma-India Theater (CBI). As something of an afterthought, the Chinese government was asked to approve this decision and accept the dispatch of an American commander to oversee the American component of the theater. On January 5, 1942, Chiang accepted these proposals, with the proviso that he remained supreme commander within China proper.

These initial decisions must have disappointed the generalissimo, for China received no promises of substantial aid or troops. His regime had been excluded from the decision-making organs forged by the Western allies. However, at least the outline of an alliance had been suggested by the formation of a military theater in China. If an important American officer served as a liaison with Chiang, a fuller relationship could develop. Yet Chiang and his representative in Washington, T. V. Soong, wanted to be certain of receiving the "right kind of American," certainly not another Owen Lattimore. Soong suggested to the War Department that the officer sent to China "need not be an expert on the Far East." In fact, it would be better if he were totally unfamiliar with China's military and political system. Too much knowledge, Soong asserted, would only confuse him! What Soong meant, of course, was that the KMT wanted to receive a rubber-stamp advisor, one who would expedite aid requests and refrain from challenging the status quo. Certainly the generalissimo did not anticipate the arrival of a foreign officer determined to take command of Chinese troops.[9]

The two men charged with selecting an American commander for CBI, Secretary of War Stimson and General Marshall, had deep misgivings over placing too much emphasis on China's war role. Marshall in particular retained his view of China as a backward and disorganized society, formed while a young soldier stationed in Tientsin many years before. To avoid a drain upon American resources, Stimson and Marshall preferred to send an officer who would emphasize internal Chinese military reorganization as the proper way for China to contribute to the fight against Japan. They first favored selecting Lieutenant-General Hugh A. Drum for the mission, but after he made plain his uninterest in such a backwater assignment, the idea was dropped.[10]

Taking the initiative with Stimson, Marshall then proposed one of the army's foremost China experts, who was also the general's friend. Lieutenant-General Joseph W. Stilwell had first gone to China in 1911, returning in the 1930s as an accomplished military attaché and chronicler of the Japanese assault. He not only learned the Chinese language, he also distinguished himself as an outstanding combat officer. Seemingly an inspired choice, the selection of Stilwell as American commander in China proved a disaster. Marshall had not merely ignored Soong's request to send a neophyte, he had chosen an expert's expert, a man who believed he was more qualified to run China than was Chiang Kai-shek. Widely known to his troops by the nickname "Vinegar Joe," Stilwell possessed a temperament which drove him to try to do so.

When the war began, Stilwell had rushed from California to Washington, where early indications suggested he would be among those chosen to lead forces in Europe. Discussions with fellow officers in the War Department greatly disturbed the general, for he believed that Roosevelt had fallen under the sway of the British and behaved like a pompous military amateur.[11] Stilwell expressed great surprise when, on January 14, 1942, Secretary Stimson told him that the general's "finger of destiny" pointed in the direction of China. General Marshall and Stimson explained to Stilwell that T. V. Soong (just named China's foreign minister, though he continued to live in Washington) now offered to place Chinese troops under an American command. American officials did not yet realize that while Soong proposed, Chiang disposed; and the generalissimo had no intention of delegating actual command powers to an American. More likely, Soong or Chiang thought that dangling the promise of command might sweeten the pot for the War Department's appointment.

Marshall told Stilwell that his main objectives in China would be to maintain transport along the vital Burma Road (threatened by a Japanese advance in Burma) and to "get Chinese factions together." The army chief of staff could not promise the dispatch of American combat troops. Stilwell explained that he could achieve these goals only if he acquired the authority to command American, British, and Chinese troops in the theater. He also required authority to control Lend-Lease, a commitment to arm thirty Chinese divisions, a promise of air supply if the Burma Road fell, and finally command over Chennault's small air task force which was to be drafted into the army air force. Marshall promised to support Stilwell as much as possible, and Soong indicated his approval of the program. In addition, Chiang decided to designate Stilwell as "the Generalissimo's chief of staff," a rank with an undefined power.[12]

In the weeks which followed the creation of his new command, Stilwell rushed about Washington in order to organize a staff. He even succeeded in getting the reluctant British to permit the establishment of bases and staging areas in India and Burma. Most importantly, he sought instructions from the President as to the political dimensions of his mission in China. An audience with Roosevelt and Hopkins on February 9, however, deeply disturbed the new American commander. The President and Hopkins spoke in glib generalities. Roosevelt instructed Stilwell to inform Chiang that upon Japan's defeat China would recover all lost territory. Roosevelt refused to specify what this meant, a troubling fact since few agreed on exactly what China's territory was or the circumstances under which it had been lost since the fall of the Ch'ing Dynasty. Hopkins only spoke of how thrilled Stilwell must be at the prospect of commanding Chinese troops. Since Stilwell did not yet know if the promise of command was real, he had hoped to ask the President whether the White House would back him up in a showdown. But these points were all glossed over as Roosevelt shook Stilwell's hand and rushed him out the door toward China. [13]

While Stilwell sought to clarify his authority and receive indications of a Presidential commitment, Chiang raced toward the American Treasury. The generalissimo devoted far more energy to the search for new economic support in the weeks following Pearl Harbor than to salvaging the desperate military situation confronting China along the Burma Road. Though China did face dire economic problems caused by rampant inflation and speculation, Chiang had no great interest in finding a remedy. Instead, he demanded that Washington show its support for China by granting an immediate $1 billion loan. Ambassador Gauss had the temerity to ask what the money would be used for. Chiang replied that Washington only had to provide the funds, China would find a proper use later. [14]

Perhaps as penance for the relatively paltry military support forthcoming to China, and in furtherance of the President's long-term political goals, the White House proved extremely eager to meet Chiang's financial requests. Lauchlin Currie pushed the proposal through the State and Treasury departments, both of which quickly agreed to the principle of extending $500 million to China. Yet, while Currie and Hornbeck favored the idea of a loan given with "no strings," Henry Morgenthau, Jr., continued to insist that all aid to China be tightly controlled. Unless the Chinese were held to a strict contract, the Treasury Secretary argued, the United States would receive no military or political return on its investment.[15]

The term "contract" is no exaggeration when describing Morgenthau's ideas about aid. He envisioned the direct payment of Chinese soldiers with U.S. banknotes or silver dollars. Alternatively, Morgenthau proposed to Roosevelt and Soong that America virtually buy a Chinese army by extending direct payments to soldiers in the field using a special form of currency called "demos," for democracy. In a manner certain to insult the Chinese, the Treasury head said, "Well, what I am thinking of Dr. Soong, [is] once a month to make you an advance for a month . . . so that while the boys fight they get their money, and if they don't fight, no money. . . . Morgenthau further explained that he and the President wanted to purchase "a million shock troops" willing to "do anything" the Americans wanted.[16]

Soong must have been startled by this proposal, for both its crudeness and its political implications. The generalissimo, he declared, would never accept such an arrangement. Aid must come as a lump-sum cash transfer to China, not as payment to troops.[17] What lay at the heart of the matter was the threat posed by the United States becoming paymaster to the KMT armies. This was no minor issue in an army based on forced conscription and the systematic brutalization of its troops. A major element in the continued loyalty of troop commanders to Chiang was the generalissimo's willingness to give them lump-sum funds out of which they paid the troops. The arrangement insured widespread corruption but preserved the loyalty of commanders to Chungking. The intervention of American paymasters threatened to undercut the entire system of loyalty and command.

Morgenthau, finding no support for his strict terms (General Marshall urged that the question be dropped, since Chiang had allegedly agreed to let "Stilwell run his army"), resigned himself to presenting the Chinese request to Congress. Yet, upon consulting with Soong, he could scarcely believe the foreign minister's statement that China had no particular plan to do anything with the $500 million. The point of the loan, Morgenthau explained, was "to make General Chiang happy" and, although he did not wish to press the point and "make him unhappy," Congress would have to be told about how the money would be used. Soong tossed off the remark that Congress should be informed that if China were to remain an ally, the money must be given. Fortunately for China and the administration, Congress never pressed the point and after perfunctory hearings agreed to the loan on February 9.[18]

Subsequent Chinese use of the funds confirmed Morgenthau's worst suspicions. Money was drawn out of the Treasury in large, haphazard amounts and allocated to a bond and certificate issue within China. Though supposedly a device to reduce inflation, it had the opposite result. Purchase of the bonds and certificates was restricted to powerful officials, bankers, and landlords, who were permitted to subscribe at a fixed dollar-yuan (Chinese currency) rate even though the real exchange rate changed drastically over the eighteen months the issue remained on the market. Thus in 1943, when the trading closed, speculators engaged in a wildly profitable buying spree. In three days, Mesdames Chiang and Kung purchased $50 million worth of notes. Soong and K. P. Chen bought $5 million each in their own names and more through third parties. The same covert Treasury Department investigation that brought these dealings to light revealed that finance minister H. H. Kung had transferred millions of dollars worth of gold from Chinese government accounts into his own name.[19]

Although Roosevelt and his associates were generally aware of the scope of this corruption, they made little effort to interfere. The President, concerned with larger questions, remained willing to condone this sort of impropriety among the Chinese. More important was China's postwar role. Treating China as a "great power," Roosevelt told Admiral Lord Louis Mountbatten in 1943, would inhibit aggression "during the immediate post-war period." Having a half-billion Chinese allies would be "very useful twenty-five or fifty years hence, even though China cannot contribute much military or naval support for the moment." Because of its strategic location, a friendly China could also become a sort of buffer against possible Soviet expansion in Asia.[20]

From the beginning of the war, Roosevelt groped for a China policy which would do several, sometimes contradictory, things at once. At a minimum, he wished to sustain China as an active ally, tying down several million Japanese troops on the Asian mainland. A policy of generous aid, combined with elevating China's importance in world political councils, could contribute to the acceptance of China as a great power. Meanwhile, a reformed, unified China could cooperate with the United States in insuring a stable postwar Asia. Also, the President remained largely convinced that within China the agency of transformation must be Chiang Kai-shek and his regime. Thus Chiang must be supported and indulged, with a view toward future cooperation. Until late in the war, the President ignored or misunderstood signs indicating that the U.S.-KMT alliance yielded results fundamentally opposed to the objectives of U.S. policy.

For a variety of reasons, other individuals and groups concerned with formulating and implementing China policy rejected the President's broad view. Centers of opposition—opposition based on a belief that Roosevelt was either too indulgent or too critical of the KMT—developed within the War, State, Treasury, and Navy departments and in the OSS. Often uncertain about the loyalty of his subordinates, Roosevelt frequently utilized personal representatives for missions to China, individuals not tied to special bureaucratic interests. Following the President's example of sidestepping normal procedures, many of the American factions in China themselves established special liaisons with the contesting Chinese groups.

The most significant contradictions and strains in China policy developed between the President and his aides, who in

Washington took a broad, long-term view of events, and the military and diplomatic officers stationed in China, who faced the realities of the political and military battlefield. While Roosevelt could project a future "great China," General Stilwell had to deal with a crumbling army. The staff of the American embassy, witnessing the grave political deterioration of the KMT, had little faith in predictions that a liberal China was about to assume the mantle of Asian leadership. While all acknowledged that the political future of China held tremendous importance for the United States, few Americans agreed upon exactly why this was so or which China really represented America's—or China's—best interests. Since the United States had resolved to begin a massive program of aid to a Chinese government engaged in both a foreign and civil war, the unresolved questions of basic policy could only contribute to eventual disaster.

Chapter 6
American Military Strategy and the Chinese Nationalists

MUCH LATER, DURING the "command crisis" of September 1944, a plaintive Joseph Stilwell reflected on the two-and-one-half years he had served in China. Politics, it seemed, controlled all his choices. Political considerations determined the questions of military supply, training, command, and strategy. "American aid had to take into consideration the domestic side of every move we have undertaken . . . so that the G-mo's own command will get the most benefit from it." Not merit, but loyalty to Chiang decided which Chinese units would receive aid and training. Stilwell remarked bitterly that everything done by the United States in China had as its goal "preserving China's precarious unity" under Chiang Kai-shek.[1]

Stilwell's problems in China began en route to that troubled nation in February 1942. Stopping first in India—the vital link in the ground and air routes his supplies must travel into western China—he discovered a disorganized and defeatist British command. India's Congress Party, demanding a firm British pledge of independence, refused to support the war. Both Indian and British leaders feared a possible Japanese attack, either overland or by sea. Neither the defense of Burma nor the China supply line placed high on British Field Marshal Sir Archibald Wavell's list of priorities. Stilwell came away from meeting Wavell convinced that he could not count on very much British support in creating an active military front in China. His many prejudices against British policy reconfirmed, Stilwell departed for Chungking on March 3.

The city that greeted him was itself a casualty of war. Correspondent Eric Severeid described the provisional capital as

Ugly beyond words. . . . a scorched battered fortress . . . it was a facade, hollow and without depth. . . . The colors were all gone, and the tones of Chungking were gray and black. Once the walls had been white, but when the bombing began they had camouflaged the city by simply painting each building black as one would paint his windows if he had no shutters.[2]

Before 1937 a backwater provincial city above the Yangtze gorges, the Japanese onslaught made Chungking the bloated haven for millions of refugees, among them the KMT government. Along the steep slopes of the river which cut through its heart, rats, lice, disease, starvation, and Japanese bombing haunted the populace. On the outlying hills, the wealthy and powerful barricaded themselves within villas. Chiang selected one of these villas as Stilwell's official residence, though the American commander found it a cold tomb and avoided it when possible.

From the day of his arrival, Stilwell rejected all hollow symbols of power such as the villa. During his first official meeting with Chiang, Stilwell requested the power to command the Chinese Fifth and Sixth armies, which had moved into Burma at British request. Chiang nominally acceded to this request, but privately complained of Stilwell's arrogance and failure to show the generalissimo sufficient deference. The American had not behaved at all like a "chief of staff," an advisor, but like an independent commander.[3]

When he left for the Burmese front on March 11, Stilwell was unprepared for the situation which he found there. Neither Chinese nor British commanders wished to sacrifice men and materiel for an area they considered marginal. British forces desired to withdraw to protect India, while Chinese commanders balked at serving under an American. Chiang, of course, had never given Stilwell more than nominal authority. Stilwell scurried around Burma and revisited Chungking in a vain effort to have Chiang order Chinese field commanders that Stilwell be obeyed. The verbal assurances given to Stilwell dissolved upon his return to the battlefield.

Given these circumstances, the battle in Burma during March 1942 proved disastrous in almost every way. The disorganized and defeatist Anglo-Chinese troops were no match for the well-supplied, disciplined, and highly motivated Japanese army. Stilwell found it impossible to rally his troops and soon discovered he had no real power to command the Chinese armies assigned to him. The Japanese assumed command of the air, making both resupply and movement of his forces nearly impossible. By mid-April the battle was clearly lost, and early in May the British, Indian, and Chinese units in Burma had become isolated and disorganized. Stilwell himself led one column through the jungles and mountain passes in a desperate effort to reach safety in India. When the weary and embittered survivors reached India on May 29, the general admitted publicly that the Allies had taken "a hell of a beating" in Burma.[4]

Even while defeat in Burma loomed, the major Chinese interest focused on securing additional reserves of military supplies. In Washington, T. V. Soong complained to Roosevelt that China was being treated as a "second class" ally, that the failure to include Chinese representation on the Combined Chiefs of Staff (CCS) and Munitions Assignment Board (MAB) proved this. Naval attaché McHugh in Chungking and Hornbeck in Washington echoed these complaints, warning that the United States risked alienating Chiang's "political genius and will to fight" by failing to deliver additional planes and war supplies. The entire situation, of collapse in Burma and alleged shortages in China, so frightened General Magruder that he devised a plan for an emergency evacuation of Chungking. Shortly thereafter Magruder himself tested the plan; in Stilwell's words he "snuck out" of China.[5]

Characteristically, almost as soon as he had reached the safety of India, Stilwell began to evaluate the causes of the military disaster which had overtaken him in Burma. Working furiously, he prepared a fifty-page report on the Burma campaign which graphically recounted the bungling of British and Chinese commanders. The British, he concluded, only cared about defending strategic colonies, and then only when it suited a larger imperial strategy. They balked at cooperating with China, since that nation represented a long-term nationalistic threat to colonialism. But Stilwell came down hardest on Chiang Kai-shek, especially for interfering with the American's effort to command Chinese troops. While "the wasteful and inefficient system of political juggling" of Chinese armies might be necessary to maintain Chiang's political power, it "emasculated the effectiveness of Chinese troops." The existing political and military organization of China was virtually hopeless, Stilwell wrote. Only by relying on the individual Chinese soldier, retrained, rearmed, and commanded by officers in a "New Army," could military victory be achieved.[6] Stilwell's dream of a New Army, conceived in the Burma debacle, took determined root in his mind as he prepared to return to Chungking. There he would present Chiang with "notes" calling for the complete reorganization of the armed forces which the generalissimo had spent his life building.

The subsequent struggle between Stilwell and Chiang must be understood in light of China's military structure and its relation to political power. The National Army of the Republic of China, if it could even be called an army in the Western sense, consisted of approximately 3.8 million men in three hundred largely ineffective divisions under the control of twelve regional military commanders. The loyalty and quality of the divisions varied tremendously, depending on personal and factional proclivities of the commanders. Chiang directly controlled only about thirty divisions, meaning that the bulk of his power rested on the adroit balancing of competing interests. He attempted to manipulate regional commanders by making vital funds and supplies dependent on their obedience. Troops were paid according to the whim of generals who found it quite profitable to pad their ranks with fictitious men and then to pocket the difference.

To maintain a sufficient force, the generals turned to forced conscription of a sort which made the British press gangs of the nineteenth century seem positively benign. An American army report of 1945 chronicled how Chinese soldiers were selected.

Conscription: Conscription comes to the Chinese peasant like famine or flood, only more regularly—every year twice—and claims more victims. Famine, flood, and drought compare with conscription like chicken pox with plague. . . . The virus is spread over the Chinese countryside. . . . There is first the press gang. For example you are working in the field looking after your rice . . . [there come] a number of uniformed men who tie your hands behind your back and take you with them. . . . Hoe and plow rust in the field, the wife runs to the magistrate to cry and beg for her husband, the children starve.[7]

This report went on to describe how prison officials sold petty convicts into army service. All the conscripts, tied together, were force-marched hundreds of miles to training centers.

If somebody dies, his body is left behind. His name on the list is carried along. As long as his death is not reported, he continues to be a source of income, increased by the fact that he has ceased to consume. His rice and his pay become a long lasting token of memory in the pocket of his commanding officer. His family will have to forget him.[8]

Not reform, but maintaining control over this motley army concerned Chiang most. If any other individual could distribute money and weapons or arrange the training of officers, Chiang's hold would disappear, and with it the aura of his legitimacy. Simultaneously, Chiang's methods insured that selected divisions could be rewarded and relied upon. Thus the ever loyal Hu Tsung-nan received special favors for himself and his four hundred thousand troops which stood guard over the Communists' base areas in northwest China. Troops facing the Japanese enjoyed no special bounty.

As an alternative to this military nightmare, Stilwell envisioned selecting a special group of thirty divisions to be "reformed, retrained, . . . re-equipped" and put under new command. This idea was partly a natural outgrowth of previous moderately successful efforts by German advisors who aided Chiang during the 1930s. But it was even more a product of Stilwell's conviction that, given the degree of KMT corruption which existed, "only outside influence can do anything for China." Outside influence would either come through Japan's defeat of Chiang or the reform of the Chinese armies under American sponsorship.[9]

The military reform proposals centered on the creation of two new Chinese army groups. One would be organized in India, built up from the remnants of the Chinese units which retreated from Burma. They would be supplemented by new conscripts. At the same time a second, larger group of thirty Chinese divisions would be assembled in China's western Yunnan province. Retrained, rearmed, and commanded by Chinese officers who themselves were under American guidance, the two groups would move into Burma, where, assisted by British military action, they would reopen the land route to China. This "simple" reform would create an active military front in China as well as paving the way for increased aid to flow across Burma. It also meant that a new Chinese army, not under Chiang's control or patronage, would probably emerge as the most powerful force in China. Such a scheme had already been angrily rejected by Soong at the time of the negotiations for the $500 million loan.

From the summer of 1942 on through his recall late in 1944 Stilwell's plans centered on the dual reform and Burma campaign projects. A new truck transport road through north Burma (from Ledo to Myitkyina) would be cleared by the combined attack of Chinese, British, and American forces operating out of India and Yunnan province. Stilwell rejected both Chinese and British claims that the fight for the north Burma route was unjustified because the road would be difficult and time consuming to construct and would probably be superfluous by the time of its completion. In various degrees the Chinese and British favored capturing Rangoon and south

Burma to open up the old Burma Road, while relying on air transport to supply China. Neither of America's allies proved eager to expend scarce resources on an operation they considered peripheral.

Most political and military strategists in Washington, even those in general sympathy with Stilwell, decidedly preferred to avoid the thorny issue of reorganizing Chiang's armies. They accepted the belief that America must first accumulate political capital in China. The Joint Psychological Warfare Committee of the CCS even urged that the United States and Britain merely sustain China for eventual use as an air base to bomb Japan. Meanwhile, aid efforts and propaganda should bolster the Nationalists and play down the role of "radical" groups in China. To this end, overseas branches of the KMT might be used to popularize Chiang's image. This report noted that, although it was true that Chiang was a reactionary dictator, no "suitable" conservative leader or coalition was available to replace him. Only the Communists could conceivably play this role, but they were fundamentally unacceptable. In sum, it was suggested that "Chiang and his selected group" be given "widespread publicity and acclaim in the United States." These recommendations by the CCS were a further endorsement of Roosevelt's plan to "treat China like a great power." [10]

Chiang balked at the essence of Stilwell's proposals, assuaging the American only by agreeing to permit the creation of a small Chinese force in India. Since they would be outside the country, the troops posed no immediate threat. But Chiang adamantly refused to consider reorganizing thirty divisions in Yunnan. Only when and if the Americans delivered substantial military aid would such a force be possible. [11] The generalissimo spoke indignantly of how he was asked to create new armies while the United States had failed to send promised aid. Here he had a good debating point, since the military crisis in the Middle East, marked by the fall of Tobruk on June 21, caused planners to divert aircraft and weapons from China. Without additional transport aircraft, the 10th Air Force could not carry sufficient cargo from India over the Hump of the Himalayas. The diversion of supplies also starved the small air task force which Chennault had begun to operate within China. To make matters still worse, the MAB cut China's monthly Lend-Lease allotment to thirty-five hundred tons in view of the undeliverable stockpiles accumulating in India.

Stilwell provided an easy and obvious target for Chiang's wrath. He had already proposed to meddle in the Chinese power structure, while T. V. Soong in Washington reported that Stilwell was "deliberately and disloyally" responsible for delaying aid.[12] Soong and Chiang found Stilwell to be anything but putty in their hands. They sought to salvage the situation by boosting the reputation of their favorite American officer— and Stilwell's archrival-to-be—Claire Chennault.

As early as February 1942, Chennault had resumed his contact with White House advisor Lauchlin Currie. The flier protested being placed under both Stilwell and the commander of the 10th Air Force, General Clayton Bissell—done at Stilwell's insistence. While Currie assured Chennault that the President sympathized with an air strategy, this did little to calm bitter feelings. By July Chennault warned Currie that neither Stilwell nor Marshall had any intention of creating a strong air force in China and that this would cause the United States to lose "China's good will." James McHugh, writing to Currie in support of Chennault, urged that he be given command of an independent air force in China.[13]

Very early in the war, Chennault had staked out a major claim. Already hurdling over regular lines of command to take his case to the President, the airman asserted that the adoption of his air war strategy held the key to military victory in China and the fulfillment of Roosevelt's political goals there. In making this argument, Chennault knew he could count on direct backing from the Chinese leadership. On June 26, Stilwell had been summoned to appear before Generalissimo and Madame Chiang to hear himself accused of deceit and misrepresentation. He was supposed to act as Chiang's "chief of staff," devoted to the cause of securing more Lend-Lease. Instead, he wasted time in futile combat operations and, according to Soong, had agreed to the emergency diversion of transport and combat aircraft en route to China. Chiang then obliquely threatened to make a separate peace with Japan unless Stilwell and the United States reevaluated current policy.[14]

Chiang's carefully staged dressing down of Stilwell put both the general and the United States on notice of his great dissatisfaction with American aid efforts. A few days later, the generalissimo handed Stilwell a formal note making "three demands" of the United States: (1) the dispatch to China of three American combat divisions; (2) the immediate creation of a combat air force of five hundred planes, presumably under Chennault's command; and (3) the monthly transport of five thousand tons over the Hump air route.[15] In the wake of these demands, the Chinese and American leadership sought to reach a compromise solution that solved the immediate problem while leaving the underlying disease untouched.

The two senior American officials in China, General Stilwell and Ambassador Gauss, urged Washington to concede nothing to Chiang in light of his threats. In a long message to Secretary Stimson, Stilwell attempted to explain the background of the generalissimo's demands. Chiang, he wrote, demanded military aid not for the common war effort, but merely to solidify his domestic position. He wished to strengthen his own "gang" against other KMT factions. One could not argue or reason with Chiang since he was vain, stubborn, without education, and had "no friends at all, only servants who are without exception ill at ease in his presence." At this point, the generalissimo would use all American aid as patronage to preserve the loyalty of favored army commanders. Chiang was determined to resist any reorganization of the army for fear of undercutting his own position. Yet, Stilwell lamented, a successful offense could only begin after military reform and reorganization.[16]

Stilwell's report to Stimson served both to vent the general's spleen and to educate the Secretary of War. Unless the War Department and the President vigorously supported his effort to compel Chinese military reorganization, Stilwell wrote, the massive aid which Chiang demanded would be hoarded and eventually turned against the Communists and other domestic enemies. Perhaps a bit self-conscious about his scathing denunciation of one of America's wartime allies, Stilwell apologized for the bluntness of his presentation. But, the theater commander concluded, Washington must understand the political realities of China before becoming trapped by them. [17]

As of July 1942, despite growing tensions in their relationship, Stilwell still attempted to reason with Chiang. At a meeting of the two men, the American pled with the generalissimo to accept the fact, as Stilwell saw it, that neither air power nor sophisticated weapons was the key to success in China. Although they both might be disappointed with the frugal aid reaching China, this was only one element of the picture. The key to victory over Japan, Stilwell argued again, lay in military reorganization, not technology. Finally, General Stilwell tried to clarify for Chiang the sticky issue of his own status. He was primarily the commander of all American forces in the China-Burma-India Theater. Second, he served as Lend-Lease administrator therein. The third, and smallest, hat he wore was that of aide to Chiang. The latter must remain subordinate to the former, he explained. [18]

Unmoved by Stilwell's explanations or logic, the generalissimo found the discussion only confirmed his worst suspicions about the American's meddling. Soong received instructions to press officials in Washington for the possible recall of Stilwell. Would the President be willing to send a replacement? Might a successor relinquish to the Chinese control over the distribution of Lend-Lease? General Marshall, after consulting with Roosevelt, met with Soong on July 14. In an irate reply Marshall informed Soong that Stilwell would not be recalled and that any possible successor would occupy the same role and exercise similar control of Lend-Lease. Fearing Chiang's reaction to this statement, Soong watered it down in transmission to Chungking, conveying the impression that Stilwell had somehow exceeded his authority in China.[19]

Following this episode, the relationship between Stilwell and Chiang Kai-shek took on a bitterness unrelieved until their final confrontation late in 1944. In Stilwell's diary and headquarters Chiang was referred to as the "Peanut," his wife as "Snow White"—terms originally used for code transmissions but now as epithets. Privately, Stilwell began to think of alternatives to KMT rule. "Something [must] be done to clean up this stinking gang and put some real people at the head of things." He then recounted that Chou En-lai, Communist representative in Chungking, had sought out one of Stilwell's aides (John P. Davies, a Foreign Service officer detached from the embassy to serve as a political advisor to the general) to complain of Chiang's treachery and remark, "half seriously," that the Communist forces would be proud to serve under Stilwell. Chou and other Communists in Chungking had told Davies and John Carter Vincent to beware of giving Chiang control over Lend-Lease lest the KMT use it against them.[20]

While Stilwell hoped that Washington would ignore the three demands of late June, the White House seemed determined to assuage the Chinese. Roosevelt, Hopkins, and Currie apparently feared that Chiang might carry out his thinly veiled threat to drop out of the war. Thus they decided to respond to an earlier Chinese request (in May), that Hopkins be sent to China, by sending Lauchlin Currie in his place. On his second presidential mission, of July 21–August 7, 1942, Currie tried to renew the chummy atmosphere between Chiang and Roosevelt that emerged from his visit of the previous year. He spent almost all his time conferring with Chiang and pointedly snubbed both Gauss and Stilwell. In his diary the theater commander fumed that Currie was a "queer little fellow" searching for an "easy solution" to impress his boss, the President.[21]

We possess no detailed record of Currie's discussions,

nothing that resembles his earlier report to Roosevelt. In 1972 a semiofficial Chinese Nationalist account of the Chiang-Currie meetings appeared, alluding to general talks concerning Lend-Lease, Sino-Soviet relations, Britain's policy in India, and the like. Currie reportedly confirmed that Stilwell controlled Lend-Lease—a fact Soong had hidden from Chiang—and cautioned against urging Stilwell's immediate recall. The Chinese text concludes with Currie bluntly telling Chiang that "Washington thinks it may not be a bad idea to make Manchuria a buffer state between Japan and Russia after the war." Whether this statement was genuine or merely was included to buttress the later Nationalist charge that Roosevelt "sold out China" to the Russians is unclear. In any case, Currie kept a safe distance from the Chinese Communists this time, refusing Chou En-lai's invitation for another meeting.[22]

However he felt about Currie, Chiang sensed the time was ripe during his visit to make a dramatic move indicating a will to compromise. The generalissimo announced a decision to accept Stilwell's strategy of a ground campaign to open Burma. But he only approved in theory the creation of a new thirty-division force in Yunnan, making any fight contingent on extensive British participation and American acceptance of a modified Three Demands. Chiang now asked for the dispatch of one combat division, five hundred planes, and five thousand tons of supplies per month. Currie carried this news back to Washington, personally convinced that he had solved the deadlock in China.

Currie's report to the President of August 24 revealed both the superficial nature of his judgment and its calculated appeal to Roosevelt's opinions. Currie insisted that a large measure of the past tensions and misunderstandings between China and the United States arose from personality disputes among Chiang, Stilwell, Soong, and Chennault. This could be solved by juggling the chemistry and personalities of the Americans in China. Far more important, Currie argued, was Roosevelt's opportunity to utilize Chiang's good will for achieving long-term political goals. In his judgment,

We have a unique opportunity to exert a profound influence on the development of China and hence Asia. It appears to me to be profoundly in our national interest to give full support to the Generalissimo, both military and diplomatic. I do not think we need to lay down any conditions nor tie any strings to this support . . . we can rely on him so far as lies within his power to go in the direction of our wishes in prosecuting a vigorous war policy and in creating a modern, democratic and powerful state.[23]

As in his recommendations of early 1941, Currie plotted out for the President a policy and a dream.

Fostering the development of a pro-American KMT remained central to Currie's analysis. He linked this to a concern with nationalist movements elsewhere in Asia, especially India. While in China, Currie heard of Ghandi's growing schism with the British over their refusal to commit themselves to liberate India. Writing to the President from New Delhi, Currie warned that many Indian deeply resented what they saw as American-British collusion against Asian nationalism. This misconception, he added, "endangers your [Roosevelt's] moral leadership in Asia and therefore America's ability to exert its influence for acceptable and just settlements in postwar Asia."[24]

Quite obviously, Currie believed the KMT and its leader represented legitimate nationalism in China, a force the United States must encourage and support. Therefore, he urged Roosevelt to replace the abrasive General Stilwell with a "diplomat" general willing to soothe Chiang—Chennault, possibly. At the same time, Roosevelt would do well to recall the unpopular Clarence Gauss as ambassador. Currie suggested John Carter Vincent or Owen Lattimore for the post, though his criterion seemed to be that they were his own friends, not particularly "pro-Chiang."[25] Sometime later, the Presidential advisor boosted himself as the best candidate for the embassy.

The tidy package of explanations and recommendations which Currie presented to Roosevelt reflected the radically contrasting perspectives of Stilwell and the White House. Although both envisioned a powerful China playing a major role in Asia, they thought in very different time perspectives. While Stilwell needed troops immediately to fight the Japanese, Roosevelt and Currie thought mainly about China's potential value in postwar Asia. As influenced by Currie, the President rejected Stilwell's basic tactic that all aid to Chiang be granted on a quid pro quo basis. Encouraging a "special relationship" precluded America presenting demands.

General Marshall, the buffer between Stilwell and the White House, believed that Roosevelt's postwar visions drew the President ineluctably toward supporting Chennault's and Chiang's almost mystical belief in air power. No one in the White House necessarily believed that air power alone would work, but Chiang desperately wanted it. "Since the Chinese wanted what Chennault wanted, and Roosevelt wanted to give the Chinese what they wanted, all these things fit[ted] together very neatly and required no further presidential effort or analysis."[26]

The White House decision to move in the direction of subsidizing air power in China revealed not a military but a political commitment. Air power was a sop to Chiang, a way to buy his support for broader American dictates. On October 12, 1942, the President finally responded to Chiang's Three Demands and Currie's report. He did not insist upon Chiang accepting Stilwell's thirty-division plan. On the contrary, Roosevelt promised to try to raise Hump deliveries to five thousand tons and send five hundred combat aircraft to China. Only determined opposition from Marshall and Stimson dissuaded Roosevelt from removing Stilwell.[27]

Although Chiang had not succeeded in his effort to be rid of Stilwell, he had gotten Washington to commit itself to increasing the flow of Lend-Lease supplies and providing an air force for Chennault. Stilwell's efforts would remain limited to training Chinese troops in India and devising paper plans for military reorganization within China. This denouement of the Three Demands left the generalissimo's power base and pride intact. He successfully aborted Stilwell's program, which he believed to be both foolhardy and an insult to Chinese independence. Instead of expending scarce Chinese resources against (Chiang believed) a doomed Japan, American transport planes would bridge the Burmese jungles carrying precious cargo; Chennault's combat aircraft would harass the Japanese. No foreigners would need to meddle with his subordinates or disrupt the frail patronage system.[28]

Chiang's most powerful ally in this successful extortion of American aid remained the myth of his genius and invincibility. The American public knew only the Chiang Kai-shek of *Time* and *Life* cover stories, the China of the Big Four fighting on the side of democracy. In public Roosevelt continually boosted Chiang's status as the leader of a "great power." Although later in the war a handful of dissenting journalists sought to shatter this myth, neither the public nor the American government were seriously challenged to examine their preconceptions.

Aside from Stilwell's constant complaints to the War Department, the only consistent source of critical information about the Nationalists appeared in the reports prepared by a relatively junior group of Foreign Service officers attached to the Chungking embassy and Stilwell's staff. These reports had slight impact within the State Department—an agency almost totally irrelevant to foreign policy during the war—or upon the President. They do, however, provide a unique insight into China's wartime politics, one vital to evaluating the impact of American policy.

The most senior, and most moderate, of the dissenters within the Chungking embassy was the genteel and soft-spoken Southerner, embassy counselor John Carter Vincent. From this post, during 1942 and 1943, Vincent prepared a number of detailed reports on the KMT. He depicted the Nationalists as a gaggle of selfish cliques "whose only common denominator and common objective is a desire to maintain the Kuomintang in control of the government." The cliques represented various personalities, geographic interests, and bureaucratic factions, but few differing ideas. T. V. Soong allegedly stood for the new breed of Western-trained professional bureaucrat; the Chen brothers symbolized conservative orthodoxy; various army commanders linked to the Wampoa Military Academy and secret police chief Tai Li all enjoyed a coterie of supporters. Chiang ruled because his clique controlled more troops than the others and he represented a symbol of national anti-Communism that all the factions could endorse. Vincent portrayed a Byzantine maze of political intrigue as the government of China. Only the specter of social revolution held the KMT together. China might still be saved, he wrote, but only if the present leadership was swept away and replaced by as yet undiscovered "liberal reformers."[29]

While a basis of American support for Chiang remained the belief that aid would encourage reform and participation in the war, the embassy staff gradually reached an opposite conclusion. Certain of U.S. backing, Chiang encouraged civil war to cement the loyalty of his underlings and destroy the Communists. Thus, early in 1943, another Foreign Service officer working partly for Stilwell, John Service, reported that the United Front was "definitely a thing of the past." There was no longer a question of whether civil war could be avoided, "but whether it can be delayed at least until a victory over Japan." Both parties had braced themselves for renewed fighting. The KMT, in particular, had cracked down on all political dissidents it could find. This reactionary terror, Service noted, might swing the revolution to the left, "going beyond the moderate democracy which the Chinese Communists now claim to be seeking."

Service, already emerging as one of the two Americans most concerned with understanding the CCP, feared that Washington's alliance with the KMT would earn it the hate of all other Chinese groups. In desperation or revenge, the revolutionary forces might turn "toward friendship with Russia." Service pondered ways for the United States to separate its support for the anti-Japanese effort from the KMT's domestic suppression. The war must be fought, he urged, against Japan and fascism, not for Chiang Kai-shek. Above all, the United States must not take up arms directly or indirectly against the Chinese Communists, a group Washington still knew almost nothing about. Service urged that Americans go to Yenan to discover who the revolutionaries really were.

What is the form of their local government? How "Communistic" is it? Does it show any Democratic character or possibilities? Has it won any support of the people? How does it compare with the conditions of government in Kuomintang China? . . . What is the military and economic strength of the Communists and what is their probable value to the Allied Cause?[30]

These vital questions could only be answered if an American team went to the Communist capital. Without answers, Service lamented, how could Washington possibly make an intelligent policy for the future?[31]

Following a conversation with Chou En-lai in March 1943, John Davies made a similar recommendation. Chou "reiterated his invitation of last summer for a small group of American officers to set up observer posts in Shensi and Shansi" and seemed to actually chide the Americans for not accepting his earlier offer to send observers to Yenan. How, he wondered, could Washington pass up this opportunity to gather all sorts of useful intelligence both about the Japanese and the Communists themselves? This offer, Chou insisted, was not conditional on American aid to Yenan. Although aid was desired, Chou doubted whether Chiang would ever permit it.[32] On this point, Davies and Stilwell later discovered, Chou understood Chiang much better than they had.

Simply because U.S. aid and weapons were present in China, Davies noted, they became a factor in the internal power struggle. Since General Stilwell led the American mission, he naturally became the American most deeply involved.

He is involved, whether he likes it or not, in Chinese politics. . . . By instinct, temperament and convictions, he seeks to avoid involvement in Chinese domestic politics. But the fact that he commands a military force in China, . . . and has under his control lend-lease material for distribution to China makes him, despite all of his wishes to the contrary, a Chinese political factor. . . . He cannot prevent politics from being played on him.[33]

Moreover, Stilwell's determination to reorganize Chinese forces for combat against the Japanese ran counter to Chiang's basic strategy.[34] These realities made Stilwell almost as great a threat to the generalissimo as were the Communists or Japanese.

The incisive, almost clairvoyant, reports prepared by Vincent, Service, and Davies had little impact on White House policy. Instead, Roosevelt chose to follow the course outlined by Currie, a policy highlighted by favoring Chennault and relying upon "personal diplomacy." Roosevelt's decision to exchange high-level guests with Chungking during 1942–43 made this even more apparent. In behavior vaguely reminiscent of the traditional Chinese tribute system, the President would send the Chinese Wendell Willkie while Chiang would send the President his wife.

Roosevelt had devised the idea of sending Willkie—a progressive Republican and internationalist—as a plum and peace offering during the Three Demands crisis. Willkie's China mission became part of a whirlwind global tour that took the ebullient emissary to most of the war's battlefronts. By early October 1942 he reached Chungking, to be feted as a conquering hero. Though Willkie snubbed Ambassador Gauss and General Stilwell, he greatly enjoyed the elaborate parties and parades which the Nationalist government staged on his behalf. In return for the pleasure of her company (and other unspecified gifts) Willkie reportedly promised Madame Chiang "all the planes in the world" if only she agreed to accompany him back to America. While Stilwell noted in his diary that "Gauss and Willkie hate[d] each other's guts," the presidential emissary eagerly listened to the jeremiads of Chennault and McHugh, promising to carry their case directly to the White House.[35]

Willkie also had an important impact upon American public opinion through a series of newspaper articles and the best-selling book, *One World*. His writing conveyed a compelling story of Chinese-American friendship. *One World*, in the section on China, pled on behalf of the "progressive forces in the Far East." In Willkie's opinion the KMT represented the responsible variety of Asian nationalism, a force that would lead China into the era of "industrial revolution" and greater Sino-American friendship. While not specifically anti-Communist (Willkie actually praised some Chinese Communists), the book stimulated even higher adulation of Chiang and his government.[36]

A counterpart to Wilkie appeared in the person of Madame Chiang, who sojourned in the United States from November 1942 until May 1943. The perfect symbol of the modern, Christian, Western-educated Chinese, Madame Chiang came to America for political lobbying and treatment of a chronic skin condition which T. V. Soong blamed on her husband's ill temper. As a guest in the White House, this emissary lost no opportunity to corner presidential aides, Congressmen, Senators, and Executive officials who might influence foreign policy. Speaking before a tumultuous joint session of Congress and at citizens' meetings, Madame Chiang proved an effective advertisement for her government. China, she announced, fought not only for it itself, but "for all minkind."

On the seamier side, the Roosevelts and the White House domestic staff found her a demanding and surly guest. A woman used to fawning subordinates, she snapped her fingers impatiently at maids and insisted on twice-daily changes of her satin bedsheets. Morgenthau suspected that the President could not wait to get her out of Washington, both to relieve his hard-pressed servants and to preclude the risk of her alienating China's supporters. Whatever private disenchantment she caused in the corridors of power, the public remained unenlightened. A high point of her visit was the publication of a pamphlet by International Business Machines entitled "First Lady of China."[37]

The almost carnival-like atmosphere of the Willkie and Chiang state visits bore material fruit for Chungking. Stilwell had written he feared what might happen once. "Mme. Bitch was let loose in Washington," and what the Joint Chiefs concluded about her visit confirmed Stilwell's worst fears. A policy memorandum of late January 1943 described the overwhelming impression held by the American public that China was making a great contribution to the war. The Joint Chiefs realized this was not so but feared public disillusionment were anything to occur leading to a collapse of the war effort in China. They hoped that as long as Chiang remained in power "the disaster of a Chinese surrender could be averted." This in turn required an American effort to maintain him in power.[38]

In October 1942 John Davies returned to China from a visit to Washington bearing similar bad news. After discussing Stilwell's problems with leading figures, Davies reached the inescapable conclusion that military considerations were not a major concern for China Theater planners. The planners within the War and State departments hoped merely to maintain the military and political status quo. Hearing this from Davies, Stilwell concluded, "well, we're on our own definitely and finally."[39] For the next few months the theater commander could do little more than make contingency plans for a Burma campaign that neither the British, Chinese, nor Americans had committed themselves to.

Almost as soon as the tentative plans for a March 1943 Burma offensive (ANAKIM) were formulated, the British and Chinese hedged their promises to participate. The British strictly limited the amount of naval and air support they would contribute, and Chiang declared this to be cause for the Chinese to drop out entirely. Washington refused to provide additional freight tonnages or combat aircraft to Chennault, further alienating the other allies. Furious at this pattern of broken promises, Stilwell raged in his diary: "What a break for the Limeys. Just what they wanted. Now they will quit, and the Chinese will quit, and the goddam Americans can go ahead and fight. . . . Unless we get tough and nail the G-mo down now, he'll get out of hand for good." Only an ultimatum from the President, Stilwell believed, could "offset this weaseling."[40]

No ultimatum, however, lay in the offing. In mid-January 1943 Roosevelt, Churchill, and their staffs met at Casablanca, itself only recently liberated. Despite the President's urging to come, Stalin pled the pressure of battle to avoid attending. The real cause was Soviet anger at continued delays in opening a second front. Thus the British and American leaders alone conferred on how to allocate resources for proposed offensives in Europe, the Mediterranean, the Pacific, and China.

At Casablanca, Churchill and his aides argued against an early cross-Channel invasion or a major campaign to open a Burma-China corridor. Instead, they urged a Mediterranean strategy designed to liberate Sicily and Italy. The Americans demonstrated little unity, with General Marshall favoring an invasion of Western Europe while Admiral King preferred an expanded campaign in the Pacific. Roosevelt tended to accept Churchill's position, delaying both the second front and a Burma campaign. Only dogged insistence by Marshall and King convinced the President to approve a limited Burma offensive for late 1943. To win even this limited concession, the Americans had to pledge to make up to the British in Europe supplies expended in Burma.

The Casablanca decisions showed the current running strongly against Stilwell's strategy. When the President spoke of China, he instructed the War Department and General Marshall to increase the flow of aid to Chennault, not Stilwell. Air power, he claimed, could be at least as effective against Japan as a ground campaign. This attitude provided Stilwell with little solace and less chance to maneuver.

Word of the Casablanca decisions was to be carried to Chiang by an imposing Anglo-American delegation consisting of Generals H. H. Arnold and Brehon Sommervell and Field Marshal Sir John Dill. But when they met the generalissimo, he had already prepared a new set of demands. The Nationalist government could only participate in a Burma campaign if China received twice as much Hump tonnages as before (ten thousand tons per month) and if Chennault actually possessed five hundred airplanes. The tone of these demands, Arnold noted, suggested blackmail.[41]

When Marshall received a report of this discussion from Arnold, he had renewed regard for Stilwell's past suggestions. The time had come for the Chief of Staff to disabuse the President of his misconceptions. Thus, when he passed Chiang's demands along to the White House, Marshall appended his own comments. An air strategy based on giving Chennault a major combat force, he wrote, made no military or political sense. It would not significantly hamper the Japanese and would give Chiang an exalted sense of his ability to manipulate American policy. Chennault's air bases could not even be protected by the Chinese. If China were to make a real contribution to the war effort, Burma must be retaken. And to do this Chiang must be kept on a short tether, with aid put on a strict quid pro quo basis as Stilwell suggested.

In a letter to Marshall early in March, the President explained his reluctance to adopt a stern approach toward Chiang. The United States and China were allies, both great powers. It would be counterproductive to attempt to command Chiang, a man who had struggled to become the "undisputed leader of 400,000,000 people" and who had created in China "what it took us a couple of centuries to attain." The President would not "speak sternly to a man like that or exact commitments from him as we might do from the Sultan of Morocco." In place of threats, Roosevelt preferred to indulge the generalissimo and win his support. Since this meant endorsing an air strategy in China, the President went on to order the creation of an independent 14th Air Force of five hundred planes under Chennault, and the increase of Hump deliveries toward ten thousand tons per month. Although a Burma campaign still remained possible, Roosevelt's insistence that Chennault receive a guaranteed monthly minimum of supplies reduced the likelihood of Stilwell accumulating necessary supplies.[42]

What at first appeared to be a technical, nonpolitical, and unextraordinary debate over military strategy actually masked a political chasm. Chennault and Stilwell fully understood, as did their Chinese hosts, that in China it was next to impossible to separate military and political strategies. For example, the impact of a few hundred planes and pilots on China, as compared to Stilwell's massive reorganization program, would be miniscule. Yet the debate in Washington, and Roosevelt's awareness, barely reflected this fact. For the Chinese and a growing number of Americans in China, however, this issue had become linked to overall policymaking and the smoldering civil war.

Chapter 7
Chungking Intrigues

THE DEMISE OF Stilwell's original plans for rapid military reorganization and an offensive to open the Burma Road left the China Theater in a state of limbo. The President had imposed a tenuous balance, speaking as if China were an important military ally, blocking the "get tough" policy of Stilwell and Marshall, while attempting to soothe Chiang's pride by gradually increasing Hump tonnages and assistance to Chennault's air program. During 1943 the competition between proponents of air and ground strategies, a debate with major political ramifications, grew to a dizzying intensity. In their personal and professional arguments, Stilwell and Chennault sought a wide variety of allies. As General Albert Wedemeyer, Stilwell's successor, noted later, both men continually jockeyed for power. Not only did they enlist support in Washington, but also "each tried to ingratiate himself with powerful Chinese, Chennault more successfully and deservedly so for he was a superb commander, capable of a deep loyalty to friend and principle."[1]

Complicating the strategies of Roosevelt, Stilwell, and Chennault, perhaps more than any of the three realized, was the overriding fact of China's political and military disorganization. Even had Chiang really desired to do so, the bevy of political factions which comprised the KMT made it extremely difficult for him to carry out the reforms Stilwell advocated. Large portions of the Nationalist army had only nominal ties to the generalissimo and central authorities. Many regional commanders, tied to a provincial base, could not be counted on to follow orders that involved personal sacrifice. For Chiang to give these forces American weapons or additional training was

125

unthinkable. As for the divisions personally loyal to Chiang, they were a precious commodity, not to be lightly sacrificed to a foreign experiment or lost in the jungles of Burma. As Magruder noted earlier, the generalissimo looked upon his best troops and equipment as "fixed assets," needed to maintain domestic supremacy.

Previously, Stilwell hoped that Chiang's instinct for power would prompt him to endorse military reform. In the often cited "Troubles of a Peanut Dictator" entry in his diary, Stilwell asked, "Why doesn't the little dummy realize that his only hope is the 30 division plan, and the creation of a separate, efficient, well-equipped and well-trained force?" [2] But the American, so intent on fulfilling his mission, failed to perceive the landscape from Chiang's perspective. After Japan's invasion, the KMT had surrendered its traditional base in the relatively prosperous coastal and lower Yangtze provinces. The central political role played in the KMT by bankers and the capitalists (or "national bourgeois") of the treaty ports was partly eclipsed. Now isolated far inland, the Nationalist government relied increasingly on support from large landlords and regional military commanders who controlled whole provinces. The war further disrupted a shaky economy and government bureaucracy, leading to galloping inflation (measured in hundreds of percents) and official corruption. The KMT's popular base, always weak among the peasantry, faded among intellectuals, urban workers, and lower officials. Chiang's grip on power remained only as firm as his control over army divisions. Once commanders became influenced, trained, paid, or supplied by Americans, they might slip from the generalissimo's grasp forever.

Stilwell's calculations also disregarded Chiang's fervent nationalism, a force not to be trifled with. In 1943 Chiang released two political tracts entitled "China's Destiny" and "Chinese Economic Theory." While supposedly proscribed for foreigners, the embassy staff easily acquired the books, which were later translated. The generalissimo's ideology proved a blend of feudal and fascist political theory, one which looked upon Nazi youth groups as a model for political organization. Chiang made no pretense of supporting liberal democracy, a concept he found totally alien. China's entire range of social-political-economic problems were blamed solely on the previous hundred years of imperalist pressure. The great historic role of the KMT would be to sweep away foreign privilege and restore China to an ascendant role in Asia.

If China today did not have the Kuomintang, there would be no China. Had the Revolution of the Kuomintang been defeated, it would have meant the complete defeat of the Chinese state. Briefly speaking, China's destiny rests entirely with the Kuomintang. . . . if the Kuomintang should fail in its task, China would have nothing on which to depend.[3]

These were not the words of a leader prepared to relinquish control of his army to an American. Chiang's fixation upon leading a revived China into greatness—however crude or incompetent his methods may seem in retrospect—insured that he would interpret Stilwell's behavior as the worst kind of foreign insult.

Given this attitude, it is perhaps difficult to understand Chiang's willingness in 1942 to permit Stilwell to organize Chinese troops at Ramgarh, India. Between 1942 and 1944 a total of fifty-three thousand soldiers, survivors from the first Burma campaign and many more conscripts flown over the Hump, comprised the so-called X-Force. At Ramgarh they were paid, fed, armed, and trained at no expense to Chiang. Most important, they were physically removed from China, minimizing their influence upon internal politics.[4] Although the X-Force fought admirably during the second Burma campaign, Chiang lost no time in disbanding it upon the troop's return to China. These combat veterans were dispersed among more trusted units lest they prove a locus for some rival's power.

Like most Americans in China, Stilwell revealed an ambiguous attitude toward nationalism and political intrigue. He had transcended the limited horizons of most Western visitors to China by traveling on foot through much of the country and by devoting himself to language study. Stilwell despised the officers, landlords, and petty officials who continually abused *lau pai hsing* ("old hundred names"), the common people. He made a virtual fetish out of his belief that well trained, armed, fed, and commanded Chinese soldiers were anyone's equal. Though hardly a liberal in the context of American politics, Stilwell empathized with the peasantry and knew that until the rural crisis was solved, China could not have internal peace.

At the same time, the American commander believed the peoples of Asia must follow a Western model of progress. Moreover, Chiang's stubbornness and the immediate task of defeating Japan justified a certain degree of foreign manipulation. Typical of this dichotomy was his view of the current troubles in India, where the Congress Party demanded independence from Britain. While opposed to granting immediate freedom to people he believed unsuited for self-government, Stilwell felt it was Britain's moral and practical duty to give the Indians enough education and political training to "fit them" for freedom.[5] Stilwell's determination to retrain a Chinese army stemmed in part from the belief that Western techniques held the key to China's overall progress. If Chiang's pride and selfish concern for power, whatever its philosophical justification, impeded this progress, he must be circumvented. Frustrated at every turn, Stilwell resolved his doubts about his own role as a foreigner and concluded that "the only way to get action was through bargaining and trading."[6]

By the end of 1942, after ten fruitless months, Stilwell threw himself fully into the internal Chinese power struggle. He would reward those Chinese supporting his reorganization plan and punish those in opposition. An early, though unexpected, ally appeared in the person of Foreign Minister T. V. Soong. Attracted to power like a moth to light, Soong flitted continually between Chungking and Washington. Although linked to Chiang through family, business, and politics, the generalissimo's brother-in-law always looked after his own affairs first and seemed more than casually interested in some day replacing Chiang. Soong had initially tried to undermine Stilwell's position in Washington and helped poison Chiang's opinion of the American. But when this approach failed to secure Stilwell's recall or Chennault's elevation, Soong returned to Chungking and sailed on the opposite tack. Meeting with Stilwell, the foreign minister suggested they pool efforts. Soong would support the proposed thirty-division Y-Force in Yunnan if "Soong men" received high positions in the new army. Soong urged that Stilwell appoint either General Ch'en Ch'eng or General Hsueh Yueh to lead the Y-Force, and that he cultivate, through aid, the powerful Hu Tsung-nan, whose forces blockaded the Communists. The American commander, pleased at Soong's initiative, felt that the foreign minister was "taking the pap."[7]

During the next several months, Stilwell and his aide, Colonel Frank Dorn, collaborated secretly with Soong to outmaneuver Chiang and his minister of war, General Ho Ying-chin. They lobbied to win the appointment of Ch'en Ch'eng, who was finally named Y-Force commander in March 1943. Stilwell envisioned several schemes in which Soong might manipulate Chinese politics and finances through his position in the Bank of China and by advancing his loyalists in the army.

In December 1942 Stilwell presented a more specific plan. It began with a statement of purpose, perhaps a device to rationalize the questionable tactics it required. Stilwell and Soong would cooperate to create a "powerful, independent China with a modern well organized army, and with close ties of interest and friendship to the United States." The two allies would police Asia, overseeing the elimination of the European empires. In essence, this echoed Roosevelt's sentiments. But to achieve the long-term goal, Stilwell argued, China must play an active role in the war. Its army must be reorganized and committed to a fight in Burma. Accordingly, both Chiang and Ho Ying-chin must be neutralized. Stilwell suggested that Ho be sent off on a prolonged visit to the United States. Chiang would then be induced to "appoint Dr. T. V. Soong as his executive assistant to coordinate American and Chinese activities for the improvement of the technical and supply services of the Chinese army." American supplies would be funneled through Soong to selected forces. Key units such as transport, air forces, communications, supply, etc., were to be commanded by "friendly" officers who had been trained by Americans at Ramgarh or in the proposed camps at Yunnan.[8]

Over the next two months, into January and February 1943, Stilwell developed many contingency plans, several of which suggested a coup. A draft of a cable to Marshall proposed that the United States remove all Chinese politicians and generals interfering with the war effort. Even Ho and Chiang were placed in this category. A "new strong man," possibly Ch'en Ch'eng, should be placed in power through American efforts. If, for any reason, even these actions failed to transform China into an active ally, then Washington ought to consider abandoning the theater. Intervention was justified, Stilwell wrote, because "our mission to China is not to perpetuate the Kuomintang, but to make the army a workable machine."[9] West Point, it seemed, could be the model for China's modern transformation!

Certainly the burning issue of mobilizing China to fight Japan remained foremost in Stilwell's mind as he pondered these drastic plans. But he also thought about China's destiny and its links to the United States. Could "China be the leader in East Asia after the war and through its influence and the threat of its army control the western Pacific," Stilwell asked himself. "The answer is an overwhelming YES!" It was imperative, a "matter of duty," for America to create the proper kind of postwar China, even if America (or Stilwell himself) had to guide the hand of destiny "through the fierce use of power politics and a ruthless progressive program."[10]

During the early months of 1943 plans were formulated in Stilwell's headquarters to "dispose of Chiang," to "infiltrate and control Chinese armies," and to explore cooperation with the Chinese Communists and rival Kwangsi generals—"the better elements of the disaffected minority parties." Opponents within Chiang's circle would be stripped of power. At one point Stilwell even considered requesting that General Donovan, of the OSS, arrange with Madame Chiang's American physicians to keep her "ill" in New York. This, he supposed, would minimize her interference.

Colonel Frank Dorn, Stilwell's close aide and confidant, assisted the general in planning for reorganization of Chinese forces at Yunnan and became deeply involved with high-level intrigues. As proposed by Dorn, the Chinese officers and troops of the Y-Force would be used to carry out Stilwell's Burma offensive, "*even if it means the overthrow of the entire regime* and the establishment of a coalition government in China which would be backed by American troops and the selected divisions mentioned above." As Dorn noted later, many of the conspiracies were abandoned because the Chinese political and military groups involved seemed no more capable of leading China than did Chiang.[11] Nevertheless, the generalissimo must have known a good deal about Stilwell's plunge into the Chungking power struggle.

These activities probably confirmed Chiang's worst suspicions regarding foreign meddling, disloyal subordinates, and the absolute need to control the distribution of American military supplies. As an immediate precaution, Soong was sent out of China and back to Washington. The anger felt toward Stilwell is evident in a secret report written sometime later by War Minister Ho Ying-chin. Almost 75 percent of all American tonnage entering China, Ho complained, went to American ground and air units. The remainder went to the Chinese. Even more demeaning were the constraints put on use of that aid.

The Americans want to decide what we need. As a condition for turning it over they want to train our toops. Before that is done they want to decide what troops are to be trained. After they have trained they want to keep control of them by liaison officers. All this means a great deal of trouble connected with American aid.[12]

Chiang faced a dilemma in trying to insure that the American goose laid its golden egg in his nest alone. He had to circumvent and neutralize Stilwell without alienating the general's superiors in Washington. Chiang seemed well aware of the long-term Sino-American alliance which Roosevelt wanted to cultivate. This augured well for the future. For the short term, however, Chiang required an antidote to Stilwell, a means to outmaneuver him by dividing the Americans among themselves. The generalissimo was enough of a traditionalist to recall the ancient Chinese way of pitting barbarian against barbarian. He would turn American bureaucrats, officers, and diplomats against one another, emasculating Stilwell and convincing the President that his own reputation depended on a "success" in China.

Not surprisingly, the Chinese strategy centered on boosting the activities of the American navy's special units in China (discussed below) and on casting Chennault as the president's general. Chennault, one of the war's earliest heroes, had already seen his Flying Tigers become a household term in America.[13] Unfortunately, recognition by the media did not immediately bring the flier more planes. As described earlier, during 1942 Chiang and other sympathizers in China had pled for more aircraft and supplies. Chiang's interest in Chennault had several bases. The more aid he received, the less there would be for Stilwell to dispense. By supporting a popular general with links to the White House, Chiang could retain the President's favor without having to fight in Burma or reorganize his armies. Chennault, moreover, seemed willing to plead the KMT case directly to Roosevelt.

During Willkie's visit of October 1942, Chennault escalated his campaign to gain autonomy from Stilwell. He had Willkie carry to the President a letter requesting that he be named both air force and overall commander of American forces in China. If only given one hundred and five fighters, thirty medium bombers, twelve heavy bombers, and sufficient replacements, Chennault promised to cause the "downfall of Japan" within one year! Never a man to underrate his own abilities, the flier predicted that his strategy would also create in China "a great and friendly trade market for generations." If Roosevelt would meet his needs, Chennault assured him, there "was no doubt of success." [14]

Ever since the army forced his resignation in 1936, Chennault had been in bad odor with the War Department. Marshall and Stimson, in particular, led the opposition to Chennault's covert air-war project of 1940–41. Stilwell inherited their intense personal and professional dislike of the man. As theater commander, he prepared careful reports to demonstrate the slipshod and egotistical thinking of the flier. Even if sufficient planes, fuel, and bombs could be delivered to Chennault over the Hump—something Stilwell doubted—the Japanese could quickly retaliate against American air bases in China. Chiang's motley armies could never protect exposed fields from ground attack. But a reorganized army could open the Burma Road, insure the delivery of supplies, and result in a combined air and ground offensive against the Japanese. [15]

To counter these reports, Chennault utilized every conceivable channel around Marshall and the War Department. He would make sure that Roosevelt was bombarded with contrary opinions from Americans who not only supported an air strategy, but claimed that it alone could cement cooperation between the United States and the government of China. Chennault's most valuable allies in this campaign were navy Commodore Milton Miles, naval attaché James McHugh, and the seemingly ubiquitous Joseph Alsop.

The U.S. Navy, with its China tradition going back to the Yangtze patrol gunboats and the Asiatic Fleet, bitterly resented the leading position which the army assumed in China after 1941. This resentment found expression in Milton Miles, who arrived in China in 1942 to command Naval Group China, a secret intelligence and guerrilla training program linked to the KMT secret police. In July, Miles came to feel that if Chennault replaced Stilwell his own efforts to work with the Chinese would be enhanced. He bluntly informed the Navy Department that Chennault was "the only man in China today who can lick the Japs. If Chennault were given complete authority, with no one but Washington to report to, and were given some planes, he'd clean the place out. The whole [Stilwell] mission should be changed to replace desk pushers with fighting men." Like Chennault, Miles went on to predict that such a strategy would insure the rewards of a "great post-war China market."[16]

Naval attaché James McHugh peppered Washington with similar advice, telling his audience (which included Knox, Marshall, Stimson, and Roosevelt) that the United States must commit itself fully to Chiang and Chennault. Only fools, McHugh wrote, would expect Chiang to waste troops and weapons in Burma or against the Japanese. Stilwell behaved like Chinese Gordon (a British mercenary of the 1860s who assisted the Ch'ing Dynasty in suppressing the T'aip'ing rebels), an anachronism. Chiang would save his troops and American aid for "post-war position," something Washington should accept. For the present, American strategy should rely on Chennault's air offensive.[17]

These reports, and Chiang's demands, contributed to Roosevelt's actions at the Casablanca Conference. The creation of the independent 14th Air Force seemed proof that the lobbying effort had borne early fruit.[18] The Chinese now prepared to play a master card, dealt by the skillful hand of Joseph Alsop, a man with a private line into the White House. This spirited journalist and distant cousin of the President and Eleanor Roosevelt instinctively sought out men in high places. His love affair with air power in Asia began when he signed on as an aide to China Defense Supplies and continued into the 1970s. After capture by the Japanese in Hong Kong and subsequent repatriation through a prisoner exchange, he used his political and family ties to strike up a friendship with Harry Hopkins. This connection allowed him to land a job as a Lend-Lease official in Chungking. No sooner had he reached China in December 1942 than Alsop again joined forces with Chennault and secured White House backing for appointment as a military aide to the general. Now Captain Alsop, he served as Chennault's press officer and contact with the White House.[19]

The reports which Alsop prepared for Hopkins predicted an apocalypse in Asia. Even before reaching Chungking he warned that the situation in China was "a national scandal . . . grossly dishonoring the President, Army and country." Alsop argued that the only hope for both American policy and China lay in Washington's offering support to both Chennault and his Chinese sponsor, T. V. Soong. The foreign minister again emerged as a Chennault ally, opposed to Stilwell. Rumors of Soong's defection reached Stilwell, who now found himself with even fewer supporters. After one meeting with Chennault's new aide, the theater commander thereafter referred to him as "Alslop."[20]

Before spending even two months in China, Alsop decided to rush back to Washington and warn of what he had discovered. He launched a letter campaign, bombarding Hopkins with graphic images and pseudo-facts of how Stilwell's strategy threatened to undermine the entire range of American military and diplomatic policy. In a twenty-one-page tirade dated March 1, 1943, Alsop blasted Stilwell as incompetent and oblivious to the truth that air power held the key to victory in China. Stilwell's contempt for Chiang and insistence on military reform served only to antagonize the Chinese. His meddling in politics threatened to unhinge Roosevelt's courtship of the KMT. To better fight Japan, and salvage postwar cooperation, Roosevelt must recall Stilwell and give Chennault full support.

In other letters Alsop told Hopkins why Washington should assist Chiang's gallant effort to "disband the Chinese Communists." Since the Nationalists faced internal subversion and were "threatened by Russia," Washington ought to allow Chiang to conserve his military strength for "postwar uses." At the same time, Chennault could use China as a base for a highly effective air war against the Japanese. Like his master, Alsop reduced the complex military and political problems of China to simplicity itself.[21]

These blistering attacks attracted the interest of Roosevelt and Hopkins precisely because of their simplicity. Air power might strike a blow against Japanese troops and shipping at a relatively low cost; China would appear to be making a valuable contribution to the war effort. Finally, nothing in this plan required the United States to become directly involved in Chinese politics or military reorganization. Chiang not only approved such a course, he championed it. Despite the War Department's opposition, an air strategy seemed an ideal way to placate the Chinese Nationalists. Again, in Marshall's earlier cited phrase, "all these things fit together very neatly and required no further presidential effort or analysis."

Breathing life into the air strategy required further amendments of plans for aid to China and cooperation with the British. The planned Washington Conference (TRIDENT) of May 1943 witnessed Roosevelt's apparent conversion to the new position. Chiang convinced the President to bring Chennault home to present his case personally. Only Marshall's direct insistence persuaded Roosevelt to also invite Stilwell. This hardly mattered since the President and Hopkins conferred privately with Chennault and Soong, emerging from their discussions visibly encouraged by the optimistic prediction of the air war advocates.[22]

Stilwell had prepared for the Washington Conference by composing a sheaf of policy papers which sought to prove that "China was on the verge of collapse" economically and militarily. But, he discovered, "nobody was interested in the humdrum work of building a ground force but me. Chennault promised to drive the Japs right out of China in six months, so why not give him the stuff to do it? It was the short cut to victory."[23] The British expressed distaste for both additional aid to China and a major campaign in Burma. Roosevelt decreed that Chiang's demands for air power must be met. Knowing that an air campaign would undercut operations in Burma, the British decided to support the Chennault strategy.

The final compromise decisions at TRIDENT called for both an air campaign and a limited offensive in Burma. China would receive ten thousand tons of supplies per month, from which Chennault would get a fixed minimum and Stilwell the remainder. Britain's contribution would come in the form of naval and amphibious support to operations in Burma. As with most compromise reports, it satisfied no one completely. But Chennault's flexibility was markedly increased and Stilwell's equally curtailed.[24] Beyond this, Roosevelt's tone showed his great displeasure at Stilwell, asking, at one point, whether the general was a "well man."

In an effort to counter the KMT's effective propaganda apparatus in Washington, Stilwell's aide, John P. Davies, launched a campaign of news leaks to reveal the "true situation" in China. Unexpectedly, he found an ally in Lauchlin Currie, formerly one of Chiang's most vocal supporters in the White House. Currie, however, found himself removed from the post of advising Roosevelt on Chinese affairs almost as soon as he revealed his disillusionment with Chiang. Nevertheless, during 1943 and 1944 Currie assisted dissident Foreign Service officers in their marginally successful effort to counteract the myth of KMT infallibility. When T. V. Soong learned of this, he warned Davies that there were no "secrets in Washington. . . . Rest assured . . . that no conference takes place regarding which I do not have accurate and complete information."[25]

Cut adrift by the TRIDENT decisions, Stilwell returned to China in mid-June after enjoying a visit with his family in California. He learned, with pleasure, that the British had finally shaken up their command in India by replacing the bungling Wavell. But, in China, Chiang and Ho continued to play havoc with the slow organization of the Y-Force at Yunnan by staging crises which diverted troops and supplies. Rumors spoke of an imminent KMT attack on the Communists, perhaps utilizing Chennault's heralded air craft. Stilwell took this seriously enough to warn the flier against an attack on Yenan. Emotionally, the cauldron of Chinese politics had worn down the commander. He wrote to Mrs. Stilwell a lament that after his visit with her he returned to "the manure pile. . . . Back to find Chiang the same as ever—a grasping, bigoted, ungrateful little rattlesnake." In his diary the general spoke even more bluntly. "Here I am, in this pile of shit, after forty-three years in the army."[26]

The guidelines issued after the Washington Conference left major questions of strategy and supply unresolved. Some loose ends were spliced during August, when British and American leaders met in Quebec for a conference code-named QUADRANT. Eager to trade their cooperation with the Americans for assumption of a commanding role, the British proposed creation of a new South East Asia Command (SEAC). The Americans agreed to this command, under Vice-Admiral Lord Louis Mountbatten, in return for a British pledge to increase participation in a Burma offensive. Stilwell, named Mountbatten's deputy, was now "lost in the second level of a three decker sandwich."[27] QUADRANT called for a limited north Burma offensive in November 1943, an increase in supplies to China, and the introduction of a few thousand American commandos for the projected offensive. But, on the other hand, the tone of discussion by military planners at Quebec indicated the growing likelihood that the final air and ground offensive against Japan would not come from China but from the chain of Pacific islands slowly being retaken. Discussion of China's contribution to the war centered upon Churchill's criticism of how little it had done. Roosevelt, unable to retort on the merits of the case, cranked out his stock speech on China's great importance in the postwar world and its usefulness as a buffer against Soviet expansionism in Asia.[28]

The unplesant political and military realities of the China-

Burma-India Theater still remained disguised by euphemisms. Despite America's growing involvement in China (by the end of 1943 almost one hundred thousand U.S. support and air force personnel served in the theater), almost no one on the White House staff, or in the State and War departments, bothered to examine the direction of U.S. policy or the frustrations it continually faced. Even Stilwell, who spared no effort in criticizing the impediments to military reform, speculated very little on internal Chinese politics which did not bear directly on his problems. Practically the only source of political reporting on China and America's role therein came from a handful of talented, energetic, and very junior Foreign Service officers. After serving with distinction, and seeing their dire predictions come to pass, they were later rewarded by accusations of treason, disloyalty, and incompetence.

Early in the war, Stilwell began a practice of raiding the Chungking embassy to enlist the most talented political observers as army advisors. Those chosen remained in the Foreign Service but divided their time between two masters, the State Department and Stilwell's command. Two of the most capable (and later the most persecuted) Foreign Service officers were John P. Davies and John S. Service. They, along with a few other members of the embassy staff, labored tirelessly to present a fuller picture of China to policymakers in Washington.

Throughout 1943 two underlying themes permeated reports prepared by these observers. Civil war, they concluded, had already resumed within China and, by definition, Americans played a role in it.[29] U.S. aid to the KMT and the presence of its forces in China gave implicit backing to one party. Second, the outcome of the political contest in China—and how the United States affected it—bore directly on larger questions of nationalism and decolonization in postwar Asia. Wartime China in effect was a laboratory for the development of policy to deal with the likely spate of revolutions in the future.

Service and embassy chargé George Atcheson (who replaced John Carter Vincent) paid particular emphasis to the vices of the Chinese Nationalist regime. Chiang himself provided most of the evidence, not only through his behavior but also in the political program outlined in *China's Destiny*. The future political order championed by the KMT, these Americans sought to make clear, was both anti-democratic and anti-foreign. Chiang even rejected the principles of freer international trade and investment. None of this seemed to correspond to Roosevelt's belief that he was incubating a future ideological twin to manage postwar Asia. [30]

By late 1943, Service reported, KMT officials admitted to partial collaboration with the Japanese and their puppets. Increasingly large numbers of government troops defected to the Japanese, forcing the enemy to maintain them while insuring that at the war's end these troops could redeclare their loyalty to Chiang and serve as an anti-Communist vanguard behind Japanese lines. [31] KMT military strategy, Service concluded, centered upon preparations to destroy the Communists. Until then, the Japanese presence in China actually served to contain the revolutionary forces.

More than any other political observer, John P. Davies addressed the wider ramifications of American policy in China. Davies argued his case in terms of the priorities established by the President. The KMT, he warned, was a corrupt, brutal regime lacking a popular base and possessing a "striking lack of social consciousness, of public trust and duty." The concept of pressing Chiang to reform defied reality. He had become "a political hostage to the corrupt system which he manipulates—he cannot institute sweeping reforms without destroying the balance." As the pace of civil war increased, Davies predicted that each side would seek foreign allies. The KMT would try to suck in the United States while the CCP, lacking other options, would appeal for Soviet support. If this came to pass, Washington would find itself fighting on behalf of a despised regime against an increasingly popular Communist movement under growing Soviet influence. In short, the United States risked entanglement "not only in a civil war in China" but also in a "conflict with the Soviet Union."

Despite this grim possibility, Davies postulated areas of American flexibility. For a variety of reasons, the Chinese Communists wished to improve their ties to the United States. Yenan not only feared Chiang's monopoly of American aid but desired to avoid slavish dependence on Moscow. Davies believed it vital to accept Chou En-lai's suggestion that American observers visit Yenan. This act might bolster pro-American, anti-Russian elements within the CCP and convince the Communists of American impartiality. It might even restrain Chiang's campaign to resume civil war. In any case, the United States must act quickly to strike a realistic balance between the KMT and CCP, lest Washington someday be faced by the specter of a pro-Russian, anti-American Communist government of China.[32]

The political implications of China policy stretched far beyond that nation alone, Davies argued. In reports to both Stilwell and the State Department (which paid little heed to any negative reports), he portrayed American, Soviet, and British intentions as all directed toward maximizing self-interest. The British hoped to use America's wartime support to shore up the decaying Asian empire. The Soviets, in Europe and Asia, would probably strive to expand Russia's borders, at their neighbors' expense, in a quest for greater internal security. To limit these British and Soviet ploys, Washington, too, must identify and pursue its self-interest.[33]

In Davies' opinion, the immediate international danger faced by America came from the continuing British campaign to link Washington to the maintenance of a colonial order in Asia. Churchill proved this by his insistence on the creation of SEAC under Mountbatten and determination to press for the speedy reoccupation of Singapore, Malaya, etc. Great Britain hoped to convince potential nationalist movements that Washington stood with the Empire. But, Davies argued, immediate and long-term interests required the United States to endorse de-colonization and responsible nationalism. If it did not, America could expect to inherit a slew of colonial wars.

Davies, more than any other American diplomat, thought through the complex question of how the United States might utilize China to reorder postwar Asia. He essentially endorsed the goal expressed by Roosevelt, that of treating China like a great power and encouraging it to become a policeman in East Asia. He concluded, however, that the Nationalist regime showed almost no ability, or willingness, to play its assigned role. Instead, the creation of a viable, progressive Chinese regime depended on Washington giving support to Stilwell's reform program. Only he could break the grip of reaction and initiate the vital process of regeneration.[34]

The tone of Davies' messages, as distinct from their content, may sound strikingly similar to what Alsop sent Harry Hopkins. This similarity was more than circumstantial. Davies in fact followed Alsop's lead and, during 1943, began to send reports directly to the President's top assistant. Hopkins heard from Davies that the KMT had sputtered into a downward spiral. Soon Washington would face a raging civil war, finding itself torn between supporting a corrupt client and a relatively democratic, popular, and possibly Soviet-backed movement. To salvage any part of Roosevelt's policy, Chiang must be immediately coerced into fundamental military and political reforms. If Chiang could not or would not change, Washington must consider working with the Chinese Communists. Davies, to no avail, counseled Hopkins:

We should avoid committing ourselves unalterably to Chiang. We should be ready during or after the war to adjust ourselves to possible realignments in China. We should wish, for example, to avoid finding ourselves at the close of the war backing a coalition of Chiang's Kuomintang and the degenerate puppets against a democratic coalition commanding Russian sympathy.[35]

This new version of events had little impact upon the White House before early 1944. Stilwell's plans remained in limbo, while the situation in China further deteriorated. By September 1943, Chennault's master plan for defeating Japan had already faltered. In response to air attacks, Japanese forces struck against his exposed bases. Chennault's reaction was to demand additional supplies. Meanwhile, neither Chiang nor the British had carried through on promises to prepare for a limited offensive in north Burma. Political tensions between the KMT and CCP had grown worse than ever, with rumors of an imminent formal break. Stilwell, perhaps influenced by the optimistic political reports he had read on the Communists, chose this moment to formally request that Chiang lift Hu Tsung-nan's blockade of Yenan. The Communists instead would be enlisted in a joint effort to attack the Japanese.[36]

As this happened, Stilwell found himself suddenly courted by the women behind the throne, Mesdames Chiang and Kung. Unexpectedly, they expressed a desire to help him promote such changes as eliminating Minister of War Ho Ying-chin. More than a little confused by this support, the American commander assumed that both Soong sisters and their brother had agreed to offer him an "offensive and defensive alliance." T. V. Soong's involvement in this is doubtful, since at practically the same time he and Alsop tried to induce Hopkins to abolish Stilwell's position. They urged replacing both the general and the head of the Air Transport Command (which flew the Hump) with Chinese. T. V. Soong apparently hoped to improve his own power and status by demonstrating his ability to dump Stilwell and secure Chinese control over Lend-Lease. Such an arrangement, augmenting their brother's power, would probably endanger the positions occupied by the sisters' husbands, H. H. Kung and Chiang Kai-shek. This rather Byzantine episode is subject to several interpretations, all equally bizarre. In any case, believing he had found new allies within the court, Stilwell peppered the Soong sisters and T. V. (who was again in China) with messages calling for additional military reforms and warnings that unless quick action were taken, American aid would be shifted to British operations.[37]

The generalissimo finally entered the fray in early October. Madame Chiang somberly told Stilwell that her husband knew the truth: he had collaborated with T. V. Soong and Ch'en Ch'eng to overthrow Chiang and Ho. Soong, however, had returned to China and persuaded the generalissimo of his own innocence and of Roosevelt's willingness to fire Stilwell if the Chinese insisted. This would be done, she explained. The American commander believed he had been "set up" and that the President would accede to Chiang's demand, replacing him with a "stooge." [38]

Amidst this confusion, Admiral Mountbatten, new SEAC commander, arrived in China. It seemed he hoped to keep Stilwell in China. Mountbatten immediately closeted himself with the Soong sisters and General Brehon Sommervell, who served as a SEAC representative. Stilwell then received a summons to appear before the generalissimo. After being told to reaffirm his loyalty (and forget about the Communists), a grand reconciliation followed. The entire question of plots and recall was swept under the carpet.

T. V. Soong emerged as the great loser in this puzzling affair. For most of the next year he remained in obscurity—or house arrest. This puzzled Stilwell, for the general had not yet understood the foreign minister's role. Relations between Chiang and Stilwell improved marginally, allowing plans for a Burma offensive to again proceed. At the same time, the Chinese were pleased by the growing flow of Hump tonnages arriving from India. Roosevelt, bolstered by Mountbatten's easy success, even agreed to another major air program for China. In November the President approved Operation Matterhorn, a project to bomb Japan from B-29s based in Chengtu. A promise to provide construction funds for the airfields accompanied approval of the project. [39] This costly project was later abandoned as Pacific bases became available.

This improvement in "atmospherics" solved no basic problems, of course. No one could predict whether the British or Chinese would actually fight in Burma or once again squirm out of their commitments. Upon visiting India, John Davies heard rumors of British opposition to the campaign, as well as a report that they opposed really humbling Japan. Postwar Asia, it seemed, might require Japanese power as a counter to Russia and China.[40] These reports, combined with the usual frustrations and delays, convinced Stilwell and Dorn to continue to believe in the necessity of American control over Chinese combat forces. Dorn even projected that after Japan's defeat the United States might retain control over its client army for at least a year, using its own discretion in returning command to the "Chinese government *then in power*."[41]

Clearly, by the end of 1943 at least two American China policies competed for dominance. Stilwell and his embassy supporters sought to compel fundamental political and military reforms within China. They advocated an opening toward the Communists and hoped to counter British efforts at shoring up European colonialism. In their minds, China was linked to the much larger issue of support for progressive nationalism. The President, Chennault, and some others approached the question from an opposite stance. For Roosevelt, support of Chiang remained the symbol and substance of China policy, his triumph seen as indispensable to securing China's future as a great power. Whatever doubts the President may have shared with Stilwell went unexpressed. During 1944, events within China came close—but only close—to tearing this veil from Roosevelt's eyes.

Chapter 8
The General or the Generalissimo?

THE CONVERGING FORCES of revolution, foreign invasion, and a contradictory American aid program placed an almost unbearable strain on China during 1944. Fighting reached its highest pitch since 1938, as allied forces finally entered Burma and the Japanese launched an offensive in southeast China. Chiang's continuing refusal to commit his forces against the Japanese and the growing signs of internal warfare prompted not only Stilwell but Roosevelt as well to consider a radical shift in policy. For a few months it appeared the President saw a new reality and even considered the partial abandonment of Chiang's regime. The failure to pursue this course marked a true turning point in America's Asian policy.

Ironically, at the end of 1943 the President had spoken of China in his most glowing tones. He pushed the State Department to abrogate America's "unequal treaties" with China, and Congress had been cajoled into revising, if only lightly, the racist Chinese Exclusion Act. In October Roosevelt told Admiral Leahy and Secretary Hull that China must be formally accepted as one of the Big Four, a demand which Hull carried to the Moscow Conference. Unless China gained treatment as an equal, the other allies could anticipate "terrific repercussions, both political and military." Due to American insistence, China was nominally included in the Four Power Declaration issued by only three foreign ministers from Moscow in November. As the President put his case to Admiral Mountbatten, having a half billion Chinese on our side would be "very useful" in the "immediate post-war periods." [1]

This enthusiasm continued through the preparations for the Cairo and Teheran conferences, where Roosevelt was to meet Churchill, Chiang, and Stalin. To arrange for the Chinese leader's presence, the President dispatched a personal emissary to China, Patrick J. Hurley. Here entered one of history's bizarre figures, a man on the periphery of power who for a brief time gained notoriety and influence only to recede into the shadows. Born poor in rural Oklahoma, Hurley parlayed self-education, enthusiasm, a quick wit, and a law degree into a full life. He amassed a moderate fortune as an oil company lawyer and used connections in the Republican Party to gain appointment as President Hoover's Secretary of War. Renowned for good looks, vanity, and pluck, Hurley stayed active in capital politics and reappeared during the war as one of several gadflies with whom Roosevelt felt a peculiar affinity. After a stint as ambassador to New Zealand, the President selected General Hurley to carry an invitation to Chiang and undertake a survey of the complicated Middle Eastern political situation.

While he spent only a few days in China, Hurley made a strong, favorable impression on both Stilwell and Chiang—no easy task. The emissary hosted the two rivals to an affable dinner party where he roundly denounced British imperialism and called for greater Sino-American cooperation in Asia. That night, in his normally caustic diary, Stilwell referred to Hurley as "an American of the best sort."[2] He would later have much cause to rue those words.

Hurley's upbeat manner hid some somber opinions about American policy in China. In a cable to the President, the emissary not only reported on Chiang's acceptance of the Cairo invitation but added a political commentary. He warned the President of Chiang's deep distrust of both Stalin and the Chinese Communists. The bulk of the message contained a skilfully worded endorsement of Chiang Kai-shek and his policies. The generalissimo, in Hurley's view, was a deep believer in liberty and democracy, a vigorous opponent of Communism, and a true friend of America who understood Roosevelt's immediate need to "temporize with imperialism and communism in the interests of the joint war effort." To maintain Chiang's friendship, the President ought to accept the "importance placed by the Chinese central government upon conserving its strength for maintenance of its postwar internal supremacy as against the more immediate objective of defeating Japan." This advice varied completely from what Stilwell thought to be Hurley's attitude. It did not bode well for the upcoming summit conferences. Nor did FDR's comment to his son praising Hurley's judgment. The United States, concluded the President, needed "more men like him." Hurley spoke in plain language, unlike "the men in the State Department, those career diplomats . . . half the time I can't tell whether to believe them or not."[3]

At the separate Cairo and Teheran meetings, held between November 22 and December 7, 1943, Roosevelt, Churchill, and Stalin had to resolve when the second front in Europe would be opened and whether the Soviets would enter the Pacific war. They also had to decide if the successful island-hopping campaign in the Pacific might soon enable American forces to bomb Japan from island airfields, significantly reducing China's military importance. Both a Soviet promise to enter the war and an island campaign would render China even more of a military stepchild. Realizing the difficult situation he faced, Chiang actually fell back upon Stilwell's assistance. He asked the general to join him and Madame Chiang as delegates to Cairo, where they could present a strong case for continued American support for the China theater. Stilwell, who took John Davies along as a political advisor, cooperated by drafting additional plans for aid to China and an offensive in Burma.[4]

Chiang's hope of making a favorable impression on Roosevelt and Churchill at Cairo (Stalin insisted on meeting the British and American leaders only, at Teheran) was frustrated by his own behavior and outside factors. British and American military planners could hardly have a civil discussion about Asian strategy, preferring to trade accusations. Stilwell vividly recorded how British Field Marshal Sir Alan Brooke "got nasty and [Admiral] King got good and sore. King almost climbed over the table at Brooke. God he was mad. I wished he had socked him." Churchill and his staff continued to oppose a major campaign in Burma while Chiang angered everyone by constantly reversing his position on what he favored. When the first phase of the Cairo meeting ended on November 27, the Americans thought they had secured tentative British and Chinese pledges to fight in Burma in the spring of 1944. No commitments were final, however, especially since the allies had not yet determined Soviet attitudes and plans.[5]

The ensuing discussions with Stalin, whom Roosevelt and Churchill met in Teheran on November 28, 1943, cast a changed light on earlier decisions. Not surprisingly, Stalin's concerns centered on getting the allies to fix a date for the invasion of Western Europe. When Roosevelt obliged by naming May 1944, Churchill declared this precluded a major British effort in Burma. Eager to nail down a second front, Stalin formed a de facto bloc with Churchill on this point. In consideration of the American desire to press the fight in the Pacific, however, Stalin pledged to join the war against Japan shortly after Germany's defeat. To this pledge he appended a request for certain "privileges" in Manchuria, a factor of great importance as time wore on. For the moment, however, the main advantage of Soviet entry into he war, for both Churchill and Roosevelt, was that it reduced their dependence on China's questionable strength.[6] British and American strategists then resumed their endless arguments over Burma, and by December 5 the Americans consented to scale down the projected campaign agreed to only a week earlier.

While Chiang had never approved of fighting in Burma for its merits, he must have realized the dire implications which flowed from this changed strategy. No plan for a major offensive meant no large increase in the level of Lend-Lease aid. This threatened the generalissimo's plans to stockpile aid for the future. In reply to Roosevelt's notification about the changed strategy, Chiang demanded major compensation in the form of a $1 billion loan and the expansion of Hump deliveries to twenty thousand tons per month.[7] The American response to this proved a rude awakening, for the previously pliable Roosevelt suddenly resisted Chiang's demands.

Even at Cairo, those close to the President detected his changed attitude. In a conversation with his son Elliott (present as an aide), Roosevelt remarked on his private discussions with Chiang. Reportedly he told the generalissimo to accept some aspects of Stilwell's program, including the idea of using Communist troops against Japan. Chiang ought to "form a unity government, *while the war was still being fought,* with the Communists in Yenan." The younger Roosevelt quoted his father as saying Chiang agreed to this idea, contingent upon a Soviet promise to respect the "frontier in Manchuria." This point, FDR observed, was on the "agenda for Teheran."[8]

Even more pointed than the President's remarks to his son were his meetings with Stilwell at Cairo. The general wished to see Roosevelt to inform him of some dramatic news Dorn had forwarded. No sooner had Chiang left Chungking, it appeared, than plotting for a coup had begun. A variety of individuals and factions were rumored to be active, including Ch'en Ch'eng and T. V. Soong. Reluctant to speak on his superiors' behalf, Dorn suggested cryptically that Stilwell might be able to "get the ball rolling in Cairo."[9] On December 6, 1943, Stilwell and Davies met with Roosevelt and Hopkins.

Speaking first only with Hopkins, the men were surprised to hear the presidential confidant ridicule Chiang's grandiose pretensions. He dismissed the idea of China recovering Outer Mongolia (for years a Soviet satellite) and perhaps other "lost" territories. Not only would Chiang soon be doing America's bidding, but an assertive United States would use its own judgment in deciding upon postwar territorial settlements. Washington would insist upon bases in "Formosa, the Philippines and anywhere we damned please."

Joining the group at this point, Roosevelt declared his refusal to grant China any more huge, unregulated dollar loans.

Perhaps, he quipped, the United States might make a contribution to the Chinese economy by "buying up Chinese dollars on the black market." He then hinted at the contents of the Teheran discussions, explaining to Stilwell and Davies that Stalin wanted—and he approved—special Soviet port and railroad privileges in Manchuria. While Stalin seemed willing to settle for these favors and leave Chiang otherwise alone, the generalissimo ought not to tempt fate by attacking the Chinese Communists.

Sensing that the time was right, John Davies tried to bring the discussion down to cases. What, he asked, ought the American military command to do if Chiang were overthrown? Support whoever stood "next in line," replied the President. As Davies remarked that a line had already formed, Hopkins shifted the conversation into a conspiratorial vein. The White House needed men in China who would form a "small, closely knit group that will not talk and would do what was needed to be done." Before anyone plumbed the meaning of those words, Hopkins and Roosevelt again shifted direction. FDR launched into his shopworn anecdotes about his grandfather's role in the old China trade: "Well, now, we've been friends with China for a gr-ee-at many years, I ascribe a large part of this feeling to the missionaries. You know I have a China history. My grandfather went out there. . . . he made a million dollars. . . ." Hopkins similarly digressed, asking the startled Stilwell and Davies to recommend an appropriate religion for conquered Japan. "Christ he's so terrible we came out puking," wrote an embittered Stilwell in his diary.[10]

Despite the bizarre aspects of their conversation, what took place at this and a later meeting with Roosevelt revealed that the White House was no longer completely under the spell of Chennault and Chiang. At a final private meeting between Roosevelt and Stilwell (for which General Frank Dorn's memory must serve as a record), the President gave even greater proof of his changed attitude.

When Stilwell returned to China he visited Dorn at Y-Force headquarters in Kunming and delivered a top-secret verbal order which he said came from Roosevelt. The order was to prepare a plan to assassinate Chiang Kai-shek. The President, according to Stilwell, was

fed up with Chiang and his tantrums, and said so. In fact, he told me in that Olympian manner of his "if you can't get along with Chiang, and can't replace him, get rid of him once and for all. You know what I mean, put in someone you can manage." [11]

Dorn dutifully devised a plan to sabotage Chiang's aircraft while he flew over the Hump to make an inspection tour of Chinese forces in India. When the passengers were forced to bail out, both the generalissimo and Madame Chiang would be given faulty parachutes. According to Dorn, the President never gave final authorization for Stilwell to carry out this assassination. But the very planning for such a contingency, assuming both Stilwell and Dorn had told the truth, revealed that the White House no longer saw China and Chiang as coterminous. [12]

Even without drastic intervention via coup and assassination, the United States could greatly influence the turn of political developments in China. Lend-Lease and economic aid were both vital ingredients in the complex formula which sustained Chiang in power and provided Washington with influence over that power. Beginning in December 1943 and continuing until the recall of Stilwell in October 1944, Roosevelt finally showed a resolve to exercise this American lever. Although he never expressed directly his reasons for so doing, we can surmise that the decision was based on the realization that China's importance in the struggle with Japan had become increasingly marginal. If any troops were to fight Japan in northeast Asia, they would be Soviet troops. The President now seemed to feel that Chiang could safely be pressured into toeing the American line. The China theater had to be straightened out, deals had to be made with Stalin, and civil war, which would give the Russians an excuse for intervention, had to be curtailed.

The President, with renewed support from Treasury Secretary Morgenthau, made his first stand on the issue of economic aid. It seemed absurd for Chiang to demand $1 billion from Washington. The Chinese had used less than half of the 1942 loan, were making no efforts to combat inflation, and continued to reap profits by maintaining an artificially low exchange rate between the dollar and the yuan (20 to 1). Virtually no one except Stanley Hornbeck spoke in supprt of a large new loan. Gauss maintained there was "no sound basis, political or economic, for supporting any such loan proposal at this time." Morgenthau labeled Chiang's request extortion and suggested that the United States meet its own expenses in China by exchanging currency on the black market. When Roosevelt told Morgenthau that he intended sending just that message to Chungking, the shocked Secretary remarked that Chiang, Kung, and Soong, would probably ask the President and himself to return the many personal gifts which the Chinese had sent them over the years. In private, Morgenthau fumed that he would "not loan Chiang another nickel" and that the "crook" could "go jump in the Yangtze." [13]

In early January Roosevelt formally turned down Chiang's request for economic aid, sending a message certain to sting the Chinese. Since the Chinese government had been unable to stop inflation, curb currency speculation, revise the dollar-yuan exchange rate, or agree to a full commitment to the Burma campaign, Roosevelt wrote that "a loan to China . . . could not be justified by the results that have been obtained. It is my opinion that a loan is unnecessary at this time and would be undesirable from the point of view of China and the United States." [14]

Complaining that the American position sounded like a "commercial transaction" and not the words of "one Allied nation to another," Chiang's shocked and indignant reply to Roosevelt's message not only repeated the demand for economic aid but threatened to cease assisting the construction of American bomber bases. He concluded with an ambiguous warning that China might be forced to drop out of the war. While none of the Americans took this threat seriously, they also did not want to impede construction of the bomber bases. Accordingly, a decision was made to grant minor economic concessions to Chiang and try to work out an amicable compromise on the revision of dollar-yuan exchange rates. [15]

An even more startling example of the changed attitude in the White House occurred as pressures mounted to force Chiang to fight in Burma. Although in December, following the Cairo decision, Chiang had refused to send the Y-Force into Burma, the generalissimo had simultaneously attempted to assuage Washington by granting Stilwell command over the X-Force in India. The general now planned to take the X-Force into Burma and thus bring great pressure on Chiang to follow through with the Y-Force. [16] Stilwell's scheme worked exactly as planned. During December he led the X-Force into Burma from India, spending the bulk of the next six months at the front while Washington's harsh glare fell upon Chiang, who kept the Y-Force inactive in Yunnan. Aroused by the spectacle of Stilwell's few Chinese divisions and Anglo-American commandos going it alone (and it *was* very rough going!), Roosevelt sent a flurry of cables to the recalcitrant Chiang. On January 14, 1944, for the first time, Roosevelt suggested that further delays by Chiang put the future of American aid in doubt. [17]

The problems faced in the Burma campaign came from three sources: bitter Japanese resistance, the continued immobilization of the Y-Force, and British opposition to the entire strategy. Once the battle had been joined, Mountbatten went so far as to send his aides to London and Washington to lobby for a revised strategy geared toward a naval campaign in Southeast Asia. [18] Responding in kind, Stilwell sent John Davies and General Hugh Boatner home to speak for him.

Reaching New Delhi in January 1944, Davies spoke with

155   The General or the Generalissimo?

General Albert Wedemeyer, then deputy chief of staff to SEAC and eventually Stilwell's successor. Wedemeyer quickly exposed his own political inclinations. The second front, he told Davies, should be postponed to maximize the number of Germans and Russians killing each other. In Asia, more consideration must be given to preserving Japan as a counter to Soviet expansion. Like Mountbatten, he was not impressed by the importance of fighting in Burma.[19]

The euphoria over China that had gripped Washington early in the war seemed a distant memory by 1944. Few planners harbored any great expectations about China, present or future. The formerly optimistic Currie now revealed a deep pessimism about Chiang. Neither Hull, Stimson, nor Morgenthau any longer spoke of China as a "great power." In this depressed atmosphere the President was increasingly influenced by the opinions of General Marshall, who of course had always been Stilwell's major supporter.[20] Now that most of Chiang's active supporters in Washington had lost either power or influence, critical reporting from the field achieved real importance for the first time. During early 1944 the policy critiques prepared by the embassy staff in Chungking found an attentive audience in the State, War and Treasury departments as well as in the White House.

Davies' evaluations of American policy focused increasingly on the impending collapse of Anglo-French power in Asia and the equally dramatic impact which Soviet power and Asian nationalism would have throughout the region. Whichever party emerged as China's postwar government, there was no doubt that China would be a strongly nationalistic state. The United States, Davies advised, should prepare to move "with the historical stream rather than fighting it." If American policy were not friendly toward Chinese nationalism, it might become a force allied to the Soviet Union. This fact held true *regardless* of whether the KMT or CCP emerged supreme. Chiang's regime, despite its conservative bent, might conceivabley seek Russian support. If it did not, there was still no certainty that it would be strong, pro-American, or capable of containing the Soviet Union. Davies believed the United States must insure "a favorable alignment of power when we again become involved in an Asiatic or Pacific war." Unless Washington could compel Chiang to transform his regime (something Davies doubted), it would be better to support the Communists or a liberal non-Communist coalition. Davies felt certain that any successor regime would support the United States because "no government in China can hope to survive without American support."[21]

John Service and Foreign Service officer Raymond Ludden expressed similar ideas. They viewed Chiang as "a hostage to the corrupt forces which he has so long manipulated." America's (and China's) only hope lay in Washington's willingness to support a new Chinese government which would serve as a "pro-American balance in an Asia affected by the rising tide of nationalism, possibly enjoying Russian support."[22] (It seems particularly ironic that these Foreign Service officers, who so eloquently warned of the need to contain Soviet influence in China, became the special targets of McCarthyism in the 1950s. Their final reward would be dismissal from the State Department as security risks.)

While reporting by Service, Davies, and Ludden provided an intellectual framework for new initiatives, the Japanese army compelled American action. An offensive launched along the Burma-India frontier in March threatened to cut off the Assam airfields which supplied the Hump and the X-Force under Stilwell's command. Sending the Y-Force from Yunnan into Burma now became a military necessity. Roosevelt and Marshall took this opportunity to make a new demand on Chiang. Since the generalissimo had long complained that using the Y-Force in Burma would expose central China to a Communist attack, the President now suggested that Chiang permit American observers to go to Yenan to insure that the Communists would not attack Chiang's rear. Roosevelt's larger concern, of course, was to open a dialogue with the CCP which, if nothing else, would give Washington some added leverage to deal with the KMT. At the same time, Americans could gather much needed information about the revolutionary movement. In Chiang's mind such a proposal undoubtedly raised the most fearsome possibility of all: the Americans had linked the issue of military reform to the question of how to deal with the Communists.[23]

Given the critical military situation in Burma by early April, Roosevelt and Marshall pushed hardest to compel the utilization of the Y-Force. After first merely chiding Chiang for accepting military aid while withholding his troops from combat, the White House escalated its pressures. On April 10 Marshall finally received authority to threaten Chiang with a cutoff of aid unless the Y-Force moved. Because Stilwell was in Burma, Dorn and General Thomas Hearn were empowered to inform the Chinese of the President's threat. Rather than prematurely force Chiang into a corner, they opted to permit him to save face. Dorn and Hearn postponed delivery of the message until informal notice of its contents had made the rounds in Chungking through Madame Chiang and others. Then, on April 14, War Minister Ho Ying-chin gave the order for the Y-Force to move across the Salween River into Burma. The attack began on May 11 and eventually turned the tide of the battle in Burma.[24]

After the Y-Force passed under Stilwell's control, many months of hard fighting in Burma still lay ahead. Bitter Japanese resistance slowed the advance of the Chinese armies and their associated Anglo-American commando units. Right behind the advancing front moved a corps of construction workers who cleared a road through the jungle over which trucks would eventually carry supplies into China, the so-called Stilwell Road. However, not until early 1945 did the allies break the full weight of Japanese power in Burma, by which time Stilwell had already been relieved of his command.

As the fighting in Burma escalated in the spring and summer of 1944, there arose yet another impasse in Sino-American relations. Both Stilwell and Roosevelt resumed efforts to establish contacts with Yenan, presumably to incorporate Communist forces into the Chinese government and American military aid program. This issue lay at the core of China's internal crisis and bore directly on U.S. relations with the Soviet Union. To prevent civil war—thus reducing the twin dangers of either a Communist victory or Soviet intervention—Americans looked for a way to control both Yenan and Chungking. If the United States appeared willing to balance its assistance between the Communists and Nationalists, both parties might be restrained from attacking the other. In any event, such an American stance would give Washington far greater flexibility than it had previously enjoyed. The Foreign Service officers serving in the embassy and with Stilwell had long advocated this strategy, arguing that the United States must send a mission to Yenan. This, they understood, was the ultimate test of whether the United States would sever itself from an unrealistic dependence on the KMT. It also represented a trial run for Washington's ability to come to terms with and possibly influence revolutionary nationalism in Asia.

When, in February 1944, Chiang refused Roosevelt's initial request that he permit an American team to visit Yenan, few observers were suprised. The generalissimo had no reason to accept the proposal, given the success he had previously enjoyed in rejecting all political demands.[25] But by March 1944 both Roosevelt's attitude and the situation within China were reversed. With unexpected fury the Japanese army launched yet another major offensive (Operation Ichigo) in southeastern China. Japanese forces struck hammer blows against provinces supposedly under firm KMT control. The provincial armies, which Chiang had long insisted needed none of Stilwell's reorganization, were no match for the Japanese and began disorderly retreats on all fronts. For a time, it even seemed that Chungking might be threatened. To make matters even worse, the Japanese overran the provinces in which Chennault's forward air bases were located. As Stilwell had long predicted, air bases left unprotected were easy prey to the Japanese. Now the precious aid which had built up Chennault's air force and bases was lost because there was no adequate Chinese army to defend them.

The debacle of Ichigo (which lasted through the early autumn) made its mark on the President. It seemed that Stilwell's tactics had been right, after all. If this was the case, perhaps it was also true that sending a group of Americans to Yenan was worth pressing for. At the least, it might frighten Chiang into cooperating more fully with Stilwell. By early March Roosevelt believed the time had come to press Chiang directly on the matter of a mission to Yenan. The means he chose were peculiarly influenced by domestic politics, especially the issue of running for a fourth term and choosing a vice-presidential candidate. Within the Democratic Party there was much resistance to repeating the Roosevelt-Wallace ticket. While Roosevelt liked Wallace and could certainly have compelled the party to renominate him, the President felt reluctant to antagonize conservatives, who saw Wallace as something of a "wild man" of the left. The President proved eager to send the Vice-President on a foreign mission, presumably because an extended absence from the United States would hinder any effort by Wallace to line up political support for renomination. Officially, however, Wallace still carried the esteem of high office and popularity, making him an ideal candidate to convey to Chiang the President's wish that Americans be allowed to travel to Yenan.

In preparation for his mission, Wallace sought counsel from a diverse group, including John Davies, Lauchlin Currie, John Carter Vincent, and Owen Lattimore. All offered Wallace similar advice: Chiang must mend his fences with the Communists or risk civil war and possible Russian intervention. The presence of Americans in Yenan, they expected, would contribute to an atmosphere more conducive to compromise on both sides.[26]

The President met with Wallace on May 18, 1944, the day

before he departed for Siberia and China. His instructions revealed many lingering contradictions. Roosevelt asked Wallace to speak with Chiang about readjusting the unrealistic exchange rate between Chinese and American currency. To avoid embarrassing the generalissimo, the Vice-President was told not to visit the Chinese Communists or General Stilwell but to confer with Chennault. Yet Roosevelt also urged Wallace to take along as advisors Owen Lattimore and John Carter Vincent, both of whom were sympathetic to Stilwell and critical of Chiang.

Roosevelt's advice on how to handle the thorny problem of KMT-Communist relations was vintage FDR.

He said the first rule for the Generalissimo to remember was "Nothing should be final between friends." . . . Then he quoted Al Smith as saying with regard to warring factions, "Let me get them all into the same room with good chairs to sit on where they can put their feet on the table, where they can have cold beer to drink and cigars to smoke. Then I will knock their heads together and we will settle everything." The President then said he would be happy to be called in as arbiter between the warring factions. He told me to tell the Generalissimo that it might be a good thing if "he would call in a friend." [27]

This combination of Tammany Hall wisdom and serious interest in promoting political compromise revealed Roosevelt's growing concern for the fate of China. Civil War, he told Wallace, would disrupt the agreements made with Stalin to keep Manchuria Chinese. "If the Generalissimo could not settle the communist thing, he, the President, might not be able to hold the Russians in line."

The two-week period (June 18–30, 1944) spent by Wallace in China was a curious one. T. V. Soong, rehabilitated from a year of disgrace to shepherd about this foreign liberal, joined Chiang in trying to convince the Vice-President of Communist perfidy. Wallace, however, was not impressed with their logic or performance in power. Even as they spoke, Japanese forces continued their rampage through southeast China, discrediting in their wake everything Chennault and his Chinese allies said. The Vice-President could not avoid making a comparison between the KMT and Alexander Kerensky, concluding that Chiang's clique "would almost prefer to lose the war than to see the old Chinese system upset in any way."

Wallace prepared extensive notes on his meetings with Chiang held between June 21 and 24. The Vice-President spoke freely about Roosevelt's desire to see China unified and stabilized through an internal political agreement and a pact with the Soviet Union. He even quoted to Chiang Roosevelt's story about Al Smith. The United States would be willing to mediate the internal crisis but, Wallace asserted, would play no direct part in Sino-Soviet negotiations. Much of the discussion was consumed by the generalissimo's complaints that the United States had not provided him enough economic or military aid, which had resulted in the collapse of his army's effectiveness. He identified other problems as the "uncooperative attitude" of General Stilwell and the appearance of critical articles about the KMT in the American press. These undercut both China's morale and its faith in the United States, Chiang remarked.

On the key issue of internal conflict, the generalissimo denounced the CCP as Soviet puppets, renegades, and virtual collaborators with the Japanese. Unless they accepted the primacy of the central government, a coalition was impossible. The American position, complained Chiang, showed signs of being influenced by "Communist propaganda." Roosevelt must display "aloofness" to the Communists so they would be willing to "reach a settlement with the Kuomintang." Only after continued pressure and a renewed demand from Roosevelt did Chiang agree to the request that a small group of American observers be permitted to go to Yenan. Even so, the generalissimo insisted that the Americans undertake no joint action with the Communists.[28] Although Wallace spoke forcefully enough to win Chiang's agreement to permit Americans to visit Yenan, he accepted the arguments of Alsop, Chennault, and Soong that the situation in China could not be improved so long as Stilwell remained in command. He might, Wallace suggested to the President, be replaced by General Albert Wedemeyer.

The Vice-President, who met Roosevelt in the White House on July 10, 1944, to give a final report, did warn the President of Chiang's "eastern" thought and outlook and his tendency to make the "Communist menace a scapegoat for his government's failures." While there were some progressive elements in the KMT (centered around Madame Chiang and T. V. Soong), Wallace berated Chiang for his reliance on an "unenlightened administration supported by landlords, warlords and bankers. . . ." The result was "widespread popular dislike for the Kuomintang government." At the end of this litany of criticism, Wallace could offer very little positive guidance to Roosevelt. The United States seemed trapped by circumstances beyond its control. For at this time, Wallace wrote, "there seems to be no alternative to support of Chiang. There is no Chinese leader or group now apparent of sufficient strength to take over the government." All that could be done was to try to "influence" Chiang to "adopt policies with the guidance of progressive Chinese which [would] inspire popular support and instill new vitality into China's war effort. . . ."

The Vice-President's final advice to the President had a haunting quality. He realized that the requirements of coalition warfare, domestic politics, and postwar planning all compelled a continued American involvement in China. Yet, the ally Roosevelt had embraced might not be able to deliver on any promises. Wallace cautioned the President that

Chiang, at best, is a short-term investment. It is not believed that he has the intelligence or political strength to run post-war China. The leaders of post-war China will be brought forward by evolution or revolution, and it now seems more like the latter.[29]

During the period of Wallace's visit, this warning took on added significance. Not only did he seem unable to halt the

Japanese advance in the southeast, but the generalissimo was being challenged by yet another group. A faction of warlords led by Marshal Li Chi-sen threatened to establish a separate regime in the south. These warlords, whose armies lay in the path of the Japanese offensive, were supposed to defend Chennault's bases. Nevertheless, Chiang regarded them with such suspicion that he ordered supplies to their troops cut off. Whether through collusion (as some thought) or chance, the Japanese were doing the generalissimo a favor by destroying the power base of actual and potential rivals. Stilwell and his staff knew of the separatist plotting and Chiang's decision to cut off the troops defending Chennault's bases. Since there seemed to be little chance that the southern warlords could actually establish a viable regime, Stilwell decided not to extend them any support. Instead, he preferred to press on with his campaign to gain control of the main body of Chiang's army and some Communist units.[30]

By now, of course, Stilwell had grown accustomed to Roosevelt's emissaries urging his recall. He appeared most angered by the possibility of Wedemeyer as a replacement, a soldier he considered "the world's most pompous prick."[31] But Roosevelt was in no mood now to cut down his own general in front of Chiang. It was the Chinese command, he decided, which needed to be shaken up. Marshall sensed the time had come to again lay Stilwell's familiar demands before the President, now undeterred by the waning influence of Chennault and Alsop.

Chiang's reaction to the Japanese Operation Ichigo offensive made American action imperative. The generalissimo suddenly began to demand that Chinese troops be brought back from the thick of the battle in Burma to meet the Japanese in China. Since it was highly unlikely that Chiang would really commit these troops against the Japanese, Stilwell suggested to Marhsall that Chiang be stripped of command powers. In his place Stilwell would assume complete freedom to direct China's war effort, command troops, remove recalcitrant officers, and even incorporate Communist units into his military plans. After convincing the Joint Chiefs they should back this proposal, Marshall presented the idea to the President on July 4, 1944.

The Army Chief of Staff asked Roosevelt to endorse a message which accused Chiang and Chennault of responsibility for a long chain of blunders. The President affixed his signature on July 6 to a cable warning Chiang that a "critical situation" now existed. Because of this it was imperative for Stilwell to assume "command of all Chinese and American forces . . . including the Communist forces." While acknowledging the antipathy between Chiang and Stilwell, Roosevelt insisted that unless he applied this radical remedy "our common cause w[ould] suffer a serious setback." Dramatically, the President warned that "the future of all Asia is at stake, along with the tremendous effort America has expended in that region. Therefore I have reason for a profound interest in the matter." Finally, Roosevelt concluded with a calculated insult directed at the generalissimo's passion for Chennault. "Air power alone," he stated, "cannot stop a determined enemy." [32]

Confronted by a demand that he essentially remove himself from power, Chiang began a desperate search for a way out of his quandary. At this point he could afford, openly, neither to accept nor reject Roosevel't demands. So Chiang temporized, asking the President for just a little more time before Stilwell assumed his new duties. This hiatus would allow the American general to become "familiar" with the command structure of the Chinese army. Moreover, if Americans were to become so powerful in China, surely the President would want to send a personal emissary to coordinate future military and political decisions? The generalissimo asked that Roosevelt send a special emissary and also concede to Chiang the power to veto any plans for cooperation with the Communists. [33]

The President had no desire to press for a confrontation with Chiang, especially since the Chinese leader had apparently conceded the major point. Stilwell would soon assume command powers, making the request for a presidential representative reasonable. Both Wallace and Gauss, in fact, had broached the idea of placing a high-level buffer between Stilwell and Chiang. When Roosevelt sent word to Marshall that he intended to accept Chiang's counteroffer, the Army Chief of Staff moved quickly. Fearing that the President or Hopkins might again select a hatchet man who favored dumping Stilwell, Marshall and Stimson jointly asked Roosevelt to choose Patrick J. Hurley for the mission. Stilwell, they believed, could depend on Hurley's loyalty, while the President was known to share confidence in him as well.[34]

In an odd quirk of fate, Roosevelt told Marshall he wanted Donald Nelson to accompany Hurley to China. The former chain store executive and chairman of the War Production Board was in a public row with his successor, and the President desired his absence from Washington. China seemed about as far as he could be sent, and thus Nelson became head of an economic fact-finding mission to China. The Hurley-Nelson team conferred with neither the War nor the State Department before departing. Although Roosevelt and Hurley did speak briefly, whatever words passed between them remained known only to themselves.[35]

If Hurley lacked formal instructions, his immediate actions revealed that he did possess a complex game plan. The route Hurley and Nelson took to Chungking led, strangely enough, through Moscow. There Hurley informed a surprised American embassy and Russian government that he had come on Roosevelt's behalf to secure assurances that the Chinese Communists would not receive Soviet aid or encouragement. Displaying a Soviet attitude of indifference toward the Chinese Communists (which would be repeated several times in the following two years), Foreign Minister Molotov offered Hurley assurances that the Kremlin would neither support Yenan nor oppose the KMT.[36] Believing he had secured one flank, Hurley gathered up Nelson and flew to Chungking on September 6, 1944.

In Moscow, Hurley had made the first move in a complicated strategy. Hurley and (we may surmise) Roosevelt believed that if the Russians could be depended on to support Chiang or at least remain aloof, the Chinese Communists would be dissuaded from pursuing an active revolutionary line in China. Chiang, at the same time, would feel more secure and might thus be prepared to accept some sort of meaningful political compromise with the Communists. Roosevelt had told Wallace the previous May of his belief that an American arbiter might be able to "knock some heads together" and engineer a political settlement in China. The importance of reaching a settlement lay in Rossevelt's fear that, if civil war did erupt, the Russians might be tempted to grab Manchuria. Nor could a China engulfed in civil war do very much to stabilize postwar Asia.

It must be admitted this is only a hypothesis, for neither Hurley nor Roosevelt ever explicitly revealed their goals. In fact, the White House at first gave some indications that Hurley's mission was not to be taken altogether seriously. As Hurley departed for Chungking, John Davies met with Harry Hopkins on Stilwell's behalf, to discover what the President's policy actually was. Hopkins, always a difficult man to pin down, complained to Davies of the unbearable workload under which he and his staff labored. But as Davies pushed for information, Hopkins asserted that the point of Hurley's mission was only to sweeten the bitter pill Chiang had to swallow in appointing Stilwell military commander. Nelson's presence, he said, should be ignored. Hopkins quipped that he expected the Chinese simply to "provide him with four or five girls" who would keep him quiet. Hopkins did say that the President wanted Stilwell to assume control "both over the central government's and the Communists' troops." This sudden interest in the Communists, Hopkins explained, resulted from reading the impressive initial reports coming to the White House from the American observer group which had gone to Yenan in July. Both he and the President wanted to receive all important material on the Communists, he told Davies.[37]

Hopkins' words revealed how the many threads of military

and political decisionmaking had begun to entwine. In both Washington and Chungking, Americans were now beginning to press for an arrangement to integrate Communist units into the Allied effort against Japan. This appeared to be a way out of the military quagmire in which the China Theater had become mired. It also was a possible means of forcing the major political factions in China to come to a settlement short of civil war. Both the Nationalists and Communists realized that they had entered into a competition for American favors. The prize— American materiel and political support—would be a crucial determinant in China's internal power struggle.

The Communists (whose major efforts to win American support will be described in the following chapters) approached both Hurley and Stilwell in early September. From Yenan the commander of the American Dixie Mission, Colonel David Barrett, forwarded an invitation from the Communist leadership that Hurley visit them. The message stated that Communist forces were eager to cooperate with Americans in the battle against Japan. Stilwell, too, found himself courted by Communist offers. On September 13, 1944, he met with two Communist representatives in Chungking who spoke of their willingness to place Yenan's forces under his command. Obviously impressed by the sincerity of the offer, Stilwell wrote in his diary, "Somehow we must get arms to the Communists who will fight." [38]

But before Stilwell could act he had to achieve actual command powers, something which remained very much in doubt. Chiang's agreement in principle to Roosevelt's earlier demand was not translated into fact. The generalissimo refused to surrender any powers until he was assured of personal control over Lend-Lease distribution and plans to arm the Communists. But these qualifications negated the entire purpose of Stilwell's assumption of command. Moreover, while Stilwell and Hurley negotiated during mid-September, the military situation in China further deteriorated, with Chiang again demanding that the Y-Force be pulled out of Burma.

In desperation, Stilwell fired off a warning to Marshall that, unless he was given command at once, the theater might collapse. The next day, September 16, Stilwell called in Soong and "got down to plain words." If he was not given full command powers immediately, and unless Ch'en Ch'eng and Pai Chung-hsi (an old KMT rival of Chiang) were named minister of war and chief of staff respectively, he would urge Washington to "withdraw entirely from China and set up base elsewhere."[39]

Stilwell's message reached Marshall and Roosevelt on September 16, 1944, while they attended the OCTAGON Conference in Quebec. It was a difficult time for the President in many ways. He and Churchill continued bickering over policy, especially colonial affairs, and the question of how to treat Germany after it surrendered. Churchill demanded that the President "leave his Indians alone" and in return Great Britain would "leave the President's Chinese alone." At dinner, both the President and Mrs. Roosevelt revealed their fears concerning China as they complained of the Chiang entourage's imperial "pretensions and extravagances."[40]

Reacting to Stillwell's warnings, Marshall's staff in Quebec drafted a message, which Roosevelt approved, rebuking Chiang. The time for stalling, it declared, had passed and unless Stilwell was given complete power to command troops, United States aid would be terminated. Blaming Chiang for courting "catastrophic consequences," the reprimand intoned that it was "evident to all of us here . . . that all your and our efforts to save China are to be lost by further delays."[41]

Stilwell delivered this ultimatum in person to Chiang on September 19, interrupting a private meeting between the generalissimo and Hurley. The consummate joy of revenge felt by Stilwell was expressed in the poem he wrote to commemorate the occasion.

> I've waited long for vengenace——
> At last I've had my chance.
> I've looked the Peanut in the eye

And kicked him in the pants.

The old harpoon was ready
With aim and timing true,
I sank it to the handle,
And stung him through and through.

The little bastard shivered,
And lost the power of speech,
His face turned green and quivered
As he struggled not to screech.

For all my weary battles,
For all my hours of woe,
At last I've had my innings
And laid the Peanut low.

I know I've still to suffer,
And run a weary race,
But oh! the blessed pleasure!
I've wrecked the Peanut's face.[42]

Believing he now had the President's full support, Stilwell could at last "play the avenging angel."

While Stilwell may have felt secure in this new role, he had won a Pyrrhic victory. During the following weeks it became clear that Patrick Hurley had secretly taken it upon himself to work with Chiang in ridding the generalissimo of the tiresome American general. Hurley's motives and methods are shrouded in mystery. His own records reveal his collusion with Chiang but fail to adequately explain his reasons for this. Hurley's behavior over the next year does show that he believed it imperative to sustain Chiang in power. He feared that any American decision either to work directly with the Communists or to topple Chiang would open up China to the several dangers of a Communist victory, European meddling, or Soviet expansion. Thus a man almost totally ignorant of the actual situation in China took it upon himself to once again steer American policy firmly in the direction of sustaining Chaing's unchallenged supremacy in China. It is a dubious testament to Hurley's skills that he managed to accomplish this task.

On September 23, when he still believed Hurley was supporting him, Stilwell sent Hurley a proposal that they jointly confront Chiang. Stilwell desired to travel to Yenan, where he would make "proposals to the Reds." The Communists would be asked to acknowledge Chiang's nominal authority while accepting Stilwell as an actual field commander. Communist forces would then be deployed north of the Yellow River and given supplies to equip five divisions. Further aid to Chaing's armies would only be granted after delivery had been made to the X, Y, and Communist divisions. Upon receiving this memorandum, Hurley accorded Stilwell's long-desired strategy only a two-word response, penciling on the bottom the words "TOO LATE." Once again Chaing had successfully split the opposition, persuading another presidential emissary to dump Stilwell. Hurley decided to back the generalissimo and press Roosevelt to withdraw his previous demands.[43]

The day after Stilwell had sent this abortive proposal to Hurley, the latter received a message from Chiang and Soong for Roosevelt. The tone revealed that they expected Hurley to endorse the position it contained. The Chinese note ruefully droned that, while Chiang had accepted the principle of an American commander, he could never accept Stilwell in this position. To do so would be to "knowingly court inevitable disaster." Hurley appended his own comments to the Chinese message, telling the President that Stilwell himself had become the central problem in China. If Stilwell were to be removed, the President's desire that Chiang undertake serious new military and political initiatives would be assured. Finally, Hurley announced that Chiang's decision was final and that he, Hurley, concurred in it.[44]

The matter rested uneasily for the week between September 25 and October 1, 1944. The President delayed responding the Chiang-Hurley ultimatum of September 24, uncertain what course to take. Stilwell hoped that the President was standing firm and took the opportunity to suggest to Ho Ying-chin that if Chiang followed through on command powers he, Stilwell, would consider postponing aid to the Communists. This uneasy quiet was broken on October 1, when Hurley told Stilwell that H. H. Kung (who was in the United States) had passed on an informal message from Hopkins to Chiang saying that Roosevelt was willing to sacrifice Stilwell. Although Hopkins vehemently denied his assertion, Stilwell was moved to such anger that he condemned in his diary "old Rubberlegs" (Roosevelt) for cutting his throat again. Whatever the truth about Hopkins' role, Chiang took advantage of the rumor to repeat his demand that Roosevelt relieve Stilwell. This issue, declared Chiang, was ultimately one of China's sovereignty.[45]

The President now faced a major policy decision, one which might ultimately determine the future course of Sino-American relations. Marshall and Stimson had urged him to take a hard line and Chiang had balked. From Chungking, Hurley gave assurances that no really deep problems even existed, that once Stilwell was removed all would go smoothly. On October 4 Donald Nelson suddenly appeared back in Washington, trumpeting praises of Hurley to Wallace and others surrounding the President. According to Nelson, Hurley and Chiang had practically solved all outstanding political and military problems before Stilwell had barged in with Marshall's message signed by Roosevelt demanding that Stilwell immediately be given command. Wallace found Nelson's presentation very persuasive, leading him to ponder why Stilwell and Marshall desired to "completely alienat[e] the Generalissimo, and lose[e] all of eastern China."[46]

Nelson's criticism and Wallace's consternation seemed to speak to the President's dilemma. In the midst of a crisis, Hurley offered an easy and immediate solution. This was important, for in only a few weeks the President faced an election for a fourth term in which he campaigned on the basis of his proven record in war and international diplomacy. He was struggling to shape a future world governed by a consortium of the Great Powers and a United Nations Organization whose principles were peace and compromise. To break with China, one of the heralded Big Four, on the eve of the election seemed the height of political folly, however justified the break might be. Whatever had to be done in China would have to be done later, after Stilwell was gone, after the election had been won, and after the issue was out of the headlines. Nevertheless, Roosevelt was so deeply pained by the problem in China that Stimson found him unable to discuss it rationally.

What the President offered Chiang on October 5, in reply to the demand for Stilwell's recall, was another compomise. Chiang could remain supreme in China if Stilwell were permitted to retain full command over the X and Y forces fighting in Burma. But Roosevelt made no threat to cut off aid if Chiang refused. Picking up this omission, both Chiang and Hurley rejected the President's offer in another joint message they sent on October 10. No halfway measures would suffice. Stilwell must leave China and must not command any Chinese troops in Burma. Roosevelt, Hurley declared, must immediately choose between supporting an expendable general or the "indispensable" leader of China.[47]

Hurley's messages to Roosevelt during the final stages of the command crisis revealed a skillful technique. Hurley emphasized the desperate (though not hopeless) situation in China and defended Chiang as the only leader who could prevent that nation's collapse. But since Chiang and Stilwell were "fundamentally incompatible" FDR had to choose between the two. "There is," claimed Hurley, "no other issue between you and Chiang Kai-shek." When Hurley learned that Stilwell had cabled Marshall his own opinion that "it is not a choice between throwing me out or losing CKS and possibly China. It is a case of losing China's potential effort if CKS is allowed to make rules now," Hurley again tried to simplify the issue. In a second message of October 10 the emissary wrote FDR

My opinion is that if you sustain Stilwell in this controversy you will lose Chiang Kai-shek and possibly you will lose China with him. . . .

If we permit China to collapse, if we fail to keep the Chinese army in the war, all the angels in heaven swearing that we were right in sustaining Stilwell will not change the verdict of history. America will have failed in China. . . . I respectfully recommend that you relieve General Stilwell and appoint another American general to command all the land and air forces in China under the Generalissimo.[48]

Hurley had raised an insidious issue—responsibility for "the loss of China"—which Roosevelt was loathe to accept. Chiang may well have known how far he could push the issue at this time for yet another reason. Hurley transmitted many of the most sensitive messages to FDR via the naval radio in Chungking. The U.S. Navy group in China, commanded by Commodore Miles, worked closely with the KMT secret police chief, General Tai Li. Many Americans suspected that both Hurley and Miles supplied the Chinese with copies of secret U.S. correspondence. (This question is discussed in chapter 11.)

On October 18, Roosevelt made the expedient decision to recall Stilwell. Hurley was asked to suggest the names of a possible successor and FDR soon selected General Albert Wedemeyer from among the nominees. In appointing the new commander, Roosevelt announced the division of the CBI Theater into a separate China Theater and Burma-India Theater. Wedemeyer would serve as commander of American forces and as the generalissimo's chief of staff but would not be expected to command any Chinese forces.

On October 21, after composing a sheaf of farewell letters to his friends and adversaries in China, Stilwell left his command. He would never again return to China. Gauss, now more superfluous than ever, soon resigned, with Hurley shortly assuming the title of ambassador. Chiang had accomplished one of the most crucial victories in his remarkable career.

Upon his arrival in Washington only George Marshall met Stilwell. Their discussion convinced Stilwell that he was to be kept "out of the way and muzzled until after the elections."

Henry Stimson admitted to his diary that he, among others, was treating Stilwell terribly shabbily. Nevertheless the administrations prority was "to keep him out of reach of all newsmen and not give them an opportunity to catch and distort any unwary word just before [the] election."[49]

Chapter 9
The Yenan Connection

THE HOST OF reversals which surrounded Stilwell's recall convinced a reluctant President that his policy in China resembled a double bind. The same aid and support which might make China a valuable military factor propelled the KMT regime toward renewed civil war and greater repression. This further reduced China's marginal role in the war and seemed certain to produce a long struggle in East Asia which might lead to a Communist victory or tempt Soviet intervention. Keenly aware of this dilemma, Roosevelt initiated new contacts aimed at managing both the Soviet Union and Chinese Communists. He hoped to secure (at a price, to be sure) Russian support for the Nationalists while opening a dialogue with the Communists, which might convince the revolutionaries to accept an American-sponsored coalition under Chiang's leadership.

Despite his greatly diminished faith in Chiang's abilities, the President still believed in the need to insure stability in postwar China. Even if that nation could not play the exalted role of a "great power" or "world policeman," it seemed crucial to prevent the break-up of China and the consequences of a massive, prolonged civil war. Since the greatest challenge to China's unity might come from Soviet intervention or a Communist victory, Roosevelt strove to coopt both forces. He sought to trade American approval of Soviet privileges in Manchuria for a general Russian commitment to avoid involvement in Chinese politics. At the same time, a Chinese Communist Party, cut off from Moscow and offered an American olive branch, might be pressed to compromise with the KMT. While flawed in both conception and execution, this strategy dominated Roosevelt's thinking until his death. Had the revolutionary crisis within China not been so profound, or had American behavior been much more flexible, the plan might even have succeeded.

As early as the Teheran Conference, Roosevelt and Stalin indicated their willingness to bargain over China. The Soviet leader noted his intention of declaring war on Japan shortly after Germany's defeat. While Russia would support the Nationalist regime, she expected the allies to look with favor upon the return of Manchurian port and railroad privileges which had lapsed with the Bolshevik Revolution. The President indicated his approval of such a deal, repeating the point when he met Stilwell and Davies in Cairo. Apparently, when necessary, Roosevelt would speak to Chiang as he might to "the Sultan of Morocco."

The following May—1944—as Henry Wallace was to begin his journey to China, Roosevelt discussed Moscow's attitude toward China with his hand-picked ambassador to the Kremlin, W. Averell Harriman. He wished Harriman to convey a message to Stalin that emphasized Roosevelt's belief that Chiang

was the only man who could hold China together and for that reason his government should not be undermined. If China broke apart and civil war flared up, effective resistance to the Japanese would end. The President hoped Stalin would be patient in working out a solution between Chiang and the Chinese Communists.[1]

Obviously, Roosevelt feared more than a Japanese advance in the face of civil war, since he told Wallace that if civil war broke out he might not be able to "hold the Russians in line."

This concern with damping the flames of civil war and securing Soviet nonintervention became even clearer with time. En route to Chungking in August 1944, Roosevelt's latest emissary to China, Patrick J. Hurley, made a detour to Moscow. There he called upon Foreign Minister Molotov and extracted a pledge that the Soviets would support Chiang and discourage Chinese Communist revolutionary activities. In November, just after Stilwell's recall, the President again conferred with Harriman, asking whether he could continue to rely on Stalin's cooperation in the search for a peaceful solution in China. Harriman thought "Stalin would cooperate in bringing pressure on the Communists to accept any reasonable deal that the Generalissimo might offer prior to the opening of the Russian campaign [against Japan]."[2]

All these references suggest Roosevelt believed that Soviet behavior might influence China in two distinct but related ways. Like most Americans, the President assumed an extremely close bond between Moscow and the CCP. If so, a clear demonstration of Soviet support for the KMT would bring great pressure on the Communists to accept some form of compromise political solution. Roosevelt thought Stalin could be induced to support this policy for a basic reason—national self-interest. Russia's historical concern with China centered far more directly upon acquiring control over Manchuria's ports and railroads than upon spreading Communism into China. By America agreeing to the reacquisition of these special rights in Manchuria, Stalin might well be willing to forgo political involvement in the rest of China.[3]

Ironically, though Roosevelt certainly overestimated Soviet influence in the CCP, he probably held an accurate view of how Stalin rated his priorities in China. Ever since the confusing period of the 1920s, Soviet–Chinese Communist relations were marked by misunderstanding, hostility, and dissent. After 1927 little if any Russian aid reached the Communist guerrillas. By contrast, Moscow granted the KMT hundreds of millions of dollars worth of military credits following Japan's 1937 invasion. Given the CCP's, and especially Mao's, penchant for ideological and military independence, it hardly seems likely that Stalin bore them any personal good will. Considering the Soviet dictator's immense concern for all forms of security, the prospect of a unified, powerful Chinese Communist neighbor may not have been very appealing. A divided China, or one ruled by a tottering KMT regime dependent on

Moscow's favor, may well have seemed to Stalin as an ideal arrangement. Later revelations by Yugoslav and Chinese Communist sources suggest Stalin worked to hamper a complete Communist victory in China after 1945.[4]

While our knowledge of Soviet policy toward the Chinese Communists is quite limited, we possess a far more complete record of American efforts to influence the revolutionary movement in China. During 1944 Americans, both symbolically and literally, broke through the KMT blockade of Yenan and initiated a period of intense contact with the Communists. The goals of these contacts varied widely, as they were undertaken by a diverse group of journalists, Foreign Service officers, army personnel, and OSS agents. At some level, all hoped to use the promise of American friendship as a means to influence and contain the direction of civil war and revolution.

The first Americans to break the KMT wartime blockade were a small group of journalists who had covered the war from Chungking. Frustrated by the constraints of KMT censorship, and enticed by pro- and anti-Communist propaganda which described the guerrilla war in north China, the journalists pressed a reluctant KMT to permit a delegation to travel to Yenan. Perhaps fearful of what the journalists might write if their request was refused, Chungking agreed in March 1944 to sanction the trip. Between mid-July and October, a half-dozen or so reporters representing a variety of American and British papers visited Yenan. The most prolific and incisive of the lot were Harrison Forman, Gunther Stein, Brooks Atkinson, and Theodore H. White. Their reports emphasized the simple fact that in the Communist region a popular government led the peasants in an active guerrilla campaign against the Japanese. But even these statements frightened the KMT censors who ravaged the copy before permitting it to leave China. The experience so rattled the Nationalists that by October all further visits by foreign journalists to Yenan were banned. American readers enjoyed only the barest glimpse of what Edgar Snow called "the other side of the river."[5]

The journalists' excursion represented only private American interest in the Communists. By the summer of 1944 Roosevelt was prepared to press for an oficial mission to Yenan. In June Henry Wallace formally told Chiang of Roosevelt's demand that an American delgation be permitted to meet the Communists. John Service had stressed the significance of such a project in his discussions with Wallace in Chungking. An American mission, the Foreign Service officer argued, might relieve the United States of its total dependence on the Nationalists. With American support, the Communists could emerge as a vehicle for transforming China into a viable, pro-American ally. Washington must quickly demonstrate a will to aid any Chinese group which would fight Japan and promise to cooperate with the United States. As something of an afterthought, Service remarked that this involved only "very modified and indirect intervention in Chinese affairs."[6] While Service envisioned a far more profound relationship with the Communists than did Roosevelt, his enthusiasm reflected the new mood among a wide array of American officials concerned with China.

Reluctantly bowing to pressure, Chiang authorized the dispatch of a small American mission to Yenan. The United States Army Observer Group (informally called Dixie because of its location in "rebel territory") began filtering into the Communist capital by early July. Led by Colonel David D. Barrett, this small group (fluctuating between one and two dozen men) of military observers and technicians was supplemented by a sprinkling of embassy political officers, OSS operatives, and apparently an informer working for Naval Group China and the KMT secret police. Each component of the group has a distinct function. Barrett supervised the mission, though he later became involved in several military schemes. Political advisors Raymond Ludden and John Service were expected to investigate the nature of Communist policies toward the United States and Soviet Union. The OSS officers were to explore the possibilities of utilizing Communist guerrilla forces against

Japan. Both these political and military questions quickly embroiled the Dixie Mission and Washington more deeply in the incipient civil war. This new proximity permitted the Chinese Communists and a small group of Americans to confront problems fundamental to the future of China and Asia.

Before July 1944 few Americans knew virtually anything about Chinese Communist views of the United States. The little that was known came second hand. As early as 1936 Mao had told Edgar Snow that he included America as a potential ally against Japan. In the two years before the Pearl Harbor attack the Communist press berated Washington for giving China (which in this case meant the KMT) far too little aid, and for implicity encouraging a "Far Eastern Munich" between the KMT and Tokyo. When the United States entered the war, however, the CCP applauded the American war effort and portrayed the United States as a progressive ally against fascism. More specifically, the Communists applauded both Roosevelt and Wallace as progressive heroes fighting against American reactionaries.[7]

Chou En-lai, who served as the CCP representative in Chungking, did everything imaginable to court the personal friendship of Americans. He continually invited embassy staff and journalists to informal discussions and weekly teas, even sending birthday cards on occasion. Chou's public demeanor seemed confirmed by the text of a speech he gave in Yenan in August 1943, somehow obtained by American military intelligence. The CCP's unofficial foreign minister told his audience that before long the United States would grow weary of the incompetent Nationalists. They would look to the Communists for assistance in fighting Japan. At that time it might be possible for Yenan to secure American political recognition and military aid.

Chou proceeded to discuss another major political theme, the relationship between the CCP and the Soviet Union. He declared that the Communists led an independent revolutionary movement, that the history of the Party was marked by

"Comrade Mao's idea to form a line for Chinese Communism—to make Marxism and Leninism Chinese."[8] Chou's speech coincided with the major "thought reform" campaign then being waged to purge pro-Soviet elements from leading positions in the Party. The fact that he linked discussion of this with the prospect of American cooperation seemed to reveal his desire to maintain a pragmatic and independent stance.

The American observer most sensitive to this point, both before and after he joined the Dixie Mission, was John Service. His childhood in China gave him an unusual insight into Chinese thought and politics. Between July and November 1944 Service prepared extensive, incisive, reports from Yenan. In March 1945 he again visited the Communist capital, at which time he was removed at the insistence of Patrick Hurley. His reports provide a unique glimpse into the shattered dawn of American–Chinese Communist cooperation.

Probably nothing better characterized the atmosphere of the mission and his reports than did a single sentence written on July 28. "We have come into a different country and are meeting a different people."[9] The Communist capital of Yenan seemed both a city and a state of mind nearly opposite to Chungking. Nestled in the loess hills of north China, it reflected the élan and optimism of an emerging new society. Relations between the city residents, peasants, and Communist officials appeared relaxed and informal. Party leaders walked about without noticeable protection, while Chairman Mao would frequently appear at impromptu weekend dances to which all might come. Not only American observers but Mao Tse-tung himself came to look upon the Yenan period as the "golden age" of Chinese Communism.

Service seemed able to speak with almost everyone in Yenan, from Mao down to the most junior Communist official. All voiced one thought: a desire to cooperate with the United States in the struggle to defeat Japan and build a new China. Service believed the Communists espoused a moderate revolutionary program, well suited to China and deserving of American support. The Communists were willing to work with both Chiang and Washington provided this meant a real sharing of power.[10] Giving the Americans every sign of their interest in furthering cooperation, Yenan radio even began to beam English-language broadcasts to San Francisco.

This symoblic act preceded the really significant initiative which Mao undertook on August 23, 1944. In what appears to be a remarkably personal and open manner, the leader of the Communist Party spoke with Service about the opportunity for cooperation with the United States. The defeat of Japan, he remarked, would turn the KMT back to the path of civil war. Chiang's party, Mao asserted, was an "amorphous body . . . divided into jealous cliques" that were all "anticommunist and antidemocratic." They were united only by "their selfish determination to perpetuate their own power." Any hope for preventing civil war depended on the ability of outside powers to restrain the Kuomintang. "Among these, by far the most important is the United States." American policy, Mao told Service, was of vital concern to the "democratic peoples of China." The Communists' broad terms for political compromise in China included the basic demand that the Chinese government "broaden its base to take in all important groups . . . to convene a provisional (or transitional) National Congress." Delegates from all parties should attend this congress which would then reorganize the government and make new laws until a formal constitutional structure was created.

Mao wished to know if "the American government" were willing to make such a proposal and to "force the Kuomintang to" accept it. In addition the Chairman specifically desired information on Washington's current attitude toward the Communists. "Does it recognize the Communist Party as an active fighting force against Japan? Does it recognize The Communists as an influence for democracy in China?" On what basis would Washington choose sides in a civil war? How would it insure that the KMT would not use American aid against the Communists? Mao felt the Ulnited States was mistaken in exclusively supporting the KMT. Neither political nor military results justified American policy. The Communist leader had some tough advice for Washington:

Chiang is stubborn. But fundamentally he is a gangster. That fact must be understood in order to deal with him. We have had to learn it by experience. . . . You must not give way to his threats and bullying. Do not let him think you are afraid; then he will press his advantage.[11]

The United States ought not to "cultivate, baby, or placate Chiang" any longer. The United States must "tell Chiang what he should do."

The Chinese Communists, Mao declared, were deeply interested in encouraging friendship between themselves and Washington. Naturally, they would be grateful for any wartime aid that might be offered. The Communists did not expect Russian help, Mao explained, but neither would the Soviets "oppose American interests in China if they are constructive and democratic." A progressive postwar China would be a stabilizing force in Asia and a vast economic area for the United States as well. "Even the most conservative American businessman can find nothing in our program to take exception to," Mao told Service. Imparting to Service the impression that Yenan could deliver what America wanted, Mao left the added implication that he preferred to deal with Washington rather than Moscow.

America does not need to fear that we will not be cooperative. We must cooperate and we must have American help. This is why it is so important to us Communists to know what you Americans are thinking and planning. We cannot risk crossing you—cannot risk conflict with you.[12]

While Mao may well have exaggerated the compatibility of long-term Communist and American goals, and may have laid on a bit heavily some references to the China Market, there is little reason to doubt the sincerity which underlay his remarks. This does not mean Mao should be interpreted as a "liberal," a mere agrarian reformer, or a crypto-capitalist. Broad cooperation with the United States seemed very much in Yenan's self-interest. At this stage in their history, the Communists lacked very much of a "sophisticated" foreign policy. They were in the midst of a military struggle for survival against both the Japanese and the KMT, while simultaneously developing a strategy to press forward with an agrarian revolution. Relations between the CCP and Moscow were at best tenuous. Mao's ongoing purge of CCP members with a background of Soviet training made this clear.

Furthermore, the Chinese Communist outlook must have been influenced by the basic question of who could give them outside political and military support. For at least the short run, the United States seemed by far the best prospect. It alone might provide aid and restrain Chiang's drive to precipitate full-scale internal warfare. Since Mao surely believed that time was on his side, encouraging cooperation or a modus vivendi with Washington seemed the only prudent course. Whatever Mao's deeper thoughts about U.S.–Chinese Communist relations may have been, nothing in his ideological baggage or current requirements argued against greater cooperation and friendship. Considering Mao's fundamental commitment to nationalism, it is difficult to believe he wanted to limit his options to dependence on the Soviet Union. When these factors are added to the personal élan and enthusiasm shown by Americans in Yenan, we can see several genuine reasons which underlay the Communist approach to the United States.

Yet, in many ways the Dixie Mission contained the seeds of its own destruction. Dixie consisted of a mere handful of talented, energetic, but very junior army, OSS, and State Department officers. They were responsible for conducting what amounted to a full range of diplomacy with an insurgent movement. Their own exuberance tended to amplify the already distorted view the Communists had of the Mission's importance. Since the Communists wanted American friends, they attributed wide-ranging powers to their guests. Every nuance of conversation, every pistol given as a personal gift, could be interpreted as a promise from Washington. Even though Hopkins spoke to Davies of his own and Roosevelt's interest in reports from Yenan, this remained something of a curiosity in the White House. The President seemed primarily interested in intelligence gathering and utilizing Dixie as a lever to maneuver both Chinese factions into a crude coalition. Neither Roosevelt's words nor actions indicated he planned to support the Communists, either independently or against the KMT.

Nevertheless John Service realized immediately that Mao's thoughts were potentially as important to the United States as to Yenan. Communist power was undeniably growing, the base of its support being extended among the peasantry. The danger of civil war continually increased and with it grew the likelihood of some form of Russian intervention. If, as seemed probable, the Communists were going to control at least part of China permanently, then Washington must consider the advantages of dealing with this reality. Moreover, Service noted, American aid to Yenan would "affect the nature, policies and objectives of the Chinese Communist Party, which was of vital, long term concern to the United States." [13]

Even before Service came to suggest the possibility of independent American military cooperation with the Communists, members of the OSS team in Yenan broached the proposal. By August 7 the OSS had already begun detailed discussions with Communist military personnel about assistance which might be given to OSS operations and training which OSS might provide to Communist units. In its earliest form this plan envisioned the creation of an American training program in Yenan teaching selected students communications, demolition, and espionage skills. Sometime in September, joint OSS and specially trained and equipped Communist units might begin anti-Japanese operations. [14]

By August 30, OSS personnel had actually started simple training classes in the use of American explosives and small arms. These demonstrations were attended by over one thousand officers and men of the 18th Group (Communist) Army. The Americans in charge of these demonstrations were quite impressed by the enthusiasm and skills of their audience.[15]

The reports from Yenan by Service and his OSS counterparts arrived in Stilwell's headquarters and in Washington just as the command crisis between Stilwell and Chiang approached its climax. Deeply troubled by the possibility that once in command Stilwell would aid Yenan, Chiang called in Ambassador Gauss on August 31 to complain about American meddling with the Communists. The generalissimo protested certain unspecified military and political complications which were arising out of the Dixie Mission. Gauss and the China expert of the State Department, John Carter Vincent, apparently hoped Chiang would learn a lesson from this. Vincent expected the generalissimo to realize that time was on Yenan's side, that unless he reached a peaceful accommodation with the Communists he was finished.[16] This optimistic hope was not borne out by Chiang's behavior.

As the crisis over command built up, Service's Yenan reports increasingly reflected the central dispute over military aid. OSS activities had obviously given rise to Communist hopes for further aid. Stilwell's desire to command Chinese troops in combat was widely known, and on September 25 Communist military commander Chu Teh announced his support for the appointment of an American commander over all Chinese armies. Chu also warned Service that a cabal led by KMT secret police chief Tai Li and elements in the American Naval Group China was planning to sabotage the Dixie Mission because of its support for the Communist position.[17] Until he learned of Stilwell's recall, Service's reports from Yenan continued to call for American political and military support of Yenan. American aid, he argued, would actually restrain civil war and would certainly prevent any Communist tendency to turn toward the Russians. By mid-October, Service looked forward to the creation of a new Chinese government in which the Communists held real power and received a proportional share of American aid. This, Service suggested, was the only possible arrangement which might lead to success for American policy.[18]

To Colonel David Barrett, the generally apolitical head of the mission to Yenan, Mao made much the same point as he had to Service. The United States, out of its own self-interest, should not commit itself to Chiang's survival. Commitment would only promote civil war, which the Nationalists would probably lose. Their defeat would be seen by most Chinese as a defeat for America as well.[19]

Reports from Dixie were widely circulated among embassy and military staff in China, so widely that they even got back to the Nationalists through friendly elements in the Navy Department. As mentioned earlier, when John Davies spoke with Harry Hopkins in September 1944, the presidential aide remarked that both he and Roosevelt were impressed by the reports and encouraged by the Communists' apparent willingness to cooperate with U.S. forces. The Treasury Department's agents in Chungking, Irving Friedman and Solomon Adler (who shared a house with Service), forwarded copies of important reports on the Communists, along with their own comments, to Morgenthau and his aide, Harry Dexter White. Friedman noted that the reports from Yenan were having a stirring effect upon Americans in China, that "U.S. military men here vie for the opportunity to go up there and see the situation for themselves." Both Friedman and Adler endorsed the general policies advocated by John Service, stressing that it was now up to Washington to decide whether the United States was going to face the Communists as a friend or enemy.

Friedman particularly worried over the implications of the Hurley-Nelson mission, which had recently (September 1944) arrived in Chungking. At the very moment a line was being opened toward Yenan, Hurley gave evidence of a new American effort to prop up an unpopular and failing regime. Despite these warnings, there is no indication that Morgenthau was moved to intervene on Stilwell's behalf. All his thoughts and energies at this time seem to have been devoted to get Roosevelt to accept a harsh program for postwar Germany.[20]

By October it seemed clear that Communist-American contacts, aid to Yenan, and the demand for Stilwell's recall were part of the same issue. Stilwell's political advisor, John Davies, drove home this point in messages to his chief. Davies was convinced that American policy in China was doomed unless the Joint Chiefs could be induced to support a new military effort under Stilwell. To seize the initiative, Davies and Dorn developed a plan to land American forces in north China in cooperation with the Communists. Communist forces would be provided with American arms and enlisted under American command. This held the key to both military and political success, Davies asserted. He wanted Stilwell's permission for himself and Dorn to fly to Yenan to develop this plan.[21]

Before any of what Service, Davies, or the OSS advocated was accomplished, Stilwell himself was removed from China. Suddenly, in October 1944, an entirely new political and military line emanated from the Chungking embassy and the China Theater headquarters. Roosevelt, who had appeared to be steering in the directuon of a new policy, again changed course. The U.S. government would pursue a policy of utilizing Soviet interests to undercut the Communists in China. Within China itself, virtually unqualified political support would be given Chiang Kai-shek. This support was not, however, given in order to encourage civil war and the destruction of the Communists. Rather, it assumed, once Yenan was deprived of any hope of foreign aid, Chiang would be prepared to offer more generous terms than before and the Communists would have no choice but to accept.

By itself, however, Stilwell's removal did not break the gathering momentum within China to effect a Communist-American alliance. The Dixie Mission, members of the embassy staff, OSS officers, and elements within the American army staff in China continued to push strenuously for the acceptance of the Communists into the American camp. The Communists themselves redoubled their efforts to win support, appealing to every American agency and individual they could contact. Yet all of this effort was foredoomed by decisions already reached by the President. Foremost among these actions was the permanent retention of Hurley as ambassador to China and the elevation of General Wedemeyer as American theater commander. In tandem, they purged the American ranks of Communist sympathizers and sought to bolster Chiang's position amidst all the contending Chinese factions.

Almost from the moment of his arrival in China, Patrick Hurley took it as his mission to achieve the unification of all Chinese military and political groups under the leadership of Chiang Kai-shek. The existing Nationalist regime was to be preserved, with the so-called minority parties and armed groups subordinated in a vague, powerless coalition. Both Roosevelt and the State Department, informed of these policies, did little to inhibit Hurley's activities. The President, in a rambling conversation with the Cabinet in December 1944, defended Hurley, complimenting the new ambassador for the "swell job" he was doing.[22] During the few remaining months of his life, Roosevelt never had occasion to criticize Hurley.

The Communists, realizing Hurley's potential influence, began a vain effort to woo him soon after he arrived in China. In September 1944 Chu Teh extended initial feelers, inviting the President's representative to Yenan. Hurley was reluctant to accept until his own status and that of Stilwell had been clarified. After Stilwell's recall, two Communist representatives in Chungking, Lin Tsu-han and Tung Pi-wu, finally met Hurley to discuss what they called "some problems of China." The list of Communist proposals presented by these men on October 23 went far beyond anything either he or Chiang had considered. The Communists sought Hurley's aid in establishing a true political coalition to rule China. The Communist Party and others were to be legalized and allowed to participate in the national government on a basis of equality with the KMT. A "joint high command," with full Communist participation, would be established over the armed forces. Finally, there would be an equal distribution of American military aid.[23]

Hurley and Chiang thought in far more restricted terms. Four days before receiving the Communist proposals, Hurley informed Roosevelt that he was hopeful of success in his effort to place the Communists *under* Chiang's control. Chiang, more confident of Soviet support, was willing to postpone civil war. Hurley further explained that all he or Chiang was prepared to offer the Communists in return for their surrender of independent military power was a pledge of gradual democratic political evolution in the Nationalist regime. Not surprisingly, Chiang personally commended Hurley's efforts to Roosevelt.[24]

Despite Hurley's initial actions, other Americans continued to anticipate and work for direct cooperation with Yenan. During the last few days of October and early November, John Davies, Service (who was about to return to Washington), and a third Foreign Service officer, John K. Emmerson, gathered in Yenan to explore with Mao, Chou, and Chu Teh the possibility of joint Communist-American military action. The Communists again declared their great interest in military cooperation, offering to assist American units in north China.

Davies' own thoughts ran in several directions. Concerned more with long-term political developments than with immediate military strategy, his mind

turned in search of other areas of possible common interest between the United States and the Chinese Communists. How might we draw them away from future reliance on the Soviet Union and into dependence on the United States? Mao had insisted to Service that he wanted American help in industrializing a future communist China. In terms of their own interests I tried indirectly to induce Chou to spell out their concept of economic collaboration with the United States. . . .[25]

Both the Communists and Davies discussed the attractions which a stable China—Communist or otherwise—might have for American investors. With the right approach, Davies believed, the Communists were "bound to attract the attention and interest of the American ruling class." Buoyed by the Communists' favorable response to all American suggestions, Davies took the initiative of strongly urging Hurley to visit Yenan. The issue, he told the Presidential emissary, was one of preserving in East Asia a balance of power friendly to the United States.

Chou continued to impress Davies with generous offers of Communist military cooperation in any plans the United States wished to undertake in north China. The Communists even professed a desire to conduct joint staff talks with the Americans. These promises, which seemed so genuine and mutually beneficial, prompted Davies to prepare three memoranda for his superiors in Chungking and Washington. The Communists, Davies concluded, were a flexible and responsible political faction, prepared to cooperate with the United States on many issues. To work with Yenan, however, the United States would have to forego its open commitment to Chiang.[26] In Davies' view, civil war was inevitable and a Communist victory almost as certain. The issue which Washington had to face was whether it would get sucked into the battle on Chiang's side, forcing Yenan to turn toward the Soviet Union. Davies, of course, urged an immediate American decision to "tilt" toward the Communists in the coming struggle for China.

In reports he sent to the OSS theater and Washington headquarters, Captain Stelle asserted that the Communist position in North China was largely invulnerable to Japanese or KMT conquest. In time, following Japan's defeat, both their military and popular strength would grow still larger. Stelle acknowledged that the Communists were genuine revolutionaries who had "sympathy with Russia," but saw no evidence that Yenan was in thrall to Moscow. Instead, the Communist leaders appeared to believe that "the actions of the United States will determine the immediate trend of events and thus their own long term policy." Should the U.S. continue to supply the KMT after civil war crupted, Stelle warned, Yenan would seek Russian assistance "against what they would undoubtedly regard as American intervention in Chinese affairs."[27]

Naturally, not all Americans in Yenan indulged in such *Realpolitik* planning. OSS ideas of how to woo Communist cooperation sometimes took what might be seen as humorous turns. One message to Washington headquarters included a request for vitamins and "assorted children's picture books and playthings for children." The hard-nosed OSS operatives also believed that the way to a Chinese Communist's heart might be through his wife. Accordingly, Major Ray Cromley pressed Washington to quickly send "assorted magazines such as *Ladies' Home Journal, Woman's Home Companion*, and *Good Housekeeping* for the wives of Chinese army officers." Colonel Barrett expanded the request to include peanuts and "25 Parker fountain pens"—shades of cultural imperialism![28]

On November 7, ten days after receiving Davies' plea that he travel to the Communist capital, Hurley prepared to act. General Wedemeyer had arrived in China, allowing Hurley to absent himself from full-time presence in Chungking. Moreover, the President's emissary had now joined the charmed circle of Americans following in the path of the ubiquitous T. V. Soong, who had regained some of his political clout through his part in engineering the Stilwell recall. Now Soong and his remaining American supporters pushed for the creation of a Hurley-Soong alliance.

Late in October, Hurley had received a detailed twelve-page memorandum which argued in favor of linking American support to Soong and Ch'en Ch'eng. Possibly written by Joseph Alsop, this proposal urged Hurley to work through Soong and Ch'en to root out the orthodox, conservative KMT leaders and replace them with pro-American modernists. The alternative, the writer warned, was a Chinese Communist victory and Russian control of China. Here, interestingly, was a mirror vision of what Davies and Service predicted, only with the Soong camp playing the "progressive" anti-Soviet role of the Communists.[29]

Acting in accordance with these recommendations, Hurley began to collaborate closely with Soong. The foreign minister even provided Hurley with a secret code which could be used to contact him. Soong emerged as Hurley's "advisor" on the Communists and now urged that he make his journey to Yenan. What appeared to make the Nationalists more willing to see Hurley attempt this mediation was a simultaneous report that the Soviet chargé in Chungking had approached Chiang Ching-kuo, the generalissimo's son, about a possible meeting between Stalin and Chiang Kai-shek. To some in Chungking this seemed to indicate a desertion of Yenan by Stalin. All parts of the puzzle seemed to be falling perfectly into place. [30]

Responding to these political signs as well as to his own irrepressible instincts, Hurley, on November 7, without any advance notice, boarded an American plane bound for Yenan. The arriving flight was met as usual on the makeshift runway by Colonel Barrett and Chou En-lai. When Hurley emerged dressed in his splendidly tailored uniform and bedecked with medals, Chou asked Barrett the identity of the handsome American. " 'That is Major General Patrick Joseph Hurley, and he is a special emissary of President Roosevelt,' replied Barrett. . . . 'Keep him here until I can find Chairman Mao, said Chou, and he dashed off to town." Hurley's idea of protocol on this occasion was to utter a bloodcurdling Choctaw Indian war cry as he deplaned. Not surprisingly, other Americans in Yenan later overheard Mao describe Hurley as "the clown." With Hurley's spectacular presence there was no longer room for John Davies in Yenan, and he was quickly ordered to return to Chungking lest he interfere with the President's representative. [31]

Discussions between Hurley (with Barrett and an American translator and secretary) and the Communist leaders (Mao, Chou, and Chu Teh) began on November 8, 1944. Hurley told Mao he had come to Yenan as Roosevelt's personal representative to "discuss matters pertaining to China." Chiang, he claimed, approved of this mission of American mediation to promote democracy and speed the defeat of Japan through the "unification of Chinese military forces." To accomplish this goal, Hurley said, the generalissimo was prepared to recognize the legality of the Communist and minority parties and allow some form of Communist participation on the Supreme War Council.

Although Hurley had originally planned to ask the CCP to subscribe to a broad declaration in support of the Nationalist regime, the nature of Mao's remarks made it clear that any "unity proposals" must include a procedure for the true sharing of military and political power and American aid by the Communists. Consequently, Hurley revealed a new document produced by himself. This so-called Five Point Proposal called for both the CCP and KMT to pledge to work for political and military unity. The existing central government and its military organs were to be reorganized as a broad-based "Coalition National Government." This new government and the KMT would adhere to a set of principles closely paralleling the American Bill of Rights. Finally, the proposal ran, American military aid would be equally distributed by the ruling coalition.

Stunned by the largesse of this offer, Mao pressed Hurley for the source of its authorship. The American admitted it was wholly his own but believed Chiang would accept it. In fact, Hurley was even prepared to invite Mao to Chungking to speak with the generalissimo. It is almost impossible to believe that Hurley really expected the KMT to accept this proposal as even a draft of a settlement. Nevertheless, he may have hoped that the Five Points would seduce the Communists into at least sending a negotiator to Chungking, where more serious talks might begin. Realizing that his party had nothing to lose by endorsing the generous document, Mao consented to Hurley's request that the two of them sign copies of the Five Point Proposal, which were to be taken back to Chungking.[32]

Superficially at least, it seemed as if the Communists had won Hurley over to their position. He had arrived in Yenen seemingly in the KMT hip pocket. After three days he had prepared a proposal for political compromise which embodied many of the basic reforms that Yenan had demanded and all of which Chungking opposed. Whether or not Mao and his companions really believed these proposals would ever be accepted is hard to know. They did, however, take Hurley's efforts seriously enough to dispatch Chou En-lai to Chungking to begin discussions with the Nationalists.

Neither Hurley's optimism nor possibly that of Yenan was shared by other knowledgeable Americans. Both John Davies and the OSS contingent in Yenan predicted failure in the Chungking negotiations and the arrival of a new moment of truth for American policy. Davies predicated his advice to Hurley on the assumption that no coalition was going to be achieved. While it was not necessary to abandon Chiang completely, the United States should be prepared to extend de facto recognition and aid to the Communists. Only this action could prevent Yenan from falling under Soviet influence, especially if Russia entered the war through Manchuria. Support for the Communists, Davies again declared, was the best way to "align ourselves behind the most coherent, progressive and powerful force in China."[33]

Even more dramatic action was proposed by Captain Charles Stelle, with the OSS in Yenan. Forecasting the breakdown in political discussions, he urged OSS headquarters in Washington to approve the creation of a large-scale "clandestine" Secret Operations program in Yenan. Stelle hoped that either Hurley or General Wedemeyer could be persuaded to make this case with the President. Even if Chiang refused to sanction American military cooperation with Yenan, the OSS would be prepared to "carry out a disownable" military program with the Communists.[34]

The Communists themselves responded to Hurley's visit in at least one way which demonstrated that they shared many of Davies' and Stelle's doubts about Hurley. They took advantage of Treasury Representative Irving Friedman's return to Washington by handing him a letter for personal delivery to

Morgenthau. The message, written by Chou En-lai, expressed keen disappointment at the KMT's failure to reform political rule in China. The Communist spokesman hoped that the Treasury Secretary would involve himself again in China policy, taking advantage of Yenan's deep interest in all forms of economic, military, and political cooperation with the United States. Finally, Chou included an invitation that Morgenthau personally visit Yenan to solidify relations and observe the potential for cooperation between Americans and Chinese Communists.[35]

Davies' and Stelle's ideas, as well as the approach to Morgenthau, ran counter not only to Nationalist power but also to the quirks in Hurley's policy. Upon his return to Chungking Hurley was apprised of two facts: Chiang and Soong were furious at the Five Points; and it was announced on November 17 that Roosevelt had formally appointed Hurley as ambassador. The new ambassador fell increasingly under the sway of Chiang and Soong. While his papers do not specifically reflect the process of his own alienation from Yenan, the movement is clearly there. It was one of the many imponderables surrounding everything that Hurley did.

The political discussions in Chungking reached an impasse on November 21, 1944, when Chou received the KMT rejoinder to the Five Point Proposal. The three-point counteroffer was a rehash of old KMT demands calling for the CCP to submit control of its armed forces to the Nationalist government in return for some token political representation. Chou was understandably disappointed by the Nationalist offer. Even more troubling were his discussions with Hurley and General Wedemeyer, in which the Americans insisted that there were positive elements to the KMT's proposals. Unmoved, Chou resolved to break off talks and return to Yenan. When bad weather delayed his flight until December 8, the tensions both in his own mind and in Yenan escalated. Colonel Barrett was sent along with Chou to attempt to keep the door open for further negotiations.

The Communist reaction to these developments came directly from Mao through Barrett. Mao staged a careful performance, balancing threats, rage, and pleas. Why, he asked, had the Americans raised hopes for a genuine coalition in the Five Points and then asked Yenan to "tie its hands behind itself" by accepting Chiang's three points? Did the Americans take the Communists for fools? Yenan was not a basket case, dependent on the goodwill of others. If no coalition was possible, then the Communists would move to establish a separate Chinese government. The formal existence of two Chinese governments would obviously destroy all pretensions and hopes for Chinese unity.

Menacingly, Mao told Barrett that if American aid was not forthcoming, Yenan could still turn to England or Russia. This, of course, was exactly what the United States hoped to prevent. (Hurley was so disturbed by the possibility of British intervention that he held meetings with the British ambassador and warned Roosevelt about British meddling with the Communists.) Mao concluded his heated presentation to Barrett with an offer and a threat. Whatever the outcome of the political duel with the Nationalists, Mao noted, the Communists and Americans still might be able to salvage their relations through military cooperation. The Communists would cooperate in joint operations and would willingly serve alongside or even under American forces. Mao's suggestion must have been influenced by the positive indications Yenan continued to receive from the local OSS contingent.

The threat relayed by Mao was directed personally at Hurley. The ambassador had insisted that both he and Mao sign the Five Point Proposal as testimony to their reasonableness. Very well. Mao now intended to release the signed proposals and let everyone see the reasonable document which Chiang refused to endorse. This would obviously embarrass Hurley, who now insisted that Yenan accept the radically different KMT Three Points and forget the Five Points.[36]

When Barrett brought word of Mao's reaction and threat

back to Chungking on December 9, Hurley became livid with rage. "The mother—. . . ," yelled the ambassador," he tricked meh [sic]!" Hurley had now fully parted ways with the Communists. He would neither knuckle under to their threats nor admit that he himself had caused the Communists to make those threats. Instead, he would increasingly turn to his implicit alliance with Chiang and Soong and reject the advice of all those in Yenan and Chungking who seemed to be betraying him. The first victim was the one closest at hand, John Davies, the epitome of those who favored supporting the Communists. Hurley ordered Davies to leave China quickly to accept a new post in the Moscow embassy. Thus began the first purge of the many messengers who brought bad news to the ambassador.[37] In Chungking parlance, they were "Hurleyed out of China."

If Hurley and Chiang had abandoned the search for a political compromise, the Communists had not. For both positive and negative reasons the Communists were compelled to try to win and maintain America's friendship. They could not afford to allow the United States to become an unquestioning ally of Chiang any more than they could afford to ignore an opportunity to win some measure of American support for themselves. What this essentially meant was that the Communists would try to achieve military collaboration with friendly American elements without the intervention of the troublesome Hurley. This type of secret military alliance was precisely what had been advocated by the OSS in Yenan. From mid-December 1944 until early January 1945, the Communists engaged in a desperate gamble to circumvent Hurley and Chiang and establish a direct military and political liaison with Washington. It was not to America's diplomats that Yenan would look for favor, but to its soldiers.

Chapter 10
The Connection Broken

THE SIMULTANEOUS COLLAPSE of political negotiations in Chungking and Hurley's emergence as a Nationalist partisan compelled the Communists to alter radically their approach to the United States. As those Americans who supported cooperation with Yenan lost influence, the Communists desperately sought to communicate with President Roosevelt. Both in China and in Washington, however, the molders of policy chose to ignore or reject the prospect of working independently with the Communists. Despite some conciliatory gestures, American policy focused almost solely on the question of how to minimize Communist power, through either cooperation with the Soviet Union or bolstering the KMT. From December 1944 until June 1945, the pattern, so dreary and unrelieved, was punctuated only by Yenan's tenacity in struggling against the tide.

Stilwell's departure, Hurley's growing hostility, and the diminished power of the KMT in many areas as a result of the ICHIGO offense were all factors propelling the CCP to think in terms of expanded military action. During December Mao and the Communist press de-emphasized the likelihood of achieving a coalition with the KMT and stressed the need for Yenan to bolster its guerrilla forces for both independent action and possible collaboration with American forces.

When, on December 8, 1944, Chou En-lai told Hurley of his refusal to continue talks on the basis of the KMT's Three Points, he carefully avoided shutting the door on direct cooperation with the United States. In fact, Chou specifically referred to the Communists' desire to explore with Americans "concrete problems of our future military cooperation." Hurley refused to discuss joint military operations, prompting Yenan to seek out Americans opposed to the ambassador's policy.[1]

The Communists, who hoped to follow up on Stilwell's proposals for combined operations, had little success with General Albert Wedemeyer, the new theater commander. Both a politically conservative individual and an officer devoted to "regular" staff procedures, Wedemeyer preferred to cooperate with Chiang and defer to his authority. The generalissimo and Wedemeyer established a pattern of regular meetings designed to avoid personal misunderstandings. As these began in November, Chiang persuaded Wedemeyer to abandon the idea of shifting troops from the northwest (where they stood guard over the Communists) to the south, or of arming the Communists. He even got the American commander to consent to recall from Burma some units of the Y-Force. Further testing his new "chief of staff," Chiang complained that Chennault, in an effort to save his air bases, had distributed weapons to the troops of Hsueh Yueh, an old rival. On November 30 Wedemeyer agreed to order Chennault to cease any weapons distribution not authorized by Chiang, regardless of its purpose.[2]

Although he remained opposed to aiding the Communists without Chiang's approval, Wedemeyer retained some interest in utilizing Communist guerrillas against the Japanese. Thus, when Colonel Barrett submitted to headquarters a plan for "possible use of Communist guerrillas," the American commander dutifully presented them to the generalissimo. Barrett's idea of arming five thousand soldiers under American supervision infuriated Chiang. He denounced the plan as "unthinkable" and told Wedemeyer it represented how Americans in the Dixie Mission "did not quite understand Chinese conditions."[3]

Despite Wedemeyer's sincere desire to heed Chiang's edicts, a question remained whether the theater commander could actually enforce them on Americans. Both the OSS and Dixie Mission had grown accustomed to functioning on a semiautonomous basis and vigorously supported the idea of utilizing Communist forces. General William Donovan, OSS commander, was himself due to arrive in China shortly and Wedemeyer expected him to push for joint action. To preclude such a move, the army general decided to have his own staff, headed by General Robert McClure, prepare a set of contingency plans for cooperation with the Communists. In conversations with KMT General Ch'en Ch'eng, however, McClure stressed the limited scope of this plan and the fact that nothing would be done without express approval from Hurley and Chiang.[4]

The question of military cooperation, seen as crucial by the Communists, dominated every aspect of American activity in China during December and January. On December 15, 1944, John Davies, Colonel Barrett, and Colonel Willis H. Bird of the OSS flew to Yenan. The two military officers carried separate proposals for guerrilla operations. Barrett believed he was transmitting a plan approved by Hurley and Wedemeyer for the dispatch of four or five thousand American commandos to Communist territory.[5] Bird discussed with Communist leaders a separate OSS proposal to supply twenty-five thousand Red troops and establish a joint intelligence network.

Communist leaders, undoubtedly hoping that both Barrett and Bird spoke on behalf of high American authorities, found new hope. They told Bird that "the people of north China looked upon the United States as their best friend, and General Wedemeyer as the commander-in-chief, and would follow his military orders if he chose to give them." Sensing that they could work with a new American faction, the CCP rejected Hurley's renewed demand that Chou return to Chungking. All they would concede to the outraged ambassador was a promise to postpone publicizing Hurley's signature on the Five Points.[6]

When John Davies flew back to Chungking on December 17, Hurley attacked him with the charge that he had persuaded the Communists to break off further political discussions. Citing evidence from T. V. Soong, the ambassador claimed that

Davies' and Barrett's secret machinations were solely responsible for the recalcitrant Communist position, and he ordered Davies to leave China immediately and assume new duties in the Moscow embassy. In a letter to his former boss, General Joseph Stilwell, Davies dryly noted how oblivious Hurley seemed to the "vast and impersonal forces now at work in China."[7]

Denials of treason meant little to Hurley, convinced as he was that the impasse in his mediation efforts lay entirely in personal disloyalty and the undercover meddling of "British imperialism." Hurley's hope of quickly subduing his opponents, as he told the President and the State Department, was overoptimistic. As the ambassador partly realized, the Communists were convinced that American military and diplomatic officials in China were vying with Hurley for influence. This belief was reinforced when Colonel Barrett returned to Yenan on December 27 carrying additional contingency plans for cooperation, supposedly drafted by McClure. The prospect thrilled the Communist leadership, who saw it as a way of circumventing both Hurley and the KMT. Chou En-lai felt confident enough to send Hurley a hectoring message that he would never resume "abstract discussions" with the KMT until the blockade of Yenan was lifted, political prisoners were released, repression of political dissent ceased, and the Five Point Plan was accepted as the basis for all negotiations.[8] Only renewed confidence in the prospect of American military support would have led Yenan to so completely slam the door in Hurley's face.

Now that the Communists had publicly and privately committed themselves against Hurley (the Party press carried a brief, condescending notice of Hurley presenting his formal diplomatic credentials to Chiang in early January), and since they had faith in the existence of a sympathetic faction in the army and OSS, Mao and Chou prepared to take a major gamble. On January 9, 1945, they handed Major Roy Cromley (of the OSS and acting commander of Dixie) a message to be sent directly to Washington through military channels. Hurley was not to be told that the CCP wished to dispatch an "unofficial group to interpret and explain to American civilians and officials" the complex problems of China. If Roosevelt would receive them as "leaders of a primary Chinese party," Mao and Chou would travel to Washington.[9]

This startling proposal revealed the lengths to which the CCP was prepared to go in its effort to win American support and a measure of international legitimacy. The journey to Washington would put additional distance between Yenan and Moscow, simultaneously raising the status of the Communists from an insurgent group to an ally in the joint war effort. Clearly, Mao and Chou believed it absolutely necessary to circumvent the Hurley-Chiang blockade and bring their case directly to American "friends" and "progressives" of the highest order. The Communists retained a certain faith in Roosevelt, despite what they must have seen as Hurley's distortion of his policies.

Not only did the secret mission to Washington not go forward, but word of it set in motion a disastrous chain of events for the Communists. Wedemeyer's growing knowledge of the freewheeling style of the Dixie Mission and OSS prompted him, on December 29, to assert control over all OSS clandestine, guerrilla, and intelligence activities by Americans in China.[10] By itself, this would have prevented independent OSS operations with the Communists. Yenan's attempt to circumvent Hurley came to naught almost as quickly. Upon visiting Chiang's headquarters on January 13–14, 1945, the ambassador learned from members of American Naval Group China serving there some of what had happened in Yenan. The naval personnel told Hurley, in exaggerated form, about secret plans to give American supplies to the Communists and to discredit Hurley with the President.

This news confirmed Hurley's worst fears of a Chinese Communist–American conspiracy, "caused by General Stilwell, Ambassador Gauss, their agents and officials," aimed at Chiang and himself. It also seemed to explain why Yenan refused to resume negotiations under his sponsorship.[11] On January 14 the ambassador rushed off a cable to Roosevelt warning of a subversive plot against the President's policy. Disloyal Americans had convinced Mao and Chou to refuse to accept a compromise with the KMT and instead to seek direct support and recognition from Washington. Hurley urged Roosevelt to refuse to meet with the Communists and instead press on with the plan to win Soviet commitments to Chiang at the upcoming Yalta meeting. This two-pronged response, Hurley insisted, would bring the CCP back to Chungking. Finally, the ambassador asked Roosevelt to keep this information secret from presumably disloyal State Department officials.[12]

The communication of the Communist offer to Roosevelt in this format virtually insured its rejection. Once again, Hurley told the President, no real, substantive problem existed. Firm American support for the KMT would convince both parties to accept mediation and compromise. Hurley would deliver a KMT-dominated coalition and prevent a civil war. Though Roosevelt did not respond directly to the ambassador, he acted in accordance with his recommendations. Generals Marshall and Wedemeyer were ordered to investigate the army's role in any unauthorized dealings with the Communists. Marshall described Roosevelt as so angered by the incident that he considered offering a formal apology to Chiang. After patching up their bruised egos, Wedemeyer and Hurley agreed to remove from command all officers implicated in the alleged plot, beginning with McClure and Barrett. Implicitly, by his handling of the entire episode, Roosevelt sanctioned the first purge of America's "China hands."[13]

The Communists, who for six months had gotten on well with Colonel Barrett and the affable Dixie contingent, received a rude shock in mid-January. In place of Barrett, Colonel Morris De Pass, an American tied to KMT secret operations, returned to Yenan with a message from Hurley. The Communists, it declared, would not receive any American aid or political support until *after* they had reached a political compromise acceptable to Chiang Kai-shek. To do this, the Communists must return to Chungking. Apparently resigned to this failure for the moment, Mao sent word to Hurley on January 22, 1945, that Chou En-lai would resume negotiations.[14]

Now that they had seemingly forced the Communists back into line, Wedemeyer and Hurley moved to tighten control over their own staffs. Wedemeyer dressed down Chennault for his alleged continued willingness to supply Hsueh Yueh. The President, said Wedemeyer, ordered all American military officers to "support the existing Chinese government." No aid would be given to any "elements" in China which "the Generalissimo did not specifically approve," whether or not "the decision seemed wise." Henceforth, Wedemeyer instructed all army personnel in China, they were not to "assist, negotiate, or collaborate in any way with Chinese political parties, activities or persons" unless he authorized it.[15]

Hurley sought to impose a similar orthodoxy on the embassy staff by censoring their dispatches to Washington. When John Service returned from a visit to the United States, the ambassador greeted him with the warning that if he interfered with the resumption of Hurley's mediation effort, Hurley would "break him." The ambassador assembled the embassy personnel on January 16 to hear him lecture on the danger of dallying with any Communists. Americans were in China, he declared, to insure that all military and political factions were united under Chiang Kai-shek's leadership.[16] When Arthur Ringwalt, a member of the embassy staff, showed the ambassador a critical message he had already sent to Washington, Hurley fumed,

"You mean you sent them *that?* . . . Why I've *killed* men for less than that." And he actually drew a pistol. Ringwalt never knew if it was loaded. When the Ambassador had more or less simmered down and sheathed his weapon, he stated that from then on United States policy would be whatever he said it was and that his policy was against sending anything derogatory.[17]

Hurley's self-confidence was nothing short of remarkable, given the actual situation within China and the contempt most Americans there held him in. While the diplomatic critics were temporarily silenced, Treasury Department representative Solomon Adler strove to warn Morgenthau of the looming disaster. After talking with Hurley, Adler wrote the Treasury Secretary that the President's special envoy totally misunderstood and misrepresented reality. Not the Communists but the Nationalists desperately needed to be pressured by Washington. Chiang possessed a "death wish," a drive to precipitate civil war. Hurley continually pandered to Chiang's reactionary, no-compromise position. Adler hoped that Morgenthau could be induced to carry this information to Roosevelt, so that the President would put a leash on Hurley. At a minimum, American policy must not be to promise Chiang support in a civil war. Hurley must be made to stop showing T. V. Soong copies of secret messages to and from Washington. The ambassador, Adler complained, was only a "stuffed shirt playing at being a great man." His continued blunders might well lead to civil war, the complete alienation of the Communists from the United States, and China emerging as a focal point of Soviet-American conflict. [18]

Hurley's activities, so accurately reported by Adler, diminished the already slight possibility that a compromise might emerge from the resumed political discussions in Chungking. Even as he returned to the talks in late January, Chou insisted that the Five Points of November 1944 must remain the principle behind a coalition. As had been true in December, however, Chiang offered the Communists only token political appointments on powerless commissions. In return, they must abandon their independent army and base. By mid-February Chou grew weary and returned to Yenan. By March 1, 1945, Chiang ended any speculation about compromise when he announced that a KMT-controlled National Assembly would be convened the following November to map China's political future. The CCP countered with a demand that an all-party national political conference be held. In essense, the KMT would only permit the gathering of a rubber-stamp conclave while the CCP insisted that a new forum, totally distinct from the existing regime, be created.[19]

Hurley continued to remain oblivious to the implications of the broken-down talks. As if to demonstrate his contempt for Chou, on the very day Yenan called for an all-party conference, Hurley closeted himself with Chiang to reaffirm support for the generalissimo. Chiang and Hurley fed each other's fear of conspiracy, denouncing plots by embassy staff, American reporters, and British agents. Chiang warned the ambassador that all their mutual opponents, including Stilwell, Service, Davies, Barrett, and various journalists, were Communist agents. Hurley, though indicating agreement, admitted to lacking "definite proof." Chiang thanked Hurley for saving all Asia from a Communist conquest, while the ambassador assured his host that "when the war with Japan is over your well equipped divisions will have a walk over in their fight with the Communists." Learning of Hurley's statements from T. V. Soong, Joseph Alsop gloated that at last America was determined to stop the "rise of Russia."[20]

The dramatic developments in China during early 1945 coincided with the momentous Yalta summit conference of early February. There, Roosevelt and Stalin haggled to reach an agreement concerning the Far East which corresponded closely to Hurley's initiatives. Clearly, the President hoped to seal off China from Soviet political influence and in this controlled environment compel the Communists to join a KMT-dominated coalition. Roosevelt would contain the revolution from abroad, while Hurley would do so from within. As seemed to be his attitude toward Europe, the President looked to a postwar world divided among "spheres of interest." If China could not be a great power, it must be (minus Manchuria, perhaps) at least in the American sphere.

Anticipating a complicated discussion over China at Yalta, Ambassador Harriman querried the Soviet leader in December

1944 as to Moscow's attitudes. Stalin, repeating his promise to enter the war against Japan, went on to expand his previous claim for compensation. The Soviet Union expected to gain control of the Kurile Islands, southern Sakhalin, Port Arthur, Dairen, and the two major Manchurian railroads which linked the Trans-Siberian route to Vladivostok. Furthermore, both the Chinese and American governments were expected to accept the status quo in Outer Mongolia, i.e., continued Soviet domination of an allegedly independent state. (Virtually all Chinese considered Outer Mongolia Chinese territory.) When Harriman voiced astonishment at these demands, Stalin merely indicated that he and Roosevelt would have to discuss the issue at their impending meeting.[21]

The Yalta Conference, held in the Soviet Crimea early in February 1945, dealt with issues which soon became the reef upon which the Grand Alliance foundered. Questions concerning future control of Germany, Poland, the Balkans, German reparations, etc., befuddled Roosevelt, Churchill, and Stalin throughout the conference. The President, apparently resigned to the fact that he had little room to influence Soviet behavior in Eastern Europe, chose to accept its consignment to a de facto Russian sphere. In return, Roosevelt believed, he secured Soviet acceptance of a much more powerful Anglo-American sphere in the West and in East Asia. Roosevelt probably envisioned this trade-off as the best way to secure Stalin's commitment to a stable postwar order.

Probably because the area was not of crucial importance to either Soviet or American security, Roosevelt and Stalin found it simpler to compromise over China than practically anywhere else. In discussing Asia, Roosevelt's opening remarks to the Soviet leader stressed both their nations' opposition to European colonialism. The President expressed a hope that French Indochina and Korea would both be placed under a trusteeship arrangement leading to eventual independence. In keeping with this "anti-imperial" tone, though not its substance, Roosevelt urged Stalin to secure the desired Manchurian port and railroad privileges by negotiating a treaty with Chiang's government. Such a method, Roosevelt must have realized, would relieve the United States of the onus of depriving China of territory while securing a form of Soviet endorsement for the Nationalists' rule over most of China. The President hoped that the terms of a Russian lease over Manchurian ports and railroads would not formally infringe upon China's sovereignty.

Stalin's reply to these suggestions was conciliatory. He seemed quite willing to accept a China in the American camp in exchange for special Soviet privileges in Manchuria. Formal negotiations for a treaty could be arranged, he said, if T. V. Soong came to Moscow in late April. Stalin concurred with Roosevelt's statement that it would be best for Chiang to remain dominant in China, even if a KMT-CCP coalition emerged there. The Soviet ruler remarked, more or less truthfully, that ever since the 1920s he had favored creation of a United Front under Chiang's leadership. Meanwhile, professing doubts as to Chinese security, Roosevelt and Stalin agreed not to inform Chiang about their decisions for the time being.[22]

This rather facile agreement received a jolt on February 10 when Molotov gave Harriman the formal Soviet draft of its Far Eastern demands. More extensive than Stalin's verbal assurances, the draft called for a Soviet "right," not "lease," to control the Manchurian railroads and ports. Harriman protested that Roosevelt favored only "internationalization" of Port Arthur and Dairen and joint Sino-Soviet management of the railroads. Further discussions led Roosevelt and Stalin to agree upon a formula for a Soviet lease of the naval base at Port Arthur, the internationalization of Dairen, and the creation of a joint agency to operate the railroads. Roosevelt agreed to eventually inform the Chinese government of what had been given away by the terms of the Yalta agreement. Although no formal details were disclosed to Chiang until the following June, Admiral Leahy soon gathered that the substance of the deal had been leaked to the Chinese.[23]

Probably no single event in wartime diplomacy or cold war

imagery conjures up more debate than the Yalta agreements on liberated Europe and Asia. Often blamed for the "loss" of Eastern Europe and China to Communism, Yalta did nothing of the kind. The Soviet Red Army already occupied most of Eastern Europe in February 1945 and, whether Washington wished or not, would eventually launch a campaign against Japanese forces in Manchuria. Roosevelt sought to strike a bargain at Yalta, accepting the reality of an expanded Soviet sphere in hopes of securing general Soviet cooperation in postwar diplomacy. The Yalta agreements, he believed, provided the best security against Soviet expansion into Western Europe and China, while possibly helping to moderate the nature of Soviet control of Eastern Europe. Whatever its success in protecting Western Europe against possible military attack, the belligerent, anti-Soviet policy of Roosevelt's successors did nothing to ameliorate the situation in Eastern Europe or "save" China.[24] The collapse of the American-supported regime in China resulted not from Soviet-American collusion but from essentially internal causes, only compounded by incredible American bungling.

In the wake of the Yalta Conference, Ambassador Hurley and General Wedemeyer decided to return to Washington for consultations and to bolster their own positions. They worried, perhaps, that career officials in the State and War departments continued to question the policy of virtually complete commitment to the KMT. If the actions of the American embassy in Chungking are considered, this was no idle fear. Under Hurley's tight reins, the embassy staff had been pressured into modifying their reports on Chinese affairs. In something of a desperate gamble, with Hurley enroute to Washington, the staff rose in revolt and sent a collective warning to the Department of State. On February 28, 1945, all the political officers sent a cable to the Secretary of State, over the signature of chargé George Atcheson. Arriving in Washington one step ahead of Hurley, the cable warned that the ambassador's actions had compromised any chance for peace and unity in

China. The only hope for averting civil war, it argued, lay in demonstrating America's willingness to cooperate with Yenan and to press Chiang into sharing power with the CCP. As for the future, stated the authors, "We can point out the advantages of having the Communists helped by the United States rather than seeking Russian aid or intervention, direct or indirect."[25] In a letter he wrote to Treasury Secretary Morgenthau and Harry Dexter White endorsing the embassy staff's cable, Solomon Adler put the case even more succinctly: America's future in China "should not be left in the hands of a bungler like Hurley."[26]

Even the small group of OSS officers still in contact with the Communists warned General Donovan that Hurley had destroyed almost any chance for peace in China. The ambassador had linked himself, and thus the United States, completely to the KMT. He had no credibility outside Chiang's clique. Since the CCP was determined to preserve its own existence, the United States must choose whether it preferred the Communists to seek Soviet aid or assistance from the United States.[27]

These attempts to convince the President and his leading advisors to reverse Hurley's policies were joined by the Communists themselves. They still imagined that if they could send representatives directly to the United States they might be able to make contact with sympathetic officials. For both this reason and their desire to achieve an aura of political legitimacy, the CCP demanded that it be included on the Chinese delegation to the upcoming San Francisco conference of the United Nations. They requested Roosevelt to pressure Chiang to place several Communist delegates on the Chinese delegation, presumably including Chou En-lai. But, at Hurley's urging, the President deftly parried this request. On March 15, Roosevelt did ask Chiang to permit Communist participation as a sign of good faith. Chiang responded by selecting a single Communist, the aging and more obscure Tung Pi-wu, who spoke no English and could hardly fill the shoes of Chou. Having failed to win either a propaganda victory (by being refused a seat) or the presence of an effective spokesman in San Francisco, the Communists were, in the words of an OSS agent in Yenan, "neatly euchred."[28]

Finally, the Communists fell back on one of their few remaining American contacts, John Service, who had rejoined the American observer group in Yenan in March. Communist leaders pumped him for information on American policy and again used him as a sounding board for their own proposals. Reflecting, no doubt, the many disappointments of the last several months, Mao characterized American policy as an "enigma." Still, he "could not believe" this policy was "fixed and unchangeable." Surely, "America would eventually realize that support of the Central Government was not the best way to fight the war, to speed China's progress toward democracy or to ensure stability in the Far East." The chairman of the Communist Party professed to be utterly confused by the failure of the American government to realize that a postwar progressive China would be a magnet for American investment and trade. Nor could Mao understand why "America's policy seemed to waver after its good start" late in 1944. Unless the United States now resumed its pressure to force the Kuomintang to establish a more representative regime, "all that America has been working for will be lost."

Mao appeared most disturbed by the contradictions in American behavior. Those Americans visiting Yenan usually praised the Communists and expressed a desire to work with them. Yet Washington and Hurley continued to support the KMT. Although Hurley might choose to call this nonintervention, Mao thought otherwise. "There is no such thing as America not intervening in China! You are here, as China's greatest ally. The fact of your presence is tremendous." To the Communists, the United States could no longer pretend to be politically uninvolved in China, nor could it escape the consequences of that involvement.[29] In further conversations and observations, Service noted that there was again much talk about creating a formal separate government for the "liberated areas." There seemed little hope for a political coalition now that Chiang had announced his intention of calling a powerless National Assembly to meet in November 1945. It would be overwhelmingly KMT and used to rubber stamp the Generalissimo's decisions.[30]

Service's tenure in Yenan was cut short by an order from Hurley issued on March 30, that he return to Washington immediately. On April 1 Service received a gala send-off from the assembled Communist leaders, including Mao, Chou, and Chu Teh. They apparently believed (or hoped) Service had been recalled to Washington for important consultations. Throwing a plum and a compliment in Service's direction, Mao implied that if only he could stay another ten days Service would be allowed to attend the upcoming Party Congress. In any case, he asked that Service convey to Washington the Communists' pledge to fight Japan and assist American forces "whether or not they received a single gun or bullet." After Japan's defeat, the Americans and Communists should try to avoid conflict. Still, the United States must understand that the CCP could never accept Chiang's rump National Assembly and, if it were called, would retaliate by proclaiming a National United Front of their own in liberated areas.[31] On April 4, 1945, shortly after recording this information, Service departed for Washington. His forced exit severed one of the last remaining links between the Communists and the United States.

The pleas and warnings of the embassy staff, the OSS officers, and the Communists fell on either deaf or hostile ears in Washington. On March 4 Hurley had visited the State Department and been given the embassy staff's February 28 telegram. After reading it he yelled at John Carter Vincent, "I know who drafted that telegram: Service! I'll get that son of a bitch if it's the last thing I do." Although Vincent urged Joseph Grew to seriously consider the embassy staff's criticisms in his ensuing discussions with Hurley and Roosevelt, such advice was to slight avail. Grew did little more than prepare a summary for the President in case he wished to refer to it in a personal meeting with the ambassador.[32] To recover any possible loss of face, Wedemeyer and Hurley told all who would listen that the embassy staff was notoriously disloyal to both themselves and the President. The two officials explained to leading members of the State and War departments that they remained opposed to any American aid for Yenan and would remove from power any diplomatic or military personnel who advocated otherwise.[33]

Throughout March and early April, Hurley and Wedemeyer made the Washington rounds, securing support from the Joint Chiefs, the President, and the War Department. Late in March, Wedemeyer, and Commodore Milton Miles of Naval Group China all appeared before the Joint Chiefs to discuss the situation in China. These three leading Americans in China all agreed that the Communists were a minor, weak party whose "rebellion in China could be put down by comparatively small assistance to Chiang's central government." Wedemeyer went on to tell his colleagues in the War Department and Secretary Stimson that Chiang had vastly inproved the quality of his forces and would have little difficulty destroying his domestic opposition.[34]

Just how cognizant the President was of these events remains uncertain. While he did meet privately with both Wedemeyer and Hurley, we have no record of these discussions. General Wedemeyer's recollection of the meeting with Roosevelt is marked by his shock at observing the President's obvious physical degeneration. Roosevelt spoke mainly about his own opposition to a restoration of French rule in Indochina. Wedemeyer himself had to bring up the issue of the political confrontation in China, telling the President that a large-scale military conflict would probably await Japan's surrender. That apparently was the sum of their exchange.[35]

Although Patrick Hurley met with Roosevelt on at least two occasions in March, neither made notes on what passed between them. What Hurley said to the President can be partially surmised from Admiral Leahy's second-hand report of the visits. Hurley complained to Leahy that he suffered the abuse of disloyal subordinates who retained an attachment to Stilwell. Leahy seemed to share Hurley's dislike for the regular diplomatic and military staff, which had "ganged up on the new ambassador from outside the regular foreign service." Given Roosevelt's dislike for so many professional diplomats, Hurley's charges may have had a special appeal to the President.[36]

The only suggestion that Roosevelt may have been thinking along a separate line appears in an account by Edgar Snow of his last conversations with the President. Roosevelt expressed to Snow anger at Chiang's refusal to grant the Communists some minimum guarantees which would get them to join a coalition. He spoke about the need for compromise in China. Barring this, he would continue to work through "two governments" and even consider permitting American military operations in north China. But nowhere did Roosevelt give any indication that he understood the nature of the real problems in China, nor did he indicate any displeasure with Hurley or Wedemeyer. On the contrary, Roosevelt told Snow that he greatly looked forward to Hurley's impending visit in order to get the ambassador's personal viewpoint, which he valued so highly.[37]

The President no longer received any significant advice on China from Marshall and Stimson, since the War Department generally had lost interest in China. The opinions it did express were now consistent with Wedemeyer's recommendations. In the State Department few voices were raised against Hurley. The rebels among the junior officers—Davies, Service, Atcheson—either had been or soon would be removed from China. (Hurley actually required his staff to sign a "loyalty oath" promising to support the ambassador and not to send "negative reports to Washington.") The only strong opinion—besides Hurley's—which the President could hear was that being expressed in Congress. During March, Congressman Walter Judd delivered a savage speech in the House denouncing American critics of Chiang. Judd defended the generalissimo as a great patriot and loyal ally. He denounced the Communists as evil Soviet puppets who desired to create a "Red China" which would endanger the fundamental security interests of the United States. Shortly before Judd spoke John Foster Dulles, a prominent lawyer and authority on world affairs, issued a similar warning regarding any desertion of the KMT. American support for Chiang, he told the Cleveland Council on World Affairs, reflected a determination "that the 400 million of China shall not become harnessed to the predatory design of any alien power." Generalissimo Chiang had come to rely on the "ultimate support of the Christian democracies, notably the United States."[38] The fact that Dulles and Judd had transformed Chinese internal politics into virtually American domestic politics may have further inhibited any desires of the President to buck the advice of the senior aides.

Whatever hopes Yenan still retained for a presidential reversal of China policy were formally dashed on April 2. In a Washington press conference, Hurley treated his audience to a virtuoso performance. The ambassador, under public questioning, denied that the Communists had ever requested American military aid or political recognition. He insisted that only minor issues separated the Communists and Nationalists, implying that Yenan's refusal to enter a coalition was completely unwarranted. Hurley went on to lump the Communists together with various separatist movements and decadent warlord factions.[39]

Reacting quickly to the import of Hurley's statements, the April 5 edition of the Hsin-hua Jih-pao printed an editorial denouncing the ambassador's assertions. The Party organ, criticizing the linking of the Communists to the warlords, claimed that Hurley completely misunderstood and distorted the true Communist effort to collaborate with the United States against Japan. This policy, said the newspaper, could only encourage civil war and prolong China's suffering. The KMT press naturally rejoiced at Hurley's words and heralded them as confirmation of American support against the Communists.[40]

Hurley's public condemnation and ridicule of the CCP,

coupled with developments inside China, forced Yenan to begin an agonizing reappraisal of policy toward the United States. Between April 23 and June 11, the 7th Party Congress met in Yenan. Communist officials certainly argued the merits of continuing to seek American cooperation in solving China's political and military crises. While some evidence suggests that "moderates" (who preferred to court U.S. aid and support a coalition regime) debated with "hardliners" (who were determined to abandon joint action and instead push forward with military campaigns and a revolutionary program), most Communist leaders were probably deeply divided within themselves over a future course of action. Mao's "Report on Coalition Government" of April 24 reflected this dual opinion.

However, even as the Congress met, the CCP was no longer willing to ignore or remain silent in the face of mounting American provocations. In a radio address beamed to the United States, Mao warned of an American-KMT conspiracy to launch a civil war "as soon as the forces of a certain allied country have cleared a considerable part of the Chinese mainland of Japanese aggressors." He charged that the KMT hoped that "certain allied countries will do the same job in China as British General Scobie has been doing in Greece" (i.e., fighting the leftist guerrillas). Mao's concluding speech to the 7th Party Congress, which received wide circulation, identified American imperialism, personified by Hurley, as a "dead weight" on China. Somewhat hopeful, Mao continued to distinguish between reactionary leaders and progressive subordinates among American policymakers.[41]

The initial denunciations of Hurley in April and the subsequent criticisms of the United States marked the renewal of an anti-American theme which had all but disappeared since 1941. Still, Mao's remarks and those of other CCP officials tried to differentiate between friendly and hostile trends in American policy. OSS officer Charles Stelle, reporting from Yenan, explained that CCP behavior toward himself and other "friendly" Americans remained cordial. What upset the Communists most was Roosevelt's apparent connivance with Hurley. Stelle, however, believed that the Communists would still try to cooperate with the United States, since they felt they had few alternatives.[42]

By early June, however, Stelle reported a marked change in Yenan. Communist officials made no secret of their fear and confusion regarding the United States. Several developments highlighted the new atmosphere. Possibly because of the Hopkins visit to Moscow, Yenan worried about a Soviet-American deal which might cause Stalin to give little support to the CCP once Russia entered the war against Japan. More specifically, Stelle wrote, the Communists feared an imminent American landing on the China coast. American troops might then "knife into the areas of their control" and allow the "KMT armies [to] walk in behind." By June the CCP had come to feel that American operations "in their areas of control were spearheads for the KMT." (T. V. Soong, in fact, was currently badgering Stimson to approve such landings.)

Captain Stelle noted that the CCP was "going through a bad time and expects worse times to come." They felt snubbed and insulted by Wedemeyer's increasingly terse and offhand messages to them. Hurley and Wedemeyer, they believed, were working with the KMT to prevent the Communists from participating in the Japanese surrender. Hurley even claimed that Stalin supported his position. Finally, during the last few days in May, the Communists captured members of a joint OSS–KMT intellignce team operating near a Communist base area with the goal of establishing contacts with Japanese puppet forces. This seemed firm evidence that such groups (this one had been used in Sian) reflected a new American policy of collaboration with the KMT, the puppets, and the Japanese against the CCP.

According to Stelle the CCP was desperate to know whether there was "any chance that the present policy of full support for Chungking alone is subject to modification" and "what American military policy will be if the U.S. Army lands or comes into their areas." Stelle urged that Wedemeyer try to salvage CCP–U.S. relations by either sending a high-level representative to Yenan or by accepting a Communist offer that he come himself. The theater commander, however, refused both these requests. [43]

There was virtually no chance that either Stelle or the CCP would get any satisfaction from leading Americans in China or in Washington. Ambassador Hurley, anticipating a last-ditch effort by some OSS officers to help Yenan, had taken the precaution during May of warning the OSS against such action. Addressing Major Quentin Roosevelt and Colonel Willis Bird (who had discussed joint operations in Yenan the previous December), Hurley made it quite clear he would not tolerate any dissent from his directive that the United States and its agents would support only the Chiang regime. The ambassador told the two men that anyone who did not follow his orders would meet the same fate (recall and disgrace) that had befallen Stilwell, Gauss, Davies, Barrett, Service, and Atcheson. The message was undoubtedly clear. [44]

Many troubling questions emerge concerning Hurley's conduct in China and the nature of his policy. Did he continually act without sufficient authority and preempt policymaking? Whas he simply a bumbling fool, an incompetent playing at being a great man, with tragic consequences? Did he completely misunderstand the nature of political conflict in China, confusing personalities with social forces? The answer to all of these questions is a qualified yes. The qualification, however, is a major one. It is true that Hurley was vain, pompous, and ignorant of China. His suspicion of his staff ran to such deep and destructive levels that it sowed the seeds of the subsequent political purges of the Foreign Service. Moreover, Hurley was not above lying to his superiors, or at best telling them what he believed they wished to hear. For example, in November 1944 Hurley sent a personal letter to Henry Morgenthau explaining the significance of Stilwell's departure and his own rise. Hurley called the Nationalists a gang of "fas-

cists and thieves" and praised the Communists as moderate reformers who had no links to the Russians. He went on to boast
that within a month he would accomplish his mission of "unifying China under the present government." Exactly why the
United States would champion the survival of "fascists and
thieves" was not explained.

Similarly, in March 1945 Hurley sought to calm the fears
of Stilwell's old supporter, Henry Stimson. Even though Hurley had already committed himself to the Nationalist cause, he
assured Stimson such was not the case. The ambassador told
the Secretary of War that the Communists were not the genuine article, had no ties with Russia, and (like the Nationalists)
were nonideological power grabbers.[45]

Despite his deviousness and his misunderstanding of the
situation in China, Hurley generally received support from the
White House and the War and State departments in his effort
to crush Yenan's attempts to cooperate directly with the United
States. Under his direction, embassy and military staff were
purged. When one reflects on the previous activities of presidential emissaries—Currie, Willkie, and Wallace—it appears
that Hurley was in the mainstream of policy while Stilwell and
his supporters were rather the exception to the rule. Finally, it
must be remembered that two Presidents sustained Hurley in
power for almost one and one-half years, anger being reserved
for his resignation not his continuance in office. Neither Roosevelt or Truman believed they were misinformed or ill served
by their ambassador.

It would be incorrect to attribute the growing American–
Chinese Communist hostility solely or even primarily to Hurley's reckless behavior. A broad range of actions, directed by
Washington, evidenced a growing anti-Communist consensus
in American foreign policy. During April, following his meetings with Roosevelt, Hurley met with British and Soviet
leaders at the President's behest. When the ambassador spoke
with Churchill in London, the Prime Minister quickly denounced what he called the "great American illusion" about

China. He remained vehemently opposed to American calls for the dissolution of the Anglo-French empires in Asia, declaring that Hong Kong would "be eliminated from the British Empire only over my dead body."

Ironically, Hurley enjoyed a far more cordial reception in the Kremlin than at Number 10 Downing Street. Stalin met the ambassador, speaking in congenial words of his desire to help avert a Chinese civil war and sustain Chiang's preeminent position. The Soviet leader claimed to have already urged Mao to enter a KMT-dominated coalition, something the Russians thought necessary since they doubted that the CCP could govern China. In praising Chiang, Stalin said, "While there had been corruption among certain officials of the National Government of China he knew that Chiang Kai-shek was 'selfless,' a 'patriot' and that the Soviet in times past had befriended him. In short," Hurley assured the President, "Stalin agreed unqualifiedly to American policy in China. . ." [46]

In dissenting cables to the State Department, Ambassador Harriman, George Kennan, and John Davies (now serving in Moscow) all warned that Soviet policy was far more complex than Hurley understood. Kennan believed that Soviet policy toward China would be "fluid, resilient," aimed at achieving "maximum power with minimum responsibility. . . ." The Russians, he predicted, would move to dominate Manchuria and cultivate a Chinese government "friendly to the Soviet Union." Davies and Kennan did not believe the Soviets would rush in to encourage civil war. Rather, they would sit back until a winner emerged and then move to maximize Soviet interests and control. Hurley remained completely concerned with the sole issue of winning Stalin's promise not to aid Yenan. But this, Davies and Kennan realized, might be completely irrelevant to the course of events in China. Nevertheless, as late as the end of May, when Truman sent Harry Hopkins to confer with Stalin, most American officials continued to feel that civil war could be prevented as long as the Russians refused to support the Chinese Communists. [47] They simply could not envision a Chinese Communist movement of local origin.

Whatever slim possibility existed for a modification of American policy in China died in mid-April with Franklin Roosevelt. His death removed a leader to whom the CCP had turned—without notable success—for understanding. The little that was known about Harry Truman added to the rapid deterioration of Soviet-American relations over the issues of Eastern Europe and Germany and boded ill for American policy toward the Communist movement in China. Inexperienced in foreign affairs and naturally suspicious of the Soviet Union, Truman proved easily swayed by the anti-Communist opinions of advisors like Averell Harriman, Admiral Leahy, James Byrnes, Joseph Grew, and Navy Secretary James Forrestal. While Roosevelt had selectively consulted these men, Truman seemed virtually dependent upon them. Assistant Secretary of State Joseph Grew, Ambassador to Moscow Averell Harriman, and Navy Secretary Forrestal harbored deep fears of Soviet behavior in Europe and possible expansion in Asia once the Russians entered the Pacific War. They had never shared Franklin D. Roosevelt's idea of limited Soviet goals or believed that despite Stalin's pretensions as a world revolutionary leader, he primarily concerned himself with controlling a Russian empire between Germany and Manchuria. By and large these men agreed that Stalin planned to seize a foothold in northeast Asia and leave, if at all, only after establishing puppet revolutionary movements. Following Germany's defeat in May, they turned their attention toward the fate of Japan. It seemed doubtful to them that, even if Chiang prevailed, China could emerge as a stabilizing force in postwar Asia. Japan, however, if not thoroughly destroyed, might become an American ally and a barrier to Soviet or possibly Chinese Communist influence in Asia.

In May Harriman had returned to Washington to warn Truman and others of his conviction that international Communism, under Soviet direction, had begun an aggressive march.

Within a year, he predicted, at least half and possibly all Europe would be "communistic." If the United States made the terrible error of supporting "communist armies in China against Chiang Kai-shek we should have to face ultimately the fact that two or three hundred millions of people would march when the Kremlin ordered." By July Harriman had come to feel that Hitler's greatest crime was that "his actions had resulted in opening the gates of Eastern Europe to Asia."[48]

Grew and Harriman shuddered at the prospect of a massive Eurasian Communist power bloc extending all the way from eastern Germany to China. Grew pressed Truman and the War Department to devise a strategy aimed at limiting Soviet expansion in Asia by engineering a quick peace settlement with Japan. A modification of "unconditional surrender" might convince more moderate Japanese officials to spare their nation unneeded destruction, while an early surrender might also preclude Soviet intervention in Manchuria and China.[49]

Harriman reacted to the likelihood of civil war in China by initiating a scheme to place American experts on Soviet policy in the Chungking embassy where they might better assist Hurley. His first choice, made on May 9, 1945, was John Melby, who had served with the Office of War Information in Moscow. In explaining his motive for transferring Melby to China, Harriman "got right to the point." Diplomats with a "Moscow background should be stationed at strategic points around the world." Melby should expect to counteract those in the embassy who were "misbehaving by doubting that the Kuomintang is necessarily the answer to the sorry China situation." Harriman emphasized his own certainty that all Communists were the same, "wherever they are."[50]

Despite these warnings, neither President Truman nor his leading military advisors felt able to accept an open breach with Moscow or a quick peace with Japan. They doubted whether "fanatics" in Tokyo would ever surrender. Moreover, until the yet-to-be-tested secret atomic bomb had proved itself, American military planners still counted on Soviet assistance in defeating Japan. At least part of the Harriman-Grew political analysis, however, gained wide acceptance in the new administration. Revolutionary movements, in Europe or Asia, represented only manifestations of Soviet imperialism, not a genuine product of clashing social forces. Accordingly, whatever their pretensions, the Chinese Communists were indistinguishable from the Kremlin, a view which made any change in existing American policy virtually unthinkable.

Developments in the United States during June drove this point bitterly home to Yenan. The Communists, though having lost all faith in Hurley and Wedemeyer, remained somewhat hopeful that more moderate views might prevail in Washington. Even this frail prospect lay shattered on June 6 when the New York office of the leftist Asian affairs journal, *Amerasia*, was raided by the FBI. The magazine's editors and several other persons, including John Service (many of whose "secret" files were found on the premises), were charged with violations of the espionage law for possessing stolen government documents.

The arrest of the alleged spies had been preceded by a secret OSS break-in of the magazine's offices to search for incriminating material. This covert entry was approved at the highest levels. On May 28 Navy Secretary Forrestal learned from OSS sources that the editor of *Amerasia*, Philip Jaffe, possessed secret documents, some of which actually appeared in earlier editions of the journal. Forrestal worried whether the immediate arrest of these "communist spies" might embarrass President Truman, then making final arrangements to meet Stalin in Potsdam. The Navy Secretary discussed the question with Truman and the President personally authorized the break-in and subsequent arrests.[51]

Shortly before news of the *Amerasia* arrests reached Yenan, the Communists still felt close enough to certain members of the remaining Dixie Mission to solicit advice on the proper format for a radio information program they planned to beam to an American audience. Less than two weeks later,

Yenan radio excoriated the United States for a brazen imperialist policy aimed at helping Chiang win a civil war. Mao's speech of June 11, 1945 ("The Foolish Old Man Who Removed the Mountains"), which concluded the 7th Party Congress, decried the two "dead weights" of imperialism and feudalism which lay upon the Chinese people. Hurley and other unspecified American leaders were clearly identified as enemies of China plotting to send U.S. forces against the Communists' "liberated areas." Mao pledged that the CCP would fight any such American effort.[52]

Mao's general theme was elaborated specifically in a June 25, 1945, editorial in *Cheh-fang Jih-pao* concerning Service's arrest. The editorial, later beamed to the United States via radio and addressed to the American people, charged that the true friends of China—identified as the dead or powerless Roosevelt, Welles, Wallace, Gauss, and Stilwell—had been replaced in power by an imperialist and reactionary clique who advocated a "policy which does not recognize the great strength of the Chinese people and only recognizes the Kuomintang government and their reactionary leader, the despot, Chiang Kai-shek." The Communists warned that any decision to intervene on Chaing's behalf would inevitably involve Americans in a civil war. While Yenan proclaimed its continued willingness to pursue the war against Japan, it stressed that if imperialists like Hurley did not "withdraw their hands . . . then the Chinese people will teach them a lesson they deserve." Mao, according to the OSS in Yenan, repeatedly echoed the threat that if Washington continued to back Chiang, postwar American friendship with the Communists would be doomed.[53] If backed to the wall, the Communists were resolved to "go it alone."

Communist efforts to frighten the United States into reassessing its policy made little if any impression upon American officials. Few highly placed leaders retained interest in any form of cooperation with Yenan. Whatever interest they did express in China turned toward the problem of how to bolster the KMT and prevent the expansion of Communist power.

Even a previously hardnosed anti-KMT skeptic like Henry Morgenthau began to soften his opposition to additional aid to the Nationalists. During May, after meeting with Soong, Morgenthau approved renewal of the shipment of Chinese gold reserves from the United States to China. The Tresury Secretary told his startled aides that he had revised his earlier belief that the KMT leaders were "just a bunch of crooks." Soong and his party were actually genuine patriots and gallant allies. The duty of America lay in helping the Nationalist regime achieve political unification and economic development. Morgenthau then helped arrange for the shipment of four thousand trucks and forty-five million yards of cotton cloth to China.[54]

The declining status of the Dixie Mission, beginning in January 1945 and accelerating during June, typified Communist-American hostility. The departures of Barrett, Davies, Service, and Ludden eliminated the open communications channels which had contributed to the mission's early charmed existence. Colonel Morris De Pass, an intelligence officer reputedly close to the KMT secret police, succeeded Barrett as mission commander. He and a temporary successor were quickly declared persona non grata by the CCP.[55] After searching for an intelligence officer considered a "communist specialist," General Wedemeyer selected Colonel Ivan Yeaton to take command of Dixie. Yeaton, who had served in Moscow, argued *against* the grant of Lend-Lease aid to Russia early in the war. Chiang Kai-shek, after personally interviewing the proposed commander, pronounced him fit for duty in Yenan.

Although Mao, Chou, Chu Teh, Yeh Chien-ying, and Huang Hua all turned out to greet Yeaton as he arrived at their capital in July, the American officer deeply mistrusted his hosts. He suspected a lie behind everything the Chinese Communists told him and suspected that the Americans in Yenan were pawns of the CCP. Yeaton believed the primary role of Dixie should be to gather intelligence on a potentially hostile group for transmission to General Wedemeyer.[56]

Yet even such an anti-Communist could not ignore the obvious attempts made in Yenan to court the favor of Americans. Amidst all his rhetoric, Yeaton confessed to enjoying the friendly atmosphere in Yenan and the informal companionship of various Communist officials. After giving instruction on weather reporting to a group of Communist soldiers who were sending the information on to the Americans, Yeaton commented that they were "as fine a group of young men as I have ever commanded anywhere." Similarly, Yeaton enjoyed the pastoral delights of pheasant hunting with Colonel Bird and Communist military commander Chu Teh.[57]

Nevertheless, these personal pleasantries paled in importance before the deepening American involvement on behalf of Chiang. American military aid to the Nationalists grew rapidly after January 1945 despite the fact that little was being put to use against Japanese forces. The completion of the Ledo Road and expansion of Hump tonnages had dramatic effects on the supply situation. But when the Dixie Mission was officially renamed the Yenan Observer Group in July, its members were explicitly warned against giving even token gifts to the Communists.[58]

The obvious signs of deteriorating U.S. relations with the Chinese Communists, and the closely associated suspicion of Soviet designs in Europe and Asia, formed the dominant features of the new Truman administration's China policy by the summer of 1945. But even this reflected only the partial scope of U.S. activities. For three years, in fact, another group of Americans in China had pursued a far more provocative policy than Hurley or Wedemeyer yet supported. Since 1942 the shadowy Naval Group China had actually assisted the Nationalists' preparations for civil war by secretly training an army of anti-Communist guerrillas. As Japan's defeat neared, these activities assumed new importance.

Chapter 11
SACO! The Counter-
revolution in Action

WHILE IT MAY appear a contradiction, neither Hurley, Wedemeyer, nor their superiors in Washington relished the prospect of an early civil war in China. Any resumption of large-scale fighting while Japan remained undefeated would only increase the difficulty of ending the Pacific War and make Soviet assistance in Manchuria more vital. Many of Chiang's supporters actually doubted the generalissimo's ability to exterminate the Communists in battle and thus favored a political solution subordinating the CCP in a coalition. If civil war errupted and the Nationalists appeared to falter, the situation could easily become a magnet for Soviet intervention. As Roosevelt remarked to Henry Wallace in May 1944, unless Chiang "settled the Communist thing," Washington might be unable to "hold the Russians in line." Roosevelt and Truman hoped to bring China through the war as unified as possible, while augmenting the strength of the KMT and securing Soviet pledges not to assist Yenan. International support for the Nationalist regime, they hoped, might convince the CCP to accept the KMT's authority, averting both revolution and civil war in China.

This scheme ignored both Chiang's singleminded drive for military supremacy as well as the determination of the Communists to preserve their revolution in the face of foreign and domestic opposition. Furthermore, American leaders failed to understand how the actual behavior of Americans in China, as distinct from formal U.S. policy, induced the KMT to pursue a military solution and antagonized the CCP. While the resumption of civil war was probably inevitable in 1945, certain U.S. operations actually encouraged an early confrontation.

231

Since shortly after Pearl Harbor, a little-known American naval mission had assisted the KMT secret police with tools and techniques vital to the pursuit of counterrevolution. Naval Group China (later the Sino-American Cooperative Organization, or SACO) began functioning in 1942 as an aid, training, and political support team for the Nationalists. Operating under the authority of Chiang's secret police chief, General Tai Li, it served as a virtual branch of the KMT and enjoyed a source of supply and command separate from all other American elements in China. The activities of this group pushed China far along the road to civil war and involved the United States directly in the internal Chinese struggle.

In contrast to the political moderation advocated by most Americans in China (Chennault, Alsop, and McHugh were the most notable exceptions) and by official policy declarations, this naval mission bolstered the most reactionary and anti-Communist faction within the KMT coalition. Moreover, while a relatively low-level operation, this mission had a unique opportunity to sponsor political and military activities within China. Naval Group China enjoyed firm support from the Navy Department, not simply because of its political program, but because it provided an opportunity for the navy to exert influence in the army-dominated China Theater. Thus some of the power and influence accorded to Naval Group China resulted from bureaucratic rivalry unrelated to the specifics of the civil war. American naval officers hoped to gain influence in postwar China which could be parlayed into status, budgetary, and policymaking capital in postwar Washington.

The factors which underlay KMT support for the navy were more directly related to Chinese politics. Naval Group China could render exceptional services to the KMT. It agreed to provide weapons to the secret police, to train counterinsurgency forces and to support Chiang in his battles with Stilwell. Consequently, the naval mission served the Nationalists' most immediate needs and, along with Chennault, enjoyed great favor.

An additional element solidified the navy-KMT alliance. The leading naval personnel in China accepted and supported the legitimacy of nonrevolutionary nationalism. Along with such key figures as Claire Chennault, James McHugh, and Patrick Hurley, Commodore Milton Miles of SACO responsded to the symbols and programs of the KMT, seeing them as the sole legitimate expression of Asian nationalism. Only the KMT appeared as the force to counter both traditional imperialism and the new threat of violent social revolution. This political vision accepted the fundamental premise that Chiang must rule in China to insure a friendly attitude toward the United States and the prevention of either Chinese or Soviet Communist expansion. Amidst the highly unstable political and military situation in wartime China, the politicized personnel of SACO played a pivotal role in affecting both the current policies and future expectations of the two contending Chinese factions. SACO's direct involvement in China, its willingness to become a conduit for secret military programs, and its dedication to the destruction of revolutionary movements all gave it a disproportionately large impact on Chinese-American relations.

In the summer of 1941, following a series of discussions between several naval officers and the Chinese assistant military attaché in Washington, Hsiao Hsin-ju, the Navy Department first considered sending a special mission to China. It would be dispatched in conjunction with the army mission then being organized by General John Magruder. Although War Department opposition killed the plan, the navy's overall interest was sustained by Hsiao's encouragement and lively reports it received from the naval attaché in Chungking, James McHugh.

After Pearl Harbor the proposed mission was immediately revived. Rear Admiral Willis Lee, an original sponsor, persuaded Admiral King to lend his support to the project. They selected Lieutenant-Commander (later Admiral) Milton Miles, who had served on the Yangtze Patrol and with the Pacific Fleet, to lead the mission. Given the title of United States

Naval Observer and nominally attached to the Chungking embassy, his general orders were to gather intelligence and "harass" the Japanese.[1]

Before departing for China, Miles established a support staff led by Captain J. C. Metzel in the Navy Department. He also conferred extensively with Hsiao Hsin-ju, seeking assurances that the Chinese would provide assistance to this so-called Friendship Project. Hsiao was in a position to inform Miles that Chiang not only favored the naval mission but had designated his trusted aide, General Tai Li, to work personally with Miles. Hsiao knew this because he was in fact Tai Li's chief agent in the United States.[2]

The intelligence reports which Miles assembled in preparation for meeting Tai chronicled his rise through the KMT. Utilizing his Gestapo-like organization, the Blue Shirts, Tai had become a key supporter of Chiang. His goon squads engaged in political assassinations, smuggling, anti-Communist terror, and the rooting out of opposition to Chiang's rule. Since 1937 Tai had controlled the dreaded Bureau of Investigation and Statistics (BIS), whose thousands of agents struck terror among all who might oppose the Nationalists. Tai also maintained a foreign network which operated in the United States through the Chinese embassy and a Chinese bishop, Paul Yu-pin.[3]

Rather than being repelled by these reports, Miles became fascinated and absorbed by the aspects of terror and intrigue which surrounded Tai Li. Upon meeting Tai in April 1942 in China, Miles looked upon him as honest and discreet, and a man "who never had anyone shot without proper authorization." Tai in turn was anxious to work with Miles and the navy, provided he received material support and a promise that the Chinese would retain control of any proposed operations. After impressing Miles by taking him on an extended trip behind Japanese lines, Tai proposed that the navy provide aid in training fifty thousand Chinese guerrillas. By accepting these proposals the navy plunged into the arena of both Chinese internal conflict and American interservice rivalry.[4]

A necessary preliminary to any extensive aid program was to insure that navy supplies could enter China. Although Miles's mission was exempt from both army control and Lend-Lease, he still needed Stilwell's cooperation in order to bring in supplies over the Hump supply route. This restraint on the navy was not removed until 1943. Although Stilwell took an immediate, profound dislike to the proposal for covert operations, he lacked authority over Miles and could do little more than temporarily delay aid shipments and complain to General Marshall. In a subsequent report to the War Department, Stilwell analyzed the whole point of Miles's arrangements as an effort to circumvent the theater commander and expand Tai Li's "Gestapo" with American arms and training.[5]

Worried by Stilwell's negative response and eager to undercut his authority, Miles and McHugh joined Chiang and Chennault in several efforts to secure Stilwell's recall. The naval officers believed that once the army general was removed (and hopefully replaced by Chennault) they could function freely and establish intimate links with the KMT.[6] Although these initial efforts failed, Miles retained his independent status in China and continually built upon it.

The naval mission's position seemed strengthened in September 1942 when General William Donovan named Miles head of OSS in China. In fact, Donovan merely hoped to take advantage of the political connections which Miles enjoyed, while Miles resented Donovan's maneuver as actually an effort to limit his special relationship with Tai Li. Tai vigorously opposed the expansion of OSS activities in China, seeing that organization as possibly anti-KMT in political orientation.[7]

Tai's fears were justified, for both the theater command and other OSS agents resented the strain which Miles's operations put on Stilwell's supply lines in the effort to build up what they called the "Chinese Gestapo." But to insure that Miles would not be inhibited by his critics, Tai and Chiang soon demanded a new basis for the naval mission. The Chinese wanted Project Friendship to become a formal Sino-American organization with Tai Li in command. Miles, requested to draw up a contractual agreement, did so by December 31, 1942. In discussions with T. V. Soong, Miles learned that Chiang Kai-shek required Roosevelt's personal approval of the proposed new organization.[8]

The formal navy-KMT alliance which Miles and his hosts now advocated was considered by the Joint Chiefs of Staff during early 1943. In February the JCS planners recommended approval of the plan since, as a pet project of Chiang's, it would enjoy his personal favor and provide a means for Americans to tap the extensive power of the KMT secret police. As an integral part of this organization, they also requested that six transport planes be specifically allocated to supply the naval mission.[9]

Hoping to speed acceptance of his proposals, Miles flew to Washington in March 1943 to lobby on his own behalf. There, however, he found that his nominal boss, the OSS, as well as "liberals and old China hands" in the State Department opposed what the navy envisioned. Miles berated his opposition as "white supremacists and pro-British imperialists" because they questioned his efforts to work with Tai Li. He particularly hated Stilwell's political advisor, John P. Davies, who had widely decried Miles's activities. Nevertheless, strong backing from Admiral King and the Navy Department secured the JCS approval which Miles required. By April 15, 1943, both President Roosevelt's and Tai Li's signatures had been secured.[10]

The actual operating arm of Miles's Naval Group China now had a formal existence as the Sino-American Cooperative Organization (SACO) under the joint direction of Tai Li and Miles. Its powers were independent of the American theater commander, its supplies coming through the navy rather than Lend-Lease. Given an initial allocation of 150 tons per month, by early 1945 SACO planes were flying in several hundred tons of military supplies per month.[11] By August 1945 SACO operated ten guerrilla training camps, had graduated over 10,000 guerrillas, was supporting eight commando columns of

1,000 men each, supplied weapons to Tai Li's 15,000-man Loyal Patriotic Army, and claimed influence over several thousand coastal pirates. In Chungking it operated a "police training school" staffed by former FBI agents. During this period a total of between 2,500 and 3,000 Americans had served in SACO.

For SACO to fully develop its connection with Tai Li it first became necessary to clarify Miles's relationship to the OSS. In November 1943 General Donovan, troubled by the reports he received about naval activities, informed the navy he wanted the mission replaced by a regular OSS contingent. The Navy Department adamantly opposed this attempt to force its own unit out of China and refused to accept Donovan's request. Undaunted, Donovan flew to China early in December 1943 with the demand that both Miles and Tai Li submit to OSS authority. When both refused, Donovan relieved Miles of his OSS status. Donovan's subsequent efforts to have the JCS reprimand Miles and place the naval officer under OSS were rejected. Instead, Donovan himself was reprimanded by the Joint Chiefs, who reaffirmed SACO's independence. [12]

Miles saw these conflicts with OSS and the theater commander as only partly due to interservice rivalry. The real cause, he insisted, lay in conflicting attitudes toward Chiang and the KMT. The OSS and the army were tainted with "imperialist psychology" and "white supremacy." SACO, on the other hand, was an American alliance with bona fide Chinese nationalism. This assertive opposition to traditional imperialism comprised an important aspect of Miles's rhetoric and a trait which he shared with Hurley, Chennault, and McHugh. [13]

However, something even more immediate than Miles's philosophical concern for China's sovereignty lay behind the clash with Donovan. In fact, this clash was occasioned by an early attempt by Roosevelt to establish contact with Yenan. In October 1943 the President ordered Donovan to begin gathering political intelligence in Communist-controlled areas. In December Donovan made his trip to China in an apparent effort to arrange with Tai Li and Miles for an intelligence mission to be sent to Yenan which would be headed by Donovan himself. Miles and Tai Li balked at the idea, compelling Donovan to separate the OSS from SACO. Although Donovan eventually delegated another OSS officer to undertake the mission, it was superseded by the entry of the Dixie Mission into Yenan in July 1944.[14]

Miles made every effort to interject himself into the struggle between the Nationalists and Communists, even to the point of sabotaging other American projects. Earlier in 1943, when a SACO official in the Navy Department learned that a mission to Yenan was under consideration, he urged Miles to make political use of this information. Miles was advised to leak the information to the KMT in order to extract concessions "from the more conservative elements with whom we wish to deal." They might then "grant us a few favors to entice us away from what they might be inclined to believe is a slight sympathy with the leftists."[15]

The naval mission's essential power lay in its ability to play off the various contending Chinese and American factions against one another. This was most clearly shown in the events surrounding Stilwell's recall and the Communists' subsequent efforts to work secretly with the Army and the OSS. In September 1944, in the midst of the crisis over the command of Chiang's armies, Stilwell had sent John Davies to confer with Harry Hopkins. In their broad-ranging discussion previously described, Hopkins seemed to promise Stilwell complete support from the White House. Davies took this pledge as a point of departure to initiate a discussion of Miles and SACO.

I told Mr. Hopkins about Miles and his activities. Most of this information was news to Mr. Hopkins. He observed that these activities seemed to be of a character which endangered American interests. I explained that we had been reluctant to clean up the Miles situation for fear that in attempting to do so we might precipitate an army-navy dispute. Hopkins hoped that when Stilwell was confirmed in his new position, he would put Miles in his proper place.[16]

The President, however, chose to sacrifice Stilwell in a bid to sustain Chiang's loyalty.

Miles became involved in the entire recall crisis in a unique way. In early October Miles persuaded Hurley to use SACO's radio facilities for his communications with the President. The most important cable traffic between Chiang and Hurley in China and Roosevelt in Washington passed through SACO headquarters, where it probably became available to Tai Li's agents.[17] Copies of many crucial reports sent by the OSS and other members of the Dixie Mission in Yenan to Washington and Chungking headquarters found their way almost immediately to Miles. Either KMT intelligence or a SACO agent among the Dixie Americans made sure that Miles and Tai Li knew in advance of all possible challenges to their policy which might emanate from Yenan or anti-SACO Americans.[18]

Miles's access to this information and his support for Hurley became a crucial factor in the ambassador's uncovering of the Communist-OSS and army military discussions of December 1944 and January 1945. On January 13–14 SACO Americans serving in Chiang's headquarters informed Hurley that Yenan and OSS and army personnel were conducting secret contacts. SACO, serving as the middleman controlling the flow of sensitive information between Washington and Chungking, twice had blocked American efforts to improve relations with the Communists.[19]

It was Miles's idea to link the navy's fortunes to the power of Tai Li, for whom Miles and his comrades felt a "magnetic attraction." But they were not unaware of how SACO might benefit both its Chinese and American members. In the words of one SACO officer, Tai Li had taken Miles into his confidence because he "intends to use SACO as a means of modernizing his own organization." This was also why the Chinese were "100% behind Chennault . . . and not behind General Stilwell."[20]

In addition to the important hold SACO had over communications, since early 1943 Miles had been actively developing joint navy-KMT military and political projects. Among the most notorious of these was SACO's police training program. Miles first conceived of establishing a police training school late in 1942. Officially called U.S. Naval Unit No. 9, the project got under way during the summer of 1943. The idea envisioned building upon and modernizing Tai Li's existing Secret Information Training Institute in Military Affairs. Various SACO officers returned to the United States during 1943 to recruit police training personnel and police equipment. The staff, which eventually numbered around fifty, included instructors drawn from the FBI, Narcotics Bureau, Secret Service, and Treasury Department, and the New York Bomb Squad. Equipment consisted of such devices as lie detectors and police dogs.[21]

Miles reported these activities to Captain Metzel, who had remained in the Navy Department. He gloated that he had

opened a new school this morning for scientific criminal investigation: I cannot overrate the importance of continuing this school. It has a political involvement which cannot fully be put on paper. It has a tremendous far reaching field in China and the United States, both during the present war and in the postwar development. . . . the complications involved are tremendous and rather terrifying to me, but I believe they will pay major dividends.[22]

Almost immediately Stilwell went on the counteroffensive, sending John Davies to protest. Davies informed Miles that Stilwell vigorously opposed the creation of a training program for Tai Li's operatives. Miles responded by challenging Stilwell to protest to the War, State and Navy departments and to seek Miles's removal. Although both the OSS and the War Department expressed their displeasure at the navy's activities, nothing was done to stop them.[23]

No criticisms were likely to dissuade Miles from working with Tai Li. Tai, after all, had taught Miles to

hate the communists in China. They had killed the men and raped the women and made them slaves. The communists were especially hated by the peasants whose lands they had confiscated and destroyed.

General Tai Li, on the contrary,

being the liberal, democratic individual he was . . . only established concentration camps that were fully legal and the money he used to run his organization was all borrowed from savings banks . . . and he loved his mother and supported education for women.[24]

By the end of the war, SACO's police training program had graduated over five hundred specialists (and was about to enroll eight hundred more), almost none of whom received any training which could be utilized against the Japanese or common criminals. The curriculum concentrated on political crimes and means of effective repression. In Miles's own words, SACO was training the core of a Chinese national police force which would utilize the most "modern and scientific" techniques to keep the peace in China once the war was over. The modern, scientific methods SACO employed, according to its American critics, included torture, poisonings, and Miles's personal participation in mass trials conducted by Tai Li, after which political prisoners were buried alive.[25]

Both Stilwell and the embassy staff labored in vain to stop Miles. A rumor that Tai Li had suffered a falling out with Chiang over smuggling profits led Stilwell to write, "Ha, Ha, maybe our little friend Miles will learn a lesson too." A month later Stilwell warned Madame Chiang that Miles was making secret arms deals with Tai Li. Apparently the general hoped to undercut Miles by stimulating Chiang's constant suspicion of intrigue among subordinates.[26] Once the police training program had begun, Stilwell used John Davies to contact Miles but ceased almost all personal communications with him. Stilwell's rancor continually grew, fueled by the knowledge expressed by General Hearn that Miles hoped to "provoke the Reds" at a time when Stilwell was trying to get both sides to "bury the hatchet."[27] In fact, SACO contributed much more than political provocations. It actually assisted Chiang and Hurley in their efforts to oust Stilwell and continue the repression of the Communist forces.

The replacement of General Stilwell by General Albert Wedemeyer did not yield the results Miles had anticipated. Though a committed anti-Communist, Wedemeyer, like Hurley, was anxious to prevent any premature outbreak of civil war. He feared it would jeopardize the entire resistance to Japan and might actually result in a Chinese Communist victory or Russian intervention. For the duration of the war, Wedemeyer preferred the status quo. To add to Miles's frustration, Wedemeyer, a firm believer in orderly staff procedures, found SACO's independence within the theater intolerable. Soon after assuming command, the general began a campaign to bring Miles under his authority.

Wedemeyer moved against SACO on many fronts. By January 1945 he had largely succeeded in bringing the OSS under his control. He again brought Donovan and Miles together, unsuccessfully attempting to get both to agree on a coordinated policy which Wedemeyer would supervise. Admiral King's intervention, however, once again rescued Miles and SACO from being placed under the army. Wedemeyer was more successful in an area which he did control. On January 11, 1945, he notified Miles that henceforth SACO tonnage coming over the Hump would be restricted to something under two hundred tons per month.[28]

Wedemeyer also met directly with Tai Li, attempting to discover the nature of SACO's undercover activities. The general told Tai Li he was prepared to seek JCS authority to control all American equipment and personnel in SACO. He did not want to destroy the organization, only to place it under the theater commander. But Wedemeyer did reveal his concern that American equipment and personnel were being used for purposes other than fighting Japan. Tai insisted that all SACO activities, with the exception of the police training program, contributed to the anti-Japanese effort. This did not square fully with rumors Wedemeyer had heard, especially charges that SACO was emphasizing the training of assassins and political police. The theater commander insisted that U.S. personnel not participate in the assassination of Communists. Tai Li urged him not to worry any further, for "Americans would not be asked to do that. Their job was to train the Chinese to do it."[29]

Miles believed that Wedemeyer opposed SACO because he was "handicapped by a prejudice against Orientals." In fact, Wedmeyer's motives were much like Stilwell's. Miles's activities risked a premature provocation of Yenan and linked the United States to a completely unsavory character. Wedemeyer learned from the embassy staff that SACO was largely out of control. Miles would brag to both Americans and Chinese of how he employed poison and joined Tai Li in officiating at political trials. He boasted that he "personally hated all Communists, that in China they should be eliminated, and that he would be glad to assist therein."[30]

In part, Wedemeyer's dislike of Miles and Tai Li reflected a personal code of honor and morals. Miles insisted upon an alliance with a Chinese who went far beyond the acceptable bounds of anti-Communism. Notorious as an assassin, torturer, dope smuggler, and thief, Tai totally lacked the veneer of enlightened Christianity in which Chiang and the Soongs had wrapped themselves. Tai shunned most foreigners, refusing to pander to them as did T. V. Soong and Madame Chiang. As Wedemeyer reported to a friend:

If the American public ever learned that we poured supplies to a questionable organization such as Tai Li operates, without any accounting, it would be unfortunate indeed. . . . I rather question the Navy's concern for the Chinese attitude. Miles has been Santa Claus out here for a long time and just between you and me Chennault has given supplies to a certain warlord friend without accounting for them. . . .[31]

---

243   SACO! The Counterrevolution in Action

Americans like Wedemeyer and John Carter Vincent hoped to support pro-American mandarins, not infamous thugs. Tai lacked the grace which might have brought him far wider American support.[32]

Army-SACO relations continued to deteriorate during the early part of 1945. In March, Wedemeyer, Miles, and Hurley were all brought back to Washington to meet with higher authorities in an effort to reconcile their differences. In addition to their individual lobbying in the War, State, and Navy departments, the three leading Americans in China argued their cases before the Joint Chiefs on March 27.

The general atmosphere of the meeting was established by the primary question asked by the Joint Chiefs: How great a danger did the "communist rebellion" pose to Chiang and the American war effort? Hurley, Wedemeyer and Miles all agreed that the so-called rebellion would be easily suppressed by Chiang as long as he continued to receive American aid. The discussion then turned to the conflict between Wedemeyer and Miles, specifically whether Miles should be placed under the theater commander. Wedemeyer rather ingenuously claimed there were no personal or political differences between himself and Miles. He only desired to smooth the chain of command and insure that all resources were effectively employed against Japan. Miles countered with the argument that, since SACO enjoyed a unique position in China, it alone could tap major portions of Nationalist power. Already, Miles claimed, he and Tai Li had trained thirty thousand guerrillas and had made preparations to process an additional sixty thousand. Were SACO's status to be altered in any way or its operations tampered with, Chiang had warned of "undesirable results." The undesirable results, of course, would affect the KMT, not the Japanese. After prolonged army-navy feuding, the JCS finally decided to support Wedemeyer and modify the SACO agreement to bring it under the theater commander's authority.[33]

Wedemeyer, who formally received his new power on

April 6, immediately undertook to choke off some of SACO's activities. Additional limits were placed on SACO-bound Hump and Ledo Road tonnage. Orders went out for SACO to cease training and equipping Tai Li's units not directly engaged in anti-Japanese activities.[34] But SACO's organizational structure still remained intertwined between naval personnel and Tai's forces. It proved extremely difficult to enforce theater directives or determine exactly what use was made of SACO equipment.

Consequently, in June Wedemeyer appointed an army inquiry board to investigate charges that SACO Americans had participated in anti-Communist operations, something the Communists had been charging for several months. The final report, issued on August 22 (following Japan's surrender), presented no definite evidence that SACO Americans had actually taken up arms against Yenan. There was, however, much evidence that American weapons were being supplied to SACO Chinese with the knowledge that they were to be used in fighting Communists. The bulk of the arms and equipment was impossible to trace, as it had been given to Tai Li under such irregular conditions that no records were kept of transfers.[35]

Both in Chungking and in Washington, SACO personnel tried as best they could to counter Wedemeyer's crusade. Miles increasingly defined SACO's mission in terms not only of the struggle against Chinese Communism, but also of America's future global position. He encouraged his unit to consider what they must do in the field of "after the war planning." Miles envisioned a global struggle among the United States, England, and the Soviet Union for control of world resources and markets. China, which had the "biggest postwar markets," would emerge as the prize in the competition between Moscow, London and Washington. SACO's support for the KMT would not only aid an American victory but would insure special privileges for the navy in postwar China and give the navy an edge in gathering anti-Soviet intelligence. In an emotional appeal to his men, Miles prophesied:

I do not know whether we will see it in our time, but it is going to happen as sure as God made the little green apples. Russia will run the Near East, India, and China—if not physically then politically. China is facing the danger of turning Russian red in the future.[36]

In Washington, Captain J. C. Metzel led SACO's effort to induce the Navy Department to expand aid to Chiang and directly help his political strategy. Metzel argued that American troops should assist Chiang in the reoccupation of Japanese-held territory after the war. This joint action would preclude the Communists' plan to expand their territory. In addition, Metzel urged the Joint Chiefs to commit American power to the termination of all special foreign rights in China except those enjoyed by the United States.

Metzel's plans envisioned a joint American-Nationalist acceptance of Japan's surrender in China. Neither Russia nor England would be permitted to participate. In addition, the United States would have to end any pretense of supporting a Nationalistic-Communist coalition government. In Metzel's words:

We might just as well face the facts and act accordingly. To my mind this means forgetting the impossible and bending our energies to a practicable solution—namely by producing a strong unified China by serving notice on the Communists that the central government is our ally . . . and that any threat to our ally is a threat to the United States and that we will not tolerate any other army in the theater.[37]

Unable to oppose Wedemeyer directly, Miles relied on subterfuge to mobilize SACO strength against the Communists. During July and August, SACO guerrillas moved through Japenese-occupied territory toward China's largest cities—Nanking, Peking, Canton, and Shanghai. Traveling with Tai Li to the Shanghai area, Miles entered into an arrangement with Tu Yue-sheng, a notoraous gangster and kingpin of the Shanghai underworld. Miles and Tu became "fast friends," following Chiang's orders which "placed Mr. Tu under SACO. He controls a lot and we expect good results." Miles believed these links with KMT gangsters were required to counter the policies of Wedemeyer and the OSS, both of whom he claimed were "working with the Communists."[38]

During the last few weeks of the war, the drive to reoccupy cities and coastal territory increased. Wedemeyer, fearful of SACO's overt involvement in civil conflict, ordered Miles not to permit any SACO American military operations in Communist areas.[39] Despite these direct commands, Miles moved his forces directly into the battle. On August 12 he dispatched a cable to SACO Americans instructing them that Chiang and Tai Li had ordered their forces to fight to prevent Communist movement into Japanese-held territory. Miles ordered that

SACO Americans . . . proceed with their authorized Chinese unit commanders. Carry with you complete radio equipment and go fully armed. Keep this secret from all your outside friends. Send all possible arms and ammunition to the Loyal Patriotic Army as soon as possible . . . and continue logistic support.

Several hours later, Miles repeated these instructions, adding that his first message was "probably going to get me a general court martial for disobedience to orders." Accordingly, the recipients were admonished to "burn this after swearing your units to secrecy."[40]

On August 16, following the Japanese surrender, Miles repeated his order that SACO Americans assist Tai Li. Miles actually joined Tai in a policy of collaborating with Japanese and puppet forces to regain control of Shanghai. They undertook joint operations with Chou Fu-hai, Wang Ching-wei's successor, who won high praises from Miles as an anti-Communist patriot. SACO Americans also facilitated the Nationalists' recapture of coastal cities by arming a fleet of junks and seizing harbor areas.[41] However, by the middle of September the expanding scope of the civil war was fast overtaking Miles's policy, his relations with Wedemeyer, and his health.

It is ironic that Miles and Wedemeyer engaged in their final clash following the Japanese surrender. After August 15

Wedemeyer himself felt freed from many of the contstraints under which he had previously labored. Both he and his headquarters staff came to advocate direct and massive American assistance to Chiang's crash campaign to garrison north China and parts of Manchuria (these developments will be discussed in the following chapter). Nevertheless, the personal enmity between Wedemeyer and Miles continued unabated until Miles was forcibly removed from China.

Wedemeyer had come to see Miles as an "ego maniac" who visualized himself as a "White savior of China." Accordingly, the general pressed the War Department to agree to the speedy termination of most SACO activities in China. Although Miles hoped to regroup SACO into a permanent postwar naval mission, Wedemeyer recommended that the United States not permit any of its personnel to work with Tai Li.[42] Although T. V. Soong and Hurley both spoke in praise of Miles, the forces being marshaled against SACO were too powerful.[43]

The Wedemeyer-Miles confrontation was cut short by Miles's failing mental health. While many of his critics in China had long considered Miles "unstable," by August he was showing overt signs of mental deterioration. By his own admission, the SACO commander had become addicted to stimulants and tranquilizers and began to suffer from paranoid fears that the army had hatched a plot to "get him."[44] Angered and worried by Miles's behavior, Wedemeyer called in Generalissimo and Madame Chiang to discuss the future of SACO and the navy in China. Chiang made an impassioned plea on Miles's behalf, describing him as honest, dedicated, and hard working. The generalissimo wanted him to lead the proposed postwar naval mission in China. Angered by Chiang's intervention, Wedemeyer refused to soften his position and vowed to prevent the return of Miles to China in any capacity.

Just how much the KMT valued SACO's services was made apparent by the Chaings' continued boosting of Miles. Madame Chiang personally offered to patch up things between Wedemeyer and Miles, if the former would only relent. She went on to describe the "good work" Miles had done in China. "Losing him would be a pity." The conference became quite tense when Madame Chaing ominously told Wedemeyer that unless Miles were allowed to serve in China the generalissimo would have to reevaluate his past favorable impression of Wedemeyer. At another point Madame Chiang announced that she simply would "not translate" Wedemeyer's negative remarks about Miles to her husband! Wedemeyer insisted that his words be translated and left the Chiangs in no doubt that Miles had no future in China if he (Wedemeyer) were to command the expected postwar American army mission.[45]

Shortly after Wedemeyer's argument with the Chiangs, Miles sealed his own fate. He called a press conference in Shanghai at which he planned to announce that he did not recognize Wedemeyer's authority in the theater and thereby "blow the lid off." The lid which had blown off was obviously Miles's own, and navy medical staff quickly hustled him out of China and back to Washington.[46] Without Miles's presence the role of SACO quickly diminished.

After undergoing medical treatment in the United States, Miles rejoined the still functioning SACO staff in the Navy Department and pushed for a formal decoration for Tai Li. This move was made in anticipation of Tai's possible appointment as commander of an enlarged Chinese navy. Miles and Metzel used a familiar argument. Tai was a possible successor to Chiang and as such the United States should curry his favor with medals and promises of special aid. In turn, the Chinese might grant the navy special privileges in China. Following renewed State and War Department protests, however, the navy leadership refrained from recommitting itself to either Miles or Tai Li.[47]

Tai Li's death in a plane crash in March 1946 (variously attributed to the Communists, the OSS, and Dr. Sun Yat-sen's spirit, as it crashed near his tomb) ended the debate over the navy's support for him. Miles went on to serve in various naval capacities in Latin America. While posted as an attaché in

Chile, he even managed to compile an intelligence file on one particularly active leftist and future president, Dr. Salvador Allende.

SACO eventually resurfaced as a veteran's organization, reputedly linked to the China lobby. In 1974 it again became an issue in Chinese politics, when the government of the People's Republic of China initiated a mass campaign to denounce the wartime collaboration between SACO and the KMT. The Chinese press carried gruesome reports on the mangled human remains which had been unearthed at SACO's "Happy Valley" headquarters near Chungking.[48]

Although in the end Miles's organization had been purged from China, it left a bitter legacy. Much of what Miles did was opposed by his superiors only because it had been done both crudely and prematurely. SACO's essential policy had been to help prepare the KMT for civil war. By the summer of 1945 the theater commander in China, General Wedemeyer, had begun independently to make similar plans. The secret war that Miles had begun on a limited scale Wedemeyer would continue on a massive scale, involving millions of KMT troops and, for a time, vast American resources.

Chapter 12
The Japanese Surrender

BY JUNE 1945 the war in the Pacific approached its inevitable, bloody conclusion. Most Chinese, the first victims of Japanese aggression but now peripheral to the major war effort, must have felt some sense of vindication as they learned of American planes pounding Japan's cities into rubble. Had Generalissimo Chiang not been correct in his belief that American technology, not reorganized Nationalist armies, would win the war? Now, within China, the invading forces began to withdraw northward and toward major cities and ports, hoping to strengthen their lines for a final battle or retreat to Japan. Yet the approaching end of the war of resistance provided slight cause for rejoicing in China. All understood that Japan's surrender would signal the resumption of widespread civil war.

Theoretically, alternatives to civil war still existed. The Communists, now in possession of substantial territory, population, and administrative skill, seemed eager to find a place in a national political structure. In his speech, "On Coalition Government," given to the 7th Party Congress, Mao expressed the belief that the CCP could make substantial power gains through political competition with the KMT. If the record of Nationalist rule over the previous eight years foretold the future, Mao had a sound basis for this expectation. Perhaps more important, preventing or at least postponing civil war would reduce the likelihood of direct American involvement on behalf of the KMT.

Chiang no doubt understood Mao's outlook. He too realized that the Communists' strength had grown immensely, that they now controlled a regular army of several hundred thousand troops and many more local guerrillas. The CCP had developed the administrative capacity to rule an area comprising perhaps a fifth of China and, by August 1945, a population approaching one hundred million people. Moreover, the Soviet Union was bound to enter the war against Japan, thus becoming a major factor in northeast China. Should the Russians eventually choose to assist the Communists, Chiang's ability to destroy them would be severely undermined. Typically, the generalissimo saw only one prudent course—he must move quickly to destroy the Communists before the Russians might decide to intervene on their behalf and while the United States continued to assist the Nationalists with massive military aid. Even though Wedemeyer, Hurley, and Miles appeared willing to support this hard line, Chiang could not be certain how Washington would act following Japan's defeat and the shift within China to civil war.

The Truman administration shared many of Chiang's fears regarding Yenan and possible Soviet intervention. Washington, however, still prefered to explore the path of a possible political accommodation with the Soviet Union, a device aimed at isolating Yenan without precipitating civil war. The mechanism for this strategy had been forged at Yalta, where Roosevelt and Stalin agreed to promote Soviet interests in Manchuria in return for a Sino-Soviet Treaty. Early in June President Truman met with T. V. Soong to inform China's foreign minister of the Yalta agreements and the need for Soong to begin negotiations with Stalin. Despite pleas from Chiang and Soong, Truman declined to take a direct role in the upcoming Moscow negotiations for a treaty.[1] This formal refusal, however, was mitigated by Ambassador Harriman's willingness to serve as an informal advisor to Soong, keeping the President and State Department fully informed on the discussions.

While Soong and the Soviet leadership haggled in Moscow during early July, neither side made concessions acceptable to the other. Soong refused to concede formally the independence of the Soviet satellite of Outer Mongolia and declared that Soviet influence in Manchuria must be limited to joint management and use of the two ports and railroads. Stalin's position was precisely the reverse: he demanded formal recognition of Mongolian independence and Soviet management and control of the ports and railroads. Even more troubling was the new Soviet demand that the Russians be permitted to establish special military zones surrounding Dairen and Port Arthur. Stalin was prepared, however, to make a major concession in exchange for these favors. He would give Chiang a "Treaty of Friendship and Alliance" which pledged recognition of Chinese sovereignty in Manchuria and exclusive Soviet support for Chiang's government.[2] It appeared that, in return for economic control of Manchuria, the Soviet leader would disown the Chinese Communists.

Stalin departed for his Potsdam meeting with the British prime minister and President Truman on July 13. He and Soong had been unable to reach an agreement despite Harriman's attempt to convince the Chinese negotiator that he was unlikely to get any better terms, especially after the Red Army entered Manchuria. The American ambassador in Moscow also argued with Soong that the proposed treaty contained the vital pledge to "support only the National Government and that all military forces of China must come under the control of that government." This fact, combined with Stalin's promise not to station Soviet troops along the railroad lines, convinced Harriman that the Chinese and Americans should accept the agreement currently offered by Moscow. Soong, however, banked on the hope that at Potsdam Truman might find a reason for opposing the Russian demands and backing a stiff Chinese resistance. Accordingly, he was willing to postpone any treaty until after the upcoming conference and Stalin's return from Germany.[3]

The final meeting of the wartime Big Three took place in the Berlin suburb of Potsdam late in July 1945. Amid the grotesque ruins of the Third Reich, Stalin greeted the new American President and the British prime minister, Winston Churchill (who was replaced by Clement Attlee in the midst of the conference after an electoral defeat). Stalin quickly renewed his pledge of Soviet entry into the war against Japan, estimating the date as early or mid-August. Truman and his new Secretary of State, James F. Byrnes—a Democrat from South Carolina who rose to great power while serving as FDR's head of the office of War Mobilization and who had hoped to obtain the vice-presidential nomination in 1944—pressed Stalin for a confirmation that the "spirit" of the Yalta accords would be respected in China. Specifically, they wanted his assurance that the Soviet demands for rail and port privileges would not be used to negate either Chinese sovereignty or the Open Door in Manchuria.

Stalin seemed unperturbed by the American concerns, assuring Truman and Byrnes that he would do nothing to contradict their expectations. Upon returning to Moscow he expected to reach a speedy and amicable accord with Soong. According to Truman and Byrnes, Stalin attempted to show his support for Chiang by openly denouncing before them the Chinese Communists. They were nothing but "a bunch of fascists," remarked Joseph Stalin.[4]

This superficial Soviet-American agreement was at best illusory. Beneath the surface calm the entire basis of the wartime alliance, especially as it would apply to China and the war against Japan, had undergone a complete and unalterable change. The United States and the Soviet Union were already at loggerheads over Soviet domination of Eastern Europe. At Potsdam neither side had shown much willingness to reach a compromise on the issues of how to establish "democratic" governments in liberated Europe or to assess German reparations. This behavior, seen by Truman and his advisors as clear evidence of Stalin's perfidy and expansionist designs, profoundly undercut their faith in his willingness to cooperate in China. Soviet involvement in northeast Asia, they feared, would lead either to Soviet conquest or support of puppet revolutionary movements like the Chinese Communists. But any plan to exclude the Soviets from helping to defeat Japan required a substitute for the Soviet military assistance which American military leaders believed desirable, if not required, for victory. Miraculously, at this very moment, such power was produced by the successful test explosion of an atomic weapon in the desert of New Mexico.

After four years of secret development, the United States possessed a super weapon which its leaders were determined to use to shorten the war. The bomb was essentially viewed as a military tool, one which could be used as other new forms of mass destruction had been used by all the belligerents. Unavoidably, because of the bomb's power and the timing of its use, it became something of a political weapon as well. This is not to say that American leaders wanted to drop the bomb on Japan primarily to blackmail the Soviet Union to mend its ways in Europe and elsewhere. But Truman and his top advisors were consciously aware of the likely political ramifications arising from the bomb's use and exclusive possession by the United States. Probably nowhere was the case more clear than in China.

Early in June, as Secretary of War Stimson conferred with President Truman, their conversation focused on the political aspects of the atomic bomb. Stimson noted that the Interim Committee (a high-level group advising the President on the options presented by the bomb) opposed giving any detailed atomic information to Russia until after "the first bomb had been successfully laid on Japan." Truman agreed, suggesting that the Potsdam meeting had been postponed precisely to give the United States more time in which to prepare and to use the new weapon. Although the President did not say that the bomb would be used against Japan in order to bring political pressure on the Soviet Union, he and Stimson did agree that the maintenance of an American atomic monopoly (by refusing to share information) might considerably speed "the settlement of the Polish, Rumanian, Yugoslavian and Manchurian problems."[5] The "Manchurian problem" to which the two men referred concerned the Soviet demands for control over the region's railroads and the ports of Dairen and Port Arthur. Truman told Stimson that Stalin had promised to respect Chinese sovereignty, but both the President and Secretary of War suspected Soviet promises might not hold up in practice.

At the Potsdam Conference the atomic bomb entered directly into the planning of American policy. On July 21, in the midst of long, unproductive discussions with the Soviets, Truman received a coded message that the bomb had been successfully tested in New Mexico. Observers noted that Truman's whole demeanor toward Stalin underwent a change, becoming more belligerent and pushy. This impression was borne out by the new attitude toward the Far East expressed by members of the American delegation.

Accompanying Byrnes at Potsdam was Walter Brown, a journalist and close friend of the Secretary. He kept a daily diary of the conference ("Walter Brown's Book") which Byrnes later incorporated into his own notes and papers. On July 18 Brown noted that while Byrnes had previously hoped that a Russian declaration of war against Japan would emerge from the meeting at Potsdam, he now expected that the United States and Great Britain would choose to issue a joint statement "giving the Japs two weeks to surrender or face destruction. (Secret Weapon will be ready at that time.)" This threat took actual form in the Potsdam Declaration, issued by the United States and Great Britain alone.

Two days later, Brown recorded, Byrnes had begun an effort to completely "outmaneuver Stalin on China." The Secretary of State told Brown he hoped T. V. Soong would stand firm against Soviet demands in Manchuria, for then "the Russians will not go into the war." Byrnes hoped that, when faced with the American ultimatum or the actual atomic bombing, Japan would "surrender before Russia goes into the war and this will save China. If Russia goes into the war, he [Byrnes] knows Stalin will take over and China will suffer."[6] Here was evidence that American leaders believed Soviet entry into the war was not only unnecessary but actively undesirable.

Henry Stimson was also present at Potsdam. Though clearly not an intimate friend of the President (he had to argue for his own inclusion on the delegation), the Secretary of War carefully noted the shift in perception which the bomb seemed to bring out among the American delegates. His diary reflects the growing American disillusionment with, and suspicion of, all Soviet behavior. The Secretary himself described a fear of an enveloping global confrontation between American freedom and Soviet totalitarianism. The Soviet and American systems were "incompatible," and the "free system" must somehow try to break down the unfree system. While Stimson did not favor a military confrontation to bring this about, the sense of impending collision in his imagery could easily become the rationale for just such a conflict.

By July 24, following detailed news of the successful atomic test, Truman and Stimson discussed more precisely the proposed bombing targets in Japan. Stimson urged the President to exclude certain areas (especially cultural centers like Kyoto) because

if elimination was not done, the bitterness which would be caused by such a wanton act might make it impossible during the long postwar period to reconcile the Japanese to us in that area rather than to the Russians. It might thus, I pointed out, be the means of preventing what our policy demanded, namely a sympathetic Japan to the United States in case there should be any aggression by Russia in Manchuria.[7]

A new range of contingencies now concerned top policymakers. The bomb gave the United States the potential to end the war quickly. Even if the Soviet Union rushed in for the kill, its advance might be limited by a quick Japanese capitulation. Russian penetration into Manchuria or north China would be kept to a minimum. Walter Brown recorded Byrnes as believing the bomb might knock Japan out of the war before Russia was in a position to "press for claims against China."

During and shortly after the Berlin Conference, other

statements by Truman and his entourage confirmed how central the atomic bomb had become in their calculations of future policy. Truman admitted he was anxious to know whether "Marshall felt that we needed the Russians in the war or whether we could get along without them." As it turned out, American military planners were still uncertain about the actual combat effectiveness of the weapon, a fact which inhibited a full break with the Soviets. Nevertheless, on board the *Augusta* for the return voyage to the United States from Europe, Truman boasted to a group of officers that he was unconcerned about future cooperation with the Soviets or their assistance in the war aganst Japan because the United States "had developed an entirely new weapon of such force and nature that we did not need the Russians—or any other nation."[8]

After Potsdam there was little doubt that the United States would use the atomic bomb against Japan in an effort to end the war quickly without the need for an American invasion of Japan or very much Soviet assistance. The greatest danger in northeast Asia, Truman and his advisors now felt, was Soviet expansion. Soon after he learned of the bomb's successful test, Harriman drastically revised his attitude toward the proposed Sino-Soviet treaty. The ambassador urged strong Chinese and American resistance to Soviet demands in Manchuria, eventually recommending American military landings in Korea and Manchuria to preclude Soviet intervention.[9] The United States, Harriman believed, had the power to compel the Soviet Union to accept Washington's narrow interpretation of the Yalta accords.

Following Potsdam, in Moscow, the Russians and Chinese continued to argue over the terms of their treaty. During the first two weeks of August Soong balked at giving in to Russian demands. But now the Chinese negotiator was not alone. The United States dropped the fiction that it was merely a disinterested observer to the treaty, for Byrnes and Truman pressed Harriman to intervene directly on China's behalf.

Harriman met with Stalin and Molotov to impress them

with the American attitude. He stated that the United States interpreted the Yalta accords as defending the Open Door in general and the freedom of access to Dairen in particular. Any contrary interpretation, according to Harriman and Soong, violated the spirit of Yalta. Stalin demurred, saying that he interpreted the Yalta accords as recognizing a "predominant Soviet interest," which included the right to administer and control Dairen.

Unable to sway Stalin to modify his position, Harriman urged Washington to repudiate any treaty containing the terms desired by Russia. The situation reached crisis proportions on August 8, 1945, two days after the atomic bomb was dropped on Hiroshima and as Soviet forces began to pour across the Siberian frontier into Manchuria. Although many Americans came to interpret the timing of Soviet entry into the war against Japan as a self-serving ploy to topple an already broken enemy, the Soviets had actually planned their move well in advance of the atomic bomb's use. But whatever the circumstances of the Soviet entry, the fact remained that the Red Army would soon be in actual control of Manchuria and northern Korea and would not be limited by any treaty with the Chinese. Harriman was so alarmed at this prospect that he urged Truman and Byrnes to land American troops immediately in Dairen and Korea to accept the Japanese surrender and to prevent the establishment of a Soviet foothold.[10]

Now that Soviet forces were in Manchuria, it was imperative that the Chinese reach some agreement with the Russians to limit Soviet activites. The potential for Soviet meddling had become clear to Chiang during late July and early August, when the OSS and the Nationalists became aware of a noticeable increase in air traffic between Siberia and areas of north China under Communist control. OSS agents spotted both transport planes and some surface convoys carrying equipment for possible use by Communist forces. The Russians apparently made little effort to hide these activities. The reason for this, according to American intelligence, was that Stalin wanted to send a signal to Chiang persuading him to sign the treaty on Soviet terms or face the consequences.

This interpretation of Soviet pressure is supported by the reports sent from American observers in Yenan. They were stunned by the gloom and anger evident at the Chinese Communist headquarters. Yenan, apparently, had not been forewarned of the sudden Soviet entry into Manchuria and had thus not been able to position its own forces to best accept the Japanese surrender or confront the Kuomintang armies. A few weeks later, when the terms of the Sino-Soviet Treaty of August 14 were announced in Yenan, there was similar disbelief among the Communists. Stalin appeared to be forsaking them in return for neo-imperialist privileges in Manchuria.[11]

The final terms of the treaty agreed upon by Soong and the Soviet negotiators on August 14 revealed a softening in the Russian position. Dairen, after all, would remain under Chinese control except in time of war, when Russian authority would be asserted. The Soviet Union agreed not to exercise exclusive port privileges and would not station Russian guards on or along the Manchurian railroads. In addition to these concessions it was stated that KMT officials could enter the areas under Russian military occupation. Russian troops, in any case, would be withdrawn from Manchuria three months after Japan's surrender. Finally, Stalin pledged the Soviet Union's "moral, material, and military support to China and solely to the Chinese National Government" led by Chiang. This explicit renunciation of the Chinese Communists and reduction in the sphere of control demanded by the Soviets somewhat reduced Harriman's fears over the treaty.[12]

While the United States had not been able to prevent the entry of Soviet forces into Manchuria, American leaders took some encouragement in reading the terms of the Sino-Soviet Treaty. At least some formal limits had been attached to Russian intervention. More heartening was Stalin's apparent willingness to refrain from encouraging the Chinese Communists, a position which Washington had been trying to get the Russians to accept for over a year. This unexpected turn of events prompted both Chiang and his American supporters to press for the liquidation of the Chinese Communist "problem." Like most previous victories achieved by the KMT, however, this one was illusory. Quite apart from anything Stalin might wish or decree, Mao Tse-tung and his followers would not cease and desist from revolution. No matter what moderation of tactics Washington urged, Chiang would press for military supremacy. Great-power diplomacy could not contain civil war in China because the forces driving forward the Chinese revolution could not be stopped by limited outside intervention.

During the four days of August 6–9, 1945, a series of momentous military events altered radically the situation within China and among the allied nations. In that time the United States dropped two atomic bombs on Japan and the Soviet Union entered the Pacific War. Virtually all informed people understood that the war would soon be over, signalling the de facto end of the Grand Alliance and the unleashing of suppressed forces within China. When President Truman met his Cabinet on August 10, he directed Secretary of State Byrnes to modify the surrender terms previously offered Japan. If Tokyo agreed to recognize the supreme authority of the proposed Occupation commander, General Douglas MacArthur, the emperor would be permitted to continue as a nominal, provisional sovereign. These terms, in fact, were accepted by the Japanese on August 14.

As his words made plain, the President desired not only to stop needless further killing but sought a quick surrender so that "the Russians [could] not push too far into Manchuria." He expressed concern over the still unsigned Sino-Soviet Treaty, fearing that the Soviets might now grab Chinese territory and become politically involved. The former Vice-President and current Secretary of Commerce, Henry Wallace, found the tone of the Cabinet meeting even more hostile than its substance. He believed that "Truman, Byrnes and both the War and Navy Departments" were eager to abandon all ties with

Moscow, "the cornerstone of the peace of the future . . ."
This, Wallace feared, would "make for war eventually. . . ."[13]

Obviously, neither Truman nor his closest advisors retained trust in Soviet promises. They now felt that only KMT strength might secure a unified, non-Communist China. Japan's surrender being imminent, the burning question faced by American policymakers was how to insure that the two million Japanese and nearly one million puppet troops in China would surrender their weapons and positions to the Nationalists. Arranging the surrender became the first act of postwar China policy.

General Wedemeyer, keenly aware of this problem, sought several ways to both contain the Communists and also avert internal warfare. Late in July he proposed to Yenan that American military observe teams be attached to Communist units to monitor their movements. The CCP seemed stunned by the request, since the Americans Wedemeyer planned to send were closely linked to Tai Li's secret police. In Yenan, General Yeh Chien-ying told Colonel Yeaton that the Communists would never accept these "spies" in their midst.[14]

However the Communists might react to his proposals, Wedemeyer planned to work closely with the KMT in preparing to reoccupy China. Chiang and Soong conferred with the American commander on July 31, reaching an agreement in principle that the United States should assist in the seizure of key ports and cities in north China. American marines and other forces would hold strategic locations until Chiang's regular troops could assume control. Chiang also wanted American assistance in seizing all Korea before Russian or local Communist forces could replace the Japanese.[15]

On August 1 Wedemeyer advised the War Department of his belief that only KMT troops should be permitted to accept the Japanese surrender. However, since Chiang might temporarily be unable to muster enough trained men to assume this task, it might be necessary to bring in additional American forces and empower them to act on Chiang's behalf. This would ease future KMT troop movements and "preserve law and order." The American commander requested JCS approval for his extending all possible logistic aid to the Nationalist reoccupation effort.[16]

Immediately following the atomic bombings and the Soviet Union's invasion of Manchuria, Wedemeyer stepped up his calls for American intervention. He requested authority to "preclude the movement of Communist troops to occupy critical points" in north China and Manchuria. He wished to airlift KMT divisions to "discourage Communist movement." Rejecting the notion that these acts represented interference in China's internal affairs, Wedemeyer insisted that they be undertaken to "insure law and order" and to speed China's postwar "rehabilitation and reconstruction." While requesting this new authority from Washington, Wedemeyer's staff also developed plans for the uninterrupted flow of military aid once Japan surrendered and the Lend-Lease provisions lapsed.[17]

The JCS, in response to the series of startling new military developments in China and the Pacific, advised Wedemeyer on August 10 of a change in his orders. They instructed Wedemeyer to extend full assistance to KMT forces in their efforts to acquire all liberated territory and equipment. The Communists were to be excluded from participating in the Japanese surrender and the reoccupation. Although the JCS instructed the American commander to avoid involvement in "fratricidal warfare," he received permission to ferry Chiang's armies northward to where they were certain to clash with the Communists.[18]

The American staff under Wedemeyer worked closely with the KMT National Military Council to develop a plan for accepting the surrender of Japanese forces. Over a 150-day period the American navy and air forces would move Nationalist troops to strategic areas. Certain missions might even be undertaken by American combat divisions. These actions were essential, Wedemeyer told General Marshall, as both the KMT and CCP had begun a scramble for control of weapons and territory. Only thorough American logistic support for Chiang might "preclude widespread uprisings and disorder and . . . localize Chinese Communist efforts." By the time Japan capitulated in mid-August, the JCS had approved this plan.[19]

Reacting to Russian entry into the war, Wedemeyer agreed with most of Truman's advisors that the pattern of Soviet imperialism in Europe had begun to repeat itself in Asia. He described China's internal conflict as a facet of a world Communist conspiracy, designed to link the Soviet empire in Europe to one in East Asia. Wedemeyer urged the JCS and civilian officials in Washington to bring some form of pressure on Moscow in order to restrain the Communists in China. The JCS responded by telling the American commander that they and the State Department were formulating new policies based on the belief that "definite action on the Chinese Communist problem is a responsibility of the great powers which should be faced at once to safeguard world peace."[20]

Hurley's and Wedemeyer's constant urging that Washington cooperate with the KMT in postwar action against Yenan bore fruit immediately upon Japan's surrender. On August 15, as one of his first acts after Tokyo had agreed to end the war, President Truman issued General Order Number One. Among other things (such as naming General MacArthur as occupation commander in Japan), this order designated Chiang Kai-shek as the only authority permitted to accept the surrender in China. Thus, by American fiat, the Chinese Communists were declared ineligible to share in the victory for which they had so long struggled.[21]

Truman's decision of August 15 had been anticipated by the Communists. In a talk before Party cadres in Yenan the day before Tokyo's surrender, Mao outlined likely developments. The United States and the KMT regime appeared determined to plunge into civil war. The Communists, Mao emphasized, had no choice but to resist American power, even if it took the form of the new atomic bomb. Similarly, in the days following the surrender, the Yenan press blasted American actions, while messages to the American command declared that the CCP fully intended to participate in the disarming of enemy troops and the reoccupation of territory.[22] From the Communists' perspective, the American actions, combined with the almost simultaneous publication of the Sino-Soviet Treaty, must have come as a bitter blow, indeed.

From this moment on Wedemeyer assumed, with good reason, that armed clashes between Americans and Chinese Communists were inevitable. Although he continued to bear in mind the caution that he avoid American involvement in fratricidal warfare, he informed Marshall that he assumed his operative priority was to proceed with the redeployment of Chiang's forces.[23] Wedemeyer directed the U.S. 10th and 14th Air Forces to begin ferrying KMT armies to designated strategic points and cities along the China coast. The vast and dramatic scope of this operation was described in a letter written to General Dwight Eisenhower:

Whole armies, spearheading the reoccupation, were airlifted in American planes to Shanghai, Nanking and Peiping. From the Pacific came part of the U.S. 7th Fleet, which later assisted in carrying Chinese troops into northern China, and 53,000 marines who occupied the Peiping-Tientsin area. The air redeployment of the Chinese occupational forces, which was undertaken by the 10th and 14th Air Forces, was unquestionably the largest troop movement by air in the world's history. Thousands of Chinese soldiers were carried to key cities to accept local surrenders and disarm the enemy. Newly appointed officials for the administration of civil government as well as many technicians for essential utilities and industries, were rushed in to prevent the failure of the civilian economy. Air Transport, always the kingpin in our strategy for war, was also our chief asset in securing the peace.[24]

Although the movement of Nationalist forces proceeded rapidly in southern and eastern China, the reoccupation of Manchuria and northern China proved far more difficult. Any Nationalist entry into Manchuria depended on arrangements with the Russians for withdrawal of their troops. In north

China, Yenan's armies were determined to make a stand against both Nationalists and Americans. As Wedemeyer forged ahead with the program of ferrying Chiang's armies north, Mao condemned what he called blantant intervention in the civil war.[25] Denunciations of American "support for Chinese reactionaries in their efforts to promote civil war" became a constant theme of the Communist press and radio after August 15. Yet, while publicly denouncing Washington, the Chinese Communists also agreed to resume the previously futile political discussions in Chungking. From late August through November, first Mao and then Chou again came to Chungking as Hurley's guest to explore the possibility of a political compromise to prevent civil war.

This apparent contradiction and reversal of policy by Yenan reflected three factors. The Communists may well have desired to find an alternative to civil war. They believed the tide of history was flowing with them and that some arrangement securing their liberated areas and their armies and giving them a "legitimate" role in the central government would redound to their credit in the long run. The CCP also clearly feared the implications of expanded American aid to Chiang which civil war would fuel. Negotiations might convince Washington it should slow the pace of military redeployment and limit military aid to Chiang. The Communists stated quite openly that they were always willing to cooperate with the United States if possible.[26] Finally, Stalin's extremely ambiguous policy toward both the KMT and the Communists must have made Yenan terribly uncertain about the Russian role in postwar China.

While top American officials such as Wedemeyer, Forrestal, Harriman, and Truman apparently believed Russia planned to gobble up as much of China as it could, many American intelligence analysts thought otherwise. OSS reports on Soviet policy aims in China expressed the belief that Stalin did not want China to emerge as a fulcrum of conflict. Although the Soviets certainly would have liked to control Manchuria's transport facilities and strip it of industry, they lacked both the resources and the desire to become deeply involved in the Chinese civil war. The Russians, like the Americans, probably supported a coalition government (though one giving the Communists a more genuine role) which would "neutralize" China for the foreseeable future. Above all, Soviet security would be served best by a relatively weak, self-absorbed Chinese government posing no threat to stability or Soviet interests in northeast Asia. OSS analysts felt they could not really predict the future course of Chinese Communist–Russian relations. While the CCP might parrot Moscow's line on international questions, its domestic independence was well established, and it was unlikely that the Communists would accept any Soviet policy which violated their self-interest.[27]

Mounting evidence of Soviet complicity in the American-Nationalist strategy must have frightened the Communists. American observers in Yenan reported that the Communists seemed unprepared for the sudden Soviet entry into the war, which should have made Washington question the degree of cooperation between the two groups. Moreover, the terms of the Sino-Soviet Treaty, when published in Yenan, were hardly the stuff celebrations were made of. On August 28, *Hsin-hua Jih-pao* applauded the treaty but noted that it could only be carried out between the Soviet Union and a "democratic" Chinese government. Since the Communists hardly believed the KMT regime to be democratic, this was an implicit criticism of the treaty. The OSS interpreted the pact to mean that the Chinese Communists would be forced to rely on their own revolutionary resources. For the CCP, keeping their armies intact, not dissolving them as Chiang demanded, would assume greater importance.[28]

As Mao departed for Chungking late in August, Americans in Yenan inferred from conversations that the circumstances surrounding both American policy and Soviet behavior had caused the Communists to resume political discussions in Chungking. The Communists had scant hope of American support and little expectation that the Soviets would come to their aid. If nothing else, Mao's decision to respond to Hurley's renewed invitation revealed how critical the Communists believed their own situation to be. The resumption of negotiations was in large part an effort to induce Washington to "soften our post-war and long range policy" toward the CCP, reported the American observers in Yenan.[29]

Hurley (who, unlike Wedemeyer, did not yet feel the Russians were promoting civil war) had long supposed that, when the Communists realized they could not rely on Stalin's support, their resistance would cave in and they would resume negotiations with the Nationalists. The terms of the Sino-Soviet Treaty with its pledge of support to Chiang were published in Yenan on August 24. OSS intelligence sources even went so far as to suggest that during the last week in August Stalin sent a message to Yenan urging the Chinese Communists to resume political talks in Chungking. By August 27, following a Party meeting, the Communist leadership decided to send Mao back to Chungking. When Chiang and Hurley conferred on August 31, both agreed that Hurley's predictions had been verified—a Soviet refusal to support the CCP had forced Mao to return to the Chungking negotiations.[30]

Mao discussed the gloomy, if not quite desperate, situation faced by the Communists on August 26, within an inner Party circular. The chairman noted that the unexpected suddenness of the end of the war had allowed Chiang and his American supporters to gain the upper hand in reoccupying large cities and lines of communications. The Communists must now fight harder to gain the advantage in north China, and would probably lose ground in south China. At the same time, Mao explained, the KMT was under domestic and foreign pressure to stop China's civil war. Because of this, the CCP would resume peace negotiations. While Mao did not say so, the actions taken by the United States and Soviet Union also put great pressure on the CCP. The resumption of political discussions in Chungking promised to restrain the KMT and its American allies from overrunning the Communists. Mao declared his willingness to compromise, to substitute political struggle for armed struggle. But, he emphasized, the CCP would never compromise its own survival. In light of mounting setbacks and present hardships, the chairman emphasized the certainty of eventual, future victory, in contrast to the immediate crisis.[31]

The resumed Chungking negotiations dragged on for over two months, as indecisive as before. Discussions stalemated on the usual questions: control of liberated territory, the maintenance of independent Communist military forces, meaningful participation in the central government by Communists and other political parties, and the calling of an all-party "political consultative conference." Neither the Nationalists nor the Americans were moved by the spirit of compromise, as they felt the Communists were now on the defensive. Chiang continued to demand the dissolution of the CCP armies in return for cosmetic changes in the KMT regime.

The great hostility between Mao and Wedemeyer flared up in an argument over the Communists' killing of an American officer and the detention of several others believed to be spies. On August 25, near Suchow, the Communists had clashed with an intelligence party led by army Captain John Birch and a KMT officer. Even the surviving KMT officer attested to the fact that Birch had provoked the Communist troops, who had stopped the party for questioning. Birch had addressed the Communists as "bandits." When he was warned by the Kuomintang officer to stop this provocation, Birch reportedly said, "I want to find out how they intend to treat Americans. I don't mind if they kill me. If they do they will be finished, for America will punish them with Atomic bombs." Since the Communists were certain teams such as that led by Birch were linked to Tai Li and Nationalist espionage, Birch's macabre wish was fulfilled and he was executed. Nevertheless,

Wedemeyer refused to accept any explanation or apology offered by Mao and warned the Communist leader against further attacks on American personnel.[32]

Both General Wedemeyer and Ambassador Hurley grew increasingly troubled by the Communists' position in the Chungking negotiations. Their early hope that Soviet policy would force Yenan to accept Chiang's terms was dashed by the continued "stubbornness" exhibited by Mao and Chou. The two most powerful Americans in China could only imagine one reason for this lack of progress toward a coalition: an international Communist conspiracy. Yenan and Moscow must be partners in a secret agreement to frustrate peace in China and link East Asia to the European base of Communist power. Wedemeyer admonished Marshall that the "communist triumph" in Europe was nearly complete and the Russians must now be attempting to bring China, via Yenan, into their orbit. Since he believed that America's security depended on an "independent" China, Wedemeyer begged Marshall's support for decisive action.[33]

Hurley, too, saw Armageddon approaching in China. The ambassador began to elaborate on a theme which had haunted his personal correspondence since his arrival in China. The struggle in Asia was really a battle between "Imperialism and Democracy," between "Free Enterprise and Monopoly." French and British imperialists, like Soviet imperialists, desired to undermine Chiang's pro-American nationalism through encouragement of the civil war. He and Wedemeyer must return to Washington, he informed the State Department, to warn others of this danger and win support for their efforts to save China.[34]

This conspiratorial delusion now permeated the attitudes of Hurley and, to an extent, Wedemeyer. On September 16, Chiang Kai-shek learned that John Service (by then exonerated in the *Amerasia* affair) and George Atcheson were to be reassigned from the United States to serve with the Occupation authorities in Japan. The generalissimo, livid at this decision, told Hurley and Wedemeyer that the two hapless diplomats were enemies of China and pawns of the Communists. Obviously, Communist agents had maneuvered to send them to Japan so they could subvert American policy in East Asia. Chiang insisted that the Chinese Communists would interpret their appointment as a sign of faltering support for the KMT. As a result of the affair, Hurley assisted Chiang in writing a futile letter of protest to President Truman.[35]

The anxious atmosphere in Chungking was duplicated in much of what passed for political analysis in the United States. The influential *New York Times* printed an editorial denouncing the Communists for instigating civil war, for colluding with the Russians, and for delaying the surrender and repatriation of Japanese troops. The Communists, who equated the *Times* editorial with official American policy, responded in kind. *Hsinhua Jih-pao* again accused the American supporters of Chinese reactionaries of responsibility for all China's ills.[36]

Given the American fear of joint Soviet-Chinese Communist depredations, the political atmosphere in Washington proved responsive to requests for increased aid to Chiang Kai-shek. Planning staffs of the State, War, and Navy departments began discussions of long-term military commitments to China. Among the chief proposals was an offshoot of the Wedemeyer-Marshall idea of sending an aid mission to China accompanied by troops who would serve as advisors. Secretary of State James Byrnes advised Truman that this proposal should be adopted while an official state of war continued. This would minimize congressional criticisms and simplify the passage of legislation. Byrnes, pondering the question of how the Lend-Lease program might be continued, convinced the President to authorize a special temporary extension of Lend-Lease to China. This would be supplemented by a program granting China, as "surplus," large amounts of American materiel in China and the Pacific. These decisions yielded a substantial amount of military aid. The estimated total dollar value of Lend-Lease aid given to China *after* August 15, 1945, was

$839,950,233. Of this sum, over one-half was for deliveries made before October 15, 1945. Additional assistance came in the form of sales which allowed the Nationalists to purchase military supplies, nominally surplus, at a fraction of true value.[37]

Because of the military crisis in north China, Wedemeyer obtained permission to use American forces to reoccupy strategic areas. The presence of these American forces, Wedemeyer believed, would both deter a Communist seizure of vital transportation links and also ease the transition from Japanese to Nationalist control. Immediately upon Japan's surrender, the 3rd Amphibious Marine Corps received orders to prepare for reassignment to north China. Late in September, the Marines arrived off the port of Chefoo on the north Shantung coast. The task force under the command of Admiral Daniel E. Barbey planned to land a contingent of Marines in the city. Before this was done, however, Communist representatives informed the Americans that Chefoo had already been liberated and that there were no Japanese forces in the area. While Communist spokesmen in Chefoo parleyed with Barbey, in Yenan Chu Teh and Yeh Chien-ying protested to Colonel Yeaton that any landing in Chefoo could only be interpreted as a hostile operation which the Communists would resist.

During the first week of October the task force continued to await disembarkation. Only when it became apparent that the Communists would actually oppose American landings did Barbey and his deputies decide to seek other landing areas on the north China coast. The more than fifty thousand marines involved in this operation were prepared for "full scale combat operations, with adequate air support and available naval gun power should such be required by developments subsequent to landing."[38]

On September 30 marines landed at Tientsin, meeting no resistance from the supposedly hostile Japanese occupiers. In fact, at that moment the Japanese were in the midst of a battle with units of the Communist Eighth Route Army which surrounded the port. Dutifully, the same American marines, who only a few months before had been fighting bloody battles against the Japanese on Okinawa, assisted the Japanese and puppet forces in holding the port while advance American units moved to secure the airfields of Tientsin and Peking, which Wedemeyer needed to airlift Nationalist forces north. Marines moving into the north China port and railroad terminal of Chinwangtao found another battle raging between puppet forces and Communist troops. The Americans relieved the puppets and intermittent clashes ensued between the Communists and marines. The marines engaged additional Communist units in Tsingtao in October.[39]

What was to be done with the surrendered Japanese and puppet troops? They were placed under Nationalist authority and assigned to share duty with the marines in guarding the key rail lines over which coal was brought from north China to Shanghai. By early November it became a common sight throughout north China to see

tall American marines standing guard duty at isolated rail stations with small Japanese soldiers along the railroad . . . seemingly, the Japanese undertook their new policing with enthusiasm . . . for they knew if they did not their chances of repatriation to Japan would be lessened.[40]

Despite Washington's insistence that the marines' mission was to handle the Japanese, American soldiers clearly perceived their true role. One disgruntled marine wrote to Senator Tom Connally in November complaining of his units' meddling in Chinese battles.

We were told when enroute to Tsingtao that we were to assist in the disarming of Japanese troops in this area. Before we arrived the Chinese had the situation well in hand, and have since gone so far as to rearm some Japanese units for added protection against Chinese Communist forces. Recently we have been told that the reason for our prolonged visit is to hold the area in lieu of the arrival of General Chiang Kai-shek's Nationalist forces. In other words we are here to protect General Chiang's interests against possible Communist uprisings. Everything we do here points directly or indirectly toward keeping the Chinese Communists subdued.[41]

The Communists reacted to the American presence by increasing the frequency and vehemence of their anti-American verbal blasts. The editor of *Chieh-fang Jih-pao*, Po Ku, personally warned Colonel Yeaton in Yenan that large-scale Communist-American clashes would be inevitable due to the hostile mission of the marines. Unfortunately, Yeaton, like Wedemeyer, interpreted these statements as merely confirming Yenan's hostility and collusion with Moscow.[42]

Public statements by American officials during November only served to fuel tensions further. In a Shanghai news conference of November 8, Wedemeyer declared his determination to keep the fifty-three thousand marines operating on behalf of the Nationalists in north China. In addition, they would take all necessary steps to protect American lives and property. The new Secretary of War, Robert Patterson, issued a similar statement on November 12. A White House press release of the same day, while denying that it was U.S. policy to interfere in Chinese internal affairs, went on to endorse the earlier statements of Wedemeyer and Patterson.

The Communists, despairing of any favorable response from Washington, addressed protests and pleas to the American people to "rise up and demand the complete withdrawal of American troops from China before Christmas." If there were no marines in north China, Yenan radio declared, there would be no danger of those Americans lives which the marines were allegedly assigned to protect. The Communists again denounced current American policy as intervention on behalf of Chinese reactionaries.[43]

During the autumn months, policymakers in Washington labored to develop a strategy for dealing with the crisis in China. Save for John Carter Vincent (now head of the State Department's Division of Far Eastern Affairs), few men in

leading bureaucratic positions or among Truman's inner circle
had any deep knowledge of Chinese affairs. Most of their experience and interests related to Europe. It was no accident,
therefore, that only Vincent persistently advocated limiting
American military intervention on behalf of Chiang. The other
leading Washington luminaries who had a major impact on the
decisions of the influential State-War-Navy Coordinating Committee still urged a widening of American intervention.
(SWNCC—created a few months before Roosevelt's death to
coordinate policy through regular meetings of Cabinet secretaries and leading officials. It exercised major influence after
the transition from FDR to Truman. James Byrnes, Dean
Acheson, James Forrestal, Robert Patterson, and William
Leahy were among those who exercised major influence over
China policy.) Following late-September discussions in
Washington with T. V. Soong, Acheson and Leahy urged Truman and the JCS to permit Wedemeyer expanded freedom in
ferrying Chiang's forces to Manchuria, where they were
needed to replace Russian occupation forces. Leahy in particular feared that unless Nationalist troops were in position when
the Soviets withdrew, Manchuria would quickly fall into
Chinese Communist control. [44]

Continually escalating KMT demands for American assistance as well as uncertainty over the role which the marines
should play raised fundamental questions about future policy in
China. Both Hurley and Wedemeyer believed their personal
presence in Washington was required to direct the course of
policy discussions. Accordingly, the ambassador and the general returned to the United States late in September. Hurley,
who had never been popular among regular State Department
officials because of his slighting the department, found his reception in Washington less than overwhelmingly cordial. Since
Secretary of State Byrnes was in London attending the first
meeting of the Council of Foreign Ministers, Hurley was received by Acting Secretary Dean Acheson—by telephone.
Their conversation revealed the ambassador's mercurial per-

sonality. He told Acheson that he had full confidence in Wedemeyer and Chiang and played down the Soviet threat in China. Mostly he stressed his personal health problems, which he stated made his return to China unlikely.[45]

Although Hurley resigned late in November amid a flurry of accusations that subversives had undercut American policy, this was not the real reason. During October and November he often privately indicated a reluctance to continue his service in China. Hurley seemed concerned about his health and finances and also suspected that many Democratic officials in Washington preferred to keep a Republican ambassador in China to serve as a sacrifice in case a political disaster occurred. Quite likely, Hurley feared, he was being set up to take the heat that might result from the "loss of China."[46] Ironically, there is no evidence that this supicion was justified. Although Truman, Byrnes, and Acheson had no great personal affection for the ambassador, they never criticized his policy or behavior and strongly urged him not to resign.

In the event that Hurley decided not to return to China, the administration wanted to have a suitable replacement ready. Thus, during October and November Truman conferred with Wedemeyer, asking the general's consent to replace Hurley in case the latter resigned. Although Wedemeyer stated his reluctance to switch from warrior to diplomat, the fact that he was offered the post suggests that at the highest levels few even considered reevaluating the premises behind the existing policy in China. Personalities might be reshuffled but not, apparently, basic policy.[47]

During September and October SWNCC attempted to thrash out a definitive program for Hurley to take back to China. Through private conversations, especially with James Forrestal, Hurley made an indirect contribution to these discussions. Forrestal heard the ambassador's elaborate praise of SACO and Tai Li and vigorous denunciations of the "communistically inclined" John Service and American press corps in China. Hurley, however, was still circumspect in his criticisms of Soviet behavior. The greatest threat in China, he claimed, came in the form of an alliance among American subversives, European imperialists, and Chinese revolutionaries.[48]

Hurley's demonology had increasingly little relevance either to events in China or the decisionmaking process in Washington. By October Washington's growing concern focused on events in Manchuria. The Russians had proclaimed their intention to begin withdrawals late in October. The question remained whether Nationalist or Communist forces would replace them. Communist intentions were not obscure, for on October 6 a leading Communist official had told the Yenan Observer Group of plans to move into Manchuria on the heels of the Soviet departure.[49] Unless KMT armies were immediately available to fill the void, Manchuria might be lost to the Communists, almost without a fight. To prevent such a debacle, the United States attempted to land Chiang's armies by ship in Manchuria.

An American transport flotilla reached the Manchurian port of Dairen during the last week in October. As the city was still occupied by the Russians, it was necessary to get their permission before landing any Nationalist troops. The Soviet authorities raised numerous technical objections to the American proposal. They variously claimed that Dairen's status under the Sino-Soviet Treaty precluded the entry of Chinese troops and that other agreements had been made with the Nationalist authorities to delay any landings until mid-November. Since the Russians obviously planned to withdraw before then, this seemed to indicate their desire to have Communist troops enter in their wake. The Russian authorities suggested, as an alternative, that the Nationalists land at the Manchurian port of Hulutao. Since this port was already in Chinese Communist hands, such an operation was impossible. Communist spokesmen in Hulutao reluctantly agreed to permit the landing of American personnel but stated their determination to resist the entry of any KMT forces. Following similarly abortive efforts to land at Yingkow (where the Russians had suddenly withdrawn in favor of the Communists), the Nationalist armies were finally put ashore at Chingwangtao, between November 7 and 13. From there they were forced to march overland several hundred miles north into Manchuria.[50]

While Soviet behavior in Manchuria generally favored the Chinese Communists (as when the Russians gave them surrendered Japanese weapons), Yenan's policy was certainly not determined by Soviet largess. The Communists had begun large-scale movements into Manchuria before they were assured of Soviet assistance. Self-interest, not Soviet plotting, determined their actions. Manchuria was a vital economic region and, like the Nationalists, they were prepared to risk much to secure it. The timing of Soviet withdrawal largely depended on the speed at which they could dismantle Manchurian industrial plants for transport back to Russia as "war booty." Such behavior could not have won much favor with Yenan, especially since the Communists had anticipated utilizing Manchuria's advanced industrial base.

Symptomatic of the ambiguous Moscow-Yenan relationship was an incident occurring in September 1945, described by Colonel Yeaton. One day Communist official Huang Hua ordered all American personnel to stay away from the Yenan airfield which had been surrounded by troops: "About noon, a Soviet air force staff plane from Mukden landed. A small group of Soviet military personnel in uniform were quickly escorted to party headquarters. The next morning the plane left and the Soviet Radio Station went with them."[51]

Officials in Washington still had not determined how deeply involved in Manchuria American forces should become. Without further confirmation from his superiors, Wedemeyer was reluctant to commit himself more extensively. As of late October SWNCC had only reaffirmed the general goal of creating a "strong, united, and democratic China" by extending advisors, transport, and continued military aid to the Chiang regime. How the United States could secure this goal without more extensive involvement in the civil war had yet to be resolved.[52] In an effort to clarify the American commitment, the JCS outlined some possible options. Their report of October 22 recommended the speedy dispatch of a military aid mission. The JCS rejected the admonition, expressed by John Carter Vincent in the State Department, that Chiang be pressed to earn American support through political reform. Instead, they recommended Chiang should be made to "pay" by granting to America special economic concessions and by putting the Chinese economy under overall American guidance. Hopefully, this would give the United States favored access to strategic raw materials, markets of civilian and military equipment, and opportunities to "map and photograph" Sino-Soviet border regions.[53]

Such proposals revealed the fantasy sphere in which so many American policymakers operated. As Chiang's troops were desperately struggling to reoccupy the most vital economic regions of China, the JCS were prognosticating about the future of the China Market and planning models for economic development. The means they envisioned to bring about this military and economic miracle seemed like a throwback to Japan's Greater East Asia Co-Prosperity Sphere. In reality, Chiang's forces were barely able to keep their footholds in north China and Manchuria, while the fifty-three thousand American marines held positions which made them an increasingly vulnerable target. On November 6 the Secretaries of the State, War, and Navy departments, accompanied by aides, conferred in an effort to determine the future disposition of the marines and the level of assistance that would be supplied to Chiang in the future.

Wedemeyer had already communicated his reluctance to extend greater aid to Chiang without receiving new orders from Washington. He believed that, barring direct Soviet intervention, the Nationalists could handle the Communists in north China. Accordingly, Wedemeyer questioned the need to endanger the marines by continuing to deploy them in north China.

279   The Japanese Surrender

The assembled experts in Washington shared little of Wedemeyer's cautious concern. The War Department's John McCloy suggested that the issue involved in the marines' presence was less a military than a political expression of willingness to lend the "American flag" to Chiang's regime. This symbolism, as well as the assistance rendered by the marines in repatriating Japanese, justified their continued deployment, McCloy told Secretary of State Byrnes. In addition to the question of the marines, Byrnes wondered how the United States could justify ferrying additional armies to north China and Manchuria. McCloy argued that such transport aid was vital if Chiang were to defeat the Communists and discourage Soviet intervention. Apparently persuaded, Byrnes suggested the United States proclaim that all future transport assistance given the Nationalists would be a "non-political act," unrelated to internal Chinese affairs.

Actually, none of the assembled policymakers believed this rationale, for McCloy himself noted that such an American declaration would not alter the way in which the Communists, Nationalists, or Soviets perceived American action. Obviously, this rhetorical subterfuge could only be expected to have an impact on American opinion. McCloy suggested that as the Russians withdrew from Manchuria the United States should utilize surrendered Japanese troops and administrators to fill the gap. The Japanese, he argued, might do a better job managing Manchurian affairs than could the KMT. During this round-table discussion of alternatives, only Secretary of War Robert Patterson, Stimson's successor, expressed any misgivings over the deepening American military involvement in Manchuria.[54]

Decisions on the marines and on Manchurian intervention had to be reached quickly, for by mid-November Chiang presented a new dilemma to the Americans. He announced his intention to strip north China of many of his best troops so that they could be moved by Wedemeyer into Manchuria. This act would not only deepen American logistic involvement in Manchuria but would require the retention of the marines in north China to fill the vacuum caused by the Nationalist troop redeployments.[55]

Wedemeyer received tentative orders on November 19 which called on him to retain the marines in place throughout north China. Although they were to avoid direct military involvement, Wedemeyer was instructed to utilize the marines in a way that would "psychologically strengthen" Chiang against the Communists. To withdraw the marines, the War Department informed Wedemeyer, would undermine the policy of unifying all China under Chiang's leadership. But before any wider new commitments were undertaken, Washington solicited Wedemeyer's opinion on Chiang's ability to hold north China and Manchuria without direct American intervention.[56]

The Secretaries of State, War, and Navy met again on November 20, anxiously awaiting Wedemeyer's reply to their queries. As they had not yet received the general's response, they continued a discussion of possible options. Byrnes and Forrestal now spoke more openly of the need to keep the marines in north China to buttress the Nationalists against the Communists. Forrestal noted approvingly that Henry Luce and his network of publications had come out vigorously in support of Chiang, easing the Secretaries' position. Even the previously cautious Robert Patterson spoke in favor of an expanded mission for the marines. Sixty thousand of them, he boasted, could "walk from one end of China to the other." To be on the safe side, however, Patterson thought it might be wise to augment their numbers. Forrestal agreed, suggesting that a decision in favor of direct American military support for Chiang was simply a logical and consistent extension of Roosevelt's policy. To "withdraw as a result of Russian pressure," the Navy Secretary warned his associates, would be seen as cowardly and a strategic retreat. The resulting anarchy in China, Forrestal said, might lead to a Russian takeover and the formation of a Sino-Soviet axis which could dominate the entire world.

Despite their often bellicose references, the Secretaries were really quite wary of blundering into a large-scale land war in China. Their deliberations were permeated by an undertone of concern that Chiang's power might be far less secure than they hoped, that Washington might be on the verge of committing itself to a vast and hopeless military task. They attached three annexes to the conference minutes for further consideration. One suggested continuing to act exactly as had been the case since Japan's surrender; a second called for the withdrawal of the marines; still a third posited an escalation of aid to Chiang and more direct American efforts in the battle to gain control of north China and Manchuria. The tone of the meeting suggested that the Secretaries really considered there to be only two options: either abandon an active but indirect role in China or directly intervene against the Chinese Communists. Since the latter choice implied a major military effort—and a possible confrontation with the Soviet Union—the Secretaries decided to make their decision in light of information forwarded by Wedemeyer.[57]

The information Wedemeyer sent to the War Department and to General Marshall during the next few days confirmed many of the half-articulated fears which had been circulating around Washington. Wedemeyer provided what could only be interpreted as a gloomy assessment. The pace of civil war had increased rapidly and Chiang would be happy to draw the United States in as deeply as possible, he reported. This partly explained the reason behind the generalissimo's request for American transport of his armies from north China into Manchuria. Such movement would place many Nationalist armies in a position where they would have to be supplied by the United States or else face defeat by Communist forces. Chiang apparently believed the United States would intervene to extricate his strung-out armies from disaster.

Wedemeyer expressed grave concern over the growing chaos in China and admitted that much of the blame lay with the KMT. Despite all American advice, the generalissimo remained loyal to "those warlords and officials who have supported him in the past. Consequently, even though they are unscrupulous and/or incompetent, he appoints them to responsible positions in the government. They exploit the opportunities presented. Further they appoint worthless subordinates in lesser positions."[58]

This pattern, repeating itself throughout China, drove growing numbers of desperate Chinese into the Communist camp. As an alternative Wedemeyer favored pressing Chiang to accept the "assistance of foreign administrators and technicians" as well as military advisors who would "inaugurate economic, political and social reforms." Despite his strong antipathy toward Chinese and Soviet communism, Wedemeyer placed himself on record against direct American military intervention in the civil war. Instead, he recommended his own relief as Chiang's chief of staff and concentration on economic-military aid supplemented by the dispatch of American military advisors.

Wedemeyer also voiced doubts about the broader political course that should be adopted toward China. His great fear was that a Communist China would become the base for global Soviet-inspired aggression. It pained him that after one great war China was again "a political and economic arena" for a contest of "the world's two greatest powers." Yet Wedemeyer doubted that the Nationalists could hold both Manchuria and north China. He believed it might be necessary to establish some temporary form of international trusteeship over these two regions to preclude Soviet or Chinese Communist control. Meanwhile, American aid policy should focus on building up KMT strength in south China in anticipation of reoccupation of the north. A Communist victory over all China, he prophesized, would mean nothing less than their "control of the world."[59]

Marshall received a similar message from the theater commander. The Communists—Chinese and Russian—were blamed for fanning the flames of civil war and defying all legitimate authority. Wedemeyer indicated that he favored some formal continued American military presence in and aid to China but felt obliged to communicate his pessimistic evaluation of the Nationalist position. At present, American forces in China were targets for the Communists but could only serve a limited positive military function. The marines should be either withdrawn or permitted to fight. In short, wrote Wedemeyer, if it was U.S. policy to assure the survival of Chiang's regime in most of China, Washington must be prepared to fight both the Chinese Communists and the Soviet Union.[60]

Forrestal and Patterson both disliked this pessimistic evaluation. They doubted the situation could be quite so bleak and feared that such pessimism, if accepted, would dissuade their colleagues from continuing military efforts on Chiang's behalf. The War and Navy Secretaries urged Byrnes to join them in opposing any plan to abandon north China and Manchuria, explaining that such a move would be virtually a sellout of China. They wrote that "from the long-range military standpoint, the War and Navy Departments consider that the most important military element in the Far East favorable to the United States is a unified China, including Manchuria, friendly to the United States." Chiang's position, they insisted, was not hopeless. Additional American assistance and pledges would give the Nationalists both the resources and will to withstand the Communists. The marines would provide an added measure of support. For the United States to permit Manchuria to pass under Russian control (in this context little distinction was made between Chinese Communists and Russians), warned Forrestal and Patterson, would be to permit Russia to accomplish all Japan's wartime goals. Admiral Leahy said very much the same thing to Truman, urging the President to provide Chiang "every necessary assistance" except additional American combat troops.[61] It appeared that in Asia the specter of the Soviet Union had fully replaced Japanese imperialism.

Such recommendations revealed the most extreme reach of the American vision. Leahy, Patterson, Forrestal, and Wedemeyer feared a cataclysmic event about to occur in China, blamed it on the demon of international Communism, and desperately sought some means to prevent a disaster they feared would pull down the United States. Yet, having ended a world war only three months previously, it proved painful for these men to consider placing large numbers of American troops in combat again. Emotionally, they believed that a pro-American China was vital to the security of the United States. But they intellectually recoiled at the idea of involvement in a major Asian land war. Moreover, the confrontation with the Soviet Union in Europe thoroughly dominated their mental energies and material resources. They simply could not square their feelings for China with the reality of its marginal importance to American economic, political, and military security.

On November 26 Wedemeyer supplemented his earlier comments on the situation in China with an even more gloomy evaluation. The position of United States forces—and policy—was untenable, he warned, because:

The Chinese Communists are doing their utmost . . . to involve United States forces in military operations that definitely can be construed as offensive in nature. They hope . . . to influence public opinion in the States . . . in their contention that the United States is interfering with the internal affairs of China.[62]

Nor, explained Wedemeyer, had Chiang been of much help. The generalissimo pressed for increased American aid to "create conditions that render our military assistance against the Chinese Communists, and possibly the Soviet Communists, mandatory or inevitable." The same reasons underlay KMT efforts to delay American plans to repatriate Japanese soldiers. The Nationalists "circumvented repatriation plans because armed Japs [were] being used to protect . . . key areas" and lines of communication.

Wedemeyer asked that the War Department explain the situation fully to the President and the State Department. Put simply, it was "impossible" to unify China and Manchuria (under the Central Government) or to repatriate the Japanese "without U.S. Forces becoming involved in fratricidal warfare." The American commander insisted that his government soon decide whether to evacuate American forces from China, intervene directly and massively, or "invoke the machinery visualized in the United Nations charter, establish immediately a trusteeship over Manchuria and Korea," and under UN aegis repatriate all Japanese in China. Thereafter all foreign forces might withdraw and permit the Chinese "through processes of evolution or revolution" to decide "by whom and how they will be governed."[63]

Byrnes, Forrestal, and Patterson met again on November 27 to formulate an overall policy for Hurley and Wedemeyer to carry out. Their efforts had been hampered by Hurley's erratic behavior as he continued to postpone his return to China and again made veiled threats of resignation. Hurley must have realized that, whatever American policy became, it would no longer bear the firm impress of his hand and he would no longer be free to wheel and deal in China as before. In lengthy meetings held with Byrnes and Forrestal on November 26 and 27, the ambassador complained that he had heard reports of an impending decision to abandon Chiang. This, combined with some new criticism in the press of his role, had persuaded Hurley to resign lest he be set up as the "fall guy." Insisting that they had no plans to abandon Chiang, the two Cabinet members assured Hurley he retained both Truman's and their own confidence. They pleaded with him to return to China, and Hurley finally pledged to do so.[64]

Without Hurley's participation, the Secretaries met to formulate a policy of continued aid to Chiang. Although Forrestal still spoke in apocalyptic terms, arguing the need to throw the marines into combat and bring more direct pressures against Moscow, the State Department had drastically reevaluated its own position. James Byrnes and Dean Acheson were skeptical that pressure on the Russians could do very much to improve things in China. Stalin had already given as firm a verbal pledge to Chiang as could be expected. The current military crisis, they believed, reflected Chinese Communist strength more than Russian military intervention. This moderation, in stark contrast to the discussions which had been held before the receipt of Wedemeyer's gloomy assessment, swayed most of those present. Byrnes and Acheson now spoke of returning to the policy which had been operative before Japan's surrender. The United States, they suggested, ought to be realistic and seek the creation of a coalition government led by Chiang. If he balked at making meaningful compromises with Yenan, the United States must at least consider threatening the generalissimo with the cessation of American aid. Byrnes and Acheson appeared to understand that only political compromise could win what force of arms had failed to secure. Had they supported this basic idea before the end of the war, subsequent events might have been different.

But the fact remained that this reversal of policy only followed an abortive attempt to use limited military means to subdue the Communists. That having failed, Washington belatedly and reluctantly sponsored an alternative solution. But even now, as the top policymakers contemplated a political compromise, they decided to permit Wedemeyer to complete the movement of Nationalist armies already en route to Manchuria. Only new deployments to the contested areas would have to be reviewed by the JCS.[65]

During the last few days of November, American policy continued along this paradoxical course. A new moderation characterized the discussion among policymakers. At the same time, other decisions proposed expanded American military aid to the Nationalists. Arrangements between Soong and Wedemeyer sped the sale of surplus arms, with vast quantities of American equipment in Yunnan province suddenly passing into KMT hands. In order to minimize further direct involvement in transporting Nationalist armies into Manchuria, several American Liberty ships were quickly transferred to Nationalist government ownership.[66] Just what Truman and Byrnes had in mind for the future was difficult for anyone to know. A brake had been applied to the forces which desired a direct military commitment to Chiang. Yet the United States continued to serve as Chiang's arsenal, a fact which influenced all aspects of Nationalist and Communist policy.

The confusion over future policy grew even larger on November 27 following Patrick Hurley's stunning public resignation. Only that morning Hurley had promised Byrnes and Forrestal he would return to China. A few hours later the ambassador released a public statement attacking the President, the State Department, the British, and Communist subversives in America's midst. The unexpected shock reached Truman at an afternoon Cabinet meeting. "See what a son-of-a-bitch did to me," yelled the outraged President. Truman's anger no doubt reflected more than simple fury at Hurley's duplicity. The very nature of the ambassador's resignation virtually ensured a congressional inquiry and increased partisan political debate over the crisis in China.

In noting Truman's reaction and the subsequent Cabinet discussion, Henry Wallace recorded a situation which captured many of the essential contradictions in America's China policy. After damning Hurley, Truman warned that "unless we took a strong stand in China, Russia would take the place of Japan in the Far East." The President's fears encapsulated all of the hard-line arguments in favor of supporting Chiang and opposing the Communists. At the same meeting Truman and Byrnes agreed that the Russian goals in China appeared to be limited to the exploitation of Manchuria and that, in their own estimation, the Chinese Communists were more bandits than agents of Moscow. No one spoke up to question the several contradictions in what Truman and Byrnes had said. How, after all, could the Soviets have both limited goals and the intention of taking "the place of Japan" in China? If the Chinese Communists were independent bandits, could they also be agents of international Communism?

Wallace, at least, thought to himself that something was

dismally wrong with all he had heard. After all, if the CCP were merely brigands, why should Washington labor to form a coalition in China? If Truman really supported a coalition, why continue to arm Chiang with weapons he would surely turn upon the Communists? As Wallace guessed, the President and most of his Cabinet had relatively slight interest in proceeding with a basic reevaluation of complex policies. The "real" problem they faced was how to stem the domestic political backlash which might follow from Hurley's resignation. Agriculture Secretary Clinton Anderson capped the discussion by suggesting that General George Marshall be sent as a new special emissary to China. A hero considered far above partisan politics, Marshall would take care not to involve the United States in a foolish or hopeless war. Equally important, no one (or so it was supposed in 1945) would ever charge George Marshall with betraying China or Chiang Kai-shek.

By itself, of course, Marshall's nomination for a mission to China did nothing to settle the American position or extricate the United States from its ties to Chiang Kai-shek. Perhaps alone among the Cabinet members, Henry Wallace was deeply troubled by the fact that, while Marshall's selection might temporarily suffice to calm the President's political problems at home, it did little to resolve the basic conflicts within American foreign policy. The conversations between the President and his advisors, Wallace noted, "seemed to be as utterly contradictory as Hurley's own actions of the past month."[67]

Chapter 13
Backing into the Future

MARSHALL'S SELECTION AS the final American pro-consul to China initially achieved what Truman and most of his Cabinet hoped. It substantially muted the domestic reaction to Hurley's charges. Washington had bought that most valuable of commodities—time—in which to step back and evaluate the dimensions of the "disaster" about to overtake its policy in China. But if the Marshall mission achieved the goal of stilling domestic criticism in 1945–46, it also bore out Henry Wallace's dire lament that the United States had done little to realign its policy goals with the reality of China. In a sense, the Truman administration opted for a leap out of the fire and back into the frying pan.

In the wake of Hurley's charges, James Byrnes gave testimony before the Senate Foreign Relations Committee refuting the absurd claim that the Truman administration had conspired to sell out Chiang and China to Communism. To his credit, Byrnes defended the reputations of numerous diplomats in the face of provocative remarks by the Republican opposition. However, like the Senators he addressed, Byrnes could offer no really coherent statement about what U.S. policy and interests in China should be now that civil war loomed. Though charges of treason subsided, little else emerged from the brief Senate hearings. Most of Truman's inner circle endorsed the President's decision to send Marshall to China, though the crusty William Leahy thought there might be some truth to the charge that Byrnes and his aides were influenced by anonymous Communists. The prevalent opinion in Washington seemed to confirm Byrnes's later assertion that by November 1945 Patrick Hurley was a confirmed "mental case."[1]

Nevertheless, the retreat from more extensive American intervention was not the same thing as a decision to end all intervention. On November 28, within twenty-four hours of Hurley's resignation, Wedemeyer received word from the Secretaries of State, War, and Navy confirming his orders to continue American logistical support to Chiang. This policy, the Secretaries acknowledged, implied "at least indirect support of Chiang Kai-shek's activities against dissident forces in China. *This situation, however, is in no way any change from that existing during the past few years. . . .* only the KMT appears to have a chance to unify China, including Manchuria." Before his departure for China, General Marshall seemed to endorse this view, telling Admiral Leahy he expected the "Communist group will block all progress in negotiations. . . ." By delaying KMT reoccupation of Manchuria, Marshall explained, the CCP would assist Russian control. Clearly, the new emissary retained a very restricted vision of what forces were operating in China and what changes the United States would tolerate there.[2]

Subsequent discussions among Truman, Byrnes, and Marshall confirmed that American policy still pursued a chimera: a united, pro-American China governed by a coalition headed by Chiang. The sole point of an armistice was to permit creation of a coalition which would both subordinate the CCP and preclude wider Russian intervention into China. They dreaded civil war precisely because it might bring about Chiang's destruction and a Chinese Communist and/or Russian triumph. Even though the American leadership supported the concept of a coalition, they would not consider abandoning Chiang if he balked. All three officials agreed it should remain American policy to "proceed with the arrangement of shipping for the transfer of the armies of the Generalissimo to Manchuria . . . and into North China. . . ." Although Chiang would not be informed of this (so that Marshall could use transportation as a bargaining chip), the implications of this decision were grave.

In a meeting he held with Byrnes and Truman on December 11, 1945, Marshall explained his intentions. Were the Communist leaders to refuse to make "reasonable concessions," the United States would openly assist Chiang's armies in their movements north. No such threat, however, would be used against the Nationalists. The three men agreed that if—following a "breakdown of the efforts to secure a political unification"—the United States abandoned Chiang, "there would follow the tragic consequences of a divided China and of a probable reassumption of Russian power in Manchuria, the combined effect of this resulting in the defeat or loss of the major purpose of our war in the Pacific." Since such a development was intolerable, "the government would have to swallow its pride and much of its policy" and continue to assist the generalissimo, lamented Marshall.[3]

Despite this fear of Russian expansion, the precise nature of Soviet policy toward China remains something of a puzzle, just as it was throughout the 1940s. Russian military activity in Manchuria during 1945–46 did not consistently abet the Communists. While captured Japanese weapons and territory were often turned over to advancing Communist units, in other cases Soviet authorities dealt openly with the KMT. In many parts of Manchuria the Russians prolonged their occupation well into 1946, partly in response to KMT requests that Nationalist forces were not yet in a position to reoccupy them. The underlying Soviet policy appears to have been opportunism. Soviet forces seized and carted off industry as "war booty" and frequently pressed the KMT to agree to establishing joint Russian-Chinese corporations to manage Manchurian industry. Many Nationalist officials believed that Stalin hoped to develop Siberia and Manchuria in tandem while simultaneously promoting an alliance with the KMT.[4] However self-serving this policy was for the Russians, it is hardly prima facie evidence that Stalin anticipated or even favored a complete Chinese Communist conquest of China.

Direct Soviet-American contacts provided a somewhat clearer indication of Russian interests and intentions regarding

China. At the Moscow Foreign Ministers Conference of mid-December 1945, Molotov broached the subject of China with Byrnes. The Soviet foreign minister suggested that both powers announce a date at which they would each remove their troops from north China and Manchuria. Byrnes balked at this proposal, claiming no date could be set until all Japanese had been repatriated and the transportation lines made secure for the movement of Chiang's forces. In other words, Byrnes had declared that the American marines would not be removed until their presence was no longer deemed necessary.

Stalin proved far less interested in discussing China than Molotov. The American marines, he told Byrnes, were not really of great concern to Russia. As in the past, Stalin spoke of China in disparaging terms, ridiculing both Communists and Nationalists. The country was a mess and the Soviet leader disclaimed any overriding interest in the outcome of events there. Almost gallantly, Stalin wished General Marshall success in his upcoming mission to suppress the civil war.[5]

Apart from what Stalin and Molotov had to say to Byrnes, the Soviet dictator soon conducted an intriguing conversation regarding China with Ambassador Harriman. The American representative, then about to retire and return to Washington, met with Stalin on January 23, 1946. Harriman was surprised to hear the Russian leader tell him that late in 1945 Chiang Kai-shek's son, Chiang Ching-kuo, had come to Moscow seeking Soviet mediation in the civil war. Stalin praised the younger Chiang (who was married to a Russian woman and had been partially schooled in the Soviet Union) as capable and again asserted his own support for the Nationalist regime. (Both Chiang Ching-kuo and Chiang Kai-shek confirm the essence of Stalin's remarks. According to the Generalissimo he "urged China to adopt an independent foreign policy, leaning neither to one side nor to the other." Stalin also offered to meet Chiang either in Moscow or on the border, a suggestion the Chinese leader rejected.) The problem of the civil war and the Chinese Communists, Stalin complained, was not easily resolved by outsiders. The Soviet government could not mediate in China because Stalin was "not sure" that the Communists would accept his views. In fact, the Soviet Union had recalled its three representatives from Yenan and now had "poor contacts" with the CCP. In what appears to have been a frank statement, Stalin said, "his own impression was 'that the Communists would not agree with the position of the Soviet Government on China.' If he were to attempt mediation and fail, Stalin added, then the Soviet Government would be placed in 'an embarrassing situation.' " In any case, Stalin maintained that he personally hoped that the CCP would "reach an agreement with Chiang's government" and that the major source of conflict was the struggle for power and "personal mistrust" between the two factions.[6] This statement sounded rather similar to some of Roosevelt's earlier laments. It certainly displayed a realism only partly understood by most Americans.

The Chinese Communist reaction to Marshall's appointment proved even more favorable than the Kremlin's. Not only did the Party press applaud it, but on December 16 Chou En-lai, accompanied by a high-level Communist delegation, returned to Chungking to resume discussions with the Nationalists and meet with Marshall. In Yenan General Chu Teh seized the occasion to engage Colonel Yeaton in a two-hour conversation in which the commander of the Communist Eighth Route Army applauded the "change in American policy."

The Communists had responded as positively as they could, both to Marshall's appointment (they were well aware of his previous support of Stilwell) and to a speech made by Truman on December 17 in which he implied American support for a real opening of the Chinese government in return for Yenan's willingness to integrate their armed forces into the national army. While Yenan's willingness to go so far was hardly certain, the Communists obviously were pleased by the admission that China needed something more substantial than cosmetic political reforms. Chu Teh now expressed a renewed hope that Communist forces could cooperate with Americans in repatriating Japanese. Even Yeaton, among the harshest critics of almost everything said in Yenan, believed that if Marshall proved at all sensitive to Communist demands the Communists were "prepared to throw themselves in the lap of the United States."[7]

The sense that perhaps the United States could make a new beginning in China gained wide currency in December 1945. Not all Americans, of course, were pleased with Marshall's entry into China. General Wedemeyer, obviously chagrined at being upstaged by Marshall, confided some of his bitterness to Ivan Yeaton. In two letters of December 13 and 14 Wedemeyer produced a long account of his thirteen months of labor in China. The general noted with pride his efforts to help China and, as he viewed it, avoid being drawn into political conflict. Unlike Miles and SACO, said Wedemeyer, he had always played straight and not taken sides in the civil war. What had done him in, he claimed, were the very ambiguous policy guidelines which the State Department had worked out for him and Hurley. If things worked out, then the career officials would take credit; a failure would be blamed on him.[8] Thus, after all he had witnessed and all he had done, Wedemeyer, like Hurley, believed that China's problems were caused largely by the meddling of diplomatic officials of dubious intelligence and loyalty.

The continued confusion in both American policy and Chinese politics was epitomized by an event at the Chungking airfield where, on December 23, Marshall was scheduled to arrive. American embassy, KMT, and CCP representatives all turned out to greet the general. Just before his plane touched down, KMT police "started to chase the Communist representatives off the field" and were only dissuaded by American intervention. Then, within a few hours of Marshall's arrival as mediator, General Wedemeyer announced that he would continue to transport additional KMT troops north. To make matters still worse, General MacArthur's headquarters in Japan released a statement that there would be no more "drastic social, economic, or political changes in Japan," a decision bound to alarm the Chinese Communists. The total effect of these developments did not bode well for a peaceful solution. Nevertheless, the Communist delegation in Chungking eagerly attended a Christmas Eve party given by American army officers in honor of General Marshall.[9]

Marshall began his futile yearlong mission to China on a public upbeat, feted at first by both the Communists and the KMT. Meeting with the American envoy, Chou En-lai once again asserted the willingness of the CCP to engage in political compromise so long as the arrangements made for coalition government protected the Communists' military and political base. The Communists probably hoped for American support in arranging a cease-fire recognizing China's de facto partition. What neither Chou nor his comrades could ever agree to was any deal which compelled Yenan to abandon its independent army while also forgoing real power over a consolidated Chinese army. For them to do so would be to court the same fate meted them by the KMT in the purges of 1926–27. But the predominant feeling one gets after reading the transcripts of the initial Chou-Marshall discussions is of the Communists' earnest desire to temporize and postpone civil war.

The Communist representative told Marshall that his party had trusted in the policy of President Roosevelt and accepted the "Four Freedoms." They hoped to participate in a coalition government and stop internal warfare, but this required the formation of a real coalition regime that included Communist members. It was not enough to merely append a few Communists to impotent existing KMT organs. Finally, Chou concluded the initial discussions with the American envoy by praising the "spirit of independence of Washington's time," the "spirit of freedom and of government for the people, of the people and by the people as expressed by President Lincoln," and American industrial techniques which could help modernize a feudal economy. Chou had done everything but offer to make baseball China's national sport!

Polite but more circumspect than Chou, Chiang Kai-shek promised Marshall his cooperation in the task of stopping civil war and promoting political compromise. However, the basic position advanced by the KMT hardly varied from what it had always been. The Nationalists insisted that the Communists abandon their separate military forces and integrate them as small units in the national (KMT) army. Moreover, the Communists' political role would be essentially limited to serving as minority members of superfluous government organs. Neither in the military nor political sphere did Chiang contemplate a real sharing of power.[10]

Despite these portents, Marshall enjoyed some initial success in reducing the level of fighting in China. Certainly the general strove to be evenhanded, at least within the limits of his own prejudices, which had led him to oppose any policy of actually siding with the CCP against Chiang. At first he kept his thoughts very much to himself, causing both Chinese factions to feel uncertain about the future of American policy. This paved the way for a temporary cease-fire in contested parts of north China and Manchuria, the establishment of tripartite truce observer commissions, and a general reduction in the scale of fighting during the first months of 1946. In addition, on July 29, 1946, Marshall placed an embargo on arms shipments to China and expedited the reduction of American forces from a level of one hundred thousand down to six thousand. Yet much of this action was negated by the continued policy of extending various forms of aid solely to the Nationalist regime. A special surplus property agreement of August 30, for example, again transferred substantial stocks of American equipment to Chiang.

Even by July of 1946 major fissures had appeared in Marshall's peace mission. Temporary truces arranged in Manchuria and north China lapsed and the KMT pressed for a quick military solution to the Communist problem. Chiang, it appeared, felt that whatever its displeasure, or temporary cessation of military aid, the United States would not abandon his regime and permit a Communist victory. Continued forms of American aid to the KMT, combined with Washington's refusal to accept the CCP as a legitimate contender for power and recipient of American support, eroded the Communists' remaining faith in Marshall's role as honest broker. Certainly, Mao and his followers must have viewed with great alarm the growing American opposition to both the Soviet Union and various revolutionary movements in Europe and Asia. They could not expect very much sympathy from Washington.

By January 1947 the United States finally abandoned its mediation efforts. Truman recalled Marshall and nominated him to succeed Byrnes as Secretary of State. Marshall's parting statement from China denounced both factions for sabotaging peace, and, upon assuming his new post, the general tried to steer American policy away from any new involvements in China. Still, the agony of civil war and revolution was not over for either China or the United States. Almost three more years passed before the Communists forced their opponents off the mainland and onto the tiny bastion of Taiwan. During this period positions hardened on all sides, especially as China emerged as a partisan political issue in the United States. By 1947 the Truman administration had begun to come under attack for its alleged "softness" on Communism. Probably nowhere was it more vulnerable than on China policy. Republicans lambasted the administration first for its willingness to consider supporting a coalition including Communists, then, following Marshall's departure, for not doing enough to help Chiang defeat the Communists. With the apparent encouragement and funding of the Nationalists, a political pressure group emerged in the Congress, press, and public. This so-called China lobby urged much greater U.S. support for the KMT in its war against the Communists.

The Truman administration was put on the defensive precisely because it had gone so far in enshrining the doctrine of "containment" in Europe. Within three months of Marshall's return the United States embarked on a cold war journey whose milestones soon included the Truman Doctrine, the Marshall Plan and, eventually, NATO. Why, chanted Chiang's supporters, was only limited economic and military assistance extended to China? If Soviet "expansion" in Greece and Turkey could be resisted through generous American aid, why did the Truman administration refuse to widen the commitment to Chiang Kai-shek?

The simple fact was that by the end of 1946 few responsible officials in the administration believed that Chiang's regime could be saved from itself. A few months after Japan's surrender, a dying Joseph Stilwell visited Truman and implored him not to intervene on Chiang's behalf. Stilwell remarked that Chiang was a "crook" who deserved no American support. Truman later recalled that he shared the general's view, that as far as he was concerned, the Chiangs, the Kungs, and the Soongs "were all thieves, every last one of them." While allowing for exaggeration, Truman's harsh judgment probably reflected his contemporary view.[11] Even the corrupt regime in Greece enjoyed a popularity and efficiency greater than Chiang's. It was unlikely that the President or Marshall would ever gamble much on such an ally, especially since they believed the major Communist challenge would come in Europe.

However low the regard in which Truman and Marshall held Chiang, they could not escape the ideological and political fallout of the emerging cold war. Growing cries from Congress and the diffuse China lobby finally prodded Truman to lift the arms embargo as early as May 1947. Other forms of economic aid were resumed through various agreements. Only on the question of committing American combat troops to China did the administration refuse to budge. Yet, in writing his cover letter for the China White Paper of 1949, Dean Acheson referred to sending American forces into China as the "most attractive idea." Military realities, he noted, as well as the lack of popular American support, had simply made this unfeasible after December 1945.[12]

Events within China quickened as 1948 wore on. The pattern of Nationalist defeats became more regular, with the military initiative passing to the Communists. Marshall increasingly seemed to look upon the Communists as both Chiang's enemy and America's. He outlined the administration's new policy as a refusal to "give any implication of support, encouragement or acceptability of coalition government in China with Communist participation."[13] In April 1948 the administration approved, with some reluctance, the China Aid Act, allocating $125 million for use "at the discretion of the Chinese government." Truman and Marshall tolerated this gesture to appease Senators and Congressmen whose votes were needed for European aid programs. Moreover, they hoped granting Chiang some additional military credits might stifle the cries of those demanding more massive or direct American aid. As Marshall noted in a closed discussion before Senate and House committees, in order to destroy the Communists the United States would have to

underwrite the Chinese Government's military effort, on a wide and probably constantly increasing scale, as well as the Chinese economy. The U.S. would have to be prepared virtually to take over the Chinese Government and administer its economic, military and governmental affairs . . . It would be impossible to estimate the final cost of a course of action of this magnitude. It certainly would be a continuing operation for a long time to come. . . . it would be practically impossible to withdraw . . .[14]

By November 1948 the discussions at Truman's Cabinet meetings suggested how hopeless the entire situation had become. Marshall's comments revealed the growing political dilemma the administration faced in both reacting to Chinese events and explaining them to the American people. "The Nationalist Government," he told the Cabinet, is on its way out and there is nothing we can do to save it. We are faced with the question of clarifying [it to] the American people and by so doing deliver the knock out blow to the Nationalist Govt in China—or we can play along with the existing govt and kee[p] facts from the American people and thereby not be accused later of playing into the hands of the Communists.[15]

This attitude prevailed through the middle of 1949, to the point when Communist armies were about to run Chiang's remaining forces off the mainland. For Marshall himself the dilemma was resolved only by ill health and retirement.

In a belated attempt to explain this disaster—and forestall Republican criticism—Truman approved the release by his new Secretary of State, Dean Acheson, of a White Paper on China policy. The August 1949 policy statement contained a blistering indictment of KMT decadence, corruption, and incompetence. Chiang, it asserted, had brought defeat upon himself. No new American policy or additional aid could undo what he had done. In an apparent effort to appease convervatives and protect the administration from further cries of betrayal, Acheson appended a cover letter to the report which denounced the Communists as usurpers and puppets of the Kremlin. They had betrayed China, he declared, making their nation a Soviet "Manchukuo."[16] Once again, the U.S. government loudly and publicly slammed the door against the reality of a Communist China.

The White Paper proved a document which almost everyone could love to hate. Chiang's defenders saw it as the kiss of death which undermined any remaining hope of preventing a Communist victory, and said it bore a causal relation to the creation of the People's Republic only two months later. Mao reacted to the document almost as swiftly as its American critics, writing several articles describing American policy as a fraud. He, too, urged people to study the record, for then they would see, in Washington's own words, how the United States had clung to Chiang and proscribed real cooperation with the CCP.[17]

Shortly before and after the October 1, 1949, creation of the People's Republic, Communist intermediaries made several futile efforts to discuss with American diplomats possible future political relations. These came to naught as Secretary Acheson refused to make any conciliatory gesture. Very quickly, the few remaining American officials in China were either withdrawn or ignominiously deported. Now, when Dean Acheson, Walter Judd, and many others turned their gaze East, all they could perceive were Soviet henchmen sitting on the Dragon Throne.

Even today the effort to assess the causes and consequences of American failure in China involves a political calculus. If success was to be measured by sustaining Chiang in power, then the tactics and strategy pursued by Washington since 1938 had been unrealistic, inappropriate, and probably doomed. However if success was taken to mean preserving a unified, stable, and "pro-American" China, then not even the Communist victory necessarily proved failure. The Peking regime forged a unity and stability unknown in China since the nineteenth century. Though "pro-American" was too diffuse a term probably for anyone to define, few if any strategic American interests were threatened by a Communist China. The Sino-Soviet alliance of 1950, lasting barely ten years, was not proof of CCP subservience. As John Davies and John Service prophesied, it represented a marriage of convenience— perhaps necessity—abetted by the United States. By 1949 there seemed no way for China's new rulers to alter the pattern of American hostility.

Probably the most tragic result of the "loss of China" came in the form of the historical lesson American policymakers and politicians derived from it. Neither the rules of the global cold war nor those of the domestic political process, they concluded, permitted another non-Communist anchor in Asia to be abandoned. The situation must never again be allowed to deteriorate to the point which China had reached in 1945.

Henceforth the United States must be prepared to intervene before a revolutionary situation became desperate. This lesson found rapid application in Korea during June 1950, when the Truman administration scarcely hesitated to send troops into battle and reimpose American forces in defense of Taiwan. The simultaneous entry into the French Indochina war proved a massive test of the American will to create a puppet Asian nationalism which would sweep back the tide of social revolution.

In a haunting way Vietnam became the macabre fulfillment of Joseph Stilwell's cherished reform strategy. Advisors attached to the White House, State Department, Pentagon, and CIA did all that was humanly possible to create a pliable government and army in South Vietnam which would form the core of a bona fide nationalist regime. The level of overt and covert manipulation of the client in Saigon surpassed even Stilwell's imagination. When the approach failed, massive and direct applications of American power were rushed into the battle. And in the end, it all went the same way as China for almost the same variety of reasons. [18]

The arrogance and self-deceit of this American vision had originated in policies adopted to create a Chinese barrier to Japanese imperialism. In this effort the United States had agreed, out of necessity, to sponsor and hopefully reform the reactionary nationalism of the KMT. Before Pearl Harbor, it might be argued, such an accommodation with Chiang's regime was justified by the greater importance of stopping Japanese imperialism. However, once the United States itself became directly involved in the Pacific War and joined the Chinese power struggle, the nature of its responsibilities was fundamentally transformed.

By 1942, in the face of an increasingly popular and powerful Communist movement, the United States could not justifiably maintain that exclusive support for the KMT was either a successful or moral policy in China. The results on the political and military battlefields proved dismal and showed no likelihood of improvement. In spite of this overwhelming evidence, neither Presidents Roosevelt nor Truman nor their leading advisors proved willing or able to do more than superficially modify their policies and tactics. In the end, only the Communists' strength, the Nationalists' hopelessness, and the perceived Soviet threat in Europe saved the United States from an even more tragic intervention. For a decade, despite a nearly total misunderstanding of China's crisis and an equally murky concept of what it wished to achieve, the United States struggled to become the arbiter of change in China and Asia. Only the fury of the Chinese revolution and the passage of time could begin to erode this arrogance.

Abbreviations
and Locations of Collections
Cited in the Notes

Amerasia Papers	Senate Committee on the Judiciary, *The Amerasia Papers*
Arnold Papers	Hoover Institution on War, Revolution, and Peace, Palo Alto, Cal.
Barbey Papers	Center for Naval History, Washington, D.C.
Boatner Papers	Hoover Institution on War, Revolution, and Peace, Palo Alto, Cal.
Byrnes Papers	Clemson University Library, Clemson, S.C.
Cairo and Teheran	Department of State, *The Conferences at Cairo and Teheran, 1943*
CBI Theater, Historical Section	Department of the Army, China-Burma-India Theater, Historical Section
Chennault Papers	Hoover Institution on War, Revolution, and Peace, Palo Alto, Cal.; Manuscript Division, Library of Congress, Washington, D.C. (microfilm)
China White Paper	Department of State, *United States Relations with China, with Special Reference to the period 1944–1949*
Connelly Papers	Harry S. Truman Presidential Library, Independence, Mo.
Douglas Papers	University of Arizona, Tucson
Dulles Papers	Princeton University Library, Princeton, N.J.
Elsey Papers	Harry S. Truman Presidential Library, Independence, Mo.
Feis Papers	Manuscript Division, Library of Congress, Washington, D.C.
Forrestal Diary	Center for Naval History, Washington, D.C.
Forrestal Papers	Princeton University Library, Princeton, N.J.
FRUS	Department of State, *Foreign Relations of the United States, Diplomatic Papers, 1931——*

307

FRUS Japan 1931–1941	Department of State, *Papers Relating to the Foreign Relations of the United States: Japan, 1931–1941*
Goodfellow Papers	Hoover Institution on War, Revolution, and Peace, Palo Alto, Cal.
Hart Papers	Center for Naval History, Washington, D.C.
Hayden Papers	Michigan Historical Collections, Ann Arbor
Hopkins Papers	Franklin D. Roosevelt Library, Hyde Park, N.Y.
Hornbeck Papers	Hoover Institution on War, Revolution, and Peace, Palo Alto, Cal.
Hull Papers	Manuscript Division, Library of Congress, Washington, D.C.
Hurley Papers	Western History Collections, University of Oklahoma, Norman
Johnson Papers	Manuscript Division, Library of Congress, Washington, D.C.
Leahy Papers	Manuscript Division, Library of Congress, Washington, D.C.
Magruder Mission Material	Department of the Army, Supporting Documents, CBI Theater History
Malta and Yalta	Department of State, *The Conferences at Malta and Yalta, 1945*
McHugh Papers	Cornell University, Ithaca, N.Y.
Miles Papers	Center for Naval History, Washington, D.C.; Hoover Institution on War, Revolution, and Peace, Palo Alto, Cal.
Morgenthau Diaries I, II	Senate Committee on the Judiciary, *Morgenthau Diary, China* (2 vols.)
Morgenthau Papers	Franklin D. Roosevelt Library, Hyde Park, N.Y.
NGC Records	Department of the Navy, Center for Naval History, Records of Naval Group China
OSS-Yenan Documents	Department of the Army, Modern Military Records Branch, OSS-Yenan Documents
PPF	President's Personal File
PSF	President's Secretary's File
Quebec	Department of State, *The Conference at Quebec, 1944*

Roosevelt Papers	Franklin D. Roosevelt Library, Hyde Park, N.Y.
Soong Papers	Hoover Institution on War, Revolution, and Peace, Palo Alto, Cal.
Stilwell CBI Correspondence	Department of the Army, China-Burma-India Theater, Records
Stilwell Papers	Hoover Institution on War, Revolution, and Peace, Palo Alto, Cal.
Stilwell Report on CBI	Department of the Army, History of the China-Burma-India Theater
Stimson Papers	Yale University Library, New Haven, Conn.
Stuart Papers	Hoover Institution on War, Revolution, and Peace, Palo Alto, Cal.
Wallace Papers	Manuscript Division, Library of Congress, Washington, D.C.
Washington and Casablanca	Department of State, *The Conference at Washington, 1941–1942 and Casablanca, 1943*
White Papers	Princeton University Library, Princeton, N.J.
Willauer Papers	Princeton University Library, Princeton, N.J.
Yarnell Papers	Center for Naval History, Washington, D.C.; Manuscript Division, Library of Congress, Washington, D.C.
Yeaton Manuscript	Hoover Institution on War, Revolution, and Peace, Palo Alto, Cal.
Young Papers	Hoover Institution on War, Revolution, and Peace, Palo Alto, Cal.

Notes

Chapter 1. Images of China

1. Harold R. Isaacs, *Scratches on Our Minds: American Images of China and India* (New York: John Day, 1958). For a description of the wary view American business interests took of China during the 1930s, see Dorothy Borg, *The United States and the Far Eastern Crisis of 1933–1938* pp. 258–62; and Mira Wilkins, "The Role of U.S. Business," in Dorothy Borg and Shumpei Okamoto, eds., *Pearl Harbor as History.*

2. Lucien Bianco, *Origins of the Chinese Revolution, 1915–1949* (Stanford, Cal.: Stanford University Press, 1971). This short study offers perhaps the most lucid treatment of the interplay of social and political factors contributing to the Chinese revolution.

3. Statement by Henry Stimson, January 7, 1932, *FRUS Japan 1931–1941*, I, 76; Henry L. Stimson and McGeorge Bundy, *On Active Service in Peace and War*, p. 236; Memoranda by Stimson, February 11, 19, 25, 1932, *FRUS 1932*, III, 287, 341, 440; Stimson to Senator William Borah, *FRUS Japan 1931–1941*, I, 80, 83.

4. Nelson Johnson to Stanley Hornbeck, April 12, 1934, Johnson Papers; Hornbeck to Johnson, Feburary 24, 1936, *ibid.*

5. Johnson to E. C. Carter, May 27, 1933, *ibid.*

6. James C. Thomson, *While China Faced West: American Reformers in Nationalist China, 1927–1937* (Cambridge, Mass.: Harvard University Press, chs. 1, 8, describes the evolving friendship between the KMT and American missionaries. A description of political conditions in China during the period of Nationalist ascendancy is found in Lloyd Eastman, *The Abortive Revolution*, and Hung-mao Tien, *Government and Politics in Kuomintang China, 1927–1937* (Stanford, Cal.: Stanford University Press, 1972).

7. O. Edmund Clubb to Johnson, April 1932, Dept. of State, Decimal File, China, 893.00b/927.

8. Report by Walter Adams, April 17, 1934, Dept. of the Army, G-2 Regional File.

9. See Borg, *Far Eastern Crisis*, pp. 202–7; O. Edmund Clubb, *The Witness and I*, provides an account of this episode.

10. Borg, *Far Eastern Crisis;* undated diary entry of 1935–36, "Communism in China," Box 21, Stilwell Papers; Report by Stilwell, January 9, 1936, Dept. of the Army, G-2 Regional File; Edgar Snow, *Red Star Over China.*

11. Frank Lockhart to Cordell Hull, December 13, 1936, Dept. of State, Decimal File, China, 893.00/13753; Lockhart to Hull, December 20, 1936, *FRUS 1936*, IV, 440–41.

12. A discussion of the complex interplay of Soviet and Chinese Communist policy at Sian is found in Lyman Van Slyke, *Enemies and Friends*, pp. 75–91.

13. Loy Henderson to Hull, December 14, 1936, Dept. of State, Decimal File, China, 893.00/13761; Report of December 14, 1936, Dept. of the Army, G-2 Regional File; extensive selections of reporting on Sian appear in *FRUS 1936*, IV, 414–58. See especially p. 439 and Hull to Johnson, December 14, 1936, Dept. of State, Decimal File, China, 893.00/13764 A.

14. Admiral Harry E. Yarnell to Admiral William Leahy, May 1, 1937, Yarnell Papers, Library of Congress; Report by Stilwell, December 21, 1936, Dept. of the Army, Military Intelligence Division Reports, 1917–41.

15. Johnson to Hull, February 23, 1937, Dept. of State, Decimal File, Sino-Japanese War, 793.94/8517; Johnson to Hull, April 20, 1937, Dept. of State, Decimal File, China, 893.00/14096; Report by Stilwell, March 11, 1937, Dept. of the Army, Military Intelligence Division Reports, 1917–41.

16. Yarnell to Bruce Leighton, June 4, 1937, Yarnell Papers.

17. Memorandum of Statement by Hull, July 16, 1937, *FRUS 1937*, I, 697.

18. Willys Peck to Hull, July 19, 1937, *ibid.*, III, 206; Memorandum of Conversation by Maxwell Hamilton, July 10, 1937, *ibid.*, p. 132; Memorandum by Hornbeck, July 12, 1937, *ibid.*, p. 144; Johnson to Hull, August 12, 1937, *ibid.*, p. 385; Hornbeck to Johnson, July 17, 1937, Johnson Papers.

19. An excellent analysis of the controversy surrounding the Quarantine Speech and Burssels Conference is found in Borg, *Far Eastern Crisis*, pp. 366–441; Memorandum by Grew, November 18, 1937, *FRUS Japan 1931–1941*, I, 415; Memorandum by Hornbeck, July 27, 1937, *FRUS 1937*, III, 279; Memorandum by Hamilton, October 12, 1937, *ibid.*, 596.

20. Cordell Hull, *Memoirs*, I, 445, 544–45, 554; historian and former State Dept. official Herbert Feis, later recalled that "one other thought figured in the guidance of American policy. Decisive success in the use of compulsion might have some undesired results. If Japan were brought to a sudden collapse it might no longer be an effective opponent of communism in Asia. Unless the retreat from Manchuria were well managed, the communists might win control of the land, not China. This gave cause for wishing a settlement by consent, rather than by coercion." Feis does not specify whether the State Dept. feared the spread of Soviet and/or Chinese Communism. In any case, the Chinese Communists apparently failed to qualify as Chinese. See Herbert Feis, *The Road to Pearl Harbor*, pp. 6–7.

21. Manny Koginos, *The Panay Incident, Prelude to War* (West Lafayette, Ind.: Purdue University Press, 1967).

Chapter 2. The Economics of Containment, 1938–40

1. Johnson to Hornbeck, December 30, 1937, Hornbeck Papers; Johnson to Hull, December 18, 1937, Dept. of State, Decimal File, China, 893.00/14192.

2. Yarnell to Johnson, July 21, 1937, Yarnell Papers; Yarnell to Senator Guy Gillette, July 22, 1937, *ibid.*; Yarnell to Leahy, February 11, March 25, March 27, August 10,

October 15, 1937, *ibid.;* Johnson to Hull, November 3, 1937, *FRUS 1937,* III, 654; Yarnell to General Bowley, November 28, 1937, Yarnell Papers; Yarnell to Paul V. McNutt, January 14, 1938, *ibid.;* Yarnell to Admiral Thomas Hart, September 2, 1938, *ibid.;* Yarnell to Leahy, November 25, 1938, and January 23, 1939, *ibid.;* Yarnell to Gillette, January 13, 1939, *ibid.;* Yarnell to Hornbeck, March 10, 1939, *ibid.*

3. Leahy to Franklin Roosevelt, January 6, 1938, PSF, China, Box 27, Roosevelt Papers; Memorandum for Roosevelt, Feburary 19, 1938, *ibid.*

4. Kenneth Shewmaker, *Americans and Chinese Communists, 1927–1945,* p. 101; Evans F. Carlson, *Twin Stars Over China,* p. 49.

5. Carlson to Le Hand, November 1, 7, 29, 1937, December 24, 1937, March 4, 1938, PPF 4951, Roosevelt Papers; Carlson to Johnson, December 18, 1938, Johnson Papers; Carlson to Le Hand, August 15, September 23, November 15, 1938, PPF 4951, Roosevelt Papers.

6. Carlson to Le Hand, August 14, 1937, PPF, 4951 Roosevelt Papers; Harold Ickes, *Secret Diary,* pp. 327–28; Edgar Snow, *Journey to the Beginning.*

7. Carlson to Johnson, September 20, 1938, Johnson Papers; H. E. Overesch to Yarnell, September 22, 1938, Yarnell Papers.

8. Johnson to Hornbeck, March 22, October 26, November 3, 1938, Hornbeck Papers; Diary entry of August 19, 1938, Leahy Papers.

9. Hornbeck to Alexander Cadogan, April 13, 1938, *FRUS 1938,* III, 141–43; John Carter Vincent to Hornbeck, July 23, 1938, *ibid.,* pp. 234–37.

10. Hull to American Embassy, London, January 6, 1938, Dept. of State, Decimal File, China, 893.51/6654; memorandum of conversation between Sumner Welles and Counselor of Chinese Embassy, January 8, 1938, *ibid.,* 893.51/6584; Johnson to Hull, February 8, 1938, *ibid.,* 893.51/6590; Johnson to Hull, February 27, 1938, *ibid.,* 893.51/6593; Johnson to Hull, April 26, 1938, *FRUS 1938,* III, 157; Johnson to Hull, June 15, 1938, Dept. of State, Decimal File, China, 893.51/6618; Johnson to Hull, July 1, 1938, 893.51/6638.

11. Hull to Joseph Kennedy, July 13, 1938, *FRUS 1938,* III, 536; memorandum by Hornbeck, August 11, 1938, Dept. of State, Decimal File, China, 893.51/6676; memorandum of a conversation by Hornbeck, July 15, 1938, *FRUS 1938,* III, 538.

12. William Bullitt to Roosevelt, August 8, 1938, Dept. of State, Decimal File, China, 893.51/6673½.

13. H. H. Kung to K. P. Chen, August 30, 1938, Young Papers; Chen to Kung, October 11, 1938, *ibid.*

14. Morgenthau to Roosevelt, October 17, 1938, PSF, Box 82, Roosevelt Papers.

15. Chen to Kung, November 17, 1938, Young Papers; Herbert Feis to Hull, November 12, 1938, Dept. of State, Decimal File, China, 893.51/6736⅛.

16. Memorandum by Maxwell Hamilton, November 14, 1938, Dept. of State, Decimal File, China, 893.51/6736^2/8; Memorandum by Hull, November 14, 1938, *ibid.,* 893.51/6736^4/8.

---

313   **2. The Economics of Containment**

17. Hornbeck to Roosevelt, November 14, 1938, PSF, Box 27, Roosevelt Papers.

18. Diary entries of November 29, 30, 1938, 153:336, 366–69, Morgenthau Papers.

19. Statement by Japanese government, November 3, 1938, *FRUS Japan 1931–1941*, I, 477; memorandum of conversation by Counselor of the Embassy in Japan, November 19, 1938, *ibid.*, 801.

20. Johnson to Hull, November 16, 1938, *FRUS 1938*, III, 377.

21. Diary entry of November 30, 1938, 153:300–302, Morgenthau Papers.

22. Press releases of December 15, 19, 1938, *FRUS 1938*, III, 586, 588; Diary entry of December 27, 1938, 158:223, Morgenthau Papers.

23. Grew to Hull, December 19, 1938, *FRUS 1938*, III, 589.

24. Memorandum by Hornbeck, May 16, 1939, Dept. of State, Decimal File, China, 893.51/6908.

25. Peck to Hull, December 19, 1938, *ibid.*, 893.51/6754; *Chung-yang Jih-pao* (Central Daily), December 17, 18, 19, 20, 1938.

26. K. C. Li to Kung, December 23, 1938, Young Papers.

27. Memoranda by Hornbeck, January 13, January 25, 1939, *FRUS 1939*, III, 482, 489. For an extensive file of Hornbeck's intradepartmental memoranda see Box 424, Hornbeck Papers.

28. Vincent to Hornbeck, January 20, 1939, *FRUS 1938*, III, 483–85; Johnson to Roosevelt, February 27, 1939, *ibid.*, 512–14.

29. White to Morgenthau, May 10, 1939, Senate Committee on the Judiciary, *Morgenthau Diaries*, I, 7, 13 (this printed collection of selected China-related materials from the manuscript diaries at Hyde Park is a valuable source for reconstructing the aid program of the Treasury Department).

30. Memorandum of Morgenthau-Chen conversation, October 4, 1939, *ibid.*, pp. 17–22; memorandum of Group Meeting at Treasury Dept., January 10, 1940, *ibid.*, p. 76. Morgenthau generally had a stenographer present at important meetings, preserving an excellent record for historians.

31. Memorandum of conversation with K. P. Chen, April 19, 1940, *ibid.*, 112–18.

32. "Report on American Aid to China," February 7, 1942, Far Eastern Section, Coordinator of Information. This document was located among a randomly organized collection of naval attaché reports at the Operational Archives, Center for Naval History, Washington, D.C.

33. Transcript of discussion, April 18, 1940, *Morgenthau Diaries*, I, 100–108; transcript of group meeting, April 30, 1940, *ibid.*, 130–36; Hornbeck to Morgenthau, April 11, 1940, *FRUS 1940*, IV, 651.

34. Chiang Kai-shek to Roosevelt, May 17, 1940, *Morgenthau Diaries*, I, 173; memorandum by Morgenthau for Roosevelt, July 1, 1940, *ibid.*, p. 174; Morgenthau to Roosevelt, July 15, 1940, *ibid.*, p. 177; memorandum of conversation with the Russian

ambassador, October 1, 1940, *ibid.*, pp. 225, 231; memorandum of conversation with Hornbeck, August 15, 1940, *ibid.*, p. 191; Morgenthau-Hull conversation, September 20, 1940, *ibid.*, pp. 209–11; Morgenthau–Jesse Jones conversation, October 2, 1940, *ibid.*, pp. 233–35. A word of explanation regarding T. V. Soong is in order. Though officially the leading Chinese official in the United States in 1940, naval attaché James McHugh reported that Soong had virtually fled Chungking for the safety of Washington. This behavior occurred frequently during the war as political battle raged within the Chiang-Soong-Kung family triumvirate. Between 1938 and 1945 Soong continued to flit between Washington and Chungking, making powerful friends and enemies in both capitals due to his wheeling and dealing. Chiang believed, with good reason as later events showed, that his brother-in-law hoped to use his influence over American aid to gain power within China. At the same time, Chiang depended on Soong's influence to win desperately needed American support. This rivalry continued long after World War II, ending only with the mens' deaths.

35. See U.S. Trade with Far East file, Box 414, Hornbeck Papers; Policy, 1940, file, Box 424, and Alliances: Germany and Italy file, Box 4, *ibid.*

36. John Morton Blum, *Morgenthau Diaries 1938–1941*, p. 356.

37. Johnson to Hull, November 9, 1940, *FRUS 1940*, IV, 688; memorandum by Hull of conversation with T. V. Soong, November 26, 1940, *ibid.*, 697; Transcript of Treasury Group Meeting, September 6, 1940, *Morgenthau Diaries*, I, 197.

38. Memorandum of conversation by Morgenthau, September 20, 1940, *Morgenthau Diaries*, I, 211; memorandum of conversation by Arthur Young, September 28, 1940, Box 88, Young Papers.

39. Johnson to Hull, October 23, 1940, *FRUS 1940*, IV, 678; Johnson to Hull, November 21, 1940, *ibid.*, 439.

40. Transcript of Treasury Group Meeting, November 29, 1940, *Morgenthau Diaries*, I, 243–50.

41. Morgenthau-Soong discussion, November 30, 1940, *ibid.*, pp. 273–77.

42. Morgenthau-Welles discussion, November 30, 1940, *ibid.*, pp. 277–87.

43. Transcript of discussion, December 1, 1940, *ibid.*, pp. 287–99.

Chapter 3. American Aid and Chinese Politics, 1939–41

1. Johnson to Hull, April 26, 1938, *FRUS 1938*, III, 158; Johnson to Hull, May 23, 1938, *ibid.*, 173; Stilwell reports of August 17 and September 14, 1938, Dept. of the Army, Military Intelligence Division Reports, 1917–41.

2. Welles to Josselyn, February 10, 1938, *FRUS 1938*, III, 78.

3. Peck to Hull, February 6, 1939, *FRUS 1939*, III, 137; Johnson to Hull, June 20, 1939, *ibid.*, pp. 189–90.

4. Johnson to Hull, August 13, 1939, *ibid.*, p. 206; Johnson to Hull, October 31, 1939, *ibid.*, p. 307.

5. Laurence Steinhardt to Hull, September 22, 1939, Dept. of State, Decimal File, China, 893.51/6985; Johnson to Hull, July 20, 1940, *FRUS 1940*, IV, 404.

6. Johnson to Hull, October 24, 1940, *ibid.*, p. 429; Johnson to Hull, October 18, 1940, *ibid.*, pp. 672–74.

7. Johnson to Hull, November 29, 1940, Dept. of State, Decimal File, China, 893.00/14599; Johnson to Hornbeck, December 12, 1940, Hornbeck Papers.

8. Johnson to Hull, December 23, 1940, *FRUS 1940*, IV, 472; Hull to Johnson, December 28, 1940, *ibid.*, p. 476.

9. Carlson to Hornbeck, December 19, 1940, Dept. of State, Decimal File, China, 893.00/14630.

10. Johnson to Hull, January 3, 1941, *FRUS 1940*, IV, 477.

11. Johnson to Hornbeck, April 11, 1941, Hornbeck Papers; Johnson to Hull, January 23, 1941, Dept. of State, Decimal File, China, 893.00/14650.

12. McHugh quoted in a memorandum by George Atcheson, April 24, 1941, *FRUS 1941*, V, 494.

13. *Ibid.*

14. Report of December 27, 1941, Far Eastern Section, G-2, Regional File.

15. Memorandum by John P. Davies, January 24, 1941, Dept. of State, Decimal File, China, 893.00/14621; memorandum of a conversation by Davies, January 29, 1941, *ibid.*, 893.00/14656; memorandum by Davies, April 12, 1941, *ibid.*, 893.00/14680.

16. Memorandum prepared in the Dept. of State, March 11, 1941, Decimal File, China, 893.00/14726; Johnson to Hull, March 10, 1941, *ibid.*, 893.00/14667; Hull to Johnson, March 13, 1941, *FRUS 1941*, V, 490–91.

17. Roosevelt to Grew, January 21, 1941, *FRUS 1941*, IV, 6.

18. Memorandum of Currie-Morgenthau conversation, January 16, 1941, *Morgenthau Diaries*, I, 348.

19. McHugh to Johnson, March 10, 1941, Johnson Papers.

20. Report by Currie to Roosevelt, March 15, 1941, PSF, Box 427, Roosevelt Papers.

21. Visit to China of Lauchlin Currie file, March 3, 1941, Dept. of State, Decimal File, 003.1193, RG 59; Currie to Roosevelt, April 25, 1941, *ibid.*; During the McCarthy period, Currie's previous involvement in China policy and his friendship with many New Dealers led anti-Communist investigators to question his political loyalty. Currie left the United States a virtual exile, and became an economic advisor to the government of Colombia.

22. Johnson to Hull, April 17, 1941, Dept. of State, Decimal File, China, 893.24/1047.

23. McHugh to Currie, April 14, 1941, McHugh Papers.

24. Transcript of Treasury Department Meeting, April 21, 1941, *Morgenthau Diaries*, I, 373.

25. McHugh to Currie, July 13, 1941, McHugh Papers.

26. Currie to Roosevelt, April 29, 1941, PSF, Box 29, Roosevelt Papers.

27. McHugh to Johnson, July 8, 1941, Johnson Papers.

28. Naval Intelligence Report, August 7, 1941, File No. 21902-P, c-9-d, Operational Archives, Center for Naval History, Washington, D.C.; McHugh to Currie, August 3, 1941, McHugh Papers; Currie to Welles, August 3, 1941, *FRUS 1941*, IV, 361.

29. Oscar Cox to Morgenthau, April 7, 1941, *Morgenthau Diaries*, I, 362.

30. See "Comment on Draft History of First Burma Campaign," Box 2, Boatner Papers; Transcript of Treasury Department Group Meeting, April 21, 1941, *Morgenthau Diaries*, I, 385–94; The so-called China lobby has experienced a geographical as well as generational expansion. Tong-sun Park, the alleged agent of the South Korean government accused of bribing American Congressmen during the mid-1970s, was a protégé of both Tom Corcoran and Anna Chennault, according to journalists in Washington. Discussions of the history of the China lobby can be found in Ross Koen, *The China Lobby in American Politics;* Stanley Bachrack, *The Committee of One Million: "China Lobby" Politics, 1953–1971* (New York: Columbia University Press, 1976).

31. McHugh to Currie, April 27, 1941, McHugh Papers; transcript of Treasury Department Group Meeting, May 12, 1941, *Morgenthau Diaries*, I, 408–18; transcript of telephone conversation with Currie, July 10, 1941, *ibid.*, pp. 339–42.

32. Charles Romanus and Riley Sunderland, *Stilwell's Mission to China*, pp. 14–17. This is the first volume of the three-volume "official" army history of the war in China. The project is a key source for all interested in the formation of military and political policy.

33. General Sherman Miles to General John Magruder, July 11, 1941, Supporting Documents, China-Burma-India Theater, Historical Section, Box 3, No. 61-A-1510 (hereafter cited as Magruder Mission Material).

34. Claire Chennault to Madame Chiang Kai-shek, October 28, 1941, Chennault Papers, Hoover Institution.

35. Hornbeck to Hull, June 10, 1941, *FRUS 1941*, IV, 263; Memorandum by Legal Advisor, Dept. of State, June 29, 1941, *ibid.*, p. 239. The most complete discussion of the informal negotiations is found in Robert Butow, *The John Doe Associates: Backdoor Diplomacy for Peace, 1941* (Stanford, Cal.: Stanford University Press, 1974).

36. The bureaucratic machinations leading to the oil embargo are discussed in Irvine H. Anderson, Jr., "The 1941 *De Facto* Embargo on Oil to Japan."

37. Memorandum by Hornbeck, September 5, 1941, *FRUS 1941*, IV, 425.

38. Memorandum by Hornbeck for Hull for use in meeting Roosevelt, November 27, 1941, Box 38, Hornbeck Papers.

39. Soong to Stimson, November 25, 1941, *FRUS 1941*, IV, 660–61.

40. Memorandum of conversation by Hull, November 29, 1941, *FRUS 1941*, IV, 685–87.

41. Blum, *Morgenthau Diaries 1938–1941*, pp. 383–85, 389–91.

Chapter 4. American Air Strategy and the Origins of Clandestine Warfare

1. Some of the most prominent New Deal critics include Charles C. Tansill, *Back Door to War* (Chicago: Regnery, 1952); Harry Elmer Barnes, ed., *Perpetual War for Perpetual Peace* (Caldwell, Idaho: Caxton, 1953); Charles A. Beard, *American Foreign Policy in the Making, 1932–1940* (New Haven, Conn.: Yale University Press, 1946), and *President Roosevelt and the Coming of the War, 1941* (New Haven, Conn.: Yale University Press, 1948). Defenders include Basil Rauch, *Roosevelt from Munich to Pearl Harbor* (New York: McClelland, 1950); Herbert Feis, *The Road to Pearl Harbor*; William L. Langer and Everett Gleason, *The Challenge to Isolation* and *The Undeclared War*.

2. See especially Barbara Tuchman, *Stilwell and the American Experience in China*.

3. Claire L. Chennault, *Way of a Fighter*, pp. 31–37, 61–71.

4. Nelson Johnson to Cordell Hull, October 23, 1940, *FRUS 1940*, IV, 678.

5. Transcript of Treasury Department Group Meeting, November 29, 1940, 333:31–74, Morgenthau diary MS.; transcript of Treasury Department Group Meeting with Sumner Welles, November 30, 1940, 333:259–85, *ibid.*; see ch. 3.

6. Department of State to Chinese Embassy, December 4, 1940, *FRUS 1940*, IV, 705.

7. Chennault, *Way of a Fighter*, p. 90; also see Chennault and Alsop correspondence with Harry Hopkins in Hopkins Papers; diary entries of August 12, September 11, October 25, December 10, 1940, vols. 30, 31, 32, Stimson Papers.

8. Soong to Morgenthau, November 30, 1940, 342A:4–7, *Morgenthau Diaries*; see entries of November 29 and 30, 1938, *ibid.*, 153:336, 366–69.

9. Memorandum of conversation by Morgenthau, December 3, 1940, *ibid.*, 342A:1.

10. Memorandum by Morgenthau of conversation with Soong, December 8, 1940, *ibid.*, pp. 2–3; memorandum by Morgenthau of conversation with Hull, December 12, 1940, *ibid.*, pp. 10–11.

11. Chiang Kai-shek to Franklin Roosevelt, December 12, 1940, and Chiang to Morgenthau, December 16, 1940, *ibid.*, pp. 15–16; memorandum by Morgenthau of conversation with Roosevelt, December 18, 1940, *ibid.*, p. 12; memorandum of conversation by Morgenthau, December 19, 1940, Morgenthau Presidential Diary, Book 3, *ibid.*, pp. 742–43.

12. Memorandum by Morgenthau of conversation with Soong, December 20, 1940, *ibid.*, pp. 18–19; transcript of Knox-Morgenthau telephone conversation, December 20, 1940, *ibid.*, pp. 20–23.

13. Notes on conference at home of Secretary Morgenthau, December 21, 1940, *ibid.*, pp. 24–26.

14. Memorandum by Morgenthau of conservation with Henry Stimson and George Marshall, December 22, 1940, *ibid.*, pp. 27–28; diary entry of December 22, 1940, vol. 32, Stimson Papers.

15. Memorandum of meeting in Secretary Hull's Office, December 23, 1940, Army Chief of Staff Secretariat, 1938–43, Standing Liaison Committee Minutes, Modern Military Records Branch, National Archives, Washington, D.C.

16. Transcript of Treasury Department Group Meeting, December 23, 1940, *Morgenthau Diary* 342:77–82; Notes on Conference, January 1, 1941, *ibid.*, 344:12–13.

17. Transcript of Treasury Department Group Meeting, May 12, 1941, *ibid.*, 397:1–21.

18. Romanus and Sunderland, *Stilwell's Mission to China*, pp. 14–17.

19. Chennault, *Way of a Fighter*, p. 99; memorandum on CAMCO, November 23, 1941, Chennault Papers, Hoover Institution.

20. Chennault, *Way of a Fighter*, pp. 101–4; Romanus and Sunderland, *Stilwell's Mission to China*, p. 18.

21. See correspondence between Currie and James McHugh for 1941 in McHugh Papers.

22. Memorandum General H. H. Arnold to Stimson, May 10, 1941, Joint Board Paper No. 355 File, Serial 691. This important document was located for the author by the staff of the Modern Military Records Branch of the National Archives; "Chinese Aircraft Requirements" as forwarded to Secretary of the Joint Board, May 23, 1941, JB 355 file.

23. Currie to Marshall, May 12, 1941, JB 355 file.

24. Currie to Frank Knox, May 28, 1941, *ibid.*

25. Memorandum from Arnold to Lovett, June 11, 1941, *ibid.*

26. Joint Board Planning Committee to Joint Board, July 9, 1941, *ibid.*

27. Notice of Joint Board approval, July 12, 1941, *ibid.*

28. Patterson and Knox to Roosevelt, July 18, 1941, *ibid.*; Roosevelt approval of July 23, 1941, *ibid.*

29. General Sherman Miles to General John Magruder, July 11, 1941, Magruder Mission Material.

30. "Memorandum for Colonel Chennault," based on conversation with Magruder's staff, October 30, 1941, Chennault Papers.

31. Currie to Chennault, July 22, 1941, *ibid.*

32. Chennault to Chiang, August 8, 1941, and September 13, 1941, *ibid.*

33. Chennault to Soong, September 4, 1941, and September 23, 1941, *ibid.*

34. Currie to Chennault, November 22, 1941, *ibid.*

35. Memorandum by Chennault entitled, "Notes on CAMCO," November 23, 1941, *ibid.*

319   4. Air Strategy and Clandestine Warfare

36. Chennault report to AVG Procurement Committee, November 16, 1941, *ibid.;* Chennault to Chiang and Currie, January 26, 1942, *ibid.;* Chennault to MacArthur, November 26, 1941, *ibid.*

37. Evidence of Japanese concern over American air aid and strategy can be found in Nobutaka Ike, *Japan's Decision for War;* see "Record of the 38th Liaison Conference of July 10, 1941" and "Document Attached to Imperial Conference of September 6, 1941," pp. 94–98, 152–56; see also transcripts based on the interrogation of Japanese officers in Dept. of the Army, Center for Military History, *Japanese Monographs* Nos. 146 and 150.

38. Willauer himself draws many parallels to his activities in China and Latin America. See Willauer Papers.

39. Chennault, *Way of a Fighter*, pp. 358–60.

40. Two recently published studies provide valuable background information on the role of CIA proprietary airlines in Asia since 1946. See Peter Dale Scott, *The War Conspiracy* (Indianapolis: Bobbs-Merrill, 1972) and Victor Marchetti and John D. Marks, *The CIA and the Cult of Intelligence* (New York: Knopf, 1974), pp. 137–47; documentation on the role of CAT and Air America from 1947 to 1961 is contained in a "Memorandum by Brig. General Edward Lansdale for General Maxwell D. Taylor," July 1961, in *The Pentagon Papers*, pp. 130–38.

Chapter 5. Allies in a New War

1. *New York Times*, December 9, 1941.

2. Han Suyin, *Birdless Summer*, pp. 235–36.

3. Report of AMMISCA to War Dept., December 10, 1941, Box 3, Magruder Mission Material; Magruder to War Dept., January 5, 1942, *FRUS 1941*, IV, 769–71; Magruder to War Dept., February 10, 1942, *FRUS 1942, China*, pp. 13–16. The Department of State issued separate volumes of China-related documents for the years 1942 and 1943.

4. McHugh to Secretary of the Navy, December 19, 1941, PSF, Box 2, Roosevelt Papers; Currie to Roosevelt, December 27, 1941, *ibid.;* McHugh to Currie, January 10, 13, 1942, McHugh Papers.

5. Gauss to Roosevelt, November 19, 1941, Dept. of State, Decimal File, China, 893.00/14827; Gauss to Hull, December 29, 1941 *ibid.*, 893.00/14834; Gauss to Hull, December 14, 1941, *FRUS 1941*, IV, 753–54.

6. Memorandum by Hopkins of Eden visit, March 27, 1943, box 138, book 7, Hopkins Papers, cited in Walter LaFeber, "Roosevelt, Churchill and Indo-China: 1942–1945," *American Historical Review*, 80 (December 1975), 1277–95; Churchill quoted in *The Diaries of Sir Alexander Cadogan, 1938–1945*, David Dilks, ed., p. 488; While Churchill and Eden were renowned for their harsh judgment of China and FDR's attitude, recent scholarship suggests that other British officials took a more measured and sympathetic view of America's China policy. See Christopher Thorne, *Allies of a Kind.* Al-

though this study appeared too late for detailed use in this work, it is a major revision of the scholarship on British-American relations in the Pacific.

7. Gauss to Hull, December 8, 1941, *FRUS 1941*, IV, 736; memorandum by Magruder on conference with Chiang, December 26, 1941, Box 3, Magruder Mission Material.

8. Roosevelt to Chiang, December 14, 1941, *FRUS 1941*, IV, 751.

9. Soong to John McCloy, January 6, 1942, Box 6, Stilwell Papers.

10. Romanus and Sunderland, *Stilwell's Mission to China*, pp. 63–70.

11. Entries of December 29, 1941, through January 13, 1942, Black and White Books, Stilwell Papers.

12. Entries of January 14, 16, 23, 1942, *ibid.*; Soong to Stimson, January 30, 1942, Box 5, *ibid.*

13. Entry of February 9, 1942, Black and White Books, *ibid.*; Romanus and Sunderland, *Stilwell's Mission to China*, pp. 79–80.

14. Gauss to Hull, December 30, 1941, Dept. of State, Decimal File, China, 893.51/7372.

15. Hull to Morgenthau, January 10, 1942, *Morgenthau Diaries*, 1:568; Roosevelt to Morgenthau, January 9, 1942, *ibid.*, p. 566; memorandum of discussion by Hornbeck, January 13, 1942, Dept. of State, Decimal File, China, 893.51/7393.

16. Record of Treasury Department group meeting with Hornbeck and Currie, January 12, 1942, *Morgenthau Diaries*, 1:576–78; Treasury Meetings of January 13, 1942, *ibid.*, pp. 587–97.

17. Soong to Morgenthau, January 21, 1942, *ibid.*, pp. 609–10.

18. Record of discussion among Morgenthau, Treasury Dept. staff, Soong, Currie, and Hornbeck, January 29, 1942, *ibid.*, pp. 645–66; record of discussion between Morgenthau and Soong, February 2, 1942, *ibid.*, pp. 694–704; notes on congressional hearings, February 9, 1942, *ibid.*, pp. 718–25.

19. Record of Treasury Dept. group meetings: April 11, 1942, *ibid.*, pp. 810–12; April 21, 1945, *ibid.*, 2:1486–88; June 29, 1945, *ibid.*, pp. 1678–83.

20. Roosevelt to Lord Louis Mountbatten, November 8, 1943, PSF, Box 38, Roosevelt Papers; J. W. Pickersgill and D. W. Forster, *The Mackenzie King Record*, I, 553.

Chapter 6. American Military Strategy and the Chinese Nationalists

1. Notes of September 1944, Box 6, Stilwell Papers.

2. Eric Severeid, *Not So Wild a Dream*, p. 310.

3. Liang Chin-tung, *General Stilwell in China, 1942–1944;* p. 3. Liang, a Chinese historian close to leading KMT figures, claimed access to KMT documents seen by no

others. This study is essentially a political response to Barbara Tuchman's biography of General Stilwell.

4. Barbara W. Tuchman, *Stilwell and the American Experience in China, 1911–1945*, pp. 329–85; Romanus and Sunderland, *Stilwell's Mission to China*, pp. 81–148. Both of these accounts contain thorough and vivid studies of military operations in Burma, 1942–44.

5. Chiang to Roosevelt, April 19, 1942, *FRUS 1942, China*, p. 33; memoranda by Hornbeck, May 7, 20, 1942, *ibid.*, pp. 40, 49, 51; Gauss to Hull, May 8, 1942, *ibid.*, p. 43; Frank Dorn, *Walkout With Stilwell in Burma*, p. 240.

6. Report by Stilwell to War Dept., June 1942, Box 4, Stilwell Papers.

7. Report from General Albert Wedemeyer to Chiang, August 5, 1945, cited in Charles Romanus and Riley Sunderland, *Time Runs Out on CBI*, pp. 369–73.

8. *Ibid.*

9. Notes of May 26, 1942, Box 5, Stilwell Papers; entry of June 19, 1942, Black and White Books, *ibid.*

10. "Suggested China Plan," March 16, 1942, CCS 385 China, Combined Chiefs of Staff Decimal File 1942–45, RG 218, National Archives, Washington, D.C.

11. Minutes of Stilwell-Chiang meeting, June 24, 1942, quoted in Romanus and Sunderland, *Stilwell's Mission to China*, pp. 169–72.

12. *Ibid.;* entry of July 1, 1942, Black and White Books, Stilwell Papers.

13. Chennault to Currie, February 5, 1942, Chennault Papers; Chennault to Currie, July 3, 1942, *ibid.;* McHugh to Currie, July 13, 1942, McHugh Papers.

14. Stilwell to Stimson and Marshall, June 1942, Box 5, Stilwell Papers.

15. Chiang to Stilwell, June 29, 1942, *ibid.*

16. Stilwell to Marshall, July 3, 1942, Stilwell CBI Correspondence; Gauss to Hull, July 11, 1942, *FRUS 1942, China*, pp. 109–14.

17. Stilwell to Stimson, June 27, 1942, Box 6, Stilwell Papers.

18. Stilwell to Chiang, July 2, 7, 1942, Box 5, *ibid.*

19. Roosevelt to Chiang, July 14, 1942, Map Room, Box 10, Roosevelt Papers; entry of July 25, 1942, Black and White Books, Stilwell Papers.

20. *Ibid.;* Gauss to Hull, July 7, 1942, *FRUS 1942, China*, pp. 98–102.

21. Currie to Roosevelt, June 26, 1945, *ibid.*, p. 88; entry of July 26, 1942, Black and White Books, Stilwell Papers.

22. Liang, *General Stilwell in China*, pp. 77–82; memorandum by Davies on visit by Currie, August 25, 1942, Dept. of State, Decimal File, 893.00/14882; Chou passed two messages to Currie, one urging continued American control over Lend-Lease, the other inviting Americans to Yenan.

23. Report by Currie to Roosevelt, August 24, 1942, Dept. of the Army, Operations Division 336, RG 165, National Archives, Washington, D.C.

24. Currie to Roosevelt, August 11, 1942, *FRUS 1942*, I, pp. 712–14.

25. Report by Currie, August 24, 1942.

26. Record of interview with General George Marshall, July 6, 13, 1949, Box 3, Supporting Documents, CBI Theater History.

27. Roosevelt to Chiang, October 12, 1942, Stilwell CBI Correspondence.

28. The Chiang-Chennault relationship was symbiotic, as both parties understood. Chennault had few supporters in the War Dept. and depended on his personal relationship with the Chiangs in order to be taken seriously. See Chennault to Madame Chiang Kai-shek, November 17, 1941, Chennault Papers.

29. Memorandum by Vincent, July 30, 1942, Dept. of State, Decimal File, China, 893.00/14876; An engaging portrait of Vincent and of many of the State Dept.'s so-called China hands is found in E. J. Kahn, *The China Hands*.

30. Report by John Service, January 23, 1943, Dept. of State, Decimal File, China, 893.00/14969.

31. *Ibid.*

32. Report by John Davis, March 23, 1943, *ibid.*, 893.00/14989.

33. Davies to Gauss, March 9, 1943, FRUS *1943*, *China*, pp. 25–29.

34. *Ibid.*

35. Gauss to Hull, October 21, 1942, *FRUS 1942*, *China*, pp. 161–62; Entries of October 1, 7, 1942, Black and White Books, Stilwell Papers.

36. Wendell Willkie, *One World*, pp. 103–5, 137–41, 152–56.

37. Diary entry of February 21, 1943, Leahy Papers; John Morton Blum, *From the Morgenthau Diaries*, III, 106; entry of January 11, 1943, Black and White Books, Stilwell Papers; Henry A. Wallace, *The Price of Vision*, entry of February 1, 1943, p. 178 (hereafter called *Wallace Diary*); International Business Machines, *First Lady of China*.

38. JCS memorandum No. 43, January 23, 1943, CCS 381, CCS Decimal File, 1942–45, RG 218.

39. Entry of October 2, 1942, Black and White Books, Stilwell Papers.

40. Entries of November 7, 10, 21, 1942, Black and White Books, Stilwell Papers; Stilwell to Marshall, November 4, 14, 1942, Stilwell CBI Correspondence; Stilwell to Marshall, November 24, December 12, 21, 1942, *ibid.*; Stilwell to Timberman, November 27, 1942, *ibid.*; Roosevelt to Chiang, December 3, 1942, *ibid.*; Chiang to Roosevelt, December 28, 1942, *ibid.*; Joseph W. Stilwell, *The Stilwell Papers*, pp. 183–84.

41. Romanus and Sunderland, *Stilwell's Mission to China*, p. 271; Dept. of State, *Washington and Casablanca*; Casablanca Conference Folder, Map Room, Box 26, Roosevelt Papers, p. 167; Chiang to Roosevelt, February 7, 1943, Stilwell CBI Correspondence.

323   6. American Strategy and the Chinese

42. Roosevelt to Marshall, March 8, 1943, in Romanus and Sunderland, *Stilwell's Mission to China*, pp. 279–82.

Chapter 7. Chungking Intrigues

1. Albert Wedemeyer, *Wedemeyer Reports!* p. 304.

2. Entry of October 5, 1942, Black and White Books, Stilwell Papers.

3. Chiang Kai-shek, "China's Destiny" and "Chinese Economic Theory" (New York, 1947).

4. Stilwell Report on CBI, i, 43. This manuscript, comprising both documents and narrative, was written by army historians under Stilwell's direction. It remained classified until the early 1970s.

5. Entry of November 7, 1942, Black and White Books, Stilwell Papers.

6. Stilwell Report on CBI, i, 65.

7. Entries of November 2, 30, 1942, Black and White Books, Stilwell Papers.

8. Memorandum by Davies, June 7, 1943, Dept. of State, Decimal File, 893.00/15038½; Stilwell Report on CBI, i, 91; Undated notes, Box 8, Stilwell Papers; Stilwell memorandum for Soong, December 27, 1942, Box 13, *ibid.*; this memorandum appears in Romanus and Sunderland, *Stilwell's Mission to China*, pp. 256–57; Stilwell to Marshall, January 5, 1943, Stilwell CBI Correspondence.

9. Memorandum by Stilwell, January 9, 1943, Box 7, Stilwell Papers.

10. Notes of February 1943, Box 8, *ibid.*

11. Entries of January 20, 21, 1943, Black and White Books, *ibid.*; Notes of February 1943, Box 8, *ibid.*; memorandum by Dorn to Stilwell, March 29, 1943, Box 8, *ibid.* Italics in original; Dorn, *Walkout with Stilwell in Burma*, pp. 79–83.

12. Report by Ho Ying-chin, May 5, 1944, Box 12, Stilwell Papers.

13. During 1942–43 at least five books appeared in the United States adulating the heroic Flying Tigers. Many more appeared in later years.

14. Chennault letter to Roosevelt, October 8, 1942, quoted in Claire Chennault, *Way of a Fighter*, pp. 212–16.

15. See Stilwell's notes on Washington Conference of May 1943, Black Book, and folder 61, Box 8, Stilwell Papers.

16. Milton Miles to Admiral Willis Lee, July 22, 1942, chapter 1, Records of Naval Group China.

17. Report by McHugh to Office of Naval Intelligence, October 5, 1942, McHugh Papers; Dorn, *Walkout with Stilwell in Burma*, pp. 81–83. Dorn notes that Sun Li-jen, Chinese commander of the X-Force, was continually implicated in plots to topple Chiang, even after the retreat to Taiwan; McHugh predicted, correctly, that the American-trained officers would soon be fired by Chiang. When General Marshall

learned that McHugh had shared his reports and opinions about Stilwell with British authorities, the attaché was removed from China. See notes by Marshall and Stimson attached to McHugh's report of October 5, 1942, 381 CTO, Case 92, Dept. of the Army, Operations Division Decimal File 1942–45.

18. Roosevelt to Chiang, March 9, 1943, Stilwell CBI Correspondence; Marshall to Stilwell, March 28, 1943, *ibid.;* Stilwell Report on CBI, I, 92–100.

19. Chennault to Roosevelt and Hopkins, December 27, 1942, Box 138, "Chinese Affairs," Hopkins Papers; Alsop to Hopkins, December 10, 22, 28, 1942, *ibid.*

20. Memorandum of conversation with Joseph Alsop, January 9, 1953, Feis Papers; entry of March 7, 1943, Black and White Books, Stilwell Papers.

21. Alsop to Hopkins, letters of March 1, 3, 5, 26, 1943, Box 138, Hopkins Papers; Soong to Hopkins, September 25, 1943, *ibid.*

22. Chiang to Roosevelt, April 10, 1943, Stilwell CBI Correspondence; Roosevelt to Chiang, April 14, 1943, *ibid.;* entry of April 18, 1943, Black and White Books, Stilwell Papers; John P. Davies, *Dragon by the Tail*, p. 264; Chennault, *Way of a Fighter*, pp. 224–26; Diary entries of May 17, 21, 1943, Leahy Papers.

23. Notes of May 1943 on Washington Conference, folder 61, Box 8, Stilwell Papers.

24. Stilwell, *Stilwell Papers*, pp. 204–6.

25. CCS meeting of May 14, 1943, *Washington and Quebec*, pp. 52–56; CCS meeting, Roosevelt and Churchill, May 14, 1943, *ibid.*, pp. 66–67; CCS meeting, Roosevelt, and Churchill, May 24, 1943, *ibid.*, 189–96; see message quoted in Romanus and Sunderland, *Stilwell's Mission to China*, p. 332; Davies, *Dragon by the Tail*, pp. 265–67; interview with John S. Service.

26. Stilwell to Marshall, July 10, 13, 1943, Stilwell CBI Correspondence; entries of June 18, 25, 1943, Black and White Books, Stilwell Papers; Stilwell, *Stilwell Papers*, p. 207.

27. CCS report to Roosevelt and Churchill, August 24, 1943, *Washington and Quebec*, pp. 1125–28; Roosevelt to Chiang, August 24, 1943, *ibid.*, pp. 1160–61; Stilwell Report on CBI, I, 119.

28. Diary entry of August 11, 1943, Leahy Papers; Pickersgill and Forster, *Mackenzie King Record*, I, 553.

29. *Chieh-fang Jih-pao* (Liberation Daily), May 28, 1943; Atcheson to Hull, July 14, 1943, Dept. of State, Decimal File, China, 893.00/15070; Stilwell to Marshall, September 14, 1943, Stilwell CBI Correspondence.

30. Atcheson to Department of State, May 31, 1943, *FRUS 1943, China*, pp. 244–48; report by Service, June 8, 1943, Dept. of State, Decimal File, China, 893.00/15038.

31. Service to Stilwell, November 13, 1943, Dept. of the Army, Army Intelligence File 1941–45, Box 323.

32. Memorandum by Davies, June 24, 1943, *FRUS 1943, China*, pp. 258–66.

33. Memorandum by Davies for Stilwell, September 17, 1943, Box 15, Stilwell Papers.

34. Davies to Stilwell, November 15, 22, 1943, *ibid.*

35. Davies to Hopkins, December 31, 1943, *FRUS 1943, China*, pp. 397–99.

36. Stilwell memorandum to Chiang, September 6, 1943, Box 5, Stilwell Papers.

37. Entry of September 13, 1943, Black Book, *ibid.;* notes of October 1943, Box 5, *ibid.;* Soong to Hopkins, September 23, 1943, Box 138, Hopkins Papers; see also Romanus and Sunderland, *Stilwell's Mission to China*, p. 375, and Tuchman, *Stilwell and the American Experience in China*, p. 498.

38. Entry of September 28, 1943, and entries of October 7–15, 1943, Black Book, Stilwell Papers; Romanus and Sunderland, *Stilwell's Mission to China*, p. 376; daily diary entries of October 5 and October 16, Stilwell Papers.

39. Romanus and Sunderland, *Stilwell's Mission to China*, p. 380; Charles Romanus and Riley Sunderland, *Stilwell's Command Problems*, p. 17; The United States failed to specify how the Chinese were to be compensated for construction of the airfields by Chinese laborers. As a result, Chiang presented the U.S. Treasury with wildly inflated bills totaling billions of dollars.

40. Entry of June 15, 1943, Black Book, Stilwell Papers; Davies, *Dragon by the Tail*, p. 276.

41. Entry of November 13, 1943, Black Book, Stilwell Papers; memorandum by Dorn for Stilwell, November 11, 1943, Box 16, *ibid.* Italics in original.

Chapter 8. The General or the Generalissimo?

1. Diary entry of October 5, 1943, Leahy Papers; memorandum of conversation with Molotov, October 21, 1943, Hull Papers; memorandum by Hull, November 1, 1943, *ibid.;* Roosevelt to Mountbatten, November 8, 1943, PSF, Box 38, Roosevelt Papers.

2. Entries of November 11, 12, Black Book, Stilwell Papers.

3. Elliott Roosevelt, *As He Saw It*, pp. 152–64; Hurley to Roosevelt, November 20, 1943, *FRUS 1943, China*, pp. 163–66.

4. Stilwell to Chiang, November 11, 1943, Stilwell CBI Correspondence.

5. Diary entries of November 22, 23, 26, 1943, Leahy Papers; Dept. of State, *Cairo and Teheran;* Romanus and Sunderland, *Stilwell's Command Problems*, pp. 49–82. For the British side see Arthur Bryant, *Triumph in the West* (New York: Doubleday, 1959), pp. 49–76; this account is based on the diaries of Field Marshal Lord Alanbrooke. See the Chinese minutes of Chiang-Roosevelt meeting, November 23, 1943, *Cairo and Teheran*, p. 322; daily dairy entries of November 23, 26, 27, Stilwell Papers.

6. Diary entries of November 28, 29, 30, 1943, Leahy Papers.

7. Diary entries of December 4, 5, 1943, *ibid.;* Roosevelt to Chiang, December 5, 1943, *FRUS 1943, China*, p. 178; Chiang to Roosevelt, December 8, 1943, Stilwell CBI Correspondence.

---

8. Roosevelt, *As He Saw It*, pp. 152–64.

9. Dorn to Stilwell, November 28, 1943, Stilwell CBI Correspondence; Solomon Adler to Treasury Dept., December 30, 1943, *Morgenthau Diaries*, II, 970; Report by John Service, February 3, 1944, Dept. of the Army, G-2 Regional File, 1933–44. This report also appears in *FRUS 1944*, VI, 319.

10. Davies, *Dragon by the Tail*, pp. 279–81; daily diary entry of December 6, 1943, and memorandum of December 6, 1943, Box 33, Stilwell Papers; Stilwell, *Stilwell Papers*, p. 251.

11. Dorn, *Walkout with Stilwell in Burma*, pp. 75–79.

12. *Ibid.*; Dorn verbally to author, May 21, 1973.

13. Morgenthau to Roosevelt, December 18, 1943, *Morgenthau Diaries*, II, 944–46; record of Treasury Dept. group meeting, December 21, 1943, *ibid.*, pp. 947–67; record of conversation between Morgenthau and White, January 18, 1944, *ibid.*, pp. 1022–24.

14. Memorandum by Hornbeck, December 27, 1943, 893.51/7725; Dept. of State, Decimal File, China, 893.51/7725; Roosevelt to Chiang, January 5, *ibid.*, 893.51/7727A.

15. Chiang to Roosevelt, January 16, 1944, *ibid.*, 893.51/7731; memorandum of group conversation on Chinese loan request, January 19, 1944, *ibid.*, 893.51/7732; record of meeting of representatives of the State, War and Treasury departments, February 14, 1944, *Morgenthau Diaries*, II, 1054–56.

16. Entries of December 18, 19, 1943, Black Book, Stilwell Papers; Stilwell to Marshall, December 17, 1943, Stilwell CBI Correspondence.

17. Roosevelt to Chiang, December 21, 1943, Stilwell CBI Correspondence; Chiang to Roosevelt, December 23, 1943, *ibid.*; Roosevelt to Chiang, December 29, 1943, *ibid.*; Roosevelt to Chiang, January 14, 1944, *ibid.*

18. Mountbatten to British Chiefs of Staff, April 14, 1944, Box 4, Stilwell Papers.

19. Davies, *Dragon by the Tail*, p. 300.

20. *Ibid.*, p. 302.

21. Memorandum by Davies, "American Policy in Asia," February 19, 1944, Stilwell Report on CBI, IIIj

22. Memorandum by Raymond Ludden, "Political Background–China," May 22, 1944, *ibid.*; Service to Gauss, March 23, 1944, Senate Committee on the Judiciary, *Amerasia Papers*, I, 575. This is a published collection of most of the several hundred documents seized by the government in the raid on *Amerasia* magazine in June 1945.

23. Chiang to Roosevelt, March 17, 1944, Stilwell CBI Correspondence; Roosevelt to Chiang, March 23, 1944, *ibid.*

24. Roosevelt to Chiang, April 3, 1944, *ibid.*; Dorn, *Walkout with Stilwell in Burma*, pp. 228–30; Romanus and Sunderland, *Stilwell's Command Problems*, pp. 310–14.

---

327   8. The General or the Generalissimo?

25. Chiang to Roosevelt, February 22, 1944, Stilwell CBI Correspondence; General Thomas Hearn to Marshall, February 23, 1944, *ibid.;* Roosevelt to Chiang, March 2, 1944, *ibid.;* Marshall to Hearn, March 4, 1944, *ibid.*

26. Wallace, *Price of Vision,* entries of March 9, March 11, May 2, May 9, 1944, pp. 311, 314, 326, 329.

27. Entry of May 18, 1944, *ibid.,* pp. 332–33.

28. Entries of June 18–30, 1944, *ibid.,* pp. 347–59; notes on the Vice-President's conversations with Chiang, PSF: Wallace, Box 190, Roosevelt Papers.

29. Wallace to Roosevelt, June 28, 1944, *FRUS 1944,* VI, 235; report by Wallace to Roosevelt, July 10, 1944, *ibid.,* p. 240; Wallace's full report, more critical of Chiang than the printed version, is found in PSF: Wallace, Box 190, Roosevelt Papers.

30. Arthur Ringwalt to Gauss, May 11, 1944, *FRUS 1944,* VI, 418; report by Ringwalt, August 10, 1944, CBI Theater, Historical Section (this is a compilation of documentary material assembled for the preparation of the theater history); Gauss to Secretary of State, August 23, 1944, *Amerasia Papers,* I, 778; Romanus and Sunderland, *Stilwell's Command Problems,* pp. 408–12; Riley Sunderland, "The Secret Embargo."

31. Daily diary entry of May 14, 1944, Stilwell Papers.

32. Marshall to Stilwell, July 2, 1944, Box 13, Stilwell Papers; Stilwell to Marshall, July 3, 1944, *ibid.;* Roosevelt to Chiang, July 6, 1944, *ibid.;* diary entry of June 1, 1944, vol. 47, Stimson Papers.

33. Chiang to Roosevelt, July 8, 1944, quoted in Romanus and Sunderland, *Stilwell's Command Problems,* pp. 385–86; Chiang to Roosevelt, July 23, 1944, *ibid.,* 414; Gauss to Hull, July 12, 1944, *FRUS 1944,* VI, 124.

34. Marshall to Stilwell, August ?, 1944, Box 17, Stilwell Papers; entry of August 3, 1944, diary vol. 48, Henry Stimson Papers.

35. Russell Buhite, *Patrick J. Hurley and American Foreign Policy,* p. 150.

36. *Ibid.,* pp. 150–52; Harriman to Hull, September 5, 1944, *FRUS 1944,* VI, 253–56.

37. Memorandum by Davies of conversation with Hopkins, September 4, 1944, Box 15, Stilwell Papers; "A story went around that, after seeing Hurley before the latter's departure, Roosevelt quipped: 'Well the next thing we hear from Pat will be his memoirs. The title will be "Alone in China." ' " Owen Lattimore quoted in Thorne, *Allies of a Kind,* p. 426.

38. Chu Teh to Patrick Hurley via Barrett, September 11, 1944, Box 97, folder 9, Patrick J. Hurley Papers; Stilwell to Marshall, late September 1944, Box 10, Stilwell Papers.

39. Memorandum for T. V. Soong, September 16, 1944, Box 27, *ibid.*

40. Pickersgill and Forster, *Mackenzie King Record,* II, 67, 71.

41. See discussion on preparation and text of letter to Chiang in Dept. of State, *Quebec,* pp. 374, 464.

---

42. Stilwell, *Stilwell Papers*, p. 334.

43. Memorandum from Stilwell to Hurley, September 23, 1944, Box 89, folder 1, Hurley Papers; daily diary entry of September 23, 1944, Stilwell Papers.

44. Aide memoire from Chiang to Hurley for Roosevelt, September 24, 1944, Box 89, folder 1, Hurley Papers.

45. Memorandum by Stilwell for Ho Ying-chin, September 28, 1944, Box 27, Stilwell Papers; Hopkins to Hurley, October 7, 1944, Box 88, folder 10, Hurley Papers; daily diary entry of October 1, 1944, Stilwell Papers; Gauss to Hull, October 5, 1944, *FRUS 1944*, VI, 264–66.

46. Wallace, *Price of Vision*, entry of October 4, 1944, pp. 386–87.

47. Entries of October 3, 4, 1944, diary volume 48, Stimson Papers; Roosevelt to Chiang, October 5, 1944, quoted in Romanus and Sunderland, *Stilwell's Command Problems*, p. 459; Chiang to Roosevelt via Hurley, October 10, 1944, Box 89, folder 2, Hurley Papers.

48. Hurley to Roosevelt, October 10, 1944, and Stilwell to Marshall, October 10, 1944, both cited in "The President and U.S. Aide to China," November 15, 1944, Elsey Papers. This 59-page report was prepared at the President's request shortly after Stilwell's recall. While not blatantly critical of Chiang, the tone of the report and the selected quotations clearly imply a belief that the KMT leader had behaved selfishly and irresponsably in the conduct of the war and utilization of American aid. Possibly, Roosevelt desired to have this report on hand should the KMT regime collapse in 1944 or 1945. Though it indicates that FDR and those around him were not totally convinced of Chiang's virtue, they were still determined to support the Generalissimo until when and if outside events brought about his downfall.

49. Daily diary entry of November 4, 1944, Stilwell Papers; Roosevelt to Hurley, October 14, 1944, Box 88, folder 8, Hurley Papers. Hurley to Roosevelt, October 15, 1944, *ibid.*; Roosevelt to Chiang, via Hurley, October 18, 1944, *ibid.*; entry of November 3, 1944, volume 48, Stimson Papers.

Chapter 9. The Yenan Connection

1. W. Averell Harriman and Ellie Abel, *Special Envoy to Churchill and Stalin, 1941–1946*, p. 311.

2. *Ibid.*, pp. 370–71.

3. A compelling discussion of Roosevelt's attitude toward Soviet foreign policy and behavior can be found in Daniel Yergin, *The Shattered Peace*.

4. Vladimir Dedijer, *Tito*, p. 322; Milovan Djilas, *Conversations with Stalin*, p. 182; In 1963 an official Chinese Communist statement spoke of past bitterness in China's relations with Stalin. The open letter to Moscow, ostensibly defending Stalin in contrast to his "revisionist" successors, declared:

"While defending Stalin, we do not defend his mistakes. Long ago the Chinese

Communists had first-hand experience of some of his mistakes. Of the erroneous "Left" and Right opportunist lines which emerged in the Chinese Communist Party at one time or another, some arose under the influence of certain of Stalin's mistakes. . . . In the late twenties, the thirties and the early and middle forties, the Chinese Marxist-Leninists represented by Comrades Mao Tse-tung and Liu Shao-chi resisted the influence of Stalin's mistakes; They gradually overcame the erroneous lines of "Left" and Right opportunism and finally led the Chinese revolution to victory."

Stated more simply, the Communists claimed that from their origins until the defeat of Chiang Kai-shek they experienced continual problems with the Soviet leader. See, "On the Question of Stalin—Comment on the Open Letter of the Central Committee of the CPSU," by the Editorial Departments of the People's Daily and Red Flag, *Peking Review,* vi (September 20, 1963), 8–15.

5. Kenneth Shewmaker, *Americans and Chinese Communists,* pp. 158–79.

6. Memorandum by Service, June 24, 1944, *Amerasia Papers,* i, 575–91.

7. Warren Cohen, "The Development of Chinese Communist Attitudes toward the United States, 1934–1945," *Orbis,* xi (Spring 1967), 219–37; Mao Tse-tung, *Selected Works,* iii, 27–29; *Chieh-fang Jih-pao,* July 4, 5, 27, October 27, November 10, 1944.

8. Transcript of speech by Chou En-lai at Yenan, August 10, 1943, Dept. of the Army, G-2 Regional File, China, 1933–44.

9. Service's reports from Yenan are reprinted in *Amerasia Papers.* Recently a well-edited compilation of Service's general reporting on the Chinese political scene has been prepared by Joseph Esherick: *Lost Chance in China: The World War II Despatches of John S. Service* (New York: Random House 1974). Report No. 1 by Service, July 28, 1944, *Amerasia Papers,* i, 681–84.

10. Report No. 2 by Service, July 28, 1944, *ibid.,* p. 684; Report No. 3 by Service, July 30, 1944, *ibid.,* pp. 690, 691–717.

11. Report No. 14 by Service, August 19, 1944, *ibid.,* p. 776; Report No. 15 by Service, August 27, 1944, *ibid.,* pp. 786–97.

12. *Ibid.*

13. Report No. 16 by Service, August 29, 1944, *ibid.,* pp. 797–800; Report No. 20 by Service, September 3, 1944, *ibid.,* pp. 823–25; Report No. 22 by Service, September 4, 1944, *ibid.,* pp. 836–42.

14. Captain Charles C. Stelle and "X" to Lt. Colonel R. Peers, August 7, 1944, OSS-Yenan Documents. (This is one of a group of OSS-Yenan documents recently released by the Central Intelligence Agency to the Modern Military Records Branch of the National Archives.) Stelle, an OSS officer, remained in Yenan for almost one year, from the summer of 1944 until the summer of 1945.

15. Memorandum to Lt. Colonel R. Peers, August 30, 1944, *ibid.,*

16. Gauss to Hull, September 4, 1944, *Amerasia Papers,* i, 826–31; Vincent to Hull, September 29, 1944, *ibid.,* ii, 947.

17. Report No. 32 by Service, September 25, 1944, *ibid.,* i, 899–904; interview with Service.

18. Report No. 34 by Service, September 28, 1944, *Amerasia Papers*, I, 939–46; Report No. 40 by Service, October 10, 1944, *ibid.*, pp. 1014–17; Report No. 44 by Service, October 14, 1944, *ibid.*, pp. 1069–79.

19. David Barrett, *Dixie Mission*. Barrett's informal memoir contains invaluable material on the atmosphere which existed between Communist and American personnel and on the subject of Hurley's first visit to Yenan.

20. Irving Friedman to White, September 14, 1944, *Morgenthau Diaries*, II, 1219–23. Many of the most penetrating reports from Yenan were forwarded to Morgenthau and White and included in Morgenthau's files. See *ibid.*, pp. 1308–1423.

21. Davies to Stilwell, October 2, 1944, Box 10, Stilwell Papers.

22. Hurley to Roosevelt, September 12, 1944, quoted in Romanus and Sunderland, *Stilwell's Command Problems*, pp. 425–26; Hurley to Secretary of State, December 24, 1944, *FRUS 1944*, VI, 745–49; Wallace, *Price of Vision*, entry of December 20, 1944, pp. 410–11.

23. Lin and Tung to Hurley, October 21, 1944, Box 97, folder 19, Hurley Papers; "List of CCP Demands," October 23, 1944, *ibid.*

24. Hurley to Roosevelt, October 19, 1944, Box 88, folder 8, *ibid.*; Chiang to Roosevelt, October 25, 1944, *ibid.*

25. Davies, *Dragon by the Tail*, pp. 342–43, 351.

26. *Ibid.*, pp. 361–63.

27. Stelle to OSS, R&A/Kunming No. 37, October 23, 1944, OSS-Yenan Documents.

28. Cromley to OSS headquarters, November 8, 1944, "Dixie Mission Manuscript History," vol. I.

29. Unsigned memorandum of October 26, 1944, Box 89, Hurley Papers.

30. Soong to Hurley, November 7, 1944, Box 97, folder 12, *ibid.*; Hurley to Roosevelt, Nov. 7, 1944, Box 88, folder 9, *ibid.*

31. Barrett, *Dixie Mission*, pp. 56–57; Davies, *Dragon by the Tail*, p. 366; Kahn, *The China Hands*, pp. 122, 124, 135.

32. Barrett, *Dixie Mission*, pp. 58–59; "Notes of Conference in Yenan," November 8, 1944, Box 97, folder 12, Hurley Papers; copy of Five Point Proposal, *ibid.*

33. Memorandum by Davies for Hurley, "American-Chinese Relations During the Next Six Months," November 15, 1944, Box 89, folder 13, *ibid.*

34. Stelle to Colonel John G. Coughlin, November 22, 1944, OSS-Yenan Documents.

35. Chou to Morgenthau, November 13, 1944, *Morgenthau Diaries*, II, 1379–86.

36. Chou to Hurley, December 8, 1944, Box 97, folder 13, Hurley Papers; Barrett to Wedemeyer, December 10, 1944, *ibid.*

37. Barrett, *Dixie Mission*, pp. 75–76; Davies, *Dragon by the Tail*, p. 383; Hurley to Chou, December 11, 1944, Box 97, folder 13, Hurley Papers; Hurley to Roosevelt, December 12, 1944, Box 93, folder 1, *ibid.*

Chapter 10. The Connection Broken

1. Chou to Hurley, December 8, 1944, Box 97, folder 13, Hurley Papers; Barrett to Wedemeyer, December 10, 1944, *ibid.;* Hurley to Chou, December 11, 1944, *ibid.;* Chou to Hurley, December 16, 1944, *ibid.;* Mao, "Our Task for 1945," December 16, 1944, *CFJP,* and *December 31, 1945, ibid.*

2. "Conferences with Generalissimo," Nos. 2–7, November 16, 21, 27, 28, 29, 1944, Box 7, Wedemeyer Files. "Conferences with Generalissimo," No. 8, November 30, 1944, *ibid.*

3. "Conferences with Generalissimo," Nos. 11 and 13, December 2, 4, 1944, *ibid.*

4. "Notes of Meeting between General Robert McClure and General Ch'en Ch'eng," December 19, 1944, Box 97, folder 14, Hurley Papers.

5. Barrett, *Dixie Mission,* p. 76; Romanus and Sunderland, *Time Runs Out on CBI,* p. 251.

6. Colonel Willis Bird to McClure, January 24, 1945, in "Wires Re.: Communists" (this is a file of documents assembled by the staff of the Modern Military Records Branch, National Archives); Chou to Hurley, December 16, 1944, Box 97, folder 13, Hurley Papers.

7. Davies, *Dragon by the Tail,* pp. 383–85; Davies to Stilwell, December 25, 1944, Box 29, Stilwell Papers.

8. Hurley to Secretary of State, December 24, 1944, *FRUS 1944,* vi, 745–49; Barrett, *Dixie Mission,* pp. 77–78; Chou to Hurley, December 28, 1944, *FRUS 1944,* vi, 755.

9. *Hsin-jua Jih-pao,* January 10, 1945; Dixie Mission to Wedemeyer, January 10, 1945, Box 98, folder 1, Hurley Papers. Additional documentation of this incident is found in "Wires Re.: Communists," Modern Military Branch, National Archives; see also Barbara Tuchman, *Notes from China,* p. 78.

10. Wedemeyer to Joint Chiefs of Staff, December 29, 1944, Box 87, folder 21, Hurley Papers.

11. Mao to Hurley, January 11, 1945, Box 98, folder 1, *ibid.;* unsigned memorandum of January 11, 1945, *ibid.;* memorandum by General Robert McClure, January 24, 1945, in "Wires Re: Communists"; Romanus and Sunderland, *Time Runs Out on CBI,* pp. 251–52.

12. Hurley to Roosevelt, January 14, 1945, *FRUS 1945,* vii, 172–77. References to the Communist effort to reach the President directly appeared in certain published material as early as the 1950s. However, they were completely overlooked by historians. See Leahy, *I Was There,* p. 289; U.S. Senate, Committee on Foreign Relations, *State Department Loyalty Investigation* (Washington, D.C.: Senate Report 2108, 81st Congress, 2nd Session, 1950), p. 1903; *Malta and Yalta,* pp. 346–51.

13. Marshall to Wedemeyer, January 15, 1945, quoted in Romanus and Sunderland, *Time Runs Out on CBI,* p. 252; Marshall to Wedemeyer, January 23, 1945, Box 98, folder 1, Hurley Papers; Wedemeyer to Marshall, January 27, 1945, *ibid;* Acting Secre-

tary of State Grew commended Hurley's handling of the entire matter (see Grew to Hurley, January 23, 1945, *FRUS 1945*, VII, 181).

14. Hurley to Mao, January 20, 1945, Box 98, folder 1, Hurley Papers; Mao to Hurley, January 22, 1945, *ibid.*

15. Memorandum of a talk with Wedemeyer, January 17, 1945, Chennault Papers; Memorandum by Wedemeyer, January 30, 1945, Box 1, Wedemeyer Files.

16. Davies, *Dragon by the Tail*, p. 402; Remarks by Hurley, January 16, 1945, Box 90, folder 16, Hurley Papers.

17. Kahn, *The China Hands*, p. 145; also see Hurley to Secretary of State, February 7, 1945, *FRUS 1945*, VII, 205–12.

18. Adler to White and Morgenthau, January 16, 1945, *Morgenthau Diaries*, II, 1411–15; Adler to White and Morgenthau, February 3, 1945, *ibid.*, pp. 1425–31; Adler to White and Morgenthau, February 12, 1945, *ibid.*, pp. 1457–65; Adler to White and Morgenthau, February 14, 1945, *ibid.*, pp. 1416–17. After the war Adler left the Treasury Department and taught economics at Harvard University. When McCarthyites accused him of being a Communist (which he may have been philosophically), he left the United States for his native England. Shortly, thereafter, he accepted an invitation to move to Peking, where he established permanent residence. Whatever his political sympathies may have been, his reporting remains a vital source of events in China.

19. *Hsin-hua Jih-pao*, January 25, 1945; *ibid.*, February 16, 1945.

20. Memorandum of conversation between Hurley and Chiang, February 16, 1945, Box 98, folder 2, Hurley Papers; memorandum of conversation by John Service, February 28, 1945, *Amerasia Papers*, II, 1372–73.

21. Harriman and Abel, *Special Envoy to Churchill and Stalin*, pp. 311, 370–71; Harriman to Roosevelt, December 15, 1944, *Malta and Yalta*, pp. 378–79.

22. Record of Roosevelt-Stalin meeting, February 8, 1945, *ibid.*, pp. 776–71; For perceptive discussions of the meaning of the Yalta agreements, see also Diane Clemens, *Yalta*, and Daniel Yergin, *Shattered Peace*.

23. Memorandum by Harriman, February 10, 1945, *Malta and Yalta*, pp. 894–97; Leahy, *I Was There*, p. 337.

24. Roosevelt's aims at Yalta are discussed most effectively in Yergin, *Shattered Peace*.

25. Atcheson to Secretary of State, February 28, 1945, *FRUS 1945*, VII, 242–46; John Service, *The Amerasia Papers: Some Problems in the History of U.S.-China Relations* (Berkeley: University of California Press, 1971), 188–91. This memoir-history was written by Service in response to the scathing personal attack upon him included in the Introduction to the Senate Judiciary Committee's *Amerasia Papers*.

26. Adler to White, February 25, 1945, *Morgenthau Diaries*, II, 1419–23.

27. Unsigned and undated memorandum to Donovan. Internal references make it appear to have been written by Charles Stelle in February or March 1945 (OSS–Dixie Mission Documents, Modern Military Records Branch, National Archives).

---

28. Roosevelt to Chiang, March 15, 1945, *FRUS 1945*, VII, 283–84; Stelle to Heppner April 12, 1945, OSS–Dixie Mission Documents.

29. Memorandum by Service of conversation with Mao, March 13, 1945, *Amerasia Papers*, II, 1400–1404.

30. See reports by Service, March 14–*March 23, 1945*, *ibid.*, pp. 1405–18, 1423–30, 1433–41, 1443–46.

31. Report by Service, April 1, 1945, *FRUS 1945*, VII, 310–17.

32. Grew to Roosevelt, March 2, 1945, State Dept. Decimal File, China; Vincent to Ballantine and Grew, March 1, 1945, *ibid.*; Drumright, Stanton, and Vincent to Grew, March 2, 1945 *ibid.*; Kahn, *The China Hands*, p. 153.

33. Memorandum by Ballantine, March 6, 1945, *FRUS 1945*, VII, 260–62; memorandum by Vincent, March 12, 1945, *ibid.*, pp. 270–72.

34. Wedemeyer to War Department, March 9, 1945, Box 1, Wedemeyer Files; entries of March 8, 9, 1945, diary vol. 49, Stimson Papers; Leahy, *I Was There*, p. 337; Wedemeyer, *Wedemeyer Reports!* p. 342; Romanus and Sunderland, *Time Runs Out on CBI*, p. 338.

35. Wedemeyer, *Wedemeyer Reports!* pp. 340–41.

36. Leahy, *I Was There*, p. 337.

37. Edgar Snow, *Journey to the Beginning*, pp. 347–48.

38. Speech by Congressman Walter Judd, March 15, 1945, *Congressional Record*, vol. 91, pt. 2 (1945), pp. 2294–2302; Dulles to Henry Luce, January 29, 1945, Box 130, Dulles Papers.

39. Transcript of Hurley's press conference, April 2, 1945, *FRUS 1945*, VII, 317–22.

40. *Hsin-hua Jih-pao*, April 5, 1945; *Shih-shih Hsin-pao*, April 4, 1945.

41. Digest of Yenan Radio, speech by Mao, May 1, 1945, *FRUS 1945*, VII, 362–65; Speech by Chu Teh, *ibid.*, pp. 388–90; Mao Tse-tung, *Selected Works*, III (Peking, 1965), 255–320.

42. Stelle to Heppner, April 12, 1945, OSS–Dixie Mission Documents.

43. Stelle to Heppner, June 6, 1945, OSS–Dixie Mission Documents; minutes of meeting with Hurley, Wedemeyer, and Chang, June 11, 1945, Box 7, Wedemeyer Files; "Conferences with Generalissimo," No. 63, June 18, 1945, *ibid.*; diary entry of May 15, 1945, vol. 51, Stimson Papers.

44. Notes on talk with Hurley, May 8, 1945. This document was released to the author by the Central Intelligence Agency under the provisions of the Freedom of Information Act.

45. Hurley to Morgenthau, November 15, 1944, *Morgenthau Diaries*, II, 1379–86; diary entry of March 8, 1945, vol. 50, Stimson Papers.

46. Buhite, *Hurley*, pp. 204–9; Memorandum by Hurley of a conversation with Stalin, April 17, 1945, *FRUS 1945*, VII, 338–40; Hurley to Secretary of State, April 14, 1945, *ibid.*, pp. 329–32.

47. Kennan to Secretary of State and Harriman, April 23, 1945, *ibid.*, pp. 342–44; Kennan to Secretary of State, April 27, 1945, *ibid.*, p. 346; Davies, *Dragon by the Tail*, p. 224; Hurley's letter to Truman, cited in Buhite, *Hurley*, pp. 204–6; memorandum of conversation between Hopkins and Stalin, May 28, 1945, *Berlin*, I, 41–52.

48. Diary entries of May 14, July 29, 1945, Forrestal Papers; John Melby, *The Mandate of Heaven*, p. 22.

49. Joseph Grew, *Turbulent Era.* II, 1423–24, 1445–46, 1457–59; James Forrestal, *The Forrestal Diaries*, pp. 52–56.

50. Melby, *Mandate of Heaven*, p. 22.

51. For a personal discussion of the case see John Service, *The Amerasia Papers*, pp. 17–52; diary entry of May 28, 1945, Forrestal Papers.

52. A complete transcript of Yenan radio broadcasts can be found in the records of the Foreign Broadcast Intelligence Service, Federal Communications Commission, RG 262, Federal Records Center, Suitland, Maryland; OSS Report No. 2986, June 1, 1945, Modern Military Records Branch, National Archives; Mao, *Collected Works, III*, pp. 321–24.

53. OSS Report No. 3154, June 30, 1945, MMR; *Chieh-fang Jih-pao*, June 25, 1945; extract of broadcast from Yenan, June 26, 1945, *FRUS 1945*, VII, 418–21.

54. Record of Treasury Department discussions, May 9, 1945, *Morgenthau Diaries*, II, 1543–59; record of group meeting at Treasury Department, May 15, 1945, *ibid.*, pp. 1562–69.

55. Upshar Evans to Assistant Chief of Staff, G-2, February 6, 1945, vol. I, ch. 5, "History of the Yenan Observer Group," Center for Military History.

56. See part 3, ch. 1, "Ivan Yeaton Manuscript," Hoover Institution. This manuscript, still in progress, consists of Yeaton's memoirs.

57. *Ibid.*

58. Memorandum on establishment of Yenan Observer Group, prepared in Headquarters, China Theater, July 28, 1945. Sent to author by Central Intelligence Agency.

Chapter 11. SACO! The Counterrevolution in Action

1. Milton Miles, *A Different Kind of War*, pp. 12–18. Miles prepared this memoir from official and personal papers he later returned to the Navy Department. See McHugh's 1941–42 correspondence with presidential aide Lauchlin Currie, McHugh Papers.

2. Undated report on Hsiao Hsin-ju, Box 89, folder 9, Hurley Papers; Miles, *A Different Kind of War*, pp. 20–22.

3. Reports on Tai Li from extensive U.S. intelligence sources are contained in ch. 38, NGC Records. This extensive collection is arranged in numbered chapters and unnumbered files. See also General Thomas Hearn to Stilwell, July 23, 1944, Stilwell CBI Correspondence; Hull to Gauss, June 14, 1944, Stilwell CBI Correspondence; Hull to

Gauss, June 14, 1944, *FRUS 1944*, VI, 99–100. See also Lloyd Eastman, *The Abortive Revolution*, for a discussion of the Blue Shirts' ideology.

4. Miles, *A Different Kind of War*, p. 56; Miles to Navy Dept., May 9, 1942, ch. 2, NGC Records; "Diary of a Trip," May–August 1942, *ibid.*

5. Miles, *A Different Kind of War*, pp. 75–77; Stilwell to Marshall, March 6, 1943, Stilwell CBI Correspondence.

6. For a discussion of Miles's and McHugh's efforts to have Stilwell recalled, see chapter 7. Despite the obvious similarity of their interests and politics, Chennault himself avoided working directly with Miles and Tai Li. The flier depended on Chinese Communist assistance to rescue downed 14th Air Force pilots and feared that his direct cooperation with Miles and Tai Li would endanger this arrangement. See Chennault, *Way of a Fighter*, p. 257.

7. "Establishment of the Office of the Co-ordinator of Strategic Services" file, NGC Records; Report on "Military Intelligence-British relations," CBI Theater, Historical Section.

8. "SACO Agreement," file, NGC Records; minutes of a meeting with T. V. Soong, December 31, 1942, *ibid.*

9. Joint Staff Planners to Joint Chiefs of Staff, February 23, 1943, Dept. of the Army, Operations Division Decimal File, 1942–45, 381 CTO.

10. Miles, *A Different Kind of War*, pp. 116–19; "SACO Agreement" file, NGC Record.

11. *Ibid.*

12. Donovan to Purnell, November 3, 1943, ch. 2. *ibid.;* Purnell to Donovan, November 6, 1943, *ibid.;* memorandum prepared at Headquarters, COMINCH, U.S. Fleet, January 5, 1944, *ibid.*

13. Miles, *A Different Kind of War*, pp. 168–72; Roy Stratton, *SACO, the Rice Paddy Navy*, p. 6. Stratton was chief of SACO supply corps in China.

14. Memorandum by General Thomas Handy, "OSS Plan for Mission to Yenan," August 10, 1944, OPD 210.684 China, RG 165.

15. Lieutenant Donald Davies to Miles, May 10, 1943, ch. 42.3, NGC Records.

16. Memorandum by John Davies of a conversation with Harry Hopkins, September 4, 1944, Box 15, Stilwell Papers.

17. Miles to Hurley, October 6, 1944, Box 88, folder 8, Hurley Papers; OSS Research and Analysis Report No. 41617, February 5, 1946. Stilwell himself was tremendously concerned when he learned that Hurley was communicating via naval radio.

18. See material contained in folder on "Chinese Communists," ch. 42.3, NGC Records.

19. The background of this incident is discussed in chap. 10.

20. "Abie" [a SACO officer] to Metzel, late 1943, ch. 4, NGC Records.

21. See reports on U.S. Naval Unit No. 9, ch. 27, *ibid.*

22. Miles to Metzel, September 1, 1943, ch. 5, *ibid.*

23. "Log of Daily Events," September 9, 1943, ch. 5.2, *ibid.;* Metzel to Miles, October 31, 1943, ch. 27, *ibid.*

24. Memorandum by Miles, August, 1945, ch. 38, *ibid.*

25. Report on Naval Unit No. 9, August 1, 1945, ch. 27, *ibid.;* John Service and Raymond Ludden to Wedemeyer, February 19, 1945, Box 11, Wedemeyer Files.

26. Entries in Black Book, August, 1943, and September 4, 1943, Stilwell Papers.

27. Hearn to Stilwell, July 14, 1944, Box 14, *ibid.;* Miles to Metzel, December 30, 1943, ch. 8, NGC Records.

28. Miles, *A Different Kind of War,* pp. 435–39; Wedemeyer to Miles, January 11, 1945, Box 1, Wedemeyer Files; Miles to Metzel, January 11, 1945, ch. 36.2.1, NGC Records.

29. Minutes of meeting with General Tai Li, January 30, 1945, Box 7, Wedemeyer Files.

30. Miles, *A Different Kind of War,* pp. 434, 474–75, 488; memorandum from Service and Ludden to Wedemeyer, February 19, 1945, Box 11, Wedemeyer Files.

31. Wedemeyer to General John Hull, July 5, 1945, quoted in Romanus and Sunderland, *Time Runs Out on CBI,* p. 254; memorandum of a talk with Wedemeyer, June 17, 1945, Chennault Papers.

32.   See memorandum prepared for John Carter Vincent, April 29, 1944, *FRUS 1944,* VI, 64–65.

33. "Minutes of a Meeting of the Joint Chiefs of Staff," March 27, 1945, RG 218; Leahy, *I Was There,* pp. 337–38.

34. War Dept. to Wedemeyer, April 6, 1945, Box 1, Wedemeyer Files; Miles, *A Different Kind of War,* pp. 457–58.

35. See section on history of the Clandestine Branch, in ms. "History of United States Forces, China Theater," Center for Military History; Wedemeyer to Marshall, June 13, 1945, Box 1, Wedemeyer Files.

36. Notes on a talk by Miles, May 29, 1945, ch. 5, NGC Records; minutes of Miles's address to SACO personnel, August 18, 1945, ch. 44, *ibid.*

37. Metzel to Edwards, May 23, 1945, ch. 42, *ibid.;* Metzel to Edwards, May 31, 1945, *ibid.*

38. Miles to Metzel, July 24, 1945, ch. 36.8, *ibid.*

39. Wedemeyer to Miles, August 1, 1945, ch. 42.3, *ibid.*

40. Miles to SACO units, August 12, 1945, ch. 39, *ibid.*

41. Miles to SACO units, August 16, 1945, *ibid.;* memorandum by Miles, August, 1945, ch. 38, *ibid.;* Miles, *A Different Kind of War,* pp. 492–95.

42. Memorandum by Wedemeyer, September, 1945, Box 2, Wedemeyer Files; Wedemeyer to War Dept., August 19, 1945, Box 3, *ibid.;* Wedemeyer to War Dept., September 14, 1945, Box 4, *ibid.*

43. Memorandum by Admiral Charles Cooke, September 18, 1945, ch. 32, NGC Records (Cooke later became a military advisor to Chiang Kai-shek on Taiwan); memorandum by James Forrestal of a conversation with T. V. Soong, August 27, 1945, *FRUS, 1945*, VII, 539; Metzel to Cooke, September 22, 1945, ch. 44, NGC Records; diary entry of September 28, 1945, Forrestal Papers.

44. Miles, *A Different Kind of War*, pp. 518, 524, 555–58; interview with John Service.

45. Minutes of meeting with Chiang Kai-shek and Madame Chiang, September 16, 1945, Box 2, Wedemeyer Files.

46. Wedemeyer to War Dept., September 22, 1945, Box 4, *ibid.*

47. Miles to Metzel to chief of naval operations, January 21, 1946, ch. 38, NGC Records; Thomas Ingles of Office of Naval Intelligence to chief of naval operations, January 21, 1946, *ibid.;* memorandum prepared in the office of the chief of naval operations, January 28, 1946, *ibid.*

48. Miles Papers, Hoover Institution. (this is a small collection of papers dealing mostly with Miles's postwar career); *New York Times*, March 26, 1974.

Chapter 12. The Japanese Surrender

1. Memorandum by Grew, June 9, 1945, *FRUS 1945*, VII, 896; Hurley to Truman, June 15, 1945, *ibid.*, p. 903; memorandum by Grew, June 19, 1945, *ibid.*, p. 906.

2. Harriman to Truman, July 3, 1945, *ibid.*, pp. 911–14.

3. See messages from Harriman to Truman, July 7–13, 1945, *ibid.*, pp. 919–34; memorandum by Harriman, July 18, 1945, *ibid.*, pp. 944–48.

4. Memorandum by Charles Bohlen of Truman-Stalin meeting of July 17, 1945, *Berlin*, II, 1582–87; Wallace, *Price of Vision*, entry of November 6, 1945, p. 506.

5. Memorandum of conference with Truman, June 6, 1945, Box 172, folder 18, Stimson Papers.

6. Entries of July 18 and July 20, 1945, "Walter Brown's Book," Byrnes Papers. Extensive similar discussions of the politics of the atomic bomb are found in Martin Sherwin, *A World Destroyed*, and Barton J. Bernstein, "Roosevelt, Truman and the Atomic Bomb, 1941–1945."

7. Notes of July 24, 1945, Box 172, folder 18, Stimson Papers; undated notes on Potsdam Conference, Box 172, folder 19, *ibid.*

8. Entries of July 24, August 3, 1945, "Walter Brown's Book," Byrnes Papers; diary entry of July 23, 1945, Stimson Papers.

9. Memoranda by Harriman for Byrnes, July 28 and July 31, 1945, *FRUS 1945*, VII, 950–54; Harriman to Truman and Byrnes, August 10, 1945, *ibid.*, pp. 967–69.

10. Harriman to Byrnes, August 7 and August 8, 1945, *ibid.*, pp. 957–58; memorandum of conversation with Stalin by Harriman, August 8, 1945, *ibid*, pp. 960–65;

Byrnes to Harriman, August 9, 1945, *ibid.*, pp. 965–66; Harriman to Truman and Byrnes, August 10, 1945, *ibid.*, p. 967.

11. Summary of OSS field reports, August 6 and September 1, 1945, CBI Theater, Historical Section; Yenan Observer Group to Wedemeyer, August 11, 12, September 2, 1945, *ibid.*

12. Harriman to Byrnes and Truman, August 11, 1945, *FRUS 1945*, VII, 967–69; Harriman to Truman and Byrnes, August 14, 1945, *ibid.*, pp. 971–73. The text of the Sino-Soviet Treaty is printed in the China White Paper.

13. Wallace, *Price of Vision*, entry of August 10, 1945, pp. 473–75.

14. Wedemeyer to Mao, July 29, 1945, vol. I, ch. 5, "History of the Yenan Observer Group," ms. at Center for Military History; statement by Yeaton, May 29, 1946, *ibid.*; "Conferences with Generalissimo," No. 68, July 30, 1945, Box 8, Wedemeyer Files; see also memorandum of a conversation between General Yeh Chien-ying and Yeaton, August 2, 1945, "History of the Yenan Observer Group," vol. I, ch. 5.

15. "Conferences with Generalissimo," No. 68A, July 31, 1945, Box 8, Wedemeyer Files.

16. Wedemeyer to War Dept., August 1, 1945, Box 8, *ibid.*

17. "Conferences with Generalissimo," No. 71, August 10, 1945, *ibid.*

18. Joint Chiefs to Wedemeyer, August 10, 1945, *FRUS 1945*, VII, 527–28.

19. See "History of the China Theater," manuscript at Center for Military History, vol. II, ch. 13, pp. 2–3; draft statement given by Hurley to Hollington Tong, August 12, 1945, Box 98, folder 9, Hurley Papers. The American-Nationalist reoccupation plans can be found in Box 4, Wedemeyer Files; Wedemeyer to Marshall, August 12, 1945, CBI Theater, Historical Section.

20. Wedemeyer to Marshall, August 14, 1945, CBI Theater, Historical Section; Joint Chiefs to Wedemeyer, August 23, 1945, *ibid.*

21. Truman to MacArthur, August 15, 1945, *FRUS 1945*, VII, 530–31; Hurley to Byrnes, August 9, 1945, *ibid.*, p. 492; Byrnes to Hurley, August 11, 1945, *ibid.*, p. 495.

22. *Chieh-fang Jih-Pao*, August 13, 1945, and *Hsin-hua Jih-pao*, August 15, 16, 1945; Yenan Observer Group to Wedemeyer, August 15, 1945, Box 98, folder 9, Hurley Papers; Wedemeyer to Marshall, August 17, 1945, *FRUS 1945*, VII, 519–20; Mao, *Selected Works*, IV, 11–26.

23. Wedemeyer to Marshall, August 19, 1945, *FRUS 1945*, VII, 531–34.

24. See "History of the China Theater," vol. II, ch. 13, pp. 8–11; report by Wedemeyer to Eisenhower, February, 1946, CBI Theater, Historical Section.

25. Mao to Wedemeyer, September 8, 1945, "History of the China Theater," vol. II, ch. 13, p. 93.

26. Report by Yenan Observer Group to Wedemeyer, August 15, 1945, CBI Theater, Historical Section.

27. Dept. of the Army, OSS Research and Analysis Report No. 2738, May 15, 1945.

28. *Ibid*. No. 3227, August 13, 1945, and No. 3247, September 7, 1945.

29. Report by Yenan Observer Group to Wedemeyer, September 2, 1945, CBI Theater, Historical Section; background on the Communist position was also provided for Hurley by the British ambassador in the form of a letter from Michael Lindsay. Lindsay, who had lived in Yenan for several years, told the British ambassador that the Communists were tremendously fearful of American military intervention and hoped that some way would be found to forestall it. See Lindsay's letter of August 24, 1945, Box 92, folder 7, Hurley Papers. See also Warren Cohen, "American Observers and the Sino-Soviet Friendship Treaty of August, 1945."

30. Hurley to Byrnes, July 10, 1945, Box 98, folder 8, Hurley Papers; Hurley to Byrnes, August 31, 1945, Box 88, folder 2, *ibid.*; summary of OSS Field Report, September 1, 1945, CBI Theater, Historical Section.

31. Mao, *Selected Works*, IV, 47–51.

32. Hurley to Byrnes, August 31, 1945, *FRUS 1945*, VII, 542–43. Theater headquarters conducted an extensive investigation of the Birch incident. Its findings appear in the John Birch File. Modern Military Records Branch, NA.

33. Hurley to Byrnes, September 1, 1945, State Dept. Decimal File, China; Hurley to Byrnes, September 2, 1945, *FRUS 1945*, VII, 546–47; Marshall to Wedemeyer, September 4, 1945, CBI Theater, Historical Section; Wedemeyer to Marshall, September 8, 1945, *ibid.*

34. Hurley to Byrnes, September 11, 1945, *FRUS 1945*, VII, 555–57. Hurley's personal papers for December 1944–November 1945 are larded with reference to British and French schemes to dominate Asia and isolate the United States. See Box 87, folders 21, 22, Hurley Papers; also Hurley to Truman, telegrams of May 20, 28, 1945, Box 94, folder 1, *ibid.*; Hurley to Truman, letter of May 13, 1945, Box 96, folder 1, *ibid.*

35. Minutes of meeting between Wedemeyer and Chiang, September 16, 1945, Box 8, Wedemeyer Files; aid memoire handed to Hurley by Chiang, September 19, 1945, Box 93, folder 1, Hurley Papers.

36. *New York Times*, August 17, 1945; *Hsin-hua Jih-pao*, August 22, 1945.

37. Memorandum by Byrnes to Truman, September 3, 1945, *FRUS 1945*, VII, 547–49; Patterson to Byrnes, January 18, 1946, OPD 400 TX, RG 165.

38. See "History of the China Theater," vol. II, ch. 13, pp. 13–14.

39. *Ibid.*, vol. III, ch. 15, pp. 53–58; Chefoo file, ser. IV, no. 28, Barbey Papers; U.S. Marine Corps, Historical Branch, *The United States Marines in North China, 1945–1949*, pp. 2–3.

40. See "History of the China Theater," vol. III, ch. 15, pp. 133–34.

41. Sgt. Sam C. McKay, Jr., to Sen. Connally, November 5, 1945, cited in Kenneth Chern, "Prelude to Cold War: The United States Senate and the Abortive China Debate, 1945," (Ph.D. dissertation, University of Chicago, 1974), p. 238.

42. Report by Yenan Observer Group to Wedemeyer, November 1, 1945, "History of the Yenan Observer Group"; Yeaton to Wedemeyer, October 6, 7, 1945, Box 15, Wedemeyer Files.

43. Transcript of Yenan radio broadcast, November 9, 1945, Foreign Broadcast Intelligence Service. United Press releases of November 8, 12, 1945.

44. Acheson to Truman, September 10, 1945, CCS 540; Leahy to JCS, September 15, 1945, *ibid.;* JCS to Wedemeyer, September 18, 1945, *ibid.*

45. Memorandum of conversation by Acheson, September 27, 1945, *FRUS 1945*, VII, 569–70.

46. Buhite, *Hurley,* pp. 258–65; Walter Robinson to Byrnes, September 27, 1945, State Dept. Decimal File, China.

47. Wedemeyer, *Wedemeyer Reports!* pp. 358, 364.

48. Diary entry of September 28, 1945, Forrestal Papers.

49. Yeaton to Wedemeyer, October 6, 1945, Box 15, Wedemeyer Files.

50. "7th Amphibious Force—Action Reports," file, December 22, 1945, Barbey Papers.

51. Part 3, ch. 1, Ivan Yeaton MS.

52. Minutes of meeting of SWNCC, October 22, 1945, *FRUS 1945*, VII, 583–90.

53. Report by JCS, October 22, 1945, *ibid.*, pp. 590–98.

54. Meeting of Secretaries of State, War, and Navy, November 6, 1945, diary entry, Forrestal Papers.

55. Wedemeyer to Marshall, November 14, 1945, *FRUS 1945*, VII, 627–28.

56. War Dept. to Wedemeyer, November 19, 1945, diary entry, Forrestal Papers.

57. Meeting of Secretaries of State, War, and Navy, November 20, 1945, diary entry, *ibid.*

58. Wedemeyer to War Dept., November 20, 1945, diary entry, *ibid.;* see Wedemeyer to Eisenhower, November 20, 1945, *FRUS 1945*, VII, 650–60.

59. *Ibid.*

60. Wedemeyer to Marshall, November 23, 1945, Box 19, Wedemeyer Files.

61. Forrestal and Patterson to Byrnes, November 26, 1945, diary entry, Forrestal Papers; diary entry of November 27, 1945, Leahy Papers.

62. Wedemeyer to Eisenhower, November 26, 1945, *FRUS 1945*, VII, 679–84.

63. *Ibid.*

64. Buhite, *Hurley,* pp. 265–68.

65. Meeting of Secretaries of State, War, and Navy, November 27, 1945, diary entry, Forrestal Papers; JCS to Wedemeyer, December 14, 1945, *FRUS 1945*, VII, 698–99.

66. Report by Adler to Robertson, December 19, 1945, *FRUS 1945*, VII, 777–83; Wedemeyer to Eisenhower, February, 1946, CBI Theater, Historical Section.

67. Wallace, *Price of Vision*, entry of November 27, 1945, pp. 519–22. Hurley's letter of resignation is printed in the China White Paper, pp. 581–84.

Chapter 13. Backing into the Future

1. Diary entry of November 28, 1945, Leahy Papers; Byrnes to Clinton Anderson, September 15, 1948, Byrnes Papers; a discussion of the Senate's reaction to Hurley's resignation is found in Kenneth Chern, "A Prelude to Cold War: The United States Senate and the Abortive China Debate, 1945" (Ph.D. dissertation, University of Chicago, 1974).

2. Message quoted in "History of the China Theater," vol. II, ch. 15, p. 104 (italics added); Marshall to Leahy, November 30, 1945, *FRUS 1945*, VII, 748.

3. Notes by Marshall on meetings with Truman, December 11, 14, 1945, *ibid.*, pp. 767–70; a recently published volume of selected materials concerning Marshall's activities in China can be found in George C. Marshall, *Marshall's Mission to China*.

4. American intelligence reports and analyses of Soviet activity in Manchuria during 1946 appear in "History of the China Theater," section entitled "Recovery of Manchuria." See also Harriman and Abel, *Special Envoy*, pp. 538–41.

5. Transcripts of Byrnes-Molotov and Byrnes-Stalin discussions, *FRUS 1945*, VII, 835–50.

6. Harriman and Abel, *Special Envoy*, pp. 531–32; O. Edmund Clubb, *Russia and China: The Great Game*, pp. 343, 355.

7. Yeaton to Wedemeyer, December 20, 1945, *FRUS 1945*, VII, 793–94; Melby, *Mandate of Heaven*, p. 63.

8. Wedemeyer to Yeaton, December 13, 14, 1945, Box 13, Wedemeyer Files.

9. Melby, *Mandate of Heaven*, pp. 65–69.

10. Marshall's initial meetings with Chiang, Soong, and Chou occurred between December 21 and December 24, 1945; *FRUS 1945*, VII, 794–813.

11. Merle Miller, *Plain Speaking*, p. 289.

12. See Acheson's Letter of Transmittal of July 30, 1949, in *China White Paper*.

13. *Ibid.*, p. 279.

14. Executive session testimony by Marshall before Senate Foreign Relations Committee and House Foreign Affairs Committee, February 21, 1948, *ibid.*, pp. 380–84.

15. Notes of Cabinet meeting of November 26, 1948 by Matthew J. Connelly, Connelly Papers. Unfortunately, Connelly's notes summarize into one or two phrases extensive Cabinet conversations on China as well as many other important topics.

16. See Acheson's Letter of Transmittal, *China White Paper*.

17. Mao, *Selected Works*, IV, 425–59.

18. For a brief but cogent discussion of China-related decisionmaking 1945–49, and its parallels to Vietnam, see Ernest R. May, *The Truman Administration and China, 1945–1949.*

13. Backing into the Future

Bibliography
Primary Sources

Government Records

Manuscripts
National Archives and Federal Records Center, Suitland, Maryland
U.S. Department of the Army
Army Intelligence File 1941–1945, RG 319
China-Burma-India Theater, Historical Section, RG 332
China-Burma-India Theater, Records, RG 332
Combined Chiefs of Staff, Records, RG 218
G-2 Regional File, 1933–44, RG 165
John Birch File, Modern Military Records Branch
Joint Chiefs of Staff, Records, RG 218
Military Intelligence Division Reports, 1917–41, RG 165
Office of Strategic Services, Yenan Documents, Modern Military Records Branch
Office of Strategic Services, Research and Analysis Reports, RG 226
Operations Division, Records, RG 165
General Joseph W. Stilwell, Correspondence and Messages, RG 332
War Plans Division, Records, RG 165
General Albert C. Wedemeyer, Files, RG 332
Wires Re: Communists, File, Modern Military Records Branch
U.S. Department of Commerce
Bureau of Foreign and Domestic Commerce, RG 151
U.S. Federal Communications Commission
Foreign Broadcast Intelligence Service, Radio Reports on the Far East, RG 262
Digest of the Chinese Press, RG 262
Yenan Radio Monitoring, RG 262
U.S. Department of State Historical Division
General Files and Decimal Files, 1933–45, RG 59
Embassy in China Files, 1941–45, RG 84
Consulate in China, Extracts from the Chinese Press (microfilm)
Other Government Depositories
Center for Military History, Washington, D.C.

345

History of the China Theater
History of the China-Burma-India Theater (Stilwell Report on CBI)
History of the Yenan Observer Group
Japanese Monograph Series
Center for Naval History, Operational Archives, Washington, D.C.
  Records of Naval Group China
  Naval Intelligence Reports, China
In addition to the above records, the Central Intelligence Agency released 64 pages of OSS and Dixie Mission documents to the author on September 24, 1975.
British Government Cabinet Records of the Second World War
  Prem 3 and Prem 4 Files (microfilm at Stanford University Library)

Published Documents

U.S. Congress
Congressional Record. 75th–79th Congresses. Vols. 83–91, 1937–45. Washington, D.C., 1937–45.
Senate Committee on the Judiciary. *The Amerasia Papers: A Clue to the Catastrophe of China.* 2 vols. Washington, D.C., 1970.
Senate Committee on the Judiciary. *Morgenthau Diary, China.* 2 vols. Washington, D.C., 1965.
U.S., Department of the Army
The Chinese Communist Movement: A Report of the United States War Department, July 1945. Ed. Lyman P. Van Slyke. Stanford, Cal.: Stanford University Press, 1968.
U.S., Department of State
Foreign Relations of the United States, Diplomatic Papers 1931. 3 vols. Washington, D.C., 1946.
—— *1932.* 5 vols. Washington, D.C., 1948.
—— *1933.* 5 vols. Washington, D.C., 1949.
—— *1934.* 5 vols. Washington, D.C., 1950–53.
—— *1935.* 4 vols. Washington, D.C., 1952–53.
—— *1936.* 5 vols. Washington, D.C., 1953–54.
—— *1937.* 5 vols. Washington, D.C., 1954.
—— *1938.* 5 vols. Washington, D.C., 1954–56.
—— *1939.* 5 vols. Washington, D.C., 1955–57.
—— *1940.* 5 vols. Washington, D.C., 1955–61.
—— *1941.* 7 vols. Washington, D.C., 1956–63.
—— *1942. China.* Washington, D.C., 1956.
—— *1943. China.* Washington, D.C., 1957.
—— *1944.* 7 vols. Washington, D.C., 1966–67.
—— *1945.* 9 vols. Washington, D.C., 1967–69.

The Conference of Berlin, 1945. 2 vols. Washington, D.C., 1960.

The Conference at Cairo and Teheran, 1943. Washington, D.C., 1961.

The Conferences at Malta and Yalta, 1945. Washington, D.C., 1955.

The Conferences at Washington, 1941–1942 and Casablanca, 1943. Washington D.C., 1968.

The Conferences at Washington and Quebec, 1943. Washington, D.C., 1970.

The Conference at Quebec, 1944. Washington, D.C., 1972.

Papers Relating to the Foreign Relations of the United States: Japan, 1931–1941. 2 vols. Washington, D.C., 1943.

Peace and War: United States Foreign Policy, 1931–1941. Washington, D.C., 1943.

United States Relations with China, with Special Reference to the Period 1944–1949. Washington, D.C., 1949 ("China White Paper").

U.S., Marine Corps, Historical Branch

The United States Marines in North China, 1945–1949. Washington, D.C., 1960.

The Pentagon Papers. New York: Bantam Books, 1971.

Roosevelt and Churchill: Their Secret Wartime Correspondence. Francis Lowenheim, Harold Langley, and Manfred Jonas, eds. New York: Saturday Review Press, 1975.

Personal Records

Julian Arnold Papers	Hoover Institution on War, Revolution, and Peace, Palto Alto, Cal.
Daniel E. Barbey Papers	Center for Naval History, Washington, D.C.
Haydon L. Boatner Papers	Hoover Institutions on War, Revolution, and Peace, Palo Alto, Cal.
James F. Byrnes Papers	Clemson University Library, Clemson, S.C.
Claire L. Chennault Papers	Hoover Institution on War, Revolution, and Peace, Palo Alto, Cal.; Manuscript Division, Library of Congress, Washington, D.C. (microfilm)
Matthew J. Connelly Papers	Harry S. Truman Presidential Library, Independence, Mo.
Lewis Douglas Papers	University of Arizona, Tucson

John Foster Dulles Papers	Princeton University Library, Princeton, N.J.
George Elsey Papers	Harry S. Truman Presidential Library, Independence, Mo.
Herbert Feis Papers	Manuscript Division, Library of Congress, Washington, D.C.
James Forrestal Diary	Center for Naval History, Washington, D.C.
James Forrestal Papers	Princeton University Library, Princeton, N.J.
Preston Goodfellow Papers	Hoover Institution on War, Revolution, and Peace, Palo Alto, Cal.
Thomas Hart Papers	Center for Naval History, Washington, D.C.
Joseph Hayden Papers	Michigan Historical Collections, Ann Arbor
Harry Hopkins Papers	Franklin D. Roosevelt Library, Hyde Park, N.Y.
Stanley Hornbeck Papers	Hoover Institution on War, Revolution, and Peace, Palo Alto, Cal.
Cordell Hull Papers	Manuscript Division Library of Congress, Washington, D.C.
Patrick J. Hurley Papers	Western History Collections, University of Oklahoma, Norman
Nelson T. Johnson Papers	Manuscript Division, Library of Congress, Washington, D.C.
William Leahy Papers	Manuscript Division, Library of Congress, Washington, D.C.
James McHugh Papers	Cornell University, Ithaca, N.Y.
Milton Miles Papers	Center for Naval History, Washington, D.C.; Hoover Institution on War, Revolution, and Peace, Palo Alto, Cal.
Henry Morgenthau, Jr. Papers	Franklin D. Roosevelt Library, Hyde Park, N.Y.
Franklin D. Roosevelt Papers	Franklin D. Roosevelt Library, Hyde Park, N.Y.
T. V. Soong Papers	Hoover Institution on War, Revolution, and Peace, Palo Alto, Cal.
Joseph W. Stilwell Papers	Hoover Institution on War, Revolution, and Peace, Palo Alto, Cal.
Henry L. Stimson Papers	Yale University Library, New Haven, Conn.
Gilbert Stuart Papers	Hoover Institution on War, Revolution, and Peace, Palo Alto, Cal.

Henry Wallace Papers	Manuscript Division, Library of Congress, Washington, D.C.
Harry D. White Papers	Princeton University Library, Princeton, N.J.
Whiting Willauer Papers	Princeton University Library, Princeton, N.J.
Harry E. Yarnell Papers	Manuscript Division, Library of Congress, Washington, D.C.
Ivan Yeaton Manuscript	Hoover Institution on War, Revolution, and Peace, Palo Alto, Cal.
Arthur Young Papers	Hoover Institution on War, Revolution, and Peace, Palo Alto, Cal.

Memoirs, Autobiographies, Diaries, Published Papers

Acheson, Dean. *President at the Creation: My Years in the Department of State*. New York: Norton, 1969.

Barrett, David. *Dixie Mission: The United States Army Observer Group in Yenan, 1944*. Berkeley: University of California Press, 1970.

Blum, John M. *From the Morgenthau Diaries: Years of Crisis, 1928–1938*. Boston: Houghton Mifflin, 1959.

—— *From the Morgenthau Diaries: Years of Urgency, 1938–1941*. Boston: Houghton Mifflin, 1965.

Bryant, Arthur. *Triumph in the West*. New York: Doubleday, 1959.

Byrnes, James. *All in One Lifetime*. New York: Harper, 1958.

—— *Speaking Frankly*. New York: Harper, 1947.

Carlson, Evans F. *The Chinese Army*. New York: Institute of Pacific Relations, 1940.

—— *Twin Stars over China*. New York: Dodd, Mead, 1940.

Chennault, Claire L. *Way of a Fighter*. New York: Putnam, 1949.

Chiang Kai-shek. *Soviet Russia in China*. New York: Farrar, Strauss & Giroux, 1965.

Churchill, Winston S. *History of the Second World War*. Vols III–V. Boston: Houghton Mifflin, 1950–51.

Clubb, O. Edmund, *The Witness and I*. New York: Columbia University Press, 1974.

Davies, John P. *The Dragon by the Tail*. New York: Norton, 1972.

Dedijer, Vladimir. *Tito*. New York: Simon & Schuster, 1953.

Dilks, David, ed. *The Diaries of Sir Alexander Cadogan*. New York: Putnam, 1971.

Djilas, Milovan. *Conversations with Stalin.* New York: Harcourt, Brace & World, 1963.

Dorn, Frank. *Walkout with Stilwell in Burma.* New York: Crowell, 1971.

Forrestal, James. *The Forrestal Diaries.* Edited by Walter Millis. New York: Viking Press, 1951.

Grew, Joseph C. *Ten Years in Japan.* New York: Simon & Schuster, 1944.

—— *Turbulent Era: A Diplomatic Record of Forty Years, 1904–1945.* Boston: Houghton Mifflin, 1952.

Han, Suyin. *Birdless Summer.* New York: Putnam, 1968.

Harriman, W. Averell and Ellie Abel. Special Envoy to Churchill and Stalin, 1941—1946. New York: Random House, 1975.

Ho Ying-chin. *The Big Circle: China's Role in the Burma Campaigns.* New York: Exposition, 1968.

Hull, Cordell. *The Memoirs of Cordell Hull.* 2 vols. New York: Macmillan, 1948.

Ickes, Harold L. *The Secret Diary of Harold L. Ickes.* 3 vols. New York: Simon & Schuster, 1953–1955.

Ike, Nobutaka, ed. and trans. *Japan's Decision for War.* Stanford, Cal.: Stanford University Press, 1967.

King, Ernest J. and Whitehill, Walter Muir. *Fleet Admiral King.* New York: Norton, 1952.

Leahy, William D. *I Was There.* New York: McGraw-Hill, 1950.

Mao Tse-tung. *Selected Works.* vol. III, Peking: Foreign Languages Press, 1965.

—— *Selected Works,* vol. IV. Peking: Foreign Languages Press, 1961.

Marshall, George C. *Marshall's Mission to China.* Intro. by Lyman Van Slyke, Arlington, Va.: University Publications of America, 1976.

Melby, John. *The Mandate of Heaven,* Toronto: University of Toronto Press, 1968.

Miller, Merle. *Plain Speaking: An Oral Biography of Harry S. Truman.* New York: Putnam/Berkley, 1973.

Miles, Milton. *A Different Kind of War.* New York: Doubleday, 1967.

Mountbatten of Burma, Vice Admiral the Earl. *Report to the Combined Chiefs of Staff by the Supreme Allied Commander, South East Asia, 1943–1945.* New York: Philosophical Library, 1951.

Peck, Graham, *Two Kinds of Time.* Boston: Houghton Mifflin, 1950.

Pickersgill, J. W. and Forster, D. W. *The MacKenzie King Record.* 3 vols. Toronto: University of Toronto Press, 1960–70.

Roosevelt, Elliott. *As He Saw It*. New York: Duell, Sloane & Pearce, 1946.

Service, John S. *The Amerasia Papers: Some Problems in the History of U.S.-China Relations*. Berkeley: University of California Press, 1971.

Severeid, Eric. *Not So Wild a Dream*. New York: Knopf, 1946.

Snow, Edgar. *The Battle for Asia*. New York: Random House, 1941.

—— *Journey to the Beginning*. New York: Random House, 1958.

—— *Random Notes on Red China, 1936–1945*. Cambridge, Mass.: Harvard University Press, 1957.

—— *Red Star Over China*. New York: Random House, 1938.

Stilwell, Joseph W. *The Stilwell Papers*. Edited by Theodore White. New York: William Sloane, 1948.

Stimson, Henry L. *The Far Eastern Crisis*. New York: Harper, 1936.

Stimson, Henry L. and McGeorge Bundy. *On Active Service in Peace and War*. New York: Harper, 1947.

Stratton, Roy. *SACO, The Rice Paddy Navy*. New York: C. S. Palmer, 1950.

Truman, Harry S. *Memoirs*. vol. II: *Year of Decisions*. New York: Doubleday, 1955.

Wallace, Henry A. *The Price of Vision: The Diary of Henry A. Wallace, 1942–1946*. Edited by John Morton Blum. Boston: Houghton Mifflin, 1973.

Wedemeyer, Albert. *Wedemeyer Reports!* New York: Henry Holt, 1958.

Welles, Sumner. *Seven Decisions That Shaped History*. New York: Harper, 1950.

White, Theodore and Annalee Jacoby. *Thunder Out of China*. New York: William Sloane, 1946.

Willkie, Wendell. *One World*. New York: Simon & Schuster, 1943.

Young, Arthur. *China and the Helping Hand, 1937–1945*. Cambridge, Mass.: Harvard University Press, 1967.

Newspapers and Periodicals

Amerasia Magazine (New York), 1938–45.
Chieh-fang Jih-pao (Yenan), 1941–45.
Chung-yang Jih-pao (Chungking), 1938–45.
Hsin-hua Jih-pao (Chungking), 1938–45.
New York Times, 1938–45.

Interview

John S. Service, March 26, 1975, San Francisco, Cal.

Secondary Sources

Adams, Frederick. *Economic Diplomacy: The Export-Import Bank and American Foreign Policy, 1934–39.* Columbia: University of Missouri Press, 1976.

Alperowitz, Gar. *Atomic Diplomacy: Hiroshima and Potsdam.* New York: Simon & Schuster, 1965.

Anderson, Irvine. *The Standard-Vacuum Oil Company and United States East Asian Policy, 1933–1941.* Princeton, N.J.: Princeton University Press, 1971.

Bernstein, Barton. "Roosevelt, Truman and the Atom Bomb, 1941–45: A Reinterpretation," *Political Science Quarterly* (Spring 1975), 90:23–29.

Borg, Dorothy. *The United States and the Far Eastern Crisis of 1933–1938.* Cambridge, Mass.: Harvard University Press, 1964.

Borg, Dorothy and Okamoto, Shumpei, eds. *Pearl Harbor as History: Japanese-American Relations, 1931–1941.* New York: Columbia University Press, 1973.

Boyle, John Hunter. *China and Japan at War, 1937–1945: The Politics of Collaboration.* Stanford, Cal.: Stanford University Press, 1972.

Buhite, Russell. *Patrick J. Hurley and American Foreign Policy.* Ithaca, N.Y.: Cornell University Press, 1973.

Butow, Robert. *The John Doe Associates: Backdoor Diplomacy for Peace, 1941.* Standord, Cal.: Stanford University Press, 1974.

Butow, Robert. *Tojo and the Coming of the War.* Princeton, N.J.: Princeton University Press, 1961.

Chern, Kenneth. "Prelude to Cold War: The United States Senate and the Abortive China Debate, 1945," Ph.D dissertation, University of Chicago, 1974.

Clemens, Diane S. *Yalta.* New York: Oxford University Press, 1970.

Clifford, Nicholas. *Retreat from China British Policy in the Far East, 1940–41.* Seattle: University of Washington Press, 1967.

Cohen, Warren. "American Observers and the Sino-Soviet Friendship Treaty of August 1945." *Pacific Historical Review* (August 1966), 35:347–350.

Cohen, Warren, "The Development of Chinese Communist Attitudes towards the United States, 1934–45." *Orbis* (Spring 1967), 11:219–37.

Crow, Carl. *400 Million Customers.* New York: Harper & Brothers, 1937.

Divine, Robert A. *The Reluctant Belligerent: American Entry into World War II.* New York: Wiley, 1965.

Deutscher, Isaac. *Russia: What Next?* London: Oxford University Press, 1953.

—— *Stalin: A Political Biography.* London: Oxford University Press, 1967.

Eastman, Lloyd. *The Abortive Revolution: China under Nationalist Rule, 1927–1937.* Cambridge, Mass.: Harvard University Press, 1974.

Feis, Herbert, *The China Tangle.* Princeton, N.J.: Princeton University Press, 1953.

—— *The Road to Pearl Harbor: The Coming of the War Between the United States and Japan.* Princeton, N.J.: Princeton University Press, 1950.

Friedman, Donald. *The Road from Isolation: The Campaign of the American Committee for Non-Participation in Japanese Aggression, 1938–1941.* Cambridge, Mass.: Harvard University Press, 1968.

Gardner, Lloyd C. *Economic Aspects of New Deal Diplomacy.* Madison: University of Wisconsin Press, 1964.

Gittings, John. *Survey of the Sino-Soviet Dispute.* London: Oxford University Press, 1964.

Gittings, John. *The World and China, 1922–1972.* New York: Harper & Row, 1974.

Heinrichs, Waldo. *An American Ambassador: Joseph C. Grew and the Development of the United States Diplomatic Tradition.* Boston: Little, Brown, 1966.

International Business Machines Corp. *First Lady of China: The Historic Visit of Madame Chiang Kai-shek to the United States.* New York: Author, 1943.

Johnson, Chalmers. *Peasant Nationalism and Communist Power.* Stanford, Cal.: Stanford University Press, 1962.

Katakoa, Tetsuya. *Resistance and Revolution in China: The Communists and the Second United Front.* Berkeley, Cal.: University of California Press, 1974.

Kahn, E. J. *The China Hands: America's Foreign Service Officers and What Befell Them.* New York: Viking, 1975.

Koen, Ross. *The China Lobby in American Politics.* New York: Macmillan, 1960.

Kolko, Gabriel. *The Politics of War.* New York: Random House, 1969.

Langer, William L. and Samuel E. Gleason. *The Challenge to Isolation, 1937–1940.* New York: Harper, 1952.

—— *The Undeclared War, 1940–1941.* New York: Harper, 1953.

Levenson, Joseph. *Confucian China and Its Modern Fate.* Berkeley: University of California Press, 1965.

Liang, Chin-tung. *General Stilwell in China, 1942–1944: the Full Story.* New York: St. Johns University Press, 1972.

Lohbeck, Don. *Patrick J. Hurley.* Chicago: Regnery, 1956.

Louis, William R. *Imperialism at Bay: The United States and the Decolonization of the British Empire 1941–45.* London: Oxford University Press, 1977.

Lowe, Peter. *Great Britain and the Origins of the Pacific War A Study of British Policy in East Asia, 1937–41.* London: Oxford University Press, 1977.

Marchetti, Victor and John D. Marks. *The C.I.A. and the Cult of Intelligence.* New York: Knopf, 1974.

Matloff, Maurice and Ernest Snell. *Strategic Planning for Coalition Warfare, 1941–1942.* Washington, D.C.: Department of the Army, 1953.

Matloff, Maurice. *Strategic Planning for Coalition Warfare, 1943–1944.* Washington, D.C.: Department of the Army, 1959.

May, Ernest. *The Truman Administration and China, 1945–1949.* Philadelphia: Lippincott, 1975.

Pelz, Stephen E. *Race to Pearl Harbor.* Cambridge, Mass.: Harvard University Press, 1975.

Pogue, Forrest C. *George C. Marshall.* Vols. I–III. New York: Viking Press, 1963, 1968, 1973.

Romanus, Charles and Riley Sunderland. *Stilwell's Mission to China.* Washington, D.C.: Department of the Army, 1953.

—— *Stilwell's Command Problems.* Washington, D.C.: Department of the Army, 1956.

—— *Time Runs Out on CBI.* Washington, D.C.: Department of the Army, 1959.

Rossinger, Lawrence. *China's Wartime Politics.* Princeton, N.J.: Princeton University Press, 1945.

Schroeder, Paul. *The Axis Alliance and Japanese-American Relations, 1941.* Ithaca, N.Y.: Cornell University Press, 1958.

Schurman, Franz. *The Logic of World Power.* New York: Pantheon Books, 1974.

Scott, Peter Dale. *The War Conspiracy.* Indianapolis: Bobbs-Merrill, 1972.

Selden, Mark. *The Yenan Way in Revolutionary China.* Cambridge, Mass.: Harvard University Press, 1971.

Selle, Earl. *Donald of China*. New York: Harper, 1948.

Sherwin, Martin. *A World Destroyed*. New York: Knopf, 1975.

Sherwood, Robert E. *Roosevelt and Hopkins: An Intimate History*. New York: Harper, 1948.

Shewmaker, Kenneth. *Americans and Chinese Communists, 1927–1945 A Persuasive Encounter*. New York: Cornell University Press, 1971.

Smith, R. Harris. *OSS: The Secret History of America's First Central Intelligence Agency*. Berkeley: University of California Press, 1971.

Spence, Jonathan. *To Change China: Western Advisors in China, 1620–1960*. Boston: Little, Brown & Co., 1969.

Sunderland, Riley. "The Secret Embargo," *Pacific Historical Review* (February 1960), 29:75–80.

Tang Tsou. *America's Failure in China*. Chicago: University of Chicago Press, 1963.

Thomson, James C. *While China Faced West: American Reformers in Nationalist China, 1927–37*. Cambridge, Mass.: Harvard University Press, 1969.

Thorne, Christopher. *Allies of a Kind: The United States, Great Britain and the War Against Japan, 1941–45*. New York: Oxford University Press, 1978.

Tien Hung-mao. *Government and Politics in Kuomintang China, 1927–1937*. Stanford, Cal.: Stanford University Press, 1972.

Tuchman, Barbara. *Notes on China*. New York: Collier, 1972.

—— *Stilwell and the American Experience in China, 1911–1945*. New York: Macmillan, 1972.

Van Slyke, Lyman P. *Enemies and Friends: the United Front in Chinese Communist History*. Stanford, Cal.: Stanford University Press, 1967.

Varg, Paul. *The Closing of the Door: Sino-American Relations 1936–46*. East Lansing: Michigan State University Press, 1973.

Watson, Mark S. *Chief of Staff: Prewar Plans and Preparations*. Washington, D.C.: Department of the Army, 1950.

Wholstetter, Roberta. *Pearl Harbor: Warning and Decision*. Stanford, Cal.: Stanford University Press, 1962.

Yergin, Daniel. *The Shattered Peace: The Cold War and the Origins of the National Security State*. Boston: Houghton Mifflin, 1977.

Index

Chennault, Gen. Claire L. (*Continued*)
mander of 14th Air Force, 122; utilizes
Alsop to influence Roosevelt's China
policy, 132-36; secret aid to warlords,
202

Chiang Kai-shek, Generalissimo: creates
Republic of China, 2; purges CCP from
first United Front, 4; requests U.S.
economic and military aid against CCP,
42-43; warns against sacrificing China for
peace with Japan, 61-62; alleged reaction
to Pearl Harbor attack, 88; demands $1
billion loan, 96-98; opposition to Stilwell's initial reform proposals, 107-9; issues Three Demands, 109; suggests that
Stilwell be relieved, 110; lack of control
over Chinese armies, 125-26; views on
nationalism and imperialism, 126-27;
demands major new loans as a result of
Cairo Conference, 150-53; prepared to
demand Stilwell's recall in 1943, 143-45;
efforts to play off Chennault against
Stilwell, 131-34; response to Roosevelt's
demands that Stilwell be given command powers, 165-75; cooperates with
Hurley, 170-74; protests Service's appointment to post in Japan, 270-71;
efforts to involve U.S. more deeply in
civil war, 270-89

Chiang Kai-shek, Mme., visit to U.S.,
119-20

China-Burma-India Theater (CBI):
created, 95; dissolved, 174

China Defense Supplies (CDS): Chinese
government Lend-Lease agent in U.S.,
54-57; predecessor of China Lobby, 55

China market, myth of, 2

China Theater, created, 174

China White Paper, issued in 1949,
300-301

Chinese army: condition of, 104; Chiang's
limited control of, 125-26

Chinese Communist Party (CCP): nearly
destroyed by Chiang, 4; re-emerges as
powerful force under Mao, 8-9; requests
U.S. mediation before New Fourth

Army Incident, 43-44; view of U.S.,
182-83; influenced by presence of Dixie
Mission and OSS in Yenan, 181-88;
interest in military cooperation with
U.S., 201-2; loses faith in political compromise with KMT, 201; abortive effort
to send Mao and Chou to U.S., 204-5;
demands representation on China's
U.N. delegation, 213-14; criticisms of
Hurley and U.S. policy, 218-19; reaction
to Amerasia Case, 226-27; 7th Party
Congress, 227; bitter view of SACO,
250; opposition to U.S. role in Japanese
surrender, 264-65; resumes peace talks
in Chungking, 266-70; conflict with U.S.
forces in north China, 274; reaction to
Marshall mission, 295-96; strained relations with Soviet Union, 179-80, 186,
220, 266-68, 278, 294-95

Chinese Exclusion Act, 2; abbrogated, 147

Chou En-lai: seeks U.S. mediation before
New Fourth Army Incident, 43; meets
secretly with Lauchlin Currie, 51; flies to
Chungking for peace talks, 197; breaks
off talks, 198; criticizes Hurley's policies,
204; resumes peace talks, 207; breaks off
peace talks, 208; meets with Marshall,
297-98

Churchill, Winston: view of China, 91; at
Washington Conference of 1943, 136; at
Cairo and Yalta Conferences, 149-50; at
Quebec Conference of 1944, 169; meets
with Hurley, 222; meets with Truman at
Potsdam, 253

Civil Air Transport (CAT), 84

Civil war in China: U.S. concern over, 231;
drift toward during summer of 1945,
251-52; full scale fighting, 299-302

Clubb, O. Edmund, early views of CCP, 9

Combined Chiefs of Staff (CCS), created
without Chinese membership, 93

Command crisis of 1944, *see* Chiang Kai-
shek; Hurley, Patrick J.; Stilwell, Joseph
W.

Currie, Lauchlin: sent by FDR on mission
to China in 1941, 47-49; influence on

FDR, 48-51; secret meeting with Chou, 51; establishes direct contacts with KMT leader through McHugh, 51; in charge of Lend-Lease, 54; convinces FDR to support secret air war plan against Japan, 78-81; mission to China in 1942, 111; endorses open-ended support for KMT and recall of Stilwell, 112-14; abandons support for KMT and Chiang, 137; advises Wallace on China, 160

Davies, John P.: early views on CCP, KMT, and United Front, 44-45; views of KMT decadence in 1942-43, 117-18; meets with Chou, 117; views of U.S. policy toward impending civil war, 139-42; suspicions of British imperialism, 139-42; urges contacts with CCP, 156-57; visits Yenan, 192-93; forced out of China by Hurley, 200; visits Yenan, 203; criticizes Hurley's view of Soviet policy toward China, 223
Dixie Mission (U.S. Army Observer Group): creation of, 181-85; declining importance of after January 1945, 228-30
Dorn, Col. Frank: role in Stilwell's military reform plans, 128-31; involvement in plan to assassinate Chiang, 153-54
Dulles, John Foster, views on KMT and CCP, 218

Emmerson, John K., visits Yenan, 192
Export-Import Bank, extends trade credits to China, 28, 32, 35-37

Foreign Service officers: general criticisms of KMT and sympathy for CCP, 115-18; joint protest to State Department over Hurley's policies, 212-13
Forrestal, James: involved in Amerasia Case, 226; fears of Soviet and Chinese Communist expansion, 224; urges expanded U.S. military involvement in civil war, 281-84
Friedman, Irving, forwards favorable views of CCP, 189

Four Power Declaration, China's nominal inclusion in, 147
14th Air Force, created for Chennault by FDR, 122

Gauss, Clarence: named ambassador to China, 53; disparaging reports on value of alliance with KMT, 89; resignation, 174
Grew, Joseph, efforts to end war, 225

Hamilton, Maxwell, opposes initial loans to China, 25-26
Harriman, W. Averell: talks with Stalin regarding China, 209-10; disagrees with Hurley's view of Soviet policy in China, 223; influence on Truman, 224-25; attempts to place Soviet Communism experts in China, 224-25; discussions with Stalin about civil war, 294; participates in negotiations for Sino-Soviet treaty, 258-60, and Yalta agreements, 210-12
Hopkins, Harry: criticizes Chiang during Cairo Conference, 151-53; rumored to have approved recall of Stilwell, 172; discusses Hurley mission, 167-68; sent by Truman to Moscow, 223
Hornbeck, Stanley: cautious reaction to Japanese aggression in 1931, 6; vigorous support of aid to China in 1938, 26
Ho Ying-chin, opposed by Stilwell, 129
Hsueh Yueh, General, supported by Soong, 129; aided by Chennault, 202
Hull, Cordell, opposes initial loans to China, 25-26; at Moscow Conference, 147
Hurley, Patrick J.: sent to China to invite Chiang to Cairo, 148; praised by FDR, 149, 217; sent as personal emissary to Chiang by FDR, 166-77; disparaged by Hopkins, 167-68; visits Moscow, 178; collaborates with Chiang to force Stilwell from China, 168-74; initial policy toward CCP, 191; visits Yenan, 194-96; signs Five Point Peace Proposal with Mao, 195-96; abandons neutral position,

urges FDR to back Stilwell in command crisis, 164-74; selected as U.S. mediator in civil war, 289; instructed by Truman, 292-95; attempts to mediate civil war, 295-99; leaves China and becomes Secretary of State, 299; opposes deeper U.S. involvement in civil war, 301

Metzel, Capt. J. C., NGC-SACO representative in Navy Department, 234

Miles, Comm. Milton (*see also* SACO): support for Chennault, 133; role in Stilwell recall, 174; opposition to Stilwell, 239; conflict with Wedemeyer, 242-45; anti-communist views, 245-46; nervous breakdown and relief from China, 248; post-WWII career, 249-50

Morgenthau, Henry, Jr.: plays leading role in sponsoring aid for China, 24-28, 32-38; angered by behavior of Soong, 36-38, 52; fears sell-out of China in 1941, 62; supports Chennault's plans for secret air war against Japan, 72-75; efforts to rigidly control 1942 gold loan to China, 95-98; plan to purchase a Chinese army, 95-98; receives reports from Dixie Mission, 189; opposition to economic aid during 1944, 154; renewed support for aid to China, 228

Moscow Conference of 1943, 147

Moscow Foreign Ministers Conference of 1945, discussion regarding China, 294

Mountbatten, Vice-Adm. Lord Louis: named commander of SEAC, 138; mediates between Chiang and Stilwell, 144

Munitions Assignment Board, Chinese excluded, 93

Nanking Decade, 7-8

Naval Group China, *see* Miles, Milton; SACO

Nazi-Soviet Pact, 30

Nelson, Donald: sent by FDR on mission to China, 166; criticizes Stilwell, 172

New Fourth Army Incident, 42

New Life Movement, 5

1911 Commercial Treaty with Japan, termination of, 30

Oil Embargo of 1941, 59

Operation Matterhorn, 144

Opium War, 1

Organization of Strategic Services (OSS): created in 1942, 66; operations with CCP, 187-88; effort to send team to Yenan in 1943, 237-38; conflict with SACO, 236-38; joint intelligence teams with KMT 220

Pact of Paris (Kellogg-Briand Pact), 4

Panay Incident, 15

Patterson, Robert, 274, 281, 284

Pearl Harbor attack, debate over, 65-67

Potsdam Conference (Berlin), 253-58

Quarantine speech, 13-14

Quebec Conference (OCTAGON), 169

Quebec Conference (QUADRANT), 138-39

Ramgarh, India, training site of X-Force, 127-28

Ringwalt, Arthur, threatened by Hurley, 207-8

Roosevelt, Elliott, reports FDR's anger at Chiang, 151

Roosevelt, Franklin D.: early lack of interest in East Asian crisis, 6; Quarantine speech, 13; approves aid to China, 27, 36-37; approves plan for air war against Japan, 74; approves creation of AVG, 77; approves JB 355, 81; vision of U.S.-China relations, 90-92, 98-99; sympathy for Chennault's strategy, 122; influenced by Currie, 112-14; decides in favor of Chennault at Washington Conference, 136-37; view of Chiang, 122-23; praise of Hurley as emissary, 148-49, 217; criticism of Chiang at Cairo, 151-52; allegedly orders assassination of Chiang, 153; opposes additional loans to China, 153-54; sends Wallace to urge negotia-

Roosevelt, Franklin D. (*Continued*)
tions between CCP and KMT, 160-62;
threatens Chiang with aid cutoff, 158;
sends Hurley and Nelson as emissaries
to China, 166; demands that Stilwell be
granted full command powers, 169;
agrees to Chiang-Hurley demand that
Stilwell be recalled, 171-74; view of
China after recall of Stilwell, 177-78;
discussions with Harriman regarding
Soviet policy in China, 178-80; rejects
appeal by Mao and Chou that they be
granted meeting with him, 206; adopts
policy of cooperating with Stalin in
China, 209-10; policy at Yalta, 209-12;
supports Hurley-Wedemeyer policy in
China, 217; death, 224
Roosevelt, Maj. Quentin, warned against
OSS aid to Yenan, 221

Service, John S.: critical evaluation of KMT
and early interest in CCP, 116-17; views
of incipient civil war and American policy, 139-43; urges contacts with CCP,
156-57; reports from Yenan as member
of Dixie Mission, 183-88; final meetings
with CCP leaders in Yenan, 214-15;
recalled at Hurley's insistence, 215; ar-
rested in Amerasia Case, 226; reassigned
to Japan, 270-71
Sian Incident, effects on U.S. policy, 10-12
Sino-American Cooperative Organization
(SACO) (also, Naval Group China and
Milton Miles), 232-34; alleged plans to
sabotage Dixie Mission, 188; informs
Hurley about CCP approaches directly
to FDR, 205; origins of naval mission,
232-34; creation of SACO, 236-37;
SACO-OSS conflict, 237; involvement in
police training and counter-insurgency
projects, 240-41; role in Stilwell recall,
174; conflict with Wedemeyer, 242-45;
role in Japanese surrender, 246-248;
attacked in 1970s by Chinese Communists, 250

Sino-Soviet Treaty, 252-53, 258-60; CCP
reaction to, 267
Snow, Edgar, 10, 20, 217
Soong Mei-ling (Mme. Chiang Kai-shek),
119-20
Soong, T. V.: lobbies for loans to China,
32-38; involved in Washington intrigues,
52-58; creates CDS, 54-57; role in selecting U.S. commander in China, 93;
negotiates for 1942 loan, 96-98; collaborates with Stilwell to undermine Chiang,
128-30; backs Chennault, 136; collaborates with Chiang and Hurley to undermine Stilwell, 170-74; advises Hurley on
policy toward CCP, 194; meets with
Truman, 252; negotiates Sino-Soviet
treaty, 252-53, 258-60
Southeast Asia Command (SEAC),
created, 138
Soviet Union, military-economic aid to
KMT, 41-42; Soviet policy in China,
179-80; at Yalta Conference, 209-12;
enters war against Japan, 259-60; *see also*
CCP, Roosevelt, Franklin D., and Sta-
lin, Joseph
Stalin, Joseph: ambiguous attitude toward
Chinese Communism, 179-80; at Tehe-
ran, 150; at Yalta, 209-12; praises
Chiang, 223; negotiates Sino-Soviet
Treaty, 258-60; discusses civil war and
Marshall Mission, 294
State-War-Navy Coordinating Committee
(SWNCC): formed, 275; debates issue of
U.S. intervention in civil war, 275-82
Stelle, Capt. Charles: reports to OSS from
Yenan, 193; analyzes CCP views of U.S.
policy, 219-20
Stilwell, Gen. Joseph W.: selected as
commander of CBI Theater, 95-96; visits
India en route to China, 101; arrival in
China, 102; defeat during Burma cam-
paign, 102-3; criticizes KMT military
structure, 104-5; plans for new strategy
in Burma, 106; urges U.S. to reject
Chiang's Three Demands, 109-10; views
on Asian nationalism and China's future,

127-30; collaborates with Soong against Chiang, 128-30; looses influence with President to Chennault at Washington Conference, 136-37; named deputy commander of SEAC, 138; threatened with recall, 143-45; meets with FDR at Cairo, 151-53; involved in plot to assassinate Chiang, 152-54; leads X-Force into Burma, 155; assumes command of Y-Force, 158; urges that he be named supreme military commander in China, 164-70; plans to cooperate with Communists, 168; recalled from China, 173-75; urges Truman to avoid involvement in civil war, 300

Stimson, Henry L.: and Stimson Doctrine, 5-6; opposes secret air war against Japan, 75-76; voices concern over use of atomic bomb, 255-58

Tai Li, Gen.: KMT sponsor of SACO, 234-35, collaborates with SACO, 236-48; death of, 249

T'ai p'ing Rebellion, 3

Teheran Conference, discussions regarding China, 150-51

Treaty Ports, 1

Truman, Harry S.: succeeds FDR, 224; influenced by anti-Communists, 224; fears of Communist expansion, 252; atomic diplomacy at Potsdam, 253-58; modifies Japanese surrender terms, 261-62; considers Wedemeyer as replacement for Hurley, 276; selects Marshall to mediate civil war, 289; instructs Marshall for mission to China, 292-93; administration's policy during civil war, 301-3

Unequal treaties, 1, end of, 147

Universal Trading Corporation, Chinese front, 25

United Front, 12; deterioration of, 39-45; effects of U.S. aid on, 43-45

U.S. Dept. of State, increasingly hostile view of Japan, 31

U.S. Dept. of the Treasury, lobbies for aid to China, 1939-40, 31-35

U.S. economic aid to China, 17-18, 24-29, 32-36, 96-98; fraud related to, 97-98; refused in 1944, 154; aid resumed in 1945, 228

U.S. policies following Japan's surrender: planning, 262-66; increased aid to KMT, 271-272; ferrying KMT troops northwards, 277-78

Vietnam, U.S. war strategy as fulfillment of Stilwell's plans, 304

Vincent, John Carter, advocates trade sanctions against Japan, 31; analyzes KMT politics, 115-16; restraining influence on intervention in civil war, 274-75

Wallace, Henry: mission to China and report to FDR, 160-64; troubled by Truman's policies, 261-62, 288-89

Wang Ching-wei: leads KMT peace faction, 23-24; establishes puppet regime, 32

Washington Conference of 1921-22, 4

Washington Conference of 1943 (TRIDENT), debate over air power in China, 136-37

Wedemeyer, Gen. Albert: views of Stilwell-Chennault rivalry, 125; opposition to Stilwell's strategy, 156; named commander of China Theater, 174; initial interest in cooperation with Communist guerrillas, 202; asserts control over U.S. military operations in China, 205-7; visits U.S., 212-13; lobbies for anti-Communist policy, 216-17; plans to cooperate with KMT to accept Japanese surrender, 262-66; criticizes Chiang's handling of Japanese surrender, 282-83; pessimistic assessment of civil war, 285-86; bitterness over Marshall Mission, 296

White, Harry Dexter: cites reasons to aid China, 31; plan to secure peace with